POLICY DYNAMICS

POLICY DYNAMICS

Edited by **FRANK R. BAUMGARTNER** & **BRYAN D. JONES**

THE UNIVERSITY OF CHICAGO PRESS Chicago & London

The University of Chicago Press, Chicago 60637
The University of Chicago Press, Ltd., London
© 2002 by The University of Chicago
All rights reserved. Published 2002
Printed in the United States of America

11 10 09 08 07 06 05 04 03 02   1 2 3 4 5

ISBN: 0-226-03940-4 (cloth)
ISBN: 0-226-03941-2 (paper)

Library of Congress Cataloging-in-Publication Data

Policy dynamics / edited by Frank R. Baumgartner and
Bryan D. Jones.
    p. cm.
    Includes bibliographical references and index.
    ISBN 0-226-03940-4 (alk. paper)—ISBN 0-226-03941-2
    (pbk : alk. paper)
    1. Political planning—United States. 2. United
States—Politics and government—1945–1989.
3. United States—Politics and government—1989–
I. Baumgartner, Frank R., 1958– II. Jones, Bryan D.

JK468.P64 P65 2002
320'.6'0973—dc21

                                2001006780

CONTENTS

PREFACE

In one way or another, and amid a great number of distractions, interruptions, moves, and other activities, we've been working on this book since we finished writing *Agendas and Instability in American Politics* almost ten years ago. We developed there some ideas, but also some techniques, that we thought could be expanded. In particular, we thought that the ideas we initially developed there could be expanded into a more robust understanding of decision making (where the political science literature had deteriorated into disagreements of whether political choice was incremental or not) and that the distinction between positive and negative feedback was a promising way to approach a more precise appreciation of public policy change. Our initial efforts to assess policy change quantitatively were crude, but we knew that in theory at least they surpassed the then-current focus on budget outlays or counts of enforcement activities. While ideas require brainpower and a pencil, assessing policy change more carefully required both a theory of measurement and the resources to do the hard work of measuring policy change consistently over long periods of time.

We began working almost immediately on an (overly) ambitious proposal to the National Science Foundation. On the second try, after demonstrating the surprising feasibility of our proposal, we were successful in gaining support in creating some very extensive databases, those that form the basis for the analysis reported in this book. It is traditional for authors to thank their funding sources, but in our case, because of the large scope of what we did, it is even more appropriate for us to point to the important role of the Political Science Program at NSF and its director, Frank Scioli. Thanks also to the three universities that have supported our research: Texas A&M, where we began the project, the University of Washington, to which Jones repaired, and Penn State, Baumgartner's new home. In exchange for the farsightedness of NSF, Texas A&M, the University of Washington, and Penn State, we have created, and we continue to update, a series of data sources reported here that have begun to provide for the study of public policy the basic infrastructure for a wide range of quantitative studies. We fervently hope that no one else will have to spend the time we and our students did in reading, coding, and documenting tens of thousands of hearings, bills, abstracts, budget documents, and media stories. If they do, we hope they will do so in a manner that can be linked to our system, thus helping to create a living data set directed at understanding long-term policy change. We trust that many will benefit from these new sources of information, increasing our understanding and the sophistication of our analyses of public policy in America. We hope that this book and the data sources whose uses our collaborators demonstrate here will prove to have been a good intellectual investment for the political science community.

It is a pleasure to acknowledge and thank the great number of students and assistants who have done the heavy lifting on this project over the years. Who knows how many authors write slowly enough so that their research assistants get jobs and then are tenured and promoted before the book comes out? In our case, we can note that Jeff Talbert, who helped design the first databases and was key in organizing a structure that remained in place for years and was duplicated by others, is now a tenured associate professor; did he write fast and get promoted just to embarrass us? Jim True solved some issues concerning the federal budget that we never would have been able to do without his help. Michael MacLeod was a long-standing project manager and helped ensure quality in a great variety of ways. Glen Krutz designed and oversaw the statutes and *Congressional Quarterly* segments of our project, developing along the way some influential ideas that have now led to an award-winning dissertation and book on omnibus legislation. Beth Leech helped do some initial thinking about how to design the *New York Times* section of our work even as she actually worked on another project related to interest groups, and then Kristi Campbell implemented and oversaw this large project. Doris McGonagle, Xinshing Liu, Yuguo Chen, Samuel Sampson, Jim Cottrill, Michelle Chin, and Jeanine Harris complete the list of Texas A&M graduate students to whom we are happy to express our thanks in print. Undergraduates at A&M who worked on the project, often under the supervision of the graduate students just named, include Ron Lorenzo, Holly Gibson, Kathryn Gunn, Angel Price, Elaine Mejia, Elizabeth Green, Kelly Lanier, David Lopez, Andrea Singley, and Sally Thurman; thanks to you as well. As should be clear from the length of this list of acknowledgments, we had quite a team working in those coding rooms and in the library back in College Station. We hope that everyone learned as much as we did. Certainly a lot of grad students got a quick introduction into the details and logistics of supervising others' work while still being responsible for the quality of it all as if the work were their own. Right, Mike?

At the Center for American Politics and Public Policy at the University of Washington, Valerie Hunt set up the web-based framework for the delivery of the data to the research community, and served as the lead research assistant on the project. Jens Feeley served as lead data manager and later lead research assistant and general problem solver on all sorts of data and coding issues that have emerged over the years. Jens and Heather Larsen supervised the Center's Undergraduate Fellows Program, a program that allowed undergraduate students to develop their own research papers from the Policy Agendas Project Data Sets and to learn large-scale data management and analysis in the social sciences in the process. Vince Fitts, Nicole Schiereck, Christi Sue, Belle Na, Ida Cohen, Les Coughran, Heather Larsen, Mark Nye, Noah Pinegar, Nathan Borgford-Powell, Jamie Howe, Mike McGrath, Stephanie McNees, and Todd Riechart all contributed to the development of the data sets and wrote papers using the data in extended research project.

At Penn State, thanks especially to Nick Semanko who worked hard but quickly to produce the figures used in this book. His standardization of a great variety of idiosyncratic authors' preferences helped greatly in producing a manuscript that is much easier to read than would otherwise have been the case. His work on the data files that can be used to replicate the work reported here also makes our web site much more useful. Nick is also the author or assistant helping to create a variety of additional analyses available on our web site. These extra resources should help anyone interested to follow up on information presented here. Michelle O'Connell worked quickly, carefully, and under tight deadlines to help clean and prepare the text and bibliography even while also working on another project on interest groups during the day. Christine Mahoney compiled the index, again as a break from other research tasks.

A great number of colleagues around the country and abroad have given us comments on this work and on the broader project of which this is a part; we particularly would like to thank Gretchen Casper, Jeff Berry, Beth Leech, Chris Deering, Mark Schneider, Pete Nardulli, Jon Bond, Joel Aberbach, John Brehm, John Aldrich, Rick Hall, Gary McKissick, Peter May, John Kingdon, Peter John, and others we are probably omitting for various bits of feedback, advice, citations, and ideas. Academics really are generous with their time and ideas; we're fortunate to be part of such a community.

Finally, this is a selection of essays written by a great variety of colleagues, former students, and others who have used the data sets we have created. Thanks to the contributors for taking the time and showing the interest to bring this book to fruition. The book produced here represents a milestone in our project, but hardly an end to it. We plan to continue together for the foreseeable future in analyzing American government and expect to follow this edited book shortly with another coauthored book dealing with many of the broad theoretical issues raised here in greater detail. Thanks to our wives, Gretchen and Diane, for putting up with it. And thanks to John Tryneski and the professional staff of the University of Chicago Press for continuing to impress us with their abilities.

CONTRIBUTORS

E. Scott Adler
*is assistant professor of political science at the
University of Colorado, Boulder.*

Frank R. Baumgartner
*is professor in and head of the political science department
at Pennsylvania State University.*

T. Jens Feeley
*is a graduate fellow of the Center for American Politics and Public Policy at the
University of Washington, Seattle.*

Jamie K. Gold
is with IXI Corporation in McLean, Virginia.

John W. Hardin
*is the assistant vice president for research and sponsored programs
at the University of North Carolina Office of the President.
He is also an adjunct assistant professor in the political science
department at the University of North Carolina, Chapel Hill.*

Valerie F. Hunt
*is a graduate fellow of the Center for American Politics and
Public Policy at the University of Washington, Seattle.*

Bryan D. Jones
*is the Donald R. Matthews Professor of American Politics
and director of the Center for American Politics and
Public Policy at the University of Washington, Seattle.*

Glen S. Krutz
is assistant professor of political science at Arizona State University.

Michael C. MacLeod
is a consultant with Hewitt Associates in Atlanta.

Matthew Potoski
is assistant professor of political science at Iowa State University.

Christina Sue

received a B.A. from the University of Washington, Seattle, in 1999 and is now in the graduate program at University of California, Los Angeles.

Nicole S. Schiereck

received a B.A. from the University of Washington, Seattle, in 1999 and is now in the graduate program at Cornell University.

Jeffery C. Talbert

is associate professor of public policy and administration and political science at the University of Kentucky's James W. Martin School of Public Policy and Administration.

James L. True

is assistant professor of political science and Jack Brooks Chair in Government and Public Service at Lamar University.

John D. Wilkerson

is associate professor of political science and associate director of the Center for American Politics and Public Policy at the University of Washington, Seattle.

PART ONE
THEORETICAL BEGINNINGS

In this book, with the help of over a dozen collaborators and fellow scholars of the public policy process, we explore some long-term trends in the development of American politics and public policy. Typically, our analyses cover the period from the end of World War II to the end of the twentieth century: about fifty years of American politics. Our work has two goals. First, we want to demonstrate the importance of a punctuated equilibrium view of politics. That is, we believe that a complete view of the development and functioning of the institutions of American government must include simultaneous attention to those mechanisms that induce equilibrium and stability (what we call here negative feedback processes) as well as those explosive properties of the political system that occasionally create major disruptions, reorganizations, and reconfigurations of the institutions of political life (positive feedback processes). Combined attention to positive and negative feedback processes shows the importance of looking at institutional structures as changing elements in the political landscape. Institutional changes are part of the same political forces that lead to and structure policy changes, so it is important that the analyst looking to explain policy outcomes spend some considerable time looking at the development of institutions rather than only studying the smooth functioning of institutions operating within periods of stability. Our first goal, then, is to focus on some large-scale theoretical questions that allow us to present a broad view of the development of the institutions and policies of American government over the second half of the twentieth century. Our punctuated equilibrium theory of politics provides the framework from which we can understand many elements of American politics that are often selectively overlooked or considered to be mutually contradictory. Stable functioning systems of negative feedback are in fact part of the same broader system of politics that makes the occasional disruption through positive feedback inevitable. These broad theoretical questions are introduced and explained in our first chapter.

A second goal of the book is to introduce readers to a wide range of data sources that we have developed and to encourage others to follow up on the studies presented here to study public policy over the long term. In chapter 2, we present in detail five large and comprehensive data sets that we have collected and which we make available on our web site (http://depts.washington .edu/ampol/agendasproject.shtml). These data, which were collected with the partial support of the National Science Foundation and are freely available to anyone, permit a wide range of analyses. The chapters that we bring together in this book illustrate many elements of our punctuated equilibrium view of American politics, but they do not complete the story. Rather, they begin the story that we expect to continue in subsequent writings and that others will complete by conducting a great variety of studies. These studies may be similar to those presented here in that they follow a given public policy over time, address the impact of the rise of new issues on various institutions of government, and show the slow evolution or the rapid revolution of different institutional procedures over time, or they may follow a different tack from the chapters included in this book. In any case, we consider this book to be a beginning of a series of studies that will explore the themes of positive feedback, negative feedback, institutional change, and punctuated equilibrium in politics. Our second goal, then, is to introduce a research approach and the data sources that we have developed in order to allow others to do their own studies as they see fit.

1

POSITIVE AND NEGATIVE
FEEDBACK IN POLITICS

FRANK R. BAUMGARTNER AND

BRYAN D. JONES

The American policy process is characterized by the dual and contrasting characteristics of stability and dramatic change. At times, government policies seem remarkably resistant to change, following standard operating procedures, working within norms of consensus among those involved, attracting little public attention, and deviating little from year to year. At other times, or in other areas of public policy, dramatic changes occur: New problems appear on the political agenda; crises require quick government response; new programs are created and old ones are terminated. The Medicare program was not created in 1965 in a wave of incrementalism, after all. Welfare reform was not just a marginal adjustment to past policies. The tobacco settlement, costing the tobacco industry hundreds of billions of dollars and putting an end to cigarette advertisements on billboards, does not reflect policy making by standard operating procedures.

Moreover, neither welfare reform nor the tobacco settlement would have occurred as they did without the operation of multiple venues for political action. In the case of welfare reform, the states took the lead. In the case of tobacco, most of the action resulted from the innovative legal theories promoted by Mississippi's attorney general. In each case, innovations and new ways of thinking about the issue were then copied by others so that large-scale national changes resulted from isolated local decisions.

THE TWO GOALS OF THIS VOLUME

Dramatic policy changes regularly occur in American politics, even if most issues most of the time are characterized by more routine developments. In this book, the chapter authors and we explore these dual characteristics of public policy, developing further evidence for the theory of punctuated equilibrium developed in our earlier work on policy change (Baumgartner and Jones 1993). This approach forces students of the policy process to integrate what have often been seen as unrelated, if not mutually antagonistic, phenomena: peaceful incrementalism and jarring change.

The chapters brought together here have in common a long-term perspective, typically looking at major issues of public policy or the institutions of government over a fifty-year period. They make use of common data sets tracing attention to public policy issues across that period. While each chapter explores a different area of public policy or a different aspect of the American institutional system, they address the issue of explaining both periods of dramatic change and those of relative stability. These are the signature characteristics of punctuated equilibrium, and the joint explanation of both contrasts sharply with the more common treatment of one to the exclusion of the other. Political scientists have traditionally focused either on the periods of rapid change (as in most studies of agenda setting and program creation) or on those of relative stability (as in most studies of policy subsystems, budgeting, implementation, or public policy more generally). One research tradition focuses on building models based on positive feedback processes; the other bases its studies on negative feedback models. In this introductory chapter, we lay out these contrasting views and explain the importance of integrating them.

This book is designed with an important theoretical ambition in mind. The study of public policy (and American politics more generally) has too often been divided into groups of scholars studying different parts of the same process. Many scholars focus their attention on explaining the smooth functioning of policy systems working within powerful and relatively stable institutional constraints. Such studies often show remarkable predictive powers and allow their authors to use sophisticated techniques of prediction and analysis. Other scholars often ask much broader questions and analyze issues over much longer periods of time or across many different institutional venues. Their work tends to have a more qualitative character, partly because the issues that they study are not clearly contained within the activities of any one institution. Students of institutions have been much more successful in modeling and in showing statistically significant predictions than have students of policy.

We want to show the importance of a combined view. Institutions, we will argue, are fundamentally endogenous to the policy process. That means that the policy process itself can alter the manner in which institutions function.

The tradition in political science, however, is to think of institutions as exogenous. When we treat institutions as exogenous, we think of them as fixed and unchanging. They are causes, but not effects, of the policies that they are involved with. They structure, but are not structured by, public policy. Since the major institutions of government generally may remain in place for decades or longer, and since their organization, structure, and rules of participation tend to induce a certain type of outcome, scholars are often well served by treating them as relatively fixed, exogenous. (In other words, institutions generally have purposes, and political scientists are well served by an emphasis on noting what those purposes are. This is an assertion that readers should find utterly uncontroversial.) The view of institutions as exogenous factors, causes but not consequences of public policy, is not so much wrong as it is incomplete.

It is deceptively easy to model the stable functioning of an institution, treating it as fixed and exogenous, but doing so ignores some important questions. Where did the institution come from? What political forces conspired to make the institution be designed in one way rather than another? How capable is the institution of exerting its authority over rival institutions? How are policies made when several institutions share jurisdiction? Do institutions evolve over time in response to new issues and the actions of competing institutions? If we want to understand the ways in which government responds to important social problems, then we must look not only at the periods during which institutions produce policies in a smooth and consistent manner, but also at those periods when the institutions themselves are reorganized, at how institutions compete with each other for control over important public policies, and at how institutional practices evolve over time. In previous work (Baumgartner and Jones 1993), we argued that American public policy is an ever-changing mosaic, with some policies quietly being handled within policy subsystems and with little public attention, but with other policies being the subject of considerable public debate and institutional struggle. A complete understanding of the process requires attention to both types of process. The chapters that follow develop these ideas in greater detail.

If we succeed in our first goal, then by the end of this book readers will have a strong understanding that a complete view of American government and public policy must include a theory of institutional development as well as an understanding of institutionally induced equilibrium. Positive and negative feedback processes lead alternately to the creation, the destruction, and the evolution of the institutions of public policy. As new issues rise to and recede from the political agenda, as old issues come to be understood in new ways, and as the institutions of government compete with each other for control over important areas of policy, institutional structures are continuously revamped, modified, and altered. While a given institution may operate according to the logic of negative feedback for long periods of time, the entire government cannot be understood in these terms alone. Looking at the operations of government over the long term, as we do here, and considering both positive and negative feedback processes, leads quickly to the conclusion that institutional design should be endogenous to our theories of government. Taking it as fixed can be useful for some limited purposes, but a larger view requires attention to the creation, modification, and evolution of the structures of government themselves.

A second goal of the book is to introduce scholars, students, and others to some straightforward techniques of studying policy change. One of the truly great failings of the policy sciences has been the inability to produce reliable longitudinal studies. Many times, as we show in chapter 2, data sets used for policy analysis are simply not equivalent across time. We have collected a series of reliable policy indicators across time, and believe that the broadest possible availability of this and similar information will help us develop a more comprehensive understanding of how public policies are formulated and changed. Each of the chapters of this book reports some original research tracing the functioning of an institution of government or a particular policy issue over time. The methods used here may be applied more broadly to other policy arenas, especially since most of the data reported are publicly available through our web site (we explain this more fully in chapter 2 and in the appendices). We want to encourage the systematic and longitudinal study of public policy, and we have made available many of the resources necessary to do that for any number of issues. If we succeed in our second goal, then many readers of this book will challenge and extend our analyses using these new data sources.

In this chapter, we introduce the most important themes that are picked up in the subsequent chapters. We begin with a discussion of negative feedback processes. These are the mechanisms that induce stability and incrementalism in public policy, and they are fundamental to most models of bureaucratic behavior, the functioning of policy subsystems, concepts of interest-group pluralism, models of democratic gridlock, and to other prominent views of the policy process. Though rarely described in the terms that we use here, all these models have in common an adherence to a negative feedback model of the political process, one where shocks to the system are dampened, where pressures from one side lead to counterpressures from another side, and in general where self-corrective mechanisms keep the system on an even keel. We then turn our attention of positive feedback models of politics — models in which ideas of momentum, bandwagon effects, thresholds, and cascades play critical roles. In these processes, dramatic and unpredictable changes to public policy are more common, as in the literatures on issue definition, agenda setting, and policy entrepreneurship. Rather than self-correction, these models are characterized by self-reinforcing processes in which change in one case makes change in the next case more likely. Like a market in which consumers prefer to own a stock that is going up in value, initial increases can become self-perpetuating, at least for a time. Many political phenomena share characteristics of positive feedback mechanisms, as for example when political leaders sense that the public, or an important segment of it, is increasingly concerned with an issue such as prescription drug coverage. The more the leaders talk about the issue, the more the public may be concerned with it, and the cycle can last for quite some time. In sum, the political system shows important characteristics of both negative and positive feedback processes, though the two do not operate at the same time for the same issue.

A complete view of the political system must include both positive and negative feedback processes because the events that make one of them possible also make the other one inevitable. Therefore any theory that focuses on one must also make room for the other. Fundamental to the differences between positive and negative feedback systems in public policy are the roles and structures of institutions. We review the important role of institutional design in promoting negative feedback processes, but also in making inevitable certain periods of institutional redesign, and therefore positive feedback processes as well. Institutions react to the changing nature of the issues that they are called upon to deal with. Sometimes institutional change is rapid and dramatic, as when new institutions are created or redesigned; at other times issues and institutions coevolve in a more gradual manner. That is, institutional structures can evolve slowly over time in reaction to the changing nature of the issues that they face. We discuss these institutional dynamics in some detail in this chapter, and several subsequent chapters then pick up these themes as well.

Many theories of politics leave no room for institutional design or change. Others have no room for the steady functioning of relatively stable systems of negative feedback. Rarely do theories of politics allow for both; we think that any complete theoretical perspective must necessarily allow for both the routine functioning of issues as they are processed by the specialized institutions of government that have been built up around them as well as for the exceptional periods when institutions themselves are created, ripped apart, or dramatically altered in the face of political mobilizations, altered understandings of underlying issues, or other factors. So we first want to encourage a broader view of the functioning of the political system and its institutional design.

A second goal of our book, as stated above, is to illustrate the uses of the many data sets we have collected in recent years. The chapters that follow give thorough descriptions of our data and illustrate how they can be used. Though this book has thirteen chapters and may seem to cover a lot of ground, it barely scratches the surface in terms of the analytical uses to which our new data sources can be put. We hope that some of our readers will be intrigued enough by what they see to follow up with studies of their own. These may be designed to explore issue areas or institutions not covered here, or they may be designed to challenge the analyses presented here. In any case, the essays included in this volume do not constitute a full test or demonstration of the theoretical ideas we want to explore. More studies — a great number of them — are necessary to do that.

American politics changed greatly in the second half of the twentieth century. During the early period covered by our data sets, that is, just after demobilizing from World War II, our government had a limited role in the economy and virtually no role in the health care system, had placed very little emphasis on public health or the environment, and had instituted no interstate highways or serious national transportation policies, no national energy policies, no space program or National Institutes of Health, and little in the way of antidiscrimination legislation. Within forty years, a new situation had evolved: not only was government bigger in absolute terms but, perhaps more importantly, it was involved in a great many more activities. Though many have noted the growth in government, few have explored the ways in which this growth has affected the nature and functioning of the government itself. Many seem to expect governmental leaders now to behave in ways reminiscent of how they worked when government was much simpler. We believe that this would be inappropriate if it were not impossible. We hope that this book will provide some initial glimpses into these wide-ranging changes, that it will prompt others to study these issues as we continue to do so ourselves, and that the combined impact of all these further studies will be an enhanced and more complete understanding of the nature of our democracy.

NEGATIVE FEEDBACK

A negative feedback system includes a homeostatic process or a self-correcting mechanism. Just as a thermostat adjusts to falling temperatures by putting out more heat, homeostatic devices work to maintain stability. Whatever the direction of the outside force, the homeostatic device operates in the opposite way; the result is to maintain steady outputs in the face of changing external pressures. The key element of any negative feedback system is simply that the system reacts to counterbalance, rather than reinforce, any changes coming in from the environment.

Negative feedback systems are extremely common in political science and in public policy. Many public policies, such as counterinflationary actions of the Federal Reserve, are explicitly designed to be homeostatic: where inflationary pressures are seen to rise, the Fed tightens credit policies, working to counterbalance the incipient inflation and to keep the economy on an even track. Unemployment compensation, antipoverty programs, price supports for farmers, and many other entitlement programs are explicitly homeostatic in that they are designed to activate automatically in response to changes in the condition they are supposed to regulate (see Boynton 1989).

Many models of congressional and bureaucratic behavior include explicit homeostatic processes. Members interested in reelection provide benefits to constituency groups that mobilize to support them, pulling back from further support when rival groups make clear their own power. The result is that the political system never leads to ever-increasing power to any single group, but rather to distributions of support that remain within certain bounds. Wlezien (1995) argues that public policy and public opinion act in such a fashion: when policy makers enact policies that are too liberal from the perspective of the general public, the public becomes more conservative. When policy is too conservative, public opinion reacts by becoming more liberal (for a similar argument see MacKuen, Erikson, and Stimson 2001). Similarly, Peltzman's (1976) model of regulatory capture models a government decision maker choosing to allocate resources to one of two groups: consumers or business. Members of these competing constituencies then support or oppose the political decision maker depending on the actions he has taken. Where the decisions veer too far in one direction, the disfavored group mobilizes to show its own power, supporting a challenging candidate, for example. With political support distributed between the two competing constituency groups, the decision maker is constrained to operate only within a certain band of action. The result is an equilibrium outcome that illustrates the negative feedback processes common to many theories of politics and policy.

Bendor and Moe (1985) present a more realistic model than Peltzman; their model includes agency leaders hoping to receive budget increases, legislators hoping for reelection, and competing interest-group coalitions hoping for certain government policies. Here, too, the key elements are essentially homeostatic: the competing interest groups provide or withdraw support from elected officials depending on the policies being produced. The elected officials then adjust their positions on future policy changes in order to maintain adequate public support to be reelected. They provide support or cutbacks to agency leaders who are producing these outcomes, basing each year's budget on the performance and outcomes generated by previous experience. The result is a closed and mutually adjusting system that ensures that policies reflect the competing interests and the relative strengths of those concerned. Bendor and Moe refer to this "pluralist equilibrium" as a "very stable balance-of-power system" (1985, 769).

Some form of negative feedback, or diminishing returns to scale, is required in any equilibrium model and is therefore a part of any neo-institutional analysis. Without countermobilization, political interests would gather ever-increasing powers until they overwhelmed the entire political system. We can see diminishing returns in any number of institutionalist models. Models of distributional politics in Congress focus on how committees may become stacked with "high demanders" working through their institutional positions to pull congressional policies to support their own constituents at the expense of the chamber preference (Fiorina 1977; Shepsle and Weingast 1987). Increasing costs accrue as the committee pulls the policy further and further from the chamber preference: as pressures grow in one direction, counterpressures from the other side are predicted to pull the system back to its stable equilibrium. In this model of congressional behavior, outcomes are expected always to remain within some range of policies acceptable to the chamber; if they were beyond the range of the acceptable, then the chamber would act to rein in the committee. Similarly in Krehbiel's (1991) informational model, specialists invest in expertise because they gain policy control. The floor grants them this control as long as their policies do not go too far from the chamber preference. The two models may predict different equilibrium outcomes, but each includes a mechanism of diminishing returns making it impossible for the committee to veer further and further from the chamber. Models of bureaucratic oversight (McCubbins and Schwartz 1984) posit an increasing likelihood that Congress will act to rein in an agency as that agency's behavior veers further from congressional preferences. Virtually all models of institutional behavior involve a strong element of diminishing returns, since this is necessary for an equilibrium analysis. (And, we might add, because it conforms to how things work in most cases most of the time.)

A focus on equilibrium analysis and an institutional rational-choice perspective is not a necessary requirement for a negative feedback process. The literature on bounded rationality, incrementalism, and administrative behavior more generally is also characterized by negative feedback systems. Standard operating procedures, rules of thumb, and decision making by incrementalism have in common a focus on the relative stability of expected policy outcomes. In the absence of dramatic revisions to the procedures themselves, decisions should be made according to a process that induces stable outcomes (see Lindblom 1960; Wildavsky 1964; Simon 1997). There are any number of nonrational or incomplete-information models of decision making that nonetheless conform to a negative feedback model. Kahneman and Tversky discuss people's aversion to risk and certain inconsistent patterns of how individuals react to the potential for gains and losses (Kahneman and Tversky 1984, 1985; see also Tversky and Kahneman 1986; Quattrone and Tversky 1988). As long as these behaviors are consistent, they can be modeled using a negative feedback and equilibrium analysis; nothing in this perspective requires or even implies a rational decision-making process. It only requires diminishing marginal returns and negative feedback to inputs; a great many patterns of behavior conform to these requirements.

Not only are the institutional approaches to congressional behavior, congressional oversight of the bureaucracy, and administrative behavior more generally dominated by models of negative feedback, but the vast literature on policy subsystems is as well. From Griffith's (1939) discussion of "policy whirlpools" though Cater's (1964) study of policy subsystems and Lowi's (1969) description of "interest-group liberalism," scholars through the decades have noted the tendency for communities of like-minded interests to dominate policy making in their areas. Those with technical expertise often have a vested interest in increased spending in a given area, and those without the expertise often have other priorities. The result, which has been noted and documented by scholars in every decade of the twentieth century, is the predominance of "iron triangles," "policy subsystems," "systems of limited participation," or "policy monopolies" in many areas of American public policy. These models of subsystem power all have in common a view that increased power stems from autonomy from the broader political system. These models also note inherent limits to this power, however. Diminishing returns are evident since a policy subsystem is not expected to grow to overtake the entire political system. Where demands grow to be too great, political leaders rein the system back in or rival subsystems attack. The result is an equilibrium outcome that may differ from the general good, but an equilibrium nonetheless.

Probably the most important negative feedback theory of American politics in general has been David Truman's "disturbance theory" (1951), the foundation of pluralism. In this view, "disturbances" to the established order — be they economic shocks, natural disasters, wars, or the actions of rival interest groups — that have large negative effects on a given social group will naturally and inevitably lead to the reaction and the mobilization of that constituency. The suffering group will organize, mobilize, and demand redress — it will "put things right." In this pluralist perspective, the self-correcting genius of American democracy was in effect a negative feedback system: any strong push in one direction could be expected to be countered by an equal and opposite push, never allowing the political system to veer too far from an underlying equilibrium. Of course the general view of the entire political system as a huge self-correcting mechanism came under strong and justified attack (for a review, see Baumgartner and Leech 1998). However, there are many areas of public policy where negative feedback systems operate over long periods of time.

We have previously noted (Baumgartner and Jones 1993) the importance of policy monopolies in creating stable policy outcomes, often for extremely long periods of time. We described the dual roles of ideas and institutions (images and venues, we called them) in buttressing these policy monopolies. Institutional structures limit who can participate in the policy debate, and powerful supporting ideas often limit the ways in which the given issue is discussed. Where the institutional venues of decision making are stable, and where a positive policy image supports a given policy, powerful negative feedback processes can operate, creating a strongly homeostatic system that generates stable policy outcomes for decades. One important element of the stable operation of policy monopolies is the policy image, or the supporting set of ideas structuring how policy makers think about and discuss the policy. Where poverty policy is considered from a perspective of helping children avoid the scourge of growing up without the best chances of success, more generous policies are supported than where the policy is considered from a perspective of cutting back on government handouts. As long as the policy image remains stable, it is difficult to justify a radical rethinking of the resulting policy. Policy images, therefore, play an important role in promoting negative feedback processes, as long as they are stable.

Institutional structures, or venues, constitute the second element of our previous explanation of the strength of policy monopolies. Where institutional rules are clear and restrictive, structuring who has legitimate standing to participate and who can be labeled an "outsider," then a group of authorities can implement a relatively stable set of policies for as long as they retain their authority. Since the leaders of government agencies typically have a vision of what policies they seek to promote, the relative autonomy of a given institution to implement the policies it favors is an important element in understanding almost any area of public policy. Where institutional structures are clear, then those promoting radical revisions from the status quo can often be dismissed as uninformed, irresponsible, or dangerous. As a result, powerful government institutions operating with autonomy and according to standard operating procedures that limit participation only to those granted authority can be a further source of the politics of negative feedback. Powerful institutions acting with set relations to the broader political system tend to produce relatively stable outcomes.

Negative feedback systems are fundamental to understanding a great variety of areas of public policy, and they are central to most theories of politics. They help explain equilibrium behavior of many kinds, and they are central to understanding the roles of voters in elections, interest groups, bureaucrats, and members of Congress. No theory of politics would be complete without an understanding of negative feedback processes. The same can be said of positive feedback processes.

POSITIVE FEEDBACK

A positive feedback mechanism includes a self-reinforcing process that accentuates rather than counterbalances a trend. If we observe such a process operating though time, we find considerable clustering of events, along with large and generally unexpected changes. Seemingly random initial events can lead to a cascade of subsequent events that dramatically change the status quo. The world of positive feedback processes is changeable, fickle, and erratic when compared with stable and predictable outcomes associated with negative feedback processes. This is because self-reinforcing processes can be explosive, as compared to self-correcting processes, which, by their nature, inhibit dramatic change.

Positive feedback systems can operate in the social sphere as well as in the physical realm. Bendor and Moe (1985) note that in a negative feedback process, "success is self-limiting" because the gains of one side lead to the mobilization of the opposing side. On the other hand, a different logic applies where positive feedback systems are operating: "In such a world, the positive feedback of the Matthew effect — 'To him who hath shall be given' — creates an unstable system of cumulative advantages" (1985, 771). (When scholars contemplate an unbalanced and hard-to-explain world, they seem compelled to turn to biblical metaphors. Mandelbrot [1982, 248–49] refers to the "Noah" and "Joseph" effects — referring to the biblical stories of floods and droughts — in explaining wild fluctuations in outcomes over time.) In any case, we note that many authors have paid attention to the different logics of positive and negative feedback systems. It is easy enough to say that positive feedback processes can be unpredictable, but what is there in the different processes at the heart of positive and negative feedback that make this occur?

Economist Brian Arthur has described elements of positive feedback in the economy. Initial success in gaining market share can make additional gains come more easily, rather than reaching a diminishing return as in a negative feedback model. Computer operating systems and widely used software packages are familiar examples of markets where the increasing returns to scale seem to operate. Part of the value of a given operating system or word processing software is not so much that it is superior to another one on technical grounds, but rather that many others use it so that files can easily be shared with colleagues and coworkers. In any situation where a consumer's choice is determined by the number of other consumers making the same choice, then positive returns to scale may operate. Whichever producer establishes an initial lead in the market may well go on to dominate the market completely, if consumers are purchasing partly on the basis of this logic. Studies of the spread of many products, such as the QWERTY keyboard, video standards (VHS or Betamax), computer operating systems, and other technologies have shown this, as have studies of fashion trends, fads, and cultural norms (see Schelling 1978; David 1985; Banerjee 1992; Arthur 1994; Axelrod 1997).

Positive returns and "lock-ins" in the economy have been challenged on both empirical and theoretical grounds (Liebowitz and Margolis 1999). On the other hand, most students of economic booms and busts point to self-sustaining bursts of optimism or pessimism (Kindleberger 1996). Studies of industrial location have noted a similar self-reinforcing trend: As a given city becomes known for the production of a particular item, the reputation can be self-perpetuating even if its initial choice was purely random. Suppliers locate nearby; a skilled and experienced workforce develops that cannot be easily replicated; economies of scale are created as the local industry grows; and these trends all reinforce each other (see Krugman 1997). Silicon Valley is Silicon Valley partly because skilled programmers already happen to live there. Why it occurred there in the first place is not necessarily all that clear. The garment district remains the garment district because anyone thinking of opening a new business in the field would find skilled workers, customers, brokers, and colleagues nearby. Reputations take hold as particular locations (be they towns, cities, areas, or neighborhoods) become known as centers for one type of industry or another. These reputations are not just based on rumor; rather there are strong and concrete incentives for all to follow this pattern, once the pattern has been established. The fact that the initial cause of the pattern may have been random or haphazard does not diminish its importance once established. However, it does make it less predictable.

A great variety of industrial standards, including railway gauges, electrical plugs, and other familiar items exhibit this characteristic: more important than making the "correct" choice on technical grounds, one simply wants to make the same choice as everyone else, so that goods can be shared more easily. Many markets exhibit positive returns to scale; one key element that they have in common is that the decisions of one depend on the decisions of those around them. Once established, great efficiencies are gained by reinforcing rather than bucking the trend. Bucking a trend is negative feedback; going along with and reinforcing a trend is positive feedback; both processes are common in different circumstances, and both play important roles in politics.

In politics, two processes are generally responsible for positive feedback; both have to do with how individuals make decisions. The first operates when people observe the behavior of others and act accordingly. Cue taking or mimicking models help us understand this type of behavior. The second operates because people, in the words of Herbert Simon (1985), are "serial information processors." They attend to only limited parts of the world at any given time. Since one cannot possibly simultaneously be attuned to all elements of the surrounding world, people use various informational short-cuts in order to make reasonable decisions. In particular, in most complex decision making settings, there are many more dimensions of choice than people can pay attention to at any given time. In other words, when faced with a complex decision that may have many underlying dimensions, people focus on one or just a few dimensions in making their choices. If, at some later point, new dimensions of the issue are shown to be important, then people may shift their attention toward that dimension of the issue. This is what Bryan Jones (1994) has called the "serial shift." When people shift attention from one element of a decision to another, they may rapidly and unpredictably change their behavior. Models of incremental decision making typically rely on an assumption of unidimensionality, but where underlying decisions involve a great number of unrelated dimensions, decisions can shift dramatically when the decision maker shifts from one dimension of evaluation to another. Both mimicking and attention shifting are important elements of decision making in many contexts, especially in governmental policy decisions. We consider each in turn.

The political advice that it is best to "go with a winner" is an apt description of how positive feedback can affect political life. Candidates for office attempting to raise money find that their perceived chances of success limit or stimulate their ability to find other supporters. Where potential donors feel the candidate has little chance of success, they may prefer to support a rival. Without money, it is hard to promote one's message, leading to a downward cycle. Conversely, where people feel that the candidate has the potential to be a legitimate contender, money may flow more easily, thus making it easier to hire the best staff, purchase media ads, travel, and develop further popular support. So the cycle can be either positive or negative, but in either case it is self-reinforcing rather than self-limiting. Donors prefer to "invest in a winner" rather than "put money down a hole." Such self-reinforcing logic helps explain why party nominations in the United States can be locked up so early, especially in recent years as candidate-centered fund-raising has become so important. Rather than a negative feedback process where early successes make subsequent victories more difficult, early successes lead to a self-perpetuating cycle. Proposals for campaign finance reforms may have at their root a dissatisfaction with precisely this element of the nominations process.

Economist Thomas Schelling (1978) was among the first to see clearly how the value people put on a good, service, or behavior often depends on how many other people around them value that same good, service, or behavior. Discussing a range of examples — crossing the street while the light is red (few will do it if they see all those around them waiting; many will if they see their neighbors all doing so); applauding in a public performance or at the end of a class (if enough begin to do it, it becomes general; if too few, it dies out); standing patiently in a line (if others are patient, so will all; if one or a few begin to surge forward, a stampede can ensue) — he notes the importance of the critical mass or the threshold effect. He writes: "What is common to all of these examples is the way people's behavior depends on *how many* are behaving a particular way, or how much they are behaving that way — how many attend the seminar how frequently, how many play volleyball how frequently, how many smoke, or double-park; how many applaud and how loudly; how many leave the dying neighborhood and how many leave the school. . . . What all the critical-mass models involve is some activity that is self-sustaining once the measure of that activity passes some minimum level" (Schelling 1978, 94–95). Schelling's examples make clear that threshold models are common in many areas of life, not only in politics.

Larry Bartels has developed a model of primary voting where voters are concerned with two things: their own views of the candidate, and their estimate of the candidate's chances of winning. Where the chances of winning are extremely low, they will not support the candidate even if they agree with her views (e.g., they do not want to "waste their vote"). Where the voters see that there is a greater chance of success, on the other hand, they become more willing to provide support. The result is "momentum" in presidential primaries and an assessment of the importance of early primary victories. Early victories lead to more press coverage, greater name recognition, easier fund-raising, less attention to competitors, and other advantages. Perhaps most importantly, they increase the chances that likely voters will consider the candidate to be "viable." This, in turn, increases voters' willingness to vote for the candidate (see Bartels 1988, 27). Of course, winning a presidential race is not purely a question of early primary victories; the candidate must retain support over the long haul. But Bartels shows how positive feedback effects are central to the electoral process.

Positive feedback processes have been seen to operate in a vast array of settings in which humans make decisions while paying attention to the decisions of those around them. Consider real estate values and how neighborhoods develop their reputations. Here again, the critical variable seems to be the degree to which a person's decision to behave in a certain way is conditioned on their estimate of the likely behaviors of those around them. Matthew Crenson (1987) has shown the impact of context in why some urban neighborhoods have so many norms of cooperation and high property values, whereas others evolve into a complete lack of coordinated action, often leading to urban decline. He uses the concept of mimicking to explain why people in some neighborhoods keep their houses and yards clean and neat, pick up litter if they see it, paint their houses, keep them in good repair, and spend money to maintain the value of their property, whereas similar people living in other neighborhoods do not engage in any of these activities. When a neighborhood benefits from a strong sense of community, residents may easily be willing to work to make it remain so — as long as they see that those around them are doing the same. When a neighborhood begins to go downhill, on the other hand, residents may see that their individual efforts are a lost cause — only a drop in the bucket, unlikely to make a difference. Worse, they may feel that any investment in their home may be wasted since the neighbors are allowing their own homes to decline in value. The main point is that behaviors are strongly conditioned by the behaviors of neighbors or colleagues, and these positive reinforcements can act equally strongly either to create a virtuous cycle of cooperation or a vicious cycle of hopelessness. Neighborhoods can shift from stable to unstable very quickly if the residents sense a shift in the attitudes of those around them.

Similar patterns of virtuous and vicious cycles is apparent in Putnam's (1993) study of civic life in Italy, in Converse and Pierce's (1986) study of participation in strikes, riots, and demonstrations during the May 1968 events in France, Lohmann's (1994) study of the demonstrations leading to the fall of the German Democratic Republic in 1991, and in Chong's (1991) work on social movements in the United States. People cannot riot or demonstrate alone, no matter how strongly they may feel compelled. Where one sees all one's neighbors ready to participate in a protest or social action, one becomes much more willing to participate oneself. Two people with the same attitudes, but living in different neighborhoods, might behave quite differently. Social movements of many kinds are characterized by sensitivity to context, and therefore by positive feedback. Dennis Chong (1991) shows the role of leadership and expected success in the civil rights movement: where many saw their neighbors participating, they overcame their fears; where few saw their neighbors participating, they were less likely to participate themselves. The participation of neighbors and the expectation of success appear to be important predictors of participation in a great variety of social and protest movements. All these models have in common a positive feedback process at their core, and they help explain the explosive nature of many social and protest movements; either they fail utterly or they can be the subject of explosive growth once they reach a certain threshold (see Granovetter 1978). Further and perhaps most importantly, virtuous cycles such as those described by Putnam or Crenson can quickly be transformed into vicious cycles as a social group crosses some threshold.

Scholars studying such disparate phenomena as revolution, rebellion, social protest, home ownership, the emergence of industrial standards, stock market pricing, the emergence of market leaders in the software industry, industrial geography, fashion, and the toy industry have all noted the exquisite sensitivity to context that humans can display. Where the behaviors of one are related to a desire or a need to conform to the behaviors of those around one, then positive feedback can occur. We can see this in everything from real estate to fashion. Who can predict what will be the next Pokémon? No one. But as long as kids want the same toys as their friends have, rather than choosing what to play with independently and in isolation from others, then we can predict that there will always be cascades and fads in the toy industry. Social cascades are an important source of positive feedback in politics as in other areas of life. Another important source is how humans process information while dealing with complex and multidimensional issues. Being unable simultaneously to pay attention to all elements of a complex decision, or not knowing all the relevant dimensions of a decision, people shift from focus to focus.

ATTENTION SHIFTING

Positive feedback processes are not limited to the mimicking actions of many individuals behaving in a group. Positive feedback also affects individual-level decision making. When people are called upon to make decisions in complex and multidimensional issues, they may be forced to focus on some elements more than others. Consider free trade. When Congress was asked to consider granting permanent normal trading relations to China in 2000, advocates on various sides of the issue argued that the issue was related to world labor standards, environmental protection, human rights, abortion, nuclear nonproliferation, America's potential democratizing influence in China, and the relative powers of the Congress and the president, among other things. Different participants in the debate, of course, pushed different elements of the issue to the forefront as they attempted to sway others' opinions on the issue. Fundamentally, however, large decisions often involve so many different dimensions of potential relevance that it can be hard, if not impossible, simultaneously to pay attention to all of them. As a practical matter, most decision makers pay attention only to a few of the underlying dimensions. At times, however, they may be forced to pay greater attention to one of the elements they had been ignoring, as when these dimensions force themselves up on the agenda because of a crisis or because of the actions of another decision maker. When this occurs, people can change their views on the issue even without changing their minds on the underlying dimensions of choice; they simply give greater weight to a dimension they had previously been ignoring.

William Riker (1984, 1986) noted that strategically minded politicians could often have dramatic effects on public debates or parliamentary voting by shifting the elements of debate from one underlying dimension to another. Jones (1994) has developed an individual decision making model involving attributes (John Zaller [1992] calls these "considerations") that underlie a set of political alternatives (such as issues before a legislature or candidates before an electorate). A decision maker can attend to only a very limited number of such attributes or considerations. If, during a debate, one's attention is shifted from one attribute to another, as Jones shows formally, a decision may be reversed.

Such reversals are a critical component of the instability that characterizes occasional positive feedback in politics. So long as one's understanding of a political issue is dominated by one attribute, there is likely to be little change (negative feedback dominates). But when new attributes come to be salient, then more substantial change is possible (positive feedback may emerge). The attention model of political debate shows the importance of the ability to focus attention on one dimension of the issue rather than on another. Where one side portrays an issue as relating to states' rights, a rival might propose that the issue really concerns racial equality. The more people participating in the debate who support one of these views over the other, the more difficult it becomes to maintain the contrary view. Political debates therefore can exhibit the signature characteristics of positive feedback, since the behavior of an individual can be closely tied to the behaviors of those around them. Individuals making complex decisions do this; social groups do it even more because both attention shifting and cue taking may occur simultaneously.

Most issues of public policy are inherently complex. Poverty has many causes; regulation of the electrical industry has a great number of impacts; military spending is related to a great number of unrelated goals; regulation of the health care industry can affect scores of different social goals. Public debates on these complex issues never simultaneously contain full discussions of all the relevant dimensions of choice; we always limit our discussion to the few dimensions that for one reason or another are on the agenda. But the future always harbors the possibility that a given element of the debate previously unattended may become more prominent. So we can see that issues of public policy typically contain the seeds of positive feedback because of the potential for attention shifts to occur. Public debates are even more prone to attention shifts and positive feedback than models of individual decision making would lead one to think, however, because public debates are social debates. That is, many of the participants in a public debate are acutely aware of the behaviors of those around them, and they want nothing more than to be on the winning side. Public debates, then, are simultaneously subject to the processes of attention shifting common to all multidimensional and complex decisions and also to the cascading and mimicking phenomena that we have noted where decisions are made in reaction to the decisions of those around oneself. The result of these twin characteristics of policy debates is that positive feedback is a fundamental feature of many policies.

POSITIVE FEEDBACK IN POLICY PROCESSES

In previous work, we have shown how changing public images of a given policy question can interact with changing institutional venues of activity to produce surprisingly rapid changes in public policy. A dominant public policy image is often unidimensional even while the underlying issue is multidimensional. Attention is often directed at only one aspect or dimension, while others are suppressed or ignored. For example, we noted that public attention toward nuclear power was once focused almost exclusively on the potential that it would produce electricity "too cheap to meter," that it represented the latest scientific advance, and other positive elements; later, of course, the image degraded considerably. At no time, however, were the many dimensions of the nuclear power industry, with its various positive and negative elements, simultaneously a part of the public discussion. This process was common, not unusual, in our study of nine different public policies.

Where a given policy monopoly begins to lose its supporting policy image, rival institutions of government which may not have been involved in the issue previously may assert their authority to become involved. The more hostile agencies that become involved, the greater the change in image; the greater the degradation of the image, the more new political leaders and agencies will want to become involved, and the cycle continues. This positive feedback mechanism explained some of the rapid shifts we observed with public policies toward nuclear power, pesticides, smoking, and other issues (see Baumgartner and Jones 1993).

The logic that applies to markets, elections, social movements, and policy change also applies to individual strategies of policy making, lobbying, and decision making within a legislature. We can establish an extremely simple model of a policy maker's willingness to spend effort on one issue rather than another. Consider the choices available to a policy maker operating under a condition of scarcity of attention. The person might be an elected official, a lobbyist, an appointed official, or a staff member giving advice to such a person; the key element is that she must choose the issues on which to spend her time, organizational resources, and energy (see Salisbury and Shepsle 1981; Browne 1995; Hall 1996). One thing she might prefer is to work on issues that have a chance of success rather than on those issues that are sure to go nowhere.

If the probability of any action on the issue is zero, then there is little reason to focus attention on the issue, since there is no expected benefit. What would cause the probability of success to rise? One important element is the expected behaviors of other relevant actors. This is why focusing events can be so important, and why policy making in Washington and elsewhere often exhibits a herdlike phenomenon characteristic of positive feedback processes. A given issue may be stalled for years, but suddenly attracts the attention of many policy makers. This can happen not because any preferences change, but only because expectations change concerning the probability of government action. With many actors simultaneously paying attention to the expected willingness of others to pay attention to the issue and to expend resources in bringing about change, they may all change in rapid response to each other, or to a commonly perceived event. So a prominent technical study, or a stochastic event such as a high school shooting bringing attention to the issue of gun control, can be important not so much because it changes anyone's mind about how serious the issue is (though this may well happen), but because it may change policy makers' calculations about the willingness of allies to become involved in the struggle. The expectation of success itself can create momentum. Of course the mobilization of one side can lead to the countermobilization of the other side, as in the negative feedback processes discussed in the previous section. In the case of gun control in the wake of the Littleton, Colorado, high school shootings, as in many other cases with such prominent focusing events, the more remarkable phenomenon is how the event mobilizes one side tremendously while it demobilizes the other. Certainly, these mobilizations do not last forever (positive feedback processes must come to an end at some point), but the important question is how much policy change may be enacted as a direct result of the heightened attention to the issue generated during this short burst of increased attention. Often, important policies are adapted remarkably quickly, even after the same issue had gone nowhere in previous years.

The willingness of a political actor to invest resources in a given lobbying struggle is likely to be related to two things: The probability of success (which is related to the expected behaviors of other actors involved), and the expected benefits. Expected benefits may change only slowly or not at all, but the expected behaviors of other relevant actors can often change dramatically and in rapid response to commonly perceived crises, focusing events, the release of studies, presidential pronouncements, or other premeditated or stochastic events. Therefore positive feedback processes, or policy bandwagons, can occur very quickly and without any change in the expected policy benefits to the various actors involved. More likely than a change in policy benefits is a change in the expected actions of others.

But why would participants expect a change in the actions of others? There can be more than one reason, but the most likely is that somehow new information has become available, and participants are trying to anticipate how others will react to it. As we have repeatedly argued, however, most so-called new information is not new at all. Rather, some aspect of available information has become more salient in the course of political debate, or some old argument suddenly has some credible new evidence to support it, or some information long known to one group of policy makers has come to the awareness of another group. As John Kingdon (1984) has argued, conditions do not automatically translate into problems; that translation occurs when previously ignored aspects of a complex situation become salient, and this occurs through the efforts of policy makers attempting to redefine public debates. So the two mechanisms that account for positive feedback effects in policy processes are intimately related. Research on how previously ignored attributes of complex public policies become salient in a policy debate, setting off a cascade of interest through the calculations of expected action described above, is currently ill-understood, however, and it remains a key item on the agenda for students of the policy process.

Most important from our perspective, large-scale decisions about institutional design are often made during periods of heightened attention to an issue; these often have substantial long-term consequences. Central to our view of the links between positive feedback processes, which are relatively rare and by definition short-lived, and negative feedback, which are more common and more long-lasting, is the role of institutional design.

INSTITUTIONAL EVOLUTION

When Aaron Wildavsky (1964) looked at federal budgetary processes and noted the importance of incrementalism, he was careful to limit his analysis of yearly budgets to units that could be directly compared. Therefore he eliminated from consideration those cases where new programs and agencies were created, radically modified, or terminated, looking instead only at the years of "steady-state" functioning of existing institutions. When Richard Fenno (1966) did his landmark study of the congressional budgetary process, he also deleted all cases that threatened "organizational integrity." One could hardly do better than these two projects as studies of steady-state budgeting. Together they demonstrated the importance of inertial forces, a finding that has been one of the most influential in the literature not just on budgeting, but on public policy overall. Of course, one might question what happens when all the observations are used.

Several scholars, including Wildavsky, have looked at more inclusive data sets and they have consistently found a combination of the same levels of incrementalism with a significant amount of nonincremental, radical change (see Davis, Dempster, and Wildavsky 1966; Jones, Baumgartner, and True 1998). In sum, the federal budgetary process is characterized by considerable incrementalism and stability, to be sure, but also by a remarkable degree of radical change. Key to the differences in these two outcomes are questions of institutional design.

Institutions are enduring rules for making decisions. At the broadest level, the Constitution establishes the rules for the American political system, and of course these have changed only rarely — our Constitution has been stable for over two hundred years. At another level, however, agencies and institutional procedures, or rules, structure the policy process in important ways. The budgetary rules observed by Wildavsky and Fenno were institutions in this sense. Institutions may be explicitly changed or they may slowly evolve. An analogy is the law — it changes explicitly when new laws are passed or old ones are amended, and it evolves more slowly through judicial interpretation and case law. Our Constitution has been amended only a few times, but its interpretation has changed dramatically over the centuries.

Invariably, institutions are created or terminated or their procedures are radically modified during periods of heightened attention to their purposes. Those involved in making these restructuring decisions typically have certain goals in mind. Therefore, institutions are typically designed to encourage participation by certain groups and discourage participation by others. Institutions are also designed to facilitate the use of some aspects of information rather than others. Institutions often promote certain issue definitions by requiring that decision makers consider to some types of information but not others. The Environmental Protection Agency looks at issues differently than the Small Business Administration; the Anti-Trust Division of the Justice Department has different staff expertise, different reporting requirements, and different priorities than does the Department of Commerce. If institutions are often created and reorganized during periods of heightened attention to a given problem, they do not disappear when public concern dies away; rather, they may be the most important legacies of agenda access. After an issue is no longer part of the public agenda, the institutions, procedures, and biases that these encourage, designed to achieve one set of goals rather than another, remain in place.

Most important social problems that government institutions may be designed to alleviate are extremely complex, but the institutions designed to attack these problems often are given the particular mandate to focus on one element of the problem. Of course, the institution may change its focus as it becomes clear that the problem has other causes that must be addressed. More typically, however, we design institutions with only a partial mandate to focus on one dimension of an inherently multidimensional problem. Welfare programs are designed to alleviate the problems of poverty, but of course their main focus is typically to distribute aid to poor people; it would be outside of their mandate to envision a radically different approach to the problem. So, if underlying social problems are largely multidimensional, but if institutions are designed to focus on one or a limited number of these dimensions but to ignore others, then it is inevitable that periodically there will be demands for institutional reorganization or for the creation of new institutions with different foci of attention. Rival institutions are created that approach the same problem from a different perspective, and in time these jurisdictional overlaps multiply. The inevitable consequence is that institutions promote simplified views of more complex social issues. Because of the limited representation of complex issues within institutional frameworks, the smooth functioning of a given set of institutions can be interrupted by periodic recognition that it is not solving the entire underlying problem. Periods of negative feedback may alternate with periods of positive feedback during which attention focuses on new aspects of the problem, and new institutions are formed to address these newly salient aspects.

If the underlying social issue that they are designed to deal with is especially complex (e.g., poverty, parity in international trade flows, parity in income between agricultural workers and city dwellers), it is unlikely that the procedures decided upon will push toward a global solution of the broader problem. One antipoverty program may be quite effective at addressing certain parts of the problem (e.g., guaranteeing the poorest families some minimum level of subsistence, or providing a breakfast or a hot lunch to schoolchildren), but when attention shifts to another element of the problem (e.g., reducing crime in poor neighborhoods), the program may not appear as successful. Calls for reform may occur, or new programs may be created in the wake of increased attention to a previously unattended dimension of the same broad social or economic problem.

So a multidimensional social issue may be subject to the same types of cycling and instability that formal theorists have discussed in relation to social choices in general. Even if a set of institutions successfully works toward achieving a certain goal, at some point in the future it could be destabilized as attention shifts to another dimension of the issue. This is more likely, of course, where the problems are complex and/or incompletely understood; it is less likely where the institution implements a straightforward technology managing a well-understood task (e.g., delivering the mail). But even in the relatively simple cases, disruptions occur. After all, the shift from a regular cabinet department (Department of the Post Office) to a quasi-independent agency (U.S. Postal Service) in the early 1970s entailed a dramatic reorganization.

Many theories of public policy focus their attention, as Wildavsky did, on the periods of smooth functioning of a given set of institutional structures. Not surprisingly, these are the theories that focus on negative feedback mechanisms, as discussed in a previous section. Other theories ask where the institutional structures come from. Invariably, they note the policy goals that institutional designers are attempting to create (or frustrate) as they structure future participation. A complete understanding of public policy must show respect for the impact of institutions as they structure behavior, but at the same time it must note that these institutional structures themselves are subject to occasional change. To do this it is generally necessary to look at public policy processes over a long period of time. More importantly, it is paramount that the analyst avoid choosing as the scope of attention only the behaviors of a single institution.

Rather than look at a single institution, it is more fruitful to choose an issue and note how various institutions become involved in its resolution. In the chapters that follow, various authors look at a range of public policies and a range of institutions. By tracing public policy over the entire postwar period, most of the chapters note periods that show a smoothly functioning negative feedback system carefully working to perpetuate a given policy goal as well as other periods when the institutional structures surrounding the issue are themselves thrown into doubt and dramatic restructurings occur. As we continue to look at a range of public policy issues and at diverse elements of the policy process, we find a consistent pattern of positive and negative feedback processes alternating irregularly in most areas of public policy. The result is a view of government comprised of a complex mosaic of ever-altering structures of limited participation and attention.

Our consideration of issues over time also allows us to observe, as several of the following chapters amply demonstrate, how issues and institutions affect each other over the long term. Many analysts have noticed the impact of institutional structures on how issues are handled and what policies are produced. However, the impact also works in the opposite direction: institutions change over time as they are forced to adapt to new issues, share jurisdiction with competing institutions, and attend simultaneously to a greater number of the underlying elements of the issues with which they deal. The result of this longer time perspective that the contributors lay out is to show both the endogenous and the exogenous sources of institutional design and evolution.

In *Analytical Politics,* Melvin Hinich and Michael Munger (1997) note that choices are a function of preferences as these interact with institutions. Changes in either preferences or the institutions through which these are expressed, therefore, can result in different choices. Changes in both preferences and institutions at the same time can be explosive, they note, since there can be an interaction effect (a multiplicative factor). Now, would one expect institutions to remain stable while preferences are changing dramatically? Sometimes. However, when the very forces that are leading to changes in preferences are simultaneously acting to promote changes in institutional structures of choice, then we may expect nonincremental, dramatic, and explosive change. Typically, scholars assume that one or the other of these two factors (preferences or institutions) is held constant so that they can model accurately the expected impact of change in the other factor. Usually, the institutions rather than the preferences are assumed to be stable; this is justified because institutional changes are often seen in the real world to be rare, slow, or both. In fact, several chapters that follow will focus on the continued interactions of issues and institutions, what we have previously referred to as the coevolution of issues and structures over time (Baumgartner, Jones, and MacLeod 2000). Positive feedback processes come about when issues are reframed, when institutional designs are altered, and when policy makers come to realize that other policy makers may be looking at old issues in new ways. In any event, this volume provides a range of studies illustrating the importance of a complete view of politics — one that gives proper weight both to the politics of negative feedback and to the related dynamics of positive feedback and dramatic change.

PLAN OF THE BOOK

In chapter 2 we complete our introductory materials, providing a detailed description of the data sets that all the remaining chapters have in common. Each chapter of part two presents a detailed study of a particular policy area: telecommunications, immigration, health care, science, and national security — with a focus on questions of multidimensionality. Each chapter in part three builds on these questions to show how institutions change in reaction to the changing nature of their policy issues and the public agenda overall. Part three does not readdress the same policy issues as part two, but rather focuses on institutional changes in the federal government. In part four, we return to our broad theoretical concerns, discussing the evidence presented in the various empirical chapters of the book and the implications of these findings.

Hopefully, the chapters will raise as many questions as they answer. That is why we have made available the full set of data from the Policy Agendas Project on our web site. Not all readers will be interested in exploring their own analyses, but for those who are so motivated, and we hope that this number will be great, these data constitute our invitation to explore the dynamics of American public policy and to note the ways in which our government has changed over the past several decades. Some will use our data to extend the analyses presented here, perhaps looking at issue areas we did not cover. Others will use the data to criticize or to amend the theoretical perspectives or the findings laid out here. We look forward to the continuing scholarly conversation and to the improved state of theory that will result.

2

STUDYING POLICY DYNAMICS

FRANK R. BAUMGARTNER, BRYAN D. JONES,
AND JOHN D. WILKERSON

All of the chapters in this book have in common the use of a series of data sets that comprise the Policy Agendas Project. The project had its genesis in previous work in which two of us used publicly available sources such as congressional hearings and the *Readers' Guide to Periodical Literature* to trace public and media attention to policy issues over the post–World War II period. In that project, we studied particular issues such as the civilian use of nuclear power, pesticides, smoking and tobacco, and other topics, covering nine issues overall (see Baumgartner and Jones 1993). In the Policy Agendas Project, we adopted a broader approach. With funding from the Political Science Division of the National Science Foundation, we began a much more ambitious project: to trace public attention to all issues, not just a few, and to cover the entire post-1947 period. The project includes data on all congressional hearings, all laws, all stories in the *Congressional Quarterly Almanac,* a sample of stories in the *New York Times Index,* and the entire federal budget. We put together these data sets with the hope of encouraging the systematic study of policy change over long periods of time.

Most of the chapters that follow supplement our data sets with additional information, and we think this is the most fruitful way for most people to make use of the data. In this chapter we lay out some of the basics of the Policy Agendas Project data sets. Our goal here is threefold. First, we explain the content, construction, and logic of the data sets. Second, we show why tracing policy activity across time depends on the availability of these data sets and others like them that ensure comparability across time. We highlight a critical warning signal to would-be policy analysts: most archived data sets are not comparable across time, even if they appear to be. In contrast with many other data sets that appear to be useful for over-time comparisons, our data sets were specifically designed to ensure consistent coding over time. We spend considerable time in this chapter explaining the difficulties of this, as well as the rarity of it. Finally, we provide information that can help other potential users — the readers of this book — to use the data sets themselves.

The critical problem with the rapidly expanding set of computerized and searchable databases covering such things as congressional hearings, media coverage, presidential papers, and other sources of historical information about various public policy issues stems from the fact that designers of these data sets have information retrieval in mind, not the creation of a consistent public record. Keyword searches, the most common form of analysis that one can do, may not reveal consistent results when done over long periods of time because vocabularies change. Indexers change their practices over the decades; keywords are multiplied so that the user can find every mention of a given word, no matter how tangential the topic may have been to the larger point. In sum, many hidden problems arise in the use of available searchable electronic databases — users must beware of what appears to be a consistent series, but which may in fact harbor many hidden inconsistencies. In order to construct a consistent time series over a period as long as those we explore here, one must pay considerable attention to the details of how data sets were created in the first place, and for what purposes they were originally collected. We show in this chapter how rare it is to find comparable data sources over long periods of time, and how we solved this problem in the construction of the Policy Agendas Project. In contrast to other sources of public policy information, our data sets were specifically designed to ensure historical continuity.

THE POLICY AGENDAS PROJECT:
FIVE DATA SETS ON U.S. PUBLIC POLICY

OVERVIEW

Each of the five data sets that make up the project is designed with a simple logic: it should be useful in and of itself to allow analysts to trace attention and government decisions over time, and it should provide enough information about the sources of the material so that anyone who wants to find out more detail about particular issues, decisions, or periods of attention can quickly find more complete information. Therefore, our practice is to gather a minimum of information about each congressional hearing, for example, but also to gather a complete set of identification materials so that the user can get more complete information from the same source materials as we used in the first place. Here we give a simple overview of each of the data sets.

The congressional hearings data set consists of over sixty-seven thousand records corresponding to each hearing held in Congress since 1947. These data were coded from the annual volumes published by the Congressional Information Service and available in most government documents sections of major libraries. Variables coded include several identification variables (CIS identification numbers, date, committees and subcommittees involved), the topic codes, a short textual summary, as well as a series of variables that indicate whether the hearing dealt with proposed legislation or was more of a fact-finding nature; whether it considered an administration proposal; whether it considered appropriations matters; whether it mentioned the creation of a new agency; the number of days the hearing lasted; and the number of sessions in the hearing.

The "CQ Stories" data set consists of a record for each article in the *Congressional Quarterly Almanac* from 1947 onward. In the cases where very long articles are broken into substantially distinct subsections (as is sometimes the case, for example, of discussions of huge omnibus bills or of the president's budget proposals), we have a separate record for each of these sections. In all, there are over twelve thousand records in this data set, which includes identification materials so that a user can find the original story; the committees and subcommittees involved; mentions of any committee reports, bill numbers, and public law numbers if applicable; and information concerning how far through the legislative process the bill proceeded (e.g., whether it passed the House, passed the Senate, was vetoed, was signed into law, or was attached to some other bill as part of an omnibus legislation). In addition, we note the length of the story. This data set is likely to be useful especially for those interested in a further check on the activities and level of interest in Congress to various issues, since the editors of CQ make efforts to cover the most important issues that Congress deals with, including those that are debated but not passed into law. Further, it is especially valuable as a sophisticated index to the *CQ Almanac* itself, since it can be used to identify all stories on a given topic or with other attributes.

Our "Public Laws" data set lists the PL number, the Congress, the sponsor of the legislation, the sponsor's party, the House and Senate report numbers (if any) concerning the bill, an indication of whether there was a conference report, whether the bill was commemorative or substantive, and whether or not the law was previously vetoed by the president. Of course, all these data sets also include a textual summary and a full four-digit set of topic and subtopic codes.

The *New York Times Index* data set consists of a sample of entries in that source, with a total of approximately thirty-six thousand records dating back to 1947. Like the other data sets, this one includes identification material, a short textual summary, and a topic code. The topics are coded only by the major topic categories rather than the 226 subtopics used in the congressional databases, however, because so many stories in the media are on questions that do not correspond exactly to what congressional hearings focus on. In addition, there are entire topic areas, such as obituaries, art and book reviews, sports, and other events that are not included in the congressional databases, as we describe in more detail below. There are a variety of filter variables in the *New York Times* data set as well designed to allow users to include or exclude local news items, international news items, and stories that have anything to do with government and public policy as opposed to those that do not, and whether the story was on page 1. For all stories that mention public policy, we also note whether the story mentions any of a number of institutions of government: the president, Congress, federal agencies, the courts, state and local governments, campaigns and elections, and interest groups.

Our data set on the federal budget is based on annual figures reported by the Office of Management and Budget in the annual budgets submitted by the president, but it is adjusted so that the spending categories are consistent over time. We report spending totals (budget authorizations) for seventy-four narrow categories of spending and seventeen major areas, as described in more detail below. Table 2.1 summarizes our data files.

TABLE 2.1 Summary of Policy Agendas Project Data Sets

Data Set	Period Covered	Source	Unit of Analysis	Number of Cases	Number of Variables
Congressional Hearings	1946–94	CIS Abstracts	hearing	67,291	20
U.S. Public Laws	1948–94	*CQ Almanac* Appendix	Public law	16,318	17
Congressional Quarterly	1948–94	*CQ Almanac*	story	12,583	37
U.S. Budget Authority	1947–97	*Budget of the United States*	OMB sub-function	115	1
New York Times	1947–94	*NYT Index*	story abstracts	36,403	20

THE TOPIC AND SUBTOPIC CODING SYSTEM

Perhaps the most important element that determines the usefulness of our data sets to a large and diverse audience is the extensive set of topic codes that we have devised. In contrast with most sources of longitudinal data, including the federal government's own reports of these materials, we have worked hard to guarantee temporal consistency for our topic categories. Typically, key-word searches, published indices, and other sources of publicly available data over time suffer from a tendency to revise or "improve" the categorization system over time. Our topic categories are consistent over time. This includes our version of the OMB budget authority; we spent over two years simply reading through the footnotes to the annual federal budget noting how OMB had altered its spending classifications over time, and we adjusted the figures so that they are consistent. OMB itself does not have a consistently defined longitudinal time series of the federal budget that goes back as far as the one we have created here. In the case of the budget data set, we use the OMB classification of seventy-four categories of spending (though we adjust it for changing definitions over time and for inflation). For each of the other data sets, we use the major topics listed in table 2.2.

New York Times stories are coded only by the major topics indicated (and since there are many categories of stories, such as book reviews, sports results, or home improvement ideas, dealing with topics on which Congress is rarely called to legislate, there are no corresponding topics in the congressional databases for a few categories that exist in the NYT database, as indicated above). Each of the congressional databases is broken down further by subtopic. For example, the major topic of health is broken down into subtopics as shown in table 2.3.

All in all, there are 27 major topic categories and 226 subtopics in our coding system, as listed in appendix 1. Users can locate all hearings, *CQ* stories, and public laws on a given subtopic or broad topic area with ease. For most categories, one or more of the budget categories used by OMB may also correspond. The U.S. government classifies spending in many ways, but the most useful system for tracking spending by topic is the functional classification system developed by OMB and reported in the annual *Budget of the U.S. Government.* Table 2.4 presents the major topic classifications used by OMB; the complete list of seventy-four detailed subtopics is presented in appendix 2.

OMB reports spending by nineteen major categories (called "functions" in OMB parlance) and also by seventy-four more detailed "subfunctions." Functions 900 (net interest) and 950 (undistributed offsetting receipts) are largely

TABLE 2.2 Major Topic Categories

1.   Macroeconomics
2.   Civil rights
3.   Health
4.   Agriculture
5.   Labor, immigration, and employment
6.   Education
7.   Environment
8.   Energy
10. Transportation
12. Law, crime, and family issues
13. Social welfare
14. Community development and housing
15. Banking, finance, and domestic commerce
16. Defense
17. Space, science, technology, and communications
18. Foreign trade
19. International affairs
20. Federal government operations
21. Public lands and water management

Additional Major Topics Used for *New York Times Index* Only
24. State and local government administration
26. Weather and natural disasters
27. Fires
28. Arts and entertainment
29. Sports and recreation
30. Death notices
31. Churches and religion
99. Other, miscellaneous, and human interest

financial categories that we typically do not analyze since they do not correspond to any substantive government activities or programs. We have, therefore, sixty-six detailed topical categories of spending in seventeen major areas of government activity, not counting the financial categories also reported by OMB. Most, though not all, of the OMB subfunctions and functions correspond closely with one or more of our subtopics and topics into which we have coded our congressional and *New York Times* materials. For most areas of spending, therefore, one can note whether spending corresponds to attention to the given topic area in the media, to congressional activities such as hearings, or to law-making activities such as new statutes. More important

TABLE 2.3 Health Care Subtopics

300	General (includes combinations of multiple subtopics)
301	Health care reform, health care costs, insurance costs and availability
303	Medicare and medicaid
306	Regulation of prescription drugs, medical devices, and medical procedures
307	Health facilities construction and regulation, public health service issues
309	Mental illness and mental retardation
310	Medical fraud, malpractice, and physician licensing requirements
311	Elderly health issues
312	Infants, children, and immunization
313	Health manpower needs and training programs
315	Military health care
332	Alcohol abuse and treatment
333	Tobacco abuse, treatment, and education
334	Illegal drug abuse, treatment, and education
349	Specific diseases
398	Research and development
399	Other

than our coding system to many users may be the fact that our data sets include a textual summary that includes a short description of each story, hearing, law, or abstract. These short summaries allow users to recode our data sets according to their own needs. Table 2.5 provides examples of records for a health subtopic from each of the data sets.

With the combination of an extensive and consistent set of topic codes in each data set and the textual summaries available for each entry, users can combine or recode the data sets to meet their needs. All in all, the extensive topic and subtopic coding is the key to making these linked data sets useful to a broad audience in public policy. In the chapters that follow, a variety of uses of these topic categories are shown.

The major topic and subtopic content codes of the Policy Agendas data set were developed through an iterative procedure that involved proposing an initial set of categories, coding congressional hearings to one and only one of these topic categories, and then modifying the categories until intercoder reliabilities were achieved at the levels of at least 95 percent for the major topic and 90 percent for the minor topic codes (see Baumgartner, Jones, and Mac-Leod 1998a). This topic system was then used to code all U.S. public laws, *Congressional Quarterly* stories, and a sample of *New York Times* stories since 1947. Similar success in reliability was achieved for these data sets.

TABLE 2.4 Major Spending Classifications Used by OMB

Code	Title
050	National defense
150	International affairs
250	General science, space, and technology
270	Energy
300	Natural resources and environment
350	Agriculture
370	Commerce and housing credit
400	Transportation
450	Community and regional development
500	Education, training, employment, and social services
550	Health
570	Medicare
600	Income security
650	Social security
700	Veterans benefits and services
750	Administration of justice
800	General government
900	Net interest
950	Undistributed offsetting receipts

Sources: See appendix 2.

We began by coding congressional hearings, and continually updated and revised our coding system until we had done several years worth of coding. After we had done about ten thousand hearings, we reached a point where few changes were needed any more; each new case fit within one of our established categories, and two coders working independently consistently coded the same cases identically over 90 percent of the time (and we achieved over 95 percent accuracy across the 19 major topics). We then went backwards in time, coding hearings all the way back to 1947. Subsequently, we followed the same procedures for all the public laws and then for all the stories in the *CQ Almanac*. Since these two sources often are broader than the congressional hearings, we more often made use of the – 00 subtopic, which includes general coverage of the entire topic area or combinations of multiple subtopics. For example, an omnibus crime bill might well cover elements of sentencing, aid to local law enforcement agencies, prison spending issues, and other subtopics. This would be coded 1200 in the Public Law and CQ Stories data sets. Congressional hearings would be coded in the same manner, but Congress is more likely to hold

TABLE 2.5 Selected Textual Summaries from Four Data Sets

Topic Code	Entry Summary

	Hearings
301	Federal health care spending
301	Health care reform and the role of medical technologies
301	Health maintenance organizations and hospitals providing managed health care
301	Health care access problems of disadvantaged and minority persons
301	Hospital financial practices and issues

	CQ Stories
301	Minority Health: a non-controversial draft bill to authorize at least $144 million in fiscal 1994 to improve the health of minorities.
301	Alternative Health-Care Proposals: alternative plans made by Congress as opposed to the Clinton plan
301	Health Care Debate Takes Off: Congress gets up to speed on the complex economics and policies driving the US health care system
301	Health care program with included tax increase on the wealthy.
301	Health care reform bill to impose national limits on health spending and expanded access to health insurance for pregnant women, children and those who worked for small businesses.

	Public Laws
301	Amend the Public Health Service Act to provide an improvement in the health of members of minority groups
301	Provide federal assistance in establishing and expanding health maintenance organizations
301	Revise and extend the program for the establishment and expansion of the health maintenance organizations
301	Enact the Health Maintenance Organization Amendments of 1978

	New York Times Index
3	Pres. Clinton's plan to save $35 billion from Medicare over next four years
3	Column article on both governmental and employers' long-term care policies and state intervention
3	Cost of health services should be distributed uniformly in all the states by financing it nationally
3	Hillary Clinton will appear before five committees of Congress during hearings on Admin's health care plan
3	Letter from Western Pennsylvania Blue Cross executive officer explains how Penn. keeps percentage of people without health insurance under 10 percent

hearings separately on each of these different elements of the bill. If they did, then the hearings would be coded according to the various relevant subtopic codes (1210 for sentencing; 1209 for police and law enforcement issues; 1205 for prisons; and 1299 for other and miscellaneous). For the *New York Times Index,* we coded only by the major topic categories and we added several categories because there are many areas of reporting that simply have no congressional counterparts (recipes, architectural reviews, sports results, obituaries, and weather reports would be some examples).

The topic categories that we developed are mutually exclusive and exhaustive. In the inevitable cases where a hearing, law, or story covered more than one topic, we coded it by the topic that was predominant. Each major topic also includes a general subtopic (always numbered −00) that includes cases where several different subtopics, all within the same major topic area, are discussed. In addition, where we noted large numbers of cross-references, we created distinct subtopic codes specifically for these cases. An example would be military health care issues: Are those defense issues or health issues? Our answer is to code them in their own category so that users can decide that question for themselves. Table 2.3 shows that category 315 is reserved for this topic, just as category 311 is reserved for elderly health issues. By creating a series of "intersection" topics, we built into our coding system a level of flexibility that users with different interests may exploit. With over 220 topics in our system, most are quite specific. Still, users should note that we allow only for a single topic code for each item. Where the case clearly crosses boundaries, we either created a new category specifically for it (if there were many such cases), or we coded the case by the topic that predominated. In cases that were evenly balanced, our rule was to use the category that is listed first in the list of topics. Our complete list of subtopics available on our web site includes an extensive explanation of each topic category with examples of cases coded into each as well as "see also" references to related subtopics where similar cases may be coded.

CUSTOMIZING AND SUPPLEMENTING PROJECT DATA

Among the greatest advantages of the Policy Agendas Project data sets is their reliability across time. The biggest problem with any single data set is that it may not suit all needs. While our coding system is reliable, a student of a particular policy area may find that it does not match exactly the aims of his or her study. We suggest three strategies: creating one's own customized set of subtopics; supplementing our data with further analysis; and searching and recoding our data based on the textual summaries. Many users will find that the data sets included here are sufficient for their needs, for example to compare attention and spending on defense to spending on domestic policies such as education, health care, or transportation. A much broader community of users will be served, however, by some combination of our data and some others.

The first possibility for customizing our data sets is quite straightforward. Appendix 1 shows the full set of topic and subtopic codes we use. While we combined various subtopics into more inclusive major topic categories, these aggregations can easily be redone, either to make our topic categories broader or narrower. Those interested in all defense-related issues, for example, might choose a set of subtopic codes that is centered within our major topic of 16 (defense), but which also includes subtopic 315 (military health care). Finding all foreign policy–related topics would require including a combination of topics 16 (defense), 18 (foreign trade), 19 (international affairs and foreign aid) and possibly a few subtopics from other areas such as 530 (immigration and refugee issues), which we code as part of the major topic of labor, immigration, and employment. The simple point is that users can easily recombine our 226 categories into customized topic areas that suit their needs. The more subtle point is that the ways in which we aggregated our 226 subtopics into 19 major topic categories might not suit all needs.

Second, our data can easily be supplemented. Each record contains the information needed to find the original source material. So, for example, one can identify every congressional hearing or CQ story focusing on immigration and refugee issues by searching on topic number 530. With this list, it is straightforward to then go to the CIS Abstracts, to the CQ Almanac, or to another source to gather information about who testified at the hearings, which legislation was considered, and what arguments were discussed, or what types of refugee issues were being debated. Several of the chapters that follow use our data sets as the base and supplement them with additional coding from the original sources.

The third way to customize our data sets is to make use of the short textual summary included in each record, illustrated in table 2.5 above. These can be searched to identify mentions of keywords in combination with our topic coding system, or instead of using our topic coding system. This may be used in two different ways: to create entire new topics (searching for all mentions of words related to the elderly, for example, as one dissertation student we supervised successfully did in order to identify all hearings dealing with issues of concern to that demographic group), or in combination with a subtopic selection in order to narrow down one or more of our subtopics to an even more precise definition. In the example above of topic code 530, immigration and refugee issues, one can read through the summary to identify one or another of those more precise topics, or to find only those cases dealing with refugees from Asia, for example.

With the combination of an extensive and consistent set of topic codes in each data set and the textual summaries available for each entry, users can combine or recode the data sets to meet their needs. All in all, the extensive topic and subtopic coding is the key to making these linked data sets useful to a broad audience in public policy. Our web site includes a full set of codebooks explaining each variable in each of the data sets, a full description of the topic codes, including examples and "see also" references, and the data sets themselves, as well as some simple annual counts from each of the data sets. In addition, users can find various updates, bibliographic information, and other useful items.

INFORMATION SYSTEMS IN THE STUDY OF POLICY PROCESSES

Recent years have seen the development of computerized search techniques and large publicly available databases of many types. These have created great new research opportunities, but also some new problems. Ironically, we often suffer from too much information, or more precisely from information that appears to be reliable at first glance, but which on deeper inspection proves to suffer from massive reliability problems. Most importantly, many large and historical data sets are designed for information retrieval, but are almost useless for the types of trend and pattern recognition that we have designed into our data sets. This is mostly because of three problems: backwards compatibility (that is, no effort is typically made to ensure that topic categories are reliable over time); overcategorization (that is, multiple keywords are used to index each item, but the keywords are not consistent and each item may be coded many times); and uniqueness (that is, each data set, collected by a different institution, agency, corporation, or scholar, uses a different set of keywords and subject categories than the others).

THREE PROBLEMS

The major problem today in quantitative policy studies involves moving from information systems based on retrieval to ones capable of trend recognition. The availability of many impressive and useful retrieval systems does not mean that they can be used for trend recognition. To do this, three critical problems must be addressed.

Backward compatibility. Analysts maintaining existing databases that have been used to monitor policy making — budgets, legislative activity, press coverage, etc.— tend to add and subtract categories over time. Normally no thought is given to making sure that previous uses of categories are consistent with present ones. This means that a category system applied in 1970 can be a quite different entity by 1995, even though it purports to assess the same material. Existing indexing systems do not value temporal consistency, but consistent categories are essential to studying policy change over time. Indexing systems must be continuously adjusted if temporal consistency is to be maintained, with all relevant material reclassified any time new categories are added. In the case of annually published indices to hearings and media coverage, however, there is no opportunity to go back and recode the previous years once the analyst decides that a new keyword or new subject category must be added. In our data sets, we did exactly this; we coded information covering the entire postwar period with the same topic categories in mind.

Overcategorization. Overcategorization is the propensity to place items in multiple nonexclusive categories. A single congressional proposal applying civil rights legislation to providers of home health care, for example, might be classified as a commerce bill, a labor bill, a health care bill, an elderly bill, *and* a civil rights bill. An important example is Legislative Indexing Vocabulary (LIV), developed by the Library of Congress. This indexing system was developed to enable congressional staff and other researchers to identify legislative actions that are relevant to their interests. This search tool is available to the public via THOMAS, the Library of Congress web site. LIV currently includes more than seven thousand subject terms, and a given bill can be coded as relevant to several dozen of these terms. While such an approach is desirable for information retrieval, it is practically useless for studying policy trends. The main purpose of the bill cannot be deciphered from the government's (or any other) indexing system. Since the purpose is to allow retrieval of all items even tangentially or incidentally related to the topic, many data sets typically are marked by extensive overcategorization. Similar problems come with the use of full text searches for keywords. A search for all bills that mention the word "cancer" would find thousands of bills, but many of these would not be primarily about that topic, but would have mentioned it only in passing, their main thrust being elsewhere. For some users, this all-inclusive search process is exactly what is needed; for others, less so. The important point is that the user should realize that all indexing systems are not equally useful for all purposes. Typically, information retrieval systems are designed to err in the direction of including too much. Most importantly, they typically do not distinguish between those cases where the keyword refers to the main topic of the item found and those where the keyword is merely one of a laundry list of topics that may have been mentioned. Of course, to find every case where a given topic was mentioned, this is exactly what some users want, so these retrieval systems play an important role and their design is not a flaw; rather, it simply needs to be understood.

Uniqueness. Even if indexing systems overcome the backward compatibility and overcategorization problems, there is an additional issue: Comparisons across data sets. One indexing system often cannot be compared to another. As a consequence, causal relations among arenas cannot be examined. For example, one might wonder if media coverage leads or lags governmental interest and activity in a policy area. This would not be possible even if both governmental activity and media coverage indexes were consistently categorized and were backward compatible unless both arenas were coded according to the same indexing system. While policy scholars emphasize "process," in fact we lack the tools needed to study the evolution of a policy idea quantitatively.

It is sometimes possible to construct parallel data sets using multiple data sources with different, but similar, categories and subject headings. For example, two of us previously constructed a series of comparable data sets tracing congressional and media attention to pesticides, nuclear power, child abuse, and certain other topics (Baumgartner and Jones 1993). In doing this, however, we were careful to construct separate lists of keywords and subject headings for each different data source (see Woolley 2000 for a discussion of the importance of making these comparisons with care). While this was possible for us to do in a small number of cases, it is not feasible to make such disparate coding systems match up across the board. While some areas of fit can often be found, there is no general solution. We solved this problem simply by applying the same coding system to all four of our data sets. (We were forced to admit defeat in our efforts to make the OMB data sets completely compatible with our other ones, though it does correspond in most categories.)

INFORMATION RETRIEVAL VS. PATTERN RECOGNITION

Providers and immediate users of most data sources are generally interested in *retrieval*, whereas students and scholars are interested in *patterns* and *trends*. The critical component for assessing trends and patterns is the reliability of the measuring instrument. If the relationship between the indicator and the measurement object changes over time, then the instrument cannot be used to follow trends. The critical component in retrieval is to make sure that the users of information find all relevant material. The expert indexer wants to make certain that a researcher interested in a topic will find and be able to recover a particular document. Librarians want an indexing system that allows them to find all relevant documents and would prefer to have this system err in the direction of providing more rather than fewer citations.

If, as is often the case, the indexed material evolves in content, then the indexer has no compunction about adding new key terms to aid the retriever of information in finding just what she wants. But it is extremely rare for the provider of information to go back in time and make sure the indexing categories are consistent. Any student of trends can make large-scale mistakes by assuming that a category this year contains the same content as last year's. Examples of this process would include something like the subject headings in the *New York Times Index* or the *Readers' Guide to Periodical Literature.* Considering a topic such as racial integration, new subject headings are often added whenever important new topics arise in the real world: so "busing" would become a relevant and widely used subject heading in the 1960s, just as "Brown v. Board of Education" would refer to many important stories on integration after, but obviously not before, 1954. There is certainly no reason why an indexer would not add new and important subject categories to allow readers to find the stories they are looking for. Our simple point is that users looking to trace changes over time must be especially aware of these changes in coding and category definitions (see also Woolley 2000).

There are three types of information systems, each of which is designed to achieve a different goal. It is useful to be aware of the goals of each type of information system. By far the most commonly used information systems are *retrieval systems,* designed to allow a user to use her knowledge to find a document, use multiple keywords to characterize each document in the system. An example is THOMAS, Congress's information system for citizens. Each bill, hearing, law, etc. is characterized by multiple categories — the Library of Congress's Legislative Indexing Vocabulary, which currently contains thousands of key terms. Because there are so many terms used to characterize each item, one has no way of tracing changes in policy categories across time.

Pattern recognition systems operate to find patterns empirically in a body of data. Designers develop computer programs embodying cluster or scaling routines that empirically search the data and report patterns. An example is Poole and Rosenthal's (1997) comprehensive study of roll call voting patterns in Congress since 1789, a research tool used regularly by congressional scholars. Their NOMINATE system basically recognizes patterns of voting in each

Congress. Pattern recognition systems, however, cannot be linked to other databases, since it is the result of a scaling procedure using roll call votes, but with no effort to categorize by topic.

Trend recognition systems rely on the highest level of designer knowledge. Expert coding systems are established, generally based on some explicit or implicit theory of the subject matter. Categories in the coding schema are exhaustive and mutually exclusive, and the coders must make key decisions about where items are to fall. An important example is the tabulation of a country's economic output by sector. Economists must maintain consistent coding categories that are exhaustive and mutually exclusive. When the economy develops in a manner that requires new categories, experts must ensure compatibility by recoding previous information according to the newly designed categories. Otherwise it will seem as if there is an explosion of new economic activity when the categories are added. A great variety of economic statistics are designed to allow comparisons over time, and the designers of these systems, such as the Bureau of the Census or the Bureau of Labor Statistics, are loath to revise their categories. Since they are careful to revise them only when necessary (and to conduct careful studies to note the measurement-induced changes in the trends they seek to trace), users can safely use these data series to analyze trends over time.

Parallel trend recognition systems are trend recognition systems in which the same indexing system is used for several different arenas — as, for example, when media coverage and congressional hearings are coded according to the same policy content system. While it is common in full-text databases to be able to search across databases using the same or similar keywords, we have discussed above how these full-text searches can often err on the side of including cases that are only tangentially related to the topic searched for. In our databases, we used the same coding process to code congressional hearings, statutes, *CQ Almanac* stories, and entries in the *New York Times Index*. Therefore, common analyses can be done comparing these disparate data sources. Table 2.6 summarizes the differences in various types of information systems.

Information systems designed for one purpose are not normally adaptable for other purposes. That is, a retrieval system is not easily adaptable to follow trends. Similarly, trend systems are not always the best devices for retrieving information. We believe that the data sets that comprise the Policy Agendas Project are the best available for the purposes that we use them for in this book. They are specifically designed to allow for parallel trend recognition, and the textual summaries that are included as parts of each record also allow users to conduct keyword searches. Of course, for some uses, a full-text keyword

TABLE 2.6 Types of Information Systems

Purpose of the System	Substantive Base of the Initial Indexing System	Example
Information retrieval	low	THOMAS, other keyword-based systems
Pattern recognition	medium	Nominate
Trend recognition	high, in one issue area	CPI, other economic indicators
Parallel trend recognition	high, in many issue areas	Policy Agendas Project

search is what is needed, and for some uses our particular topic coding system will not be appropriate.

CONCLUSION

The Policy Agendas Project consists of five linked and comparable data sets covering the entire post–World War II period. These data sets allow the systematic comparison of a variety of issues and the exploration of a number of questions that have not before been subject to systematic quantitative analysis. We believe that the ability to make comparisons across many issues and to compare the policy process more generally will lead to a variety of new understandings about the American policy process. For example, we can systematically compare issues on the dimension of their agenda status, and when we do so we observe that very few issue areas remain out of the realm of public discussion over the entire period. Similarly, when we look at budgetary incrementalism, we find that almost all areas exhibit periods of stasis as well as periods of dramatic change. Full understandings of the policy process will come with the kinds of broad-based comparisons that our new data sets allow, especially as these are compared and integrated with previous studies based on smaller sets of comparisons.

Many previous works in public policy have focused on certain patterns of behavior, such as institutionally created equilibrium behaviors leading to steady, routine, bureaucratic outputs. Others have contrasted with this literature in their studies of particular policy areas that have exhibited periods of dramatic change, reversal, or macropolitical intervention. Because of the lack of a common set of indicators, however, scholars have not been able to characterize any given pattern of behavior as particularly common, uncommon, or so rare as to be a complete anomaly. While we do not expect that the creation of these data sets will put an end to various disputes in the literature, we do hope that they will encourage broad studies of the policy process, studies that note simultaneously the importance of inertia, incrementalism, and institutionally driven patterns of stability at the same time as they note that these characteristics of many policies coexist with their polar opposites: dramatic policy changes and the creation of new institutional structures that occur from time to time in all areas of politics and public policy. As two of us wrote in a previous book, we believe that these seeming opposites are actually part of a single underlying process (Baumgartner and Jones 1993).

PART TWO

MULTIDIMENSIONALITY
AND PUNCTUATED EQUILIBRIUM
IN PUBLIC POLICY

Having laid out our theoretical perspectives in chapter 1 and a description of our shared data sources in chapter 2, we turn in this section to a series of individual studies of particular policy areas. Through detailed analyses of telecommunications policy, immigration, health care, science and technology, and national security policy over the entire post–World War II period, the chapters that follow demonstrate a series of related themes. First, every public policy of substance is inherently multidimensional, but official consideration (and public understanding) of the issue at any given time typically is only partial. That is, the institutions of government, like people in general, tend to focus exclusively on only a subset of the underlying dimensions of complex policy issues such as those discussed here. We set short-term, incomplete, and partial goals and design policies to meet them. After we focus on a particular goal for long enough, if the underlying issue is itself multidimensional, we realize that we have ignored other important goals whether or not we may have accomplished the original goal. In chapter 3, for example, Michael C. Mac-Leod shows how telecommunications policy in the United States was once designed to foster the development of a single national network based on the AT&T monopoly with a goal of providing maximal service to rural areas and a single standard of quality. Of course there were other goals, such as technical innovation, economic competitiveness, and fairness to competitors, but these were given little weight during the early period when the overriding goal was to establish the national system in the first place. As time went on, other dimensions of the issue became more important, of course. But change did not come incrementally in this case; rather the AT&T monopoly was sustained for decades through powerful forces of negative feedback. These were broken, as MacLeod demonstrates, through the rapid interactions of multiple venues of federal policy making: congressional committees, courts, challenging business competitors, and the public. In other words, a positive feedback mechanism replaced a smoothly functioning negative feedback system in the telecommunications industry when the monopoly was finally broken up. These changes, amply illustrated and explained in the telecommunications case, resulted from changing institutional pressures, to be sure. But they would not have been possible if the underlying policy questions were not themselves inherently multidimensional. The complexity of all public policy issues ensures the potential for instability in politics.

We continue our explorations of the multidimensional nature of a series of public policies in each subsequent chapter in this section of the book. As Valerie F. Hunt shows in chapter 4, immigration is variously seen as a fundamental element of the American creed, as a source for low-wage labor, as a source of strain on our public services, as an engine of economic growth and national diversity, and in many other ways. However, at any given time and within any given governmental institution, a single or a few of these diverse policy images typically hold sway. Policies are designed to promote a single or a small set of goals in immigration policy, but inevitably these cannot achieve all the diverse goals of what an ideal policy would be. So we lurch from one focus to another; the various public institutions with sway over immigration policies vie with each other for influence. Health care, science policy, national security policy similarly are linked with a great variety of different goals. The inevitable consequence of the diverse and multidimensional nature of any significant public policy is that we should not expect it to achieve a stable and global equilibrium. Rather, individual institutions or programs may for a time function smoothly to achieve some of the myriad goals that we might set for them, but it is inevitable that other goals will not be attained even if the policy works flawlessly according to its original design. As these other goals become more prominent, calls will emerge for changes in policy. The chapters that follow explore these issues in five different areas of domestic and international policy. While they do not exhaust what can be demonstrated, they do provide a great deal of information concerning the inherent multidimensionality of the underlying policy issues and they show the many implications of this simple fact.

A second theme has to do with studying policy change. This book has two goals, after all: to illustrate important ideas about positive and negative feedback in politics, and to illustrate methods of studying change over time. Each of the chapters in this section focuses on a given policy area. Using our various data sources as a starting point, the chapters in this section build on these data sources by adding information. MacLeod's study of telecommunication policy over most of the twentieth century relies on our data concerning congressional committee hearings, but he supplements this information with a wide variety of other sources including lists of witnesses at those hearings, court cases, activities of the Federal Communications Commission, and other publicly available sources. Hunt's analysis of immigration similarly uses the Policy Agendas data to begin, but she supplements it in order to create a fuller and more complete case history of her policy area. In fact, each of the authors in this section makes use of some of the data included here but none limit themselves to what we collected. In this way, these chapters illustrate an important element of the Policy Agendas Project: the data are particularly useful to provide a baseline and a starting point for the study of particular policy areas. A thorough analysis of any policy area of course requires some additional work as well.

The chapters that follow demonstrate a third important factor in the study of public policy: the value of a long time perspective, and the importance of observing institutional change as part of the process. Each chapter included here documents important changes in the degree to which particular institutions of government are active in the policy area. Some show the dramatic creation and destruction of powerful institutions of government with clearly held jurisdictional control in their area. Others show the slow accretion of competing jurisdictional rivals. In all cases, they clearly show the importance of viewing the institutional structure as a variable to be explained rather than as an assumption from which to begin a study. A project that tells the history of the Immigration and Naturalization Service will not be the same as a history of American policies toward immigration — it is an empirical question to know which institution of government, and how many, take control over a given policy. As these institutions change, and as the policies with which they deal evolve over time, we see important and long-lasting changes in policy outputs, many of which would be obscured in an analysis that began with the institutional structure rather than with the social problem itself. The chapters in part three share a particular focus on the evolution of institutional structures over time; these elements are not absent from the chapters included in this part 2, however. Multidimensional and highly complex social problems such as those discussed in this part could not be addressed in a simple institutional setting. In any case, the chapters that follow show that they rarely are.

3

THE LOGIC OF POSITIVE FEEDBACK: TELECOMMUNICATIONS POLICY THROUGH THE CREATION, MAINTENANCE, AND DESTRUCTION OF A REGULATED MONOPOLY

MICHAEL C. MACLEOD

INTRODUCTION

We often think of politics as governed by laws characterized by negative feedback. Pluralist politics, interest group liberalism, and policy subsystems involve powerful entrenched interest groups and institutional structures and procedures that diminish or counteract challenges to the status quo. As opponents to a given policy mobilize and invest resources into a political conflict, they may gain some concessions at first as privileged groups adjust to the new challenge but eventually they achieve smaller marginal returns for their efforts. Under negative feedback, shocks to the system or challenges to the status quo may result in temporary deviations from existing equilibria, but the system usually returns to its original position. Privileged groups remain privileged groups and policy communities retain a relative stability. This is the logic of negative feedback.

Why then should we be concerned about positive feedback? Because most policy subsystems have undergone rapid changes at some point in their evolution. At times, entrepreneurial actions are subject to positive feedback and small challenges to the status quo can rapidly cascade through the policy subsystem and beyond, resulting in major policy changes and the development of new institutions. Shocks are not contained as normal, but rather they are amplified resulting in major deviations from existing equilibriums. Challengers gain greater and greater returns at the margins the more resources that they invest. Eventually the challengers may either completely displace privileged groups or take an equal seat at the table with them. Policy communities are completely disrupted and do not return to anything near the status quo.

Eventually a new equilibrium is reached but it is drastically different from the balance that it replaced. As Baumgartner and Jones have written, "The points at which a political system or subsystem changes from negative to positive feedback are critical . . . [because] the politics of positive feedback follow a different logic from those of negative feedback" (Baumgartner and Jones 1993, 18).

Most accounts of positive feedback in politics come from studies of mass behavior; bandwagon effects are well known in the study of political campaigns, collective actions, and the adoption of products in markets. Like bandwagons in mass behavior, decisions by members of institutions and interest groups to challenge existing policies are heavily dependent on their expectations of success, and these expectations are based on the potential support from other actors in their policy community. While institutional gatekeeping promotes policy stability, cue taking is still prevalent and shifts in cues can lead to rapid policy destabilization under certain conditions. Changes in policy making by a single institution can set a cascade in motion that leads to dramatic policy changes; decision making by policy makers and voters follows the same logic. The focus of this chapter is on the conditions under which positive feedback is likely to occur in policy making.

TOWARD A THEORY OF POSITIVE FEEDBACK IN POLICY MAKING

One of the most important findings in the study of politics is that political systems do not respond to inputs in a linear fashion; responses to both exogenous and endogenous changes are often *nonlinear* (Simon 1947, 1983; Lindblom 1960, 1977; Jones 1975; Lowi 1979; Cobb and Elder 1983; Bosso 1987; March and Olsen 1989; Baumgartner and Jones 1993; Jones 1994; Kingdon 1995; Browne 1995; Mucciaroni 1995). Political systems rarely respond to inputs in a linear fashion because of the way that humans process information (Simon 1947, 1983, 1985; Kahneman and Tversky 1985; Jones 1994), because of the social nature of politics (Huckfeldt and Sprague 1995), and as a result of institutional structures and procedures (Shepsle 1979; North 1990) and subsystem politics (Redford 1969). Policy subsystems typically tend to diminish or counteract new inputs, although at times they will amplify the effect of new information. Stability in policy communities is usually due to negative feedback, while rapid change is usually due to positive feedback.

When policy communities are dominated by positive feedback, small events can lead to rapid policy changes. Positive feedback takes many forms in the social science literature such as bandwagons, fads, tipping points, vicious and virtuous cycles, conflict expansion, and punctuated equilibrium, but here I attempt to integrate two areas of thought: (1) positive feedback in the form of bandwagons and information cascades that occur in political campaigns and collective action movements (mass behavior); and (2) positive feedback in public policy making as a result of the interaction of institutional venues, issue definition, and interest groups. Many scholars view elite and mass decision making under two different lenses, yet the same lens applies to both. Concepts developed by scholars in these areas will be used to develop a theory of rapid policy change based on the interaction of members of government institutions and interest groups and their expectations of a successful challenge to the status quo.

POSITIVE FEEDBACK IN POLITICAL CAMPAIGNS
AND COLLECTIVE ACTION MOVEMENTS

Mass participation in politics is strongly driven by feelings of efficacy. Voters with low feelings of efficacy are likely to stay away from the polls. Three findings in studies of voting behavior are particularly important to the study of positive feedback: (1) political campaigns have the strongest impact on those who are undecided; (2) in a situation of low information about one or more candidates, individuals gather information from others like them (and this is a rational strategy); and (3) feelings of political efficacy are based on expectations of future success — individuals do not waste their votes or efforts on worthless causes (Berelson, Lazarsfeld, and McPhee 1954; Downs 1957; Wolfinger and Rosenstone 1980; Sniderman, Brody, and Tetlock 1991; Teixeira 1992; Zaller 1992; Huckfeldt and Sprague 1995). These and other scholars have shown that voters take shortcuts to gather information; they usually rely on their friends, peers, and members of their social class to gather information about candidates who are relatively unknown.[1]

Bartels's (1987) study of U.S. presidential nomination campaigns provides a good example of positive feedback in voting behavior. In the 1984 campaign Walter Mondale and Gary Hart competed for the Democratic nomination. Mondale began the race as the plurality choice for the nomination, while Gary Hart barely registered at the polls in early primaries. According to Bartels, Hart's upset victory in the New Hampshire primary led to a reversal of fortune for the candidate. Between the New Hampshire primary and Super Tuesday (a period of two weeks), National Election Study (NES) data show that voters' expressed preferences for Hart rose 20 percent, a dramatic increase (Bartels 1987). Over the next month Hart's gains gradually eroded and Mondale achieved a narrow victory. The puzzle, according to Bartels, is that voter thermometer ratings remained fairly steady for both candidates over the course of the campaign.

Bartels's explanation for this bandwagon behavior is based on the interaction of voters' predispositions and their expectations of a candidate's chances of winning:

$$\text{Probability (Hart preference)} = [\text{intercept} + (1 - \text{Mondale preference})] \, {}^{\star} \\ (\text{perception of Hart's chances}) + e$$

There are two key components in his model: "political predispositions to support a challenger (or, in my story, to oppose a front runner) are necessary but not sufficient to generate actual support. The other necessary ingredient of support is some perception that the challenger has a genuine chance to win. That is what Hart lacked before Iowa, and what he gained in New Hampshire" (1987, 15). Bartels's model clearly demonstrates the conditions under which positive feedback is likely: (1) there has to be a large block of unattached or undecided voters; (2) there has to be an expectation of success for a challenger. Under these conditions a small, random event such as an early victory can lead to a rapid change in fortune because individuals are especially receptive to information or cues from others. These features are very similar to collective actions where the success of a movement largely depends on expectations of success.

Positive feedback occurs in social situations where information is inferred from the behavior of others. Research on the impact of information cascades arose from early studies of collective action (for a review see Olson 1965; Chong 1991). These studies demonstrated that social interaction, mainly expectations about the future behavior of others, has a dramatic impact on collective outcomes. Schelling's (1978) description of a "dying seminar" provides a good example. The dying seminar refers to the way a seminar, after an initial burst of enthusiasm, dies out as fewer people turn up for each meeting. The reason for this decline is not due to a lack of interest, but rather due to the perception that others are no longer interested. This is because many individuals may simultaneously be making the same observations and altering their behaviors accordingly. If all observe that the seminar is popular, they may attend. If they observe that others are not interested, they may also withdraw, even if their own interest in the topic remains unchanged. Why spend time and effort attending a series of seminars that appears unsuccessful? The key variable is whether the behavior is driven by personal preferences alone (e.g., interest in the underlying topic) or by a combination of preferences and expectations about the behavior of others.[2] In many situations from voting to participating in a seminar, not to mention riots, collective action, and policy making, these expectations about the behaviors of others matter.

Collective actions usually involve some type of threshold or tipping point. These concepts are used to explain both decisions to enter and exit a collective action, and they are heavily based on expectations of success. The key concept in Granovetter's (1978) model is that of a "threshold" or the point at which a given actor will make a decision based on the proportion of other actors that have already done so. He notes that social interaction is crucial because individuals incorporate the actions of others into their utility structure. Granovetter makes an important distinction in his model about the relationship between participants. In this case he notes that friends have a much stronger influence on an actor than strangers do; the actions of friends will lower the threshold point for an individual for both joining a movement and exiting one.

Chong's (1991) study of the civil rights movement clearly demonstrates these threshold effects. First, Chong notes that membership in civil rights organizations rose and fell in sync with public successes or public failures. A public demonstration or action that was deemed successful led to membership increases because it lowered the threshold for joining. Conversely, a public failure led to membership decreases because it both raised the bar for joining and lowered the threshold for exiting. Second, Chong found that community or social pressure was a critical element of the decision by people to take an active role in the movement. Many people participated in marches, demonstrations, and other actions simply because they feared social ostracism if they did not participate. Social pressure was a powerful means of maintaining membership and promoting active participation and leaders of the movement used this pressure to their advantage.

Other scholars have developed explicit models that explain the conditions under which individuals are likely to jump on a bandwagon. Bikhchandani, Hirshleifer, and Welch (1992) attempt to explain why bandwagons (called "conformity" in their study) seem so fragile. The key to their model is that small shocks lead to big shifts in mass behavior "only if people happen to be very close to the borderline between alternatives" (994). In their model, individuals have two sources of information: (1) the actions of others and (2) their independent estimation of the situation. If the individual's estimation of the value of information from both sources is equal or the action of others has greater value, then cascades are almost inevitable as the number of participants increases. Like bandwagons that occur in political campaigns, information cascades are more likely to occur when individuals are indifferent between two or more alternatives, or if they are especially tuned to conforming to the expected behavior of those around them. The closer an information cascade model is to the reality of a situation, the more likely leaders are to be motivated to try to set one off, and the greater the role early leaders will play.

The main point of these studies is that positive feedback (in the form of bandwagons) occurs only under two specific conditions, both of which are necessary: (1) when there is a large group of participants, voters, or consumers who have little or no private information about the choice between alternatives (they have no strong preferences for one alternative over another); and (2) when there is some expectation of success for an outcome or alternative. These factors can also be used to explain positive feedback in policy making; expectations of success for a new policy alternative can set off a cascade of attention when enough policy actors are either opposed to the status quo or attention is shifted to a new alternative.

POSITIVE FEEDBACK IN POLICY MAKING

One of the fundamental differences between positive feedback in mass behavior and positive feedback among elites involved in policy making is that the constraints imposed by institutional norms, rules, and procedures lead to greater policy stability. Institutions promote short-term equilibriums by limiting the range of preferences of decision makers within an institution, and by focusing debate on a narrow set of alternatives (Shepsle 1979). Members of institutions usually come to support the prevailing definition of an issue. But even structure-induced equilibria (Shepsle 1979) can prove to be unstable when looked at over a period of a years or decades (see Riker 1980).

Positive feedback in policy making has been described using terms such as conflict expansion, mobilization of enthusiasm, and punctuated equilibrium, and it usually occurs when "windows of opportunity" are present (Schatt-schneider 1960; Downs 1972; Cobb and Elder 1983; Bosso 1987; Baumgartner and Jones 1993; Kingdon 1995). Recent models of policy making that develop explanations for both policy stability and policy change focus on the interaction of issue definition, interest groups, and government actors (Cobb and Elder 1983; Bosso 1987; Baumgartner 1989; Hansen 1991; Baumgartner and Jones 1993; Sabatier and Jenkins-Smith 1993; Mucciaroni 1995; Worsham 1998). The key to the policy process is the way that issues are defined and debated because issue definition largely structures the coalitions of actors in a policy community and determines the groups that accrue policy benefits. The points at which policy subsystems switch from negative to positive feedback can usually be recognized by looking at these key indicators; rapid policy changes often occur when institutional attention to an issue increases, when new participants gain access to policy making, and when issues are redefined.

For example, Schattschneider's (1960) conflict expansion model involves appeals by losers in a political conflict to other venues in the political system; here losers attempt to exploit our federal system of government by taking their case to a more receptive venue. The key to conflict expansion is finding a receptive venue because jurisdictional challenges often lead to issue redefinition. Conflict expansion involves an increase in systemic and institutional attention to an issue, an increase in the participants involved including both new interest groups and members from government institutions, and it usually results in the destruction or alteration of existing institutional structures.

Building on Schattschneider's work, Baumgartner and Jones (1993) develop a theory that accounts for both negative and positive feedback in policy making. Their term, "punctuated equilibrium," allows for both periods of stability and change. Like Schattschneider's conflict expansion model, punctuations involve the incorporation of new participants, issue redefinition, a loss of jurisdictional control, and changes in institutional structures and procedures. Again, institutional access and support are key. Studying policy reform in several areas, Mucciaroni (1995) demonstrates that if key institutional actors are committed to reform, then groups will lose current benefits. Conversely, if they are opposed to reform, even in the face of a negative issue context, groups will maintain their current benefits. For example he shows that agricultural interests were able to maintain their subsidies even in the face of poor economic performance and large budget deficits because of institutional support (see also Browne 1995). In all these studies, venues of policy making are important because members of institutions with jurisdiction over a policy area control access maintain existing policies — without a receptive venue interest groups are largely shut out of the policy process.

At another level, these indicators can be thought of as preferences and expectations of success. New policy alternatives gain momentum when preferences begin to change or attentions to preferences shift (see Jones 1994). Initial forays gain steam if expectations of success increase due to jurisdictional challenges (venue expansion), scoring a significant victory, or capitalizing on a crisis or event. One key prerequisite for positive feedback is a growing number of actors opposed to the status quo. However, in policy making, a true shift in preferences may not always be necessary to achieve major policy changes. Unlike mass beliefs, elite preferences are less volatile and more ideologically structured. Strategic manipulation of the method of aggregating preferences or manipulation of attention to preferences can also lead to rapid changes in policy making; policy changes can occur even when elite preferences remain fairly static (Simon 1985; Riker 1986; Jones 1994). Because members of institutions often hold multiple preferences on an issue and they are very strategic in their decision making, expectations of success (or political gain) can play a very important role in the decisions to support one alternative over another.

Like voters, policy entrepreneurs are strategic actors that do not want to waste their time on challenges that will be ignored (see especially Kingdon 1995, chap. 8, on this point). Actors pay careful attention to the preferences and actions of other political actors and take this into account when deciding on a course of action. Institutions are often constrained by the groups that they serve, but, more importantly, they are also constrained by the action of other institutions; it is usually difficult for a single institution to enact major policy changes without support, or at least acquiescence, from other political institutions.

Just as the interaction of individual preferences and expectations of success can explain bandwagons in nomination campaigns, so too can the combination of preferences and expectations of success be used to model elite decisions to challenge the status quo. Again, the key difference is that institutional structure and procedures and entrenched interests create anchors within policy communities that make equilibriums less fragile than in mass behavior. Policy making usually undergoes long periods of stability, but at times exhibits rapid changes. Like bandwagons in voting behavior, positive feedback in policy making occurs under certain identifiable conditions: (1) when there are a sufficient number of actors that are indifferent or opposed to the status quo;[3] and (2) when there is an expectation of success for a new alternative or a challenge to the status quo. These expectations of success are largely driven by the decisions of governmental actors with jurisdiction over a policy area (note that this is not confined to a single institution).

Note again, that institutional structures and procedures promote negative feedback. It is relatively easy for politicians to exploit structures and procedures to maintain a state of negative feedback or to head off positive feedback cycles that may be gaining steam. Here, the threshold that must be crossed to sustain a positive feedback cycle is much higher than in collective action movements or other types of mass behavior. This is mainly due to the ability of entrenched political actors to maintain the status quo by manipulating expectations of success or failure through political structures. Hence, policy studies mostly reflect incremental change, and accounts of dramatic change are few and far between.

A MODEL OF POSITIVE FEEDBACK IN POLICY MAKING

Returning to Bartels's model discussed above, decisions by groups or members of government institutions to challenge the status quo can be thought of as a function of preferences and expectations of success:

$$\text{Probability (decision to challenge the status quo)} = (\text{actor preference}) *$$
$$(\text{perception of chances of success}) + e$$

Policy preferences can be thought of as support of or opposition to an existing policy, and expectations of success are largely controlled by the decisions of members of political institutions with jurisdiction over a policy area. The main idea here is that interest groups and members of institutions are unlikely to challenge the status quo if they have low expectations of success even if they have preferences for change. Interest groups and governmental actors are heavily dependent on the political context. While groups or government officials might strongly prefer policy change, they are unlikely to act on those preferences as long as expectations of winning are low. As expectations of success increase, more and more challenges to the status quo occur (policy actors jump on the bandwagon). From this, several hypotheses about positive feedback can be drawn.

Hypothesis 1: Positive feedback is more likely to occur when a sufficient percentage of actors come to oppose the status quo either through replacement, through adaptation to changes in the environment, or because of shifts in attention to new dimensions of debate.

Hypothesis 2: Positive feedback is more likely to occur as expectations of successful challenges to the status quo increase. These expectations are heavily dependent on the decisions of governmental actors.

Hypothesis 3: If an institutional challenge to the status quo — be it new legislation, a bureaucratic ruling, or a court decision — remains unchecked by other political institutions with jurisdiction over a policy, cascades may be set in motion that lead to positive feedback and the destabilization of a policy area.

INDICATORS OF POSITIVE FEEDBACK IN TELECOMMUNICATIONS POLICY

Telecommunications policy making has undergone four distinct periods: (1) competition from 1900 to 1933; (2) a powerful monopoly from 1934 to 1969; (3) limited competition from 1970 to AT&T's breakup in 1984;[4] and (4) full competition thereafter in long-distance service and telephone equipment manufacturing. There are two main periods of positive feedback in telecommunications: (1) the period of the institutionalization of AT&T's telecommunications monopoly in the 1920s; and (2) the period of the destruction of its monopoly in the 1980s. In this paper, I specifically focus on the destruction of AT&T's monopoly due to the availability of archival data.[5]

Preferences and perceptions of institutional actors are often difficult to define let alone to measure especially over time and across institutions. Here I use surrogates for preferences and expectations. Actor preferences are tapped by coding outcomes of FCC and federal district court cases on telecommunications policy that involved allegations of antitrust violations by AT&T, and by coding the testimony of witnesses from various institutions and interest groups at congressional hearings on telecommunications policy. These measures are not perfect indicators of the preferences of policy actors but they were the best longitudinal measures that were available across the political institutions involved in telecommunications policy.[6] To double-check the validity of these measures, the results were compared with several excellent qualitative case studies of telecommunications policy; the timing of changes in the quantitative measures correspond very well to events recorded in these studies (see Temin 1987; Henck and Strassberg 1988; A. Stone 1989).

Expectations of success are tapped by coding institutional attention to an issue. While attention can be influenced by many variables, increases in institutional attention to an issue usually signal that a policy challenge is occurring; an increase in attention usually means that expectations of a successful challenge to the status quo are also increasing (see Baumgartner and Jones 1993; Kingdon 1995).

THE TELECOMMUNICATIONS POLICY ENVIRONMENT: WITNESSES AND THEIR TESTIMONY

A key prerequisite for positive feedback is a large pool of actors opposed to the status quo. While this is imprecisely defined, the key is to demonstrate that over time a growing number of actors in a policy community begin to oppose the status quo or that actors began to shift their attention to another important dimension of policy debate. Table 3.1 lists the main actors in telecommunications policy from 1934 to 1995 and the cells indicate the percentage of their statements that were supportive of AT&T's monopoly or neutral. These figures are drawn from witness lists at congressional hearings on telecommunications policy.

Table 3.1 presents a lot of information; only some of the most important

TABLE 3.1 Percentage of Witness Statements at Congressional Hearings Either Supporting AT&T's Monopoly or Neutral

Witness Type	% Support Monopoly 1934–69	% Support Monopoly 1970–83	% Support MFJ 1984–95	n
AT&T	100	100	56	61
Bell operating companies	100	70	60	48
Independent telephone cos.	13	32	60	213
Telephone equipment mfgs.	*	50	53	21
Electronic and computer	*	13	65	53
Cable TV	*	0	75	10
Broadcasting and publishing	75	53	55	54
Banking	*	*	*	*
Satellite	*	*	*	*
Western Union	67	0	*	5
Congress	83	50	60	21
FCC/ICC	100	19	60	54
DOJ	0	0	67	12
DOC/NTIA	100	33	50	18
DOD/NASA	100	100	*	9
Other exec.	*	57	80	11
State and local	86	90	70	88
Trade and professional	*	0	50	7
Labor unions	100	88	50	33
Citizen/advocacy	*	46	58	59
University/think tank		79	60	39
Other	*	*	*	*
Number of positive or neutral statements	60	185	230	
Total witness statements	81	361	374	816
Percent positive or neutral	74%	51%	61%	
Total hearings	24	55	111	190
Total number of witnesses	296	1050	1102	2448
Witnesses per hearing	12	19	10	

*Not calculated because of low n or no codable statements by the group.
Note: Individual cells represent the percentage of total witness statements for each period that were either in support of AT&T's monopoly or were neutral. Witness statements were coded as 0 = neutral; 1 = support for greater competition; or 2 = support for monopoly. Witness statements were coded neutral if they were providing background or technical information on telecommunications policy or if they provided opposing viewpoints on competition. Also note that all witness statements were coded according to topic and only those statements on topics such as regulation of long-distance service, local service, or equipment manufacturing are included. In addition, many of the witness statements were not codable because of the lack of information in the hearing abstracts. Prior to 1970, CIS included little information about witness statements. Format changes in 1970 made it much easier to code witness statements. 816 of 2,448 (33%) of witness statements were codable.

points are discussed here. First, from 1934 to 1969 most witnesses testified in support of AT&T's monopoly. The score represents the percentage of statements were supportive of AT&T's monopoly or neutral; neutrality usually involved providing background or technical testimony. AT&T's biggest supporters included the Bell operating companies, Congress, the FCC, the Department of Commerce and the National Telecommunications Information Agency (DOC/NTIA), the Department of Defense and the National Aeronautics and Space Administration (DOD/NASA), state and local government officials, and labor unions. The Bell operating companies, which provided local phone service, were owned by AT&T until 1984, so they completely supported the existing monopoly. More importantly, almost all government officials involved in telecommunications policy supported the telecommunications monopoly when testifying before Congress. Executive branch supporters included the FCC, the DOC, and the DOD. Since its creation in 1934, the FCC fully supported AT&T's monopoly because it allowed them to fulfill their legislative mandate — the 1934 Communications Act charged the FCC to ensure universal telephone service at a reasonable cost. In 1934, AT&T was the only telephone company large enough to provide nationwide service. The DOD was an important advocate for AT&T's monopoly because AT&T provided almost all of the communications equipment for the military.

Most state and local government officials testified in support of AT&T's monopoly. This category includes testimony from state public utility commissioners, members of state legislatures, the U.S. Conference of Mayors, state attorneys general, public service commissions, and the National League of Cities. From the 1920s until its breakup, AT&T was a regulated monopolist and its main regulators were the FCC and state public utility commissioners (PUCs) (A. Stone 1989). State PUCs were the most vocal advocates of telecommunications monopoly during testimony for the 1934 Communications Act. Most states wanted one company to provide universal service because most businesses wanted a single provider; many businesses complained about having to deal with several regional providers. State regulators also argued that universal service was necessary because it would allow a single provider to offset the costs of providing rural service with profits earned in urban areas (see A. Stone 1989). State regulators remained ardent supporters of AT&T's monopoly even during the breakup because they did not want to lose authority over a system of cost sharing that they controlled. Labor unions were also important supporters of AT&T's monopoly. Most of the unions in this category were comprised of AT&T, Bell, and Western Electric employees. AT&T alone employed over one million workers in all fifty states by 1970. These unions

feared that competition in telecommunications would have adverse consequences for union members such as the loss of jobs and the reduction of
wages (Temin 1987).

Opposition to the monopoly came mainly from independent telephone
companies such as MCI and IT&T, lesser-known regional independent companies such as Richmond Telephone Company, Nevada Telephone and Telegraph, Elkhart Telephone, and a myriad of peak business associations representing small independent telephone companies such as the U.S. Independent
Telephone Association, the Competitive Telephone Association, and the Colorado Independent Telephone Associations. These firms and associations
pressed for competition in telephone service but their claims were largely denied by government institutions until the 1970s. It is important to note that
AT&T had a significant number of competitors even during the height of its
monopoly, but these competitors played little role in the policy process because there were few receptive venues.

The Department of Justice was about the only venue receptive to challenges
of AT&T's monopoly from 1934 to 1969. However, it was reluctant to bring
antitrust actions during this period because of the lack of support among the
other institutions with jurisdiction over telecommunications (Henck and
Strassberg 1988). The DOJ's only antitrust suit against AT&T during this period (in 1956) was largely dropped for lack of support by other political institutions. The DOJ suit was opposed by the FCC, the DOD, and the Eisenhower
administration, which believed that a large regulated monopoly was in the
best interests of the country (see A. Stone 1989); in this case, a cascade was not
set in motion because this challenge was blocked or checked by other institutions involved in telecommunications policy. AT&T was able to maintain its
monopoly through its institutional supporters such as the FCC, DOD, DOC,
and members of Congress. From 1934 to 1969 negative feedback was operating; there were few receptive venues for AT&T's opponents and the challenges
that did occur were contained.

In the late 1960s, governmental actors (beginning with the FCC) that were
once ardent supporters of AT&T began rule in favor of its competitors. As
table 3.1 shows, only 19 percent of FCC statements at congressional hearings
on telecommunications policy from 1970 to 1983 were supportive of AT&T's
monopoly or neutral. The FCC was not the only government actor that began
to favor the deregulation of telecommunications. The DOC/NTIA also came
out in opposition to the monopoly during the 1970s. As the table shows, only
33 percent of their statements were supportive or neutral. Similarly, many
members of Congress began to argue for competition in telecommunications.

Table 3.1 shows that 50 percent of the testimony by members of Congress at hearings on telecommunications was supportive or neutral; this is big decline from the 83 percent of congressional statements that were supportive or neutral during the previous period. These figures represent substantial changes that clearly signal a window of opportunity for groups that were previously shut out of policy making to challenge the status quo.

There are a number of reasons why this shift occurred among members of institutions involved in telecommunications policy making. In addition to deregulation sweeping many other policies areas (see below), one of the reasons that support for AT&T's monopoly declined had to do with the impact of technological advances. First, the development of computer technology brought new participants into the telecommunications policy debate and created problems for the FCC and AT&T. If AT&T were to be allowed to maintain its restrictions on interconnection, then companies wanting networked computers would be forced to purchase them from AT&T. This conflict led to the computer I and II inquiries by the FCC that resulted in a complete rejection of AT&T's interconnection policies.

On another front, the development of microwave communications allowed MCI to challenge AT&T's monopoly over long-distance communication. In a narrow ruling, the FCC allowed MCI to offer long-distance service via microwave between Chicago and Saint Louis as an experiment. However, once this decision was made, MCI and others quickly flooded the FCC with applications for licenses for additional sites. Opponents emerged as technology progressed on many fronts, and this increased the pool of opponents to AT&T's monopoly (Derthick and Quirk 1985).

The final period, from 1984 through 1995, requires some explanation as well. This column of table 3.1 is based on support for the modified final judgement (MFJ). This is the judgment reached by the district court judge Harold Greene that led to AT&T's divestiture of the Bell operating companies. Each of these companies became a separate entity, and they were barred from acting in collusion. In addition, the Bell operating companies were prevented from competing in long-distance markets, equipment manufacturing, and the burgeoning information services market. Similarly, AT&T was barred from competing in the local telephone service market and in the information services market. The MFJ created competition in the long-distance service and telephone equipment manufacturing, but local service was still a monopoly controlled by thirteen Bell operating companies. The percentages here reflect support for or opposition to the modified final judgment.

Overall, the key shift leading the transition from negative feedback to positive feedback occurred among the institutions with jurisdiction over telecommunications policy. AT&T always had competitors, but for the most part they were shut out of policy making because there were few receptive venues. Once the preferences of members of institutions began to change (or they began to shift their attention to different dimensions) because of deregulation in other areas and technological advances, interest groups quickly reacted to this signal and aggressively pursued change. Shifts in the preferences of members of political institutions greatly increased expectations of successful challenges. Challenges were not contained as normal by the institutions involved in telecommunications policy but were rather amplified beginning in the 1970s. This set off a cascade of institutional attention that is typical of positive feedback.

POSITIVE FEEDBACK AND ATTENTION CASCADES

A key indicator of instability is an increase in institutional attention to an issue, and higher levels of attention are also indicative of changes in expectations (see e.g., Cobb and Elder 1983; Baumgartner and Jones 1993; Worsham 1998). An increase in attention by itself does not necessarily imply that policy changes are about to occur; however, increased levels of attention almost always indicate a challenge to the status quo or some problem with an existing policy. Higher levels of attention often indicate a shift in preferences or the introduction of a new alternative that looks promising, the entry of new participants into the process, and usually some loss of jurisdictional control (see Baumgartner and Jones 1993; Jones, Baumgartner, and Talbert 1993).

AT&T's institutional support eroded after several FCC decisions in the late 1960s and early 1970s allowing limited competition in long-distance communication; this set a cascade of institutional attention to telecommunications policy in motion. Members of institutions involved in telecommunications policy making began to see the political viability of competition and members of interest group began to flood the system with challenges to AT&T's monopoly and calls for Congress to reform the telecommunications system (Derthick and Quirk 1985). In this case, challenges to the status quo were not contained as they normally are. The FCC began to allow limited forays into competition, and the other institutions involved in telecommunications policy did not counter these incursions. Indeed, they began to support competition. The initial decisions by the FCC sparked a dramatic cascade of institutional attention to telecommunications policy that was largely driven by political actors

FIGURE 3.1 FCC CASES INVOLVING AT&T AND ANTITRUST ISSUES

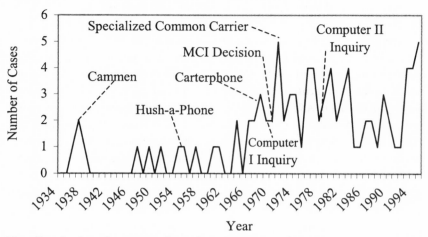

Note: Data for these figures were drawn from FCC Reports (FCC 1st covers 1934 to 1964; FCC 2d covers 1965 to 1995). To be included, a case had to involve AT&T as a defendant or plaintiff and include allegations of antitrust violations. FCC inquiries into AT&T tariffs, such as the Computer I Inquiry, are also included. From 1934 to 1964 searching the table of contents of each FCC volume and then skimming the record for the topic and outcome identified cases. From 1965 to 1995, cases were identified using a keyword search on Lexis-Nexis. The keywords included combinations of the following terms: *AT&T, Bell, Western Electric, telecommunications, telephone,* and *antitrust.* Once a list was compiled, it was compared to cases cited in several excellent qualitative studies of telecommunications policy to ensure that no major cases were overlooked (Temin 1987; Henck and Strassberg 1988; Brock 1994).

searching for new opportunities and interest groups that had previously been shut out of the policy-making process (see A. Stone 1989). Figure 3.1 shows FCC cases involving AT&T and antitrust issues from 1934 to 1995.

This figure shows distinct periods in FCC attention to telecommunications policy.[7] From its creation in 1934 until the late 1960s, the number of cases involving AT&T and antitrust issues is rather low but it increases sharply in the late 1960s and stays higher thereafter. During the height of AT&T's power from 1934 to the 1960s, the FCC received very few challenges to AT&T's monopoly. The few challenges brought by AT&T's competitors, such as *Cammen* and *Hush-A-Phone,*[8] were mostly decided in AT&T's favor — *of the twenty-three antitrust cases before the FCC between 1934 and 1969, fifteen (65 percent) were decided in AT&T's favor.*[9] The system clearly operated under negative feedback during this period.

Once the FCC began to allow limited competition in telephone equipment manufacturing and long-distance service, the number of challenges to AT&T's monopoly dramatically increased. The *Carterfone* decision in 1968, the *MCI* decision in 1969, the *Computer I Inquiry* in 1970, the *Specialized Common Carrier* decision in 1971, and the *Computer II Inquiry* in 1978 paved the way for competition in long-distance service and telephone equipment manufacturing. *Of the forty-three cases from 1970 to 1983 shown in figure 3.1, only four (9 percent) were decided in AT&T's favor.*[10] This represents a dramatic decline from the previous period.

Increasing levels of attention after the 1960s are indicative of instability; they mark the beginning of positive feedback in telecommunications. They also indicate a significant institutional shift in preferences and the beginning of a growing number of actors opposed to the status quo, a key prerequisite for positive feedback. FCC preferences changed over time as a result of the impact of deregulation in other areas of the economy (see Derthick and Quirk 1985), through replacement of key personnel (see Henck and Strassberg 1988), and because of advances in technology that made it increasingly difficult for the FCC to maintain its old restrictive policies (a point discussed above). Note that preferences changed in favor of competition as a result not only of replacement but also of a shift of attention to new dimensions of debate (deregulation and advances in technology).

Once the FCC began to allow limited competition, a number of court cases were filed by competitors seeking entry into new areas and seeking damages for being run out of markets by AT&T; many of these entrepreneurs had been largely shut out of the policy process. Federal district court cases involving antitrust concerns about AT&T exhibit a similar pattern of activity: low attention during its monopoly and a significant increase in attention as the courts began to allow limited competition. Figure 3.2 shows all federal district court cases from 1930 to 1995 that involve antitrust complaints about AT&T.

These cases were identified in two ways: (1) by a keyword search of federal district court cases using LexisNexis and (2) by a thorough review of several qualitative studies of telecommunications policy to make sure that all important cases were identified (see Temin 1987; Henck and Strassberg 1988; Brock 1994). For a list of keywords see the legend to figure 3.1.

As figure 3.2 demonstrates, the number of court cases involving antitrust complaints was also low, almost nonexistent, from the 1930s until the 1970s, when they began to increase for a period of about ten years. Again, low levels of attention are indicative of AT&T's strength. Competitors simply did not file suits because they feared losing (expectations of success were low). *Of the six*

FIGURE 3.2 FEDERAL DISTRICT COURT CASES INVOLVING AT&T AND ANTITRUST ISSUES

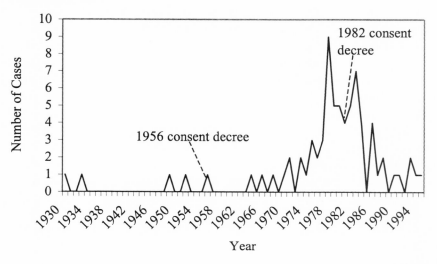

antitrust cases decided from 1934 to 1969, four (67 percent) were decided in AT&T's favor.[11] While this number may not seem startling, both the low number of cases filed and the high success rate for AT&T suggests that the federal courts were not a very receptive venue for antitrust appeals and that many groups might have decided to forgo court challenges because their expectations of success were low.

Beginning in the mid-1970s, there was a large increase in the number of cases filed against AT&T. This increase is indicative of instability and positive feedback. Once the FCC began to allow limited competition, many groups appealed to the courts to receive compensation for economic harms imposed by AT&T's monopoly or to further open markets to competition. *Of the fifty-three antitrust cases decided from 1970 to 1983, only thirteen (25 percent) were decided in AT&T's favor.*[12] Like the FCC, once the courts began to rule against AT&T there was a large increase in the number of cases filed because expectations of success increased. Here, challengers quickly jumped on the bandwagon.

The two consent decrees noted in this figure illustrate both positive and negative feedback at work. Both cases involved DOJ antitrust suits against AT&T alleging violations of the Sherman Antitrust Act. The Justice Department's antitrust suit against AT&T in 1956 was settled out of court. AT&T prevailed in this case because of its institutional supporters (A. Stone 1989). As noted earlier, almost all members of the government involved in telecommunications policy fully supported AT&T during this period. Here the political context was conducive to negative feedback, and this major challenge to AT&T's monopoly was contained. Under pressure from the DOD, FCC, and the Eisenhower White House, the DOJ dropped this suit (see A. Stone 1989).

About thirty years later, another DOJ antitrust suit led to a completely different outcome. The 1982 modified final judgment handed down by district court judge Harold Greene forced AT&T to divest itself of the Bell operating companies and Western Electric. The judgment instituted full competition in long-distance telephone service and telephone equipment manufacturing. This outcome represented a radical change in the sense that legislation pending in Congress would have required AT&T to allow competition in long-distance markets and equipment manufacturing but it would have allowed it to maintain ownership of the local Bells. The court was able to achieve this outcome because the political context was much different than in 1956; in this case, there was widespread institutional support for reform (see A. Stone 1989).

As noted in the table above, most of the institutional actors testifying before Congress about proposed legislation to reform existing policies advocated competition. As the FCC and the courts began to allow competition in telecommunications services, Congress joined the fray at the behest of AT&T. In 1976, Congress convened a round of hearings on the "AT&T Bill," a bill drafted by supporters of AT&T that was designed to restore its telecommunications monopoly. This bill eventually failed, but it signaled the beginning of a dramatic increase in congressional attention to telecommunication as it struggled to bring some coherence to the dramatic policy changes that had occurred.

Congressional hearings on telecommunications policy from 1934 to 1995 were identified using a keyword search on the Congressional Information Service (CIS) Congressional Hearing Statistical Masterfile. The keywords used to identify these hearings were "telecommunications," "telephone," "telegraph," "AT&T," "Bell," and "Western Electric" (AT&T owned Western Electric).

Like that of the FCC and the district courts, congressional attention to telecommunications policy over the last sixty years exhibits several distinct periods of attention. Figure 3.3 shows all congressional hearings on telecommunications policy from 1934 to 1995. One of the most remarkable features about this figure is the extremely low level of congressional attention to the single largest monopoly in the world from the passage of the 1934 Communications Act up until AT&T's attempt to regain its monopoly status through the introduction of legislation in Congress in the late 1970s. Over a period of forty-two years (1934 to 1976), Congress held a total of only *sixteen* hearings on telecommunications policy. Remember that AT&T controlled over 80 percent of

FIGURE 3.3 CONGRESSIONAL HEARINGS ON TELECOMMUNICATIONS POLICY

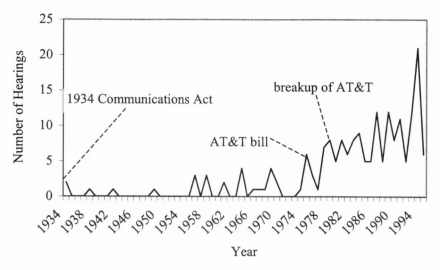

the telephone market and had annual revenues exceeding $2.5 billion by 1970 (Brock 1994). The lack of congressional hearings during this period is clearly indicative of a policy monopoly and negative feedback; Congress simply did not entertain opposition to the existing monopoly. Unlike a distributive policy that requires regular appropriations, there is no reason for Congress to hold hearings on telecommunications policy unless is it dissatisfied with existing legislation; clearly, the fact that Congress held so few hearings on telecommunications policy during much of this period suggests most members supported AT&T's monopoly and that expectations of a successful challenge were low.

As noted earlier, the first attempt by Congress to pass legislation governing telecommunications was the 1934 Communications Act. Thereafter Congress sporadically held hearings on telecommunications policy until the late 1970s, when it began a round of hearings aimed at a major overhaul of telecommunications policy. Telecommunications policy increased in importance on the congressional agenda as more groups pressed for competition and the FCC and the courts promoted it. In 1976 Congress, spurred by AT&T, began considering comprehensive telecommunications legislation. Congress had long supported AT&T's monopoly and AT&T hoped to regain a measure of control over the policy area by convincing members of Congress to pass legislation that would restore its monopoly. However, this legislation failed to gain the necessary support and other members began to introduce legislation that would deregulate telecommunications markets. Congress continued to consider legislation even after the divestiture of AT&T in 1982; many members of Congress were dissatisfied with the Court's decision, so congressional hearings continued until the passage of new legislation in 1996.

CONCLUSION

At times perceptions of success are just as important as preferences when accounting for policy outcomes. This seemingly uncontroversial statement is loaded with implications that conflict with typical notions of policy change. Decisions by interest groups and members of institutions to challenge the status quo are heavily dependent upon their perceptions of the likelihood of success. When an outsider is granted access to a policy community and scores a small victory, others reassess their fortunes. When a political institution challenges the status quo to further its goals and other political institutions support that move, policy systems can be destabilized because institutional structures and procedures no longer restrict the flow of participants, information, or alternatives that previously helped to maintain stability.

The figures cited above demonstrate a clear cascade of institutional attention: the FCC started the cascade, it spilled over into courts in the mid-1970s, and then Congress got involved in the late 1970s. Decisions by the FCC in the late 1960s and early 1970s sent signals to both government actors and interest groups that the time was right for challenges to AT&T's monopoly. This policy course was not contained by other political institutions involved in telecommunications policy, and a cascade of institutional attention ensued as expectations of a successful challenge increased. This rapid increase in institutional attention when looked at over long periods of time is indicative of a period of positive feedback that led to the destruction of AT&T's monopoly.

Like Hart's early primary victory that increased his viability in the eyes of voters, initial FCC decisions allowing limited competition dramatically increased expectations of a successful challenge to the status quo. Challenges to AT&T's monopoly by both interest groups currently shut out of telecommunications policy making and by members of institutions currently in control of telecommunications policy dramatically increased. Advances in technology led to an increase in the pool of actors opposed to the status quo, and the general deregulatory climate further amplified the initial actions of the FCC. Once the genie was released from the bottle, successful challenges invited more competition and subsequently more challenges and more successes, a positive feedback process that did not end until the collapse of AT&T's monopoly.

An easy way for policy actors to make sense of the political environment is to gauge their actions on the past actions of others and to update their beliefs accordingly. Past outcomes are tangible while future outcomes are speculative at best. Failed challenges send strong signals to members of a policy community that future challenges are unlikely to succeed. Successful challenges send the opposite signal, but again these failures or successes are tangible results that serve as an important guide for subsequent behavior. Decisions of interest groups and members of political institutions to challenge existing policies are not merely a function of their preferences, but also are heavily dependent upon their perceptions of the outcome.

NOTES

1. As Kingdon (1989) notes, legislators exhibit similar behaviors: when faced with little information about a choice between alternatives, a legislator will usually seek advice from a like-minded (ideologically similar) colleague.

2. Expectations of success based on one's calculation about the expected behavior of others is more volatile and, at times, more important than one's own preferences (see Jones 1994).

3. Rapid policy changes can also occur because of shifts in attention to preferences (see Jones 1994).

4. The 1982 consent decree that led to AT&T divestiture was not implemented until 1984.

5. There simply was not much federal attention to telecommunications policy prior to the 1930s. Most attention was at the state level, and collecting state level indicators of attention prior to the 1930s is difficult at best.

6. I did not use roll call votes to measure the preferences of members of Congress because there were very few votes on telecommunications policy between 1934 and the consent decree in 1982.

7. I use the term "attention" loosely here. While the FCC and the federal district courts (see figure 3.2) are dependent upon groups to bring antitrust claims, they to some extent controlled the number of suits brought by consistently deciding in AT&T's favor.

8. *Cammen* and *Hush-A-Phone* involved challenges to AT&T's telephone equipment monopoly.

9. Figures compiled by the author from FCC records.

10. Ibid.

11. Figure compiled by the author from federal district court records.

12. Ibid.

4

THE MULTIPLE AND CHANGING GOALS OF IMMIGRATION REFORM: A COMPARISON OF HOUSE AND SENATE ACTIVITY, 1947–1993

VALERIE F. HUNT

INTRODUCTION

The punctuated equilibrium theory provides two major conceptions that account for the dual dynamics of quietude and change in public policy. The first holds that policy issues are inherently multidimensional. As issues change over time or new ways of understanding old issues emerge on the political agenda, dominant policy decision makers will have trouble maintaining control over the scope and magnitude of changes in the policy process and outcomes. As issues change, the institutional structures designed to address them change as well. The second conception, developed by Baumgartner and Jones in *Agendas and Instability* (1993) and further developed by Bryan Jones (1994) in his research on institutional decision making, holds that shifts in attentiveness of policy decision makers leads to unpredictable and dramatic changes in policy process and outcomes. Jones argues that a change in attentiveness to a particular issue dimension can occur without an attendant change in policy preferences. Yet the shift in attentiveness can result in shifts in the policy process.

The punctuated equilibrium theory predicts that periods of dramatic change are short in duration and are invariably followed by a negative feedback process where the policy subsystem finds a new equilibrium. However, because of the potential for multidimensional issues to generate attention shifts in the policy process across different institutional venues, significant changes within a policy subsystem may recur even after a major punctuation has altered the structure and outcomes of the policy process. Two conceptions allow us to address the question "How can we explain recurrent dramatic changes in post–World War II U.S. immigration policy?" Immigration scholars offer economic (Borjas 1990, 1999; Smith and Edmonston 1997), social (Massey 1990) and interest group(Freeman 1995) models to explain the cause and impact of migration flows across national borders. Several scholars have focused on the unintended consequences of U.S. immigration policy reforms, particularly those policies addressing immigration control (see Cornelius, Martin, and Hollifield 1994). Others offer explanations for public attitudes toward immigration policies (Espenshade and Calhoun 1993; Fetzer 2000) and the public ambivalence toward different types of migrant statuses (e.g., legal versus illegal migrants, nonskilled versus highly skilled laborers, European versus non-European migrants). Although these models are useful in accounting for shifts in migration patterns and, to a certain degree, evaluations of the efficacy of particular policies, they only provide a partial picture of the overall dynamics of quietude and change within U.S. immigration policy.[1] What is missing is a *systemic* account of why these shifts have occurred.

This essay cannot address the full range of theoretical and empirical questions surrounding policy change in U.S. immigration. However, a good place to start is an exploratory analysis of long-term policy dynamics within macro-level institutions. I argue that immigration as a policy subsystem is deceptively simple. U.S. immigration appears to be a classic policy subsystem complete with the familiar firewalls around the policy gates to promote stability: constraints on the number of legitimate policy actors to a handful of business and labor interests; an entrenched bureaucracy, the Immigration and Naturalization Service (the INS, one of the oldest American bureaucracies, surpassed only by the United States Postal Service); and a well-developed and narrowly defined policy decision making jurisdiction within Congress — the House and Senate Judiciary Committees and their respective immigration subcommittees. Most important, immigration policy seems to be characterized as governed by one dominant definition of the problem of controlling borders. However, as discussed below, the immigration policy arena has several issue dimensions, making immigration more similar to health care policy (a complex policy arena with many ramifications) than to agriculture policy (a one-dimensional arena focusing primarily on the extent of subsidies offered to producers).[2]

These issue dimensions are the basis for prolonged conflict and recurring reform efforts. "Keeping a lid" on a universally accepted policy image has been problematic at best and extremely divisive across partisan and traditional coalition lines. For example, the congressional initiatives that spearheaded the 1986 Immigration Reform and Control Act (IRCA) originally addressed migration flows as a problem of employers who hired undocumented workers. However, the issue of employer sanctions quickly became redefined by political actors interested in expansionist immigration policy reform as a problem of discrimination against foreign-sounding and foreign-looking individuals. In terms of policy outcomes, the final legislation embodied several contradictory policy goals. In terms of policy *process,* the institutional agendas of the House and Senate (despite vigilant efforts of key congressional players)[3] were constantly out of step with each other.

This essay makes the case for accounting for immigration policy making as interplay between issue redefinition efforts and the congressional committee system. By examining congressional activity in immigration, we can observe when and how policy making activity between the two chambers diverges and converges and how these shifts influence long-term policy change. Specifically, we can trace the influence of committee entrepreneurial activity on shifts in issue definition and agenda change. Second, we can correlate the agenda change with policy change. To this end, this essay conducts an exploratory analysis of the congressional committee activity in immigration policy from 1947 to 1993 to trace how shifts in issue dimensions of immigration impact negative and positive feedback processes.

THEORIES OF AGENDA CHANGE, PROBLEM DEFINITION, AND POLICY CHANGE

Successful problem redefinition is crucial for shifts in structural arrangements in the policy process and content of policy outcomes. Previous research in agenda setting demonstrates that a successful redefinition of a policy problem creates opportunities for change throughout a policy arena: changes in jurisdictional authority over a policy (Baumgartner and Jones 1993; Jones, Baumgartner, and Talbert 1993; King 1997), changes in attention given by the policy system and system actors, subsequent shifts from local to centralized decision making systems (Jones 1994), and changes in legitimate policy alternatives (Kingdon 1984). Successful issue redefinition by opponents of prevailing policy conceptions and subsequent agenda change can cause changes in the makeup of coalitions (Rochefort and Cobb 1994).

When issues have several dimensions of evaluation (i.e., problem definitions), there is a greater likelihood of reversals in policy decision making (Jones 1994), shifts in structure and makeup of coalitions as well as shifts in the location of where policy decisions are made. At times, political actors will take advantage of an existing definition and use a different institutional venue to promote their cause. Thus, it is important to examine agenda change and redefinition efforts both within and across institutions. When examining multidimensional issues, congressional activity is better understood as an intrainstitutional process between the two chambers rather than as activity of the full Congress. We can observe how changes in problem definitions can influence changes in institutional dynamics.

THE CASE OF U.S. IMMIGRATION
FOR UNDERSTANDING POLICY CHANGE

U.S. immigration policy is an ideal case study for examining the influence of changes in issue (i.e., problem) definition on changes in institutional arrangements. First, immigration issues have been a part of the public and systemic agenda since the beginning of this country (King 2000; Reimers 1998). Americans consider themselves a "nation of immigrants," yet the American public has historically harbored a deep ambivalence toward each new wave of immigrant groups (Fuchs 1990; Massey 1990b; Simon 1985; Simon and Alexander 1993). Concerns about immigration have captured public attention as well as spurred public and governmental debate about acceptable policy measures for determining who and how many can immigrate to the United States (King 2000; Smith 1993).

Second, Congress is the dominant institutional decision making location for immigration policy. Article one, section eight, clause four of the United States Constitution confers power to the Congress on matters of immigration and naturalization. More specifically, the Senate and House judiciary committees and their respective subcommittees on immigration are the dominant locations for immigration policy making. However, other congressional committees, such as the Senate Foreign Relations Committee, have contested the judiciary and immigration committees' "property rights" (King 1997, 11) over immigration and have focused on competing issue dimensions such as humanitarian concerns for political refugees. The question becomes how the multidimensional nature of immigration and the congressional committee system interact to allow different dimensions to gain agenda access in different committees within Congress.

Finally, how the problem of immigration is defined has changed over time, which influenced several reforms in immigration policy reforms since the infamous 1921 and 1924 National Origins Quota Acts, federal laws codifying race-based quotas to curb migration flows from areas other than Western Europe. Immigration policy is ostensibly considered to be a national security issue of controlling borders and establishing conditions of entry and exit of immigrants by different legal classifications of residency and citizenship status. Yet underneath this dominant policy image are well-developed alternative definitions of immigration. These perceptions have recurred periodically since the early twentieth century, varying in issue salience (Calavita 1996). Each of these alternatives has demonstrated the ability to capture governmental and public attentiveness and attendant agenda space. There are three enduring issues within immigration (to be elaborated in next section). They are: (1) immigration as a national security issue of controlling borders and preserving national identity; (2) immigration as a steady, reliable labor resource to critical U.S. industries; and (3) immigration policy as a humanitarian effort for the politically and religiously persecuted from other countries.

DIFFERENT ISSUE DIMENSIONS IN IMMIGRATION POLICY

Given the scarcity of attention of policy makers (Kingdon 1984, 1989; Baumgartner and Jones 1993) and the finiteness of agenda space in the policy process, no single issue can dominate the public agenda indefinitely. The dominance of any one issue dimension depends upon whether and how long it can hold the attention of policy makers and the institutional agenda. As in other contentious policy arenas such as health care (Hacker 1997) and welfare rights (Melnick 1994), competing policy actors challenged the dominant way of understanding the policy issue. Successful challenges by policy entrepreneurs in alternative venues could result in a venue shift, which increases the opportunity for new policy outcomes.

When the issue of who should be let in and who should be kept out gains agenda access, several subissues are immediately highlighted, such as the challenge of pursuing coherent policies that address legal ("front door") and illegal ("back door") migration flows. By framing the issue as a concern over vulnerable, out-of-control borders, policies tend to be exclusionary and result in policies such as those manifested by Operation Wetback of the 1950s and Operation Hold-the-Line of the 1980s.[4] Yet when immigration is defined in labor market terms (i.e., migration streams as labor sources), subissues such as business interests' call for increased quota provisions for highly skilled labor are highlighted. This focus ushered in polices such as the bracero program (1942 to 1964), that essentially established a network of immigrant labor to western and southwest agricultural growers (see Calavita 1992).

Immigration takes on distinct issue definitions that often compete for limited agenda space and often exhibit overlapping decision making jurisdictions of different congressional committees. At times, two or more problem definitions crowd the congressional agenda. During the 1950s, the national sovereignty dimension of controlling borders from both front-door and back-door migration dominated the policy agenda while Congress quietly dealt with other politically contentious issues, such as the use of undocumented labor from Mexico by south and southwest agricultural growers, far away from the public limelight.[5] This allowed these issues to maintain agenda access within the policy domain without contesting the dominant issue dimension. Much less visible policy measures such as the "Texas proviso," a section of the 1952 McCarran-Walter Act stating that "the usual and normal practices incident to employment shall not be deemed to constitute harboring" (quoted in Hutchinson 1981, 302) resulted from this shift. In other words, Congress legislated that employers would not be held legally accountable for hiring undocumented workers. Immigration historian Lawrence Fuchs makes the following observation about the relationship between the bracero program and the INS border control policies.

> At the beginning of the Korean War in 1951, Public Law 78 established a third *bracero* program in which the Department of Labor became the labor contractor. The new *bracero* program did not stanch the accelerating flow of illegal aliens. Returning *braceros* became recruiting agents for growers by recounting the opportunities to earn good money in the U.S. Many illegal aliens were ex-*braceros* or relatives of *braceros*. The program, it turned out, was not just a replacement for illegal migration but a stimulus to it. The Border Patrol could now vigorously apprehend aliens (875,000 were caught in 1953), while employers could continue to count on large numbers getting across. (Fuchs 1990, 123)

The implication of multidimensional issues is that different committees in both chambers of Congress may focus on different issue dimensions, despite the attentiveness of the dominant venues to one policy image (e.g., the judiciary committees' predominant focus on law-and-order policy solutions). However, this attentiveness to a particular issue dimension (or small set of issue dimensions) can change over time. The judiciary committees' focus on the law-and-order dimension created highly visible border operations policies that recurred throughout the postwar period. Yet the committees continually had to shift their attention to addressing the contradictions of sustaining (even promoting) temporary migrant flows that were heavily comprised of undocumented workers. These examples demonstrate that the interaction of the predominant policy image and competing issue definitions on the one hand, and institutional venues on the other hand, can result in enduring political and policy changes.

DATA SOURCES

The Policy Agendas Project database is a series of comprehensive data sets of U.S. congressional hearings, public laws, *Congressional Quarterly Almanac* stories, and selected stories from the *New York Times* spanning over forty-five years of policy making in the United States. The data used for this study are drawn from the first three data sets by utilizing a combination of keyword searches and the topic-coding scheme developed by the Policy Agendas Project researchers. I also used secondary research on U.S. immigration reform. Finally, I conducted a close reading of the six federal statutes commonly identified in the literature as the most critical sources of policy change in immigration for the time frame of this study:[6] the 1952 Immigration and Nationality Act (the McCarran-Walter Act), the 1965 Hart-Celler Act, the 1976 Immigration and Nationality Act Amendments, the 1980 Refugee Act, the 1986 Immigration Reform and Control Act (IRCA), and the 1990 Immigration Act.

DESIGN

Congress allocated ongoing policy making attention to immigration policy matters such as migration patterns, status of new migrants, refugee issues, and the changing yet pressing labor needs of agricultural, high-tech, and service industries. As a consequence, there are reasonably lengthy time series on legislative activity both in the early stages of policy decision making (congressional hearings) and in the later stages of policy decision making (passed legislation).

Congressional hearings are a good place to identify patterns of issue redefinition efforts. For example, congressional entrepreneurs and other political actors within a policy subsystem use hearings activity to buttress their existing policy jurisdiction as well as to make claims on other policy areas where they want to get in on the action.[7] Redefinition efforts are used to lay claim to an issue, direct (or redirect) attention to an issue, and shift focus to previously discounted policy solutions. Some of these redefinition efforts are facilitated by high-profile events that focus attention on policy discontinuities.[8] For example, the 2000 national and international media coverage of the struggle between the national government and the relatives of Cuban refugee Elian Gonzalez over Elian's residency status revealed the divergence in the U.S. refugee policy toward Cubans and Haitians.

The strategy is twofold. First, I examine the level and intensity of hearings activity in the House and the Senate and compare hearings activity between the two chambers. I focus on each chamber activity as a separate process in order to discern redefinition efforts by committee entrepreneurs and shifts in subcommittee jurisdiction. Each chamber tells a part of the story of policy change as a function of problem redefinition efforts.

Second, I analyze the level and intensity of legislative output and compare it to hearings activity. I use public statutes weighted by the amount of news coverage each statute received in the *Congressional Quarterly Almanac* (*CQ*). Weighted statutes are used in this study as an indicator of the relative importance of passed legislation during a congressional period. *CQ* devotes more news coverage to controversial or important legislation than it does to less salient issues. Statutes that receive more coverage in *CQ* are more likely to be the object of redefinition efforts. Comparisons of statute activity and hearing activity provide a picture of possible redefinition efforts.

EXPECTATIONS AND FINDINGS

The first expectation for trends in the different congressional committee venues is periodic divergence in defining immigration issues. Second, immigration policy making within Congress as a whole should fit the punctuated equilibrium model of long periods of relative quiet with policy punctuations that reveal brief periods of heightened activity in outputs and hearings activity. Competition between dominant and alternative venues leads to change in policy outputs (as measured by public statutes) over time. The complexity of issues such as immigration leads to circumstances where the different underlying dimensions become salient at different times. More importantly, no single issue dimension, no matter how entrenched in the dominant decision making venue, can dominate indefinitely. Studies that look at only one government agency (like the Immigration and Naturalization Service) or a single congressional committee (like the Senate Judiciary Committee) can miss the more complete picture of the policy process, where the policy subsystem struggles with the various facets of a multidimensional issue. These struggles come into focus at different times, under different policy thrusts and in different policy venues.

EXAMINATION OF U.S. IMMIGRATION STATUTES, 1947–1993

Figure 4.1 displays the U.S. weighted public statutes by congressional years (80th–103d Congresses) for the years 1947 to 1993. The figure shows several peaks in the series in terms of importance of policy outputs. All six identified major pieces of legislation are salient in comparison to other passed legislation (to be discussed in next section). Six of the seven peaks in the time series coincide with the statutes identified as the most important immigration reforms, thereby confirming expectations about the importance of the selected statutes. The 1965 act is the most salient, with the 1990 and 1976 acts following in importance.

The 1990 Immigration Act has the highest peak after the 1965 Hart-Celler Act; this is a surprising finding. The 1990 act significantly revised the 1965 act by setting new maximum levels of immigrants from 290,000 to 675,000 per year. The 1990 act primarily addressed legal migration issues. However, the most protracted legislative battle over immigration reform concerned the 1986 Immigration Reform and Control Act (LeMay 1994; Gimpel and Edwards 1999). The fight over the 1986 act lasted over ten years before chief legislative architects Senator Alan Simpson (R-Wy.) and Congressman Romano Mazzoli (D-Ky.) were able to muster the necessary support for passage in both chambers of Congress.[9] Additionally, the reform measures included in IRCA addressed issues of both legal and illegal immigration. It is reasonable to assert that during this particular period of immigration policy reform, dominant policy actors found it difficult to keep just one dimension on the policy agenda. For these reasons it seems that the 1986 act should exhibit a larger peak than the 1990 act.

Table 4.1 summarizes the 1952 McCarran-Walter Act and the five major amendments to the act from 1965 to 1993: the 1965 Hart-Celler Act, the 1976 Immigration Act, the 1980 Refugee Act, the 1986 Immigration Reform and Control Act, and the 1990 Immigration Act. The table also includes this author's assessment of the dominant problem definition(s) embodied in each act. The assessment is based on an analysis of each policy as well as secondary research conducted on particular policies and on the legislative history of congressional policy making in immigration (Hutchinson 1981).

The 1965 Hart-Celler Act marked the first major change in immigration policy since the establishment of the infamous race-based quota system in the 1920s. Before 1965, twentieth-century immigration policy was restrictionist in

FIGURE 4.1 U.S. IMMIGRATION PUBLIC LAWS

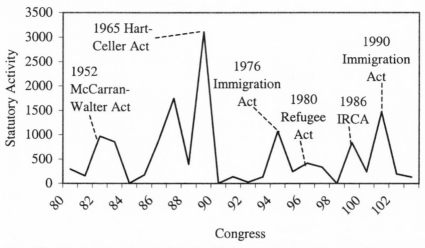

Congress

Note: The figure presents the number of public laws in the area of immigration weighted by the amount of coverage of these laws in *Congressional Quarterly*.

nature, allowing only a fraction of the number of immigrants who arrived in the previous waves of U.S. immigration of the 1840s and 1880s (DeSipio and de la Garza 1998; Massey 1990b, 1995). The 1924 National Origins Quota Act banned some nationalities altogether (migrants primarily from China and Japan) and set migration quotas for eligible countries to one-sixth of one percent of country nationals who had resided in the United States as recorded in the 1890 and 1910 censuses (Hutchinson 1981, 308). The 1965 act reversed the restrictionist era and liberalized immigration policy in unprecedented (and unanticipated) ways. The Hart-Celler Act replaced the national-origins quota system with a seven-tier preference system primarily devoted to determining migration levels based on different kinship relations (e.g., first-tier preference was for unmarried children of U.S. citizens while the second-tier preference included spouses and unmarried children of permanent resident aliens). The second significant change embodied in the 1965 act was that it opened the door to fundamental changes in the size and composition (in terms of country of origin) of migration flows. By shifting the primary policy focus from national-origins quotas to family reunification quotas,[10] Congress opened the door to redefining "immigrant" and the problem of immigration.

The 1976 act further liberalized the visa system by applying the twenty-thousand-per-country visa limits to Western Hemisphere countries. The

TABLE 4.1 Six Major U.S. Immigration Public Statutes, 1952 to 1990

Legislation	Key Provisions	Problem Definition
1952 McCarran-Walter Act	Maintained the national-origins quota system. Broadened the definition of excludable and deportable aliens.	Immigration as a national sovereignty concern of controlling entry and exit of aliens and protecting U.S. from subversive ideologies.
1965 Hart-Celler Act	Reversed the national-origins quota system and established a seven-tier preference system based on family reunification and needed employment skills. Also set a 20,000-per-country limit for immigrants from Eastern Hemisphere.	Immigration as a problem of setting policy criteria for legal migration that was commensurate with U.S. heritage as "a nation of immigrants."
1976 Immigration Act	Applied the 20,000-per-country limit to the Western Hemisphere.	Problem of controlling legal migration from Latin America and Canada.
1980 Refugee Act	Established an overall system for refugee admissions and resettlement. Removed refugees from the preference system.	Immigration as concern of U.S. upholding its humanitarian and political commitments to ideological allies by opening its borders to displaced persons.
1986 Immigration Reform and Control Act (IRCA)	Established employer sanctions for knowingly hiring undocumented workers. Provided amnesty for illegal residents who had resided in U.S. before 1982. Increased border enforcement.	Problem of controlling the nation's borders from illegal migration.
1990 Immigration Act	Increased yearly immigration limits to 675,000 (after 1995). Established a diversity visa program to promote immigration from underrepresented countries.	Problem of diversifying the composition of legal migration flows.

Refugee Act of 1980 formalized ad hoc policy toward refugee migration. However, the consequence of this extension of the twenty-thousand-per-country limits created an instant backlog of immigrant applicants from Mexico and elsewhere in Latin America (Tichenor 1994). Heightened attention was given to addressing refugees from Indochina and refugee resettlement financing to states and localities. The IRCA focused on illegal immigration to the United States and established employer sanctions to ameliorate the pull of migrants to the United States for employment. The 1990 act significantly increased the overall ceiling for annual legal migration (from 290,000 per year to 675,000 per year) and addressed the composition change of immigrant flows by adding "diversity" visas designed to increase migration from Ireland.

While most of the legislative changes have generally been in the direction of liberalizing immigration policy measures, there has been strong and consistent support for a restrictionist approach to limit the number of immigrants and control the diversity of the composition of immigrant streams. Each of these changes was a result of significant political struggle and countermobilization efforts of policy actors within Congress. The countermobilization efforts to set the agenda for immigration can be traced as divergent policy making activity in the two chambers of Congress, activity that is influenced by shifts from positive to negative feedback forces in the policy process.

POSITIVE AND NEGATIVE FEEDBACK PROCESSES IN U.S. IMMIGRATION POLICY REFORM

A practical way of analyzing the negative and positive feedback processes in U.S. immigration is to take the 1965 Hart-Celler Act as the key policy punctuation and examine policy making processes before and after 1965 (see figure 4.1). Figure 4.1 shows that the Hart-Celler Act marked a period of dramatic policy change. The period before 1965 can be characterized as a period of policy stability and reinforced by negative policy feedback processes. The period after 1965 can be characterized as experiencing dramatic policy change and reinforced by positive feedback processes. The period also saw several policy changes as a result of lurches in attentiveness to new subissues that emerged on the political and public agendas. We will discuss each period in turn.

Periods of positive feedback exhibit the following characteristics: an influx of new political actors and new political ideas, the creation of new programs and agencies to implement the new policy provisions, new policy outcomes representing a departure from the previous way of doing things, and a change in the location or number of legitimate institutional venues for policy decision making. Immigration reform in the period between the 1965 act and the 1990 act follows this pattern of waves of policy enthusiasm.

As noted, the Hart-Celler Act marked a shift in attentiveness from immigration as a problem of controlling "unwanted migration" from southern Europe and Asia (namely China and Japan) to the new issue dimension of defining immigration as a matter of family reunification. The resulting changes in the policy dismantled the national-origins quota system — the statutory provisions prescribing conditions for entry — and replaced it with a preference system that defined conditions of entry based on relationships to native and naturalized citizens. The wave of enthusiasm generated by the Hart-Celler Act also resulted in the influx of new political actors into the policy subsystem. The greater importance of the Hart-Celler Act is that it laid the foundation for the policy subsystem to become attentive to new dimensions of evaluation in immigration. In other words, the Hart-Celler Act created opportunities for subissues to emerge and reemerge on the policy agenda. In future rounds of policy reform, the principle of family reunification gave legitimacy to political actors such as the black and Hispanic congressional caucuses to call for more expansive policy reforms.

The period ushered in the creation of federal agencies and programs. The Office of Refugee Resettlement of the Department of Health and Human Services was developed to address local resettlement and integration issues of new migrants. New interest group organizations (also called nongovernmental organizations, or NGOs) either emerged or became political actors as a result of policy reforms. The American Immigration Lawyers Association (AILA), the Mexican American Legal Defense and Education Foundation (MALDEF), and the National Immigration Forum are all powerful players that have supported expansive provisions such as immigrant health care, increases in per-country visa limits, and concerns about unfair labor practices.

The policy reforms after 1965 resulted from lurches in attentiveness of policy actors to new contentious subissues on the national policy agenda that the congressional judiciary committees could not suppress. The reforms also resulted from countermobilization efforts of political actors interested in restricting legal immigration and generating tougher measures to deal with undocumented immigration. This interplay of new issue dimensions, political actors, and alternative congressional committee venues created a policy making environment where the judiciary committees were continually forced to address issues they had been able to contain during the pre-1965 era. The 1986 Immigration Reform and Control Act is a good example of how the

FIGURE 4.2 COMMITTEE COMPETITION OF U.S. IMMIGRATION HEARINGS IN HOUSE AND SENATE

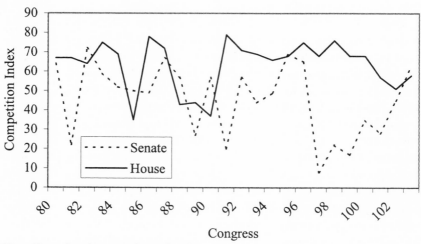

Congress

Note: House hearings: 393; Senate hearings: 248.

emergence of contentious subissues disrupted the policy subsystem. Figure 4.1 shows that IRCA was a significant policy reform.

Figure 4.2 illustrates the competition in the hearings activity across committees; it shows the degree of political contentiousness surrounding the policy process. IRCA was the first post-1965 legislation that specifically addressed illegal migration. However, policy makers found it difficult to disentangle the dimension of illegal migration from the dimension of the need for short-term migrant labor streams. The ressultant policy reflected this conflict in issue dimensions. While on the face of it IRCA was enacted to control illegal immigration, the law also provided a very generous amnesty program for undocumented aliens who had resided in the United States since 1982. Some three million undocumented aliens utilized the amnesty program to become naturalized citizens or permanent resident aliens. The second restrictionist measure in IRCA provided for sanctions to employers who hired undocumented migrant workers. However, the sanctions had very few enforcement provisions.

Despite the official congressional attentiveness to immigration as an issue of maintaining national identity, there was an equally potent image and policy reality of immigration as an issue of maintaining cheap and available sources of labor for agricultural and service industries (see Calavita 1984, 1992; Easterlin 1980).[11] This issue dimension was subordinate to the policy image of national sovereignty and border control. As expected under the punctuated equilibrium model, competing issues are kept off the decision agenda of the predominant venue in order to maintain control of the policy process.

The 1980 and 1990 policy reforms also reflect two different shifts in attention to enduring subissues in immigration. First, Congress and the nation turned their attention to the growing global issue of political refugees. Second, political actors began to focus on the changes in the composition of immigrant streams (i.e., the shift from European to Asian and Latin American migration to the United States) and the impact of these changes on U.S. national identity. The 1980 Refugee Act was primarily a congressional response to both domestic and international pressures to attend to global refugee populations. Congress had delegated much of refugee policy making to the presidency. Refugee issues that had essentially been of low issue salience during the immediate post–World War II period, merged with Cold War ideology and gained prominence. Refugee issues were determined by U.S. foreign policy goals of promoting liberal democracy abroad. In the wake of Cold War ideology, decisions about refugees and political asylum seekers became a foreign policy tool deployed to support U.S. allies and to discredit communist regimes. For example, the Cuban Refugee Assistance Act was largely a response to communist leader Fidel Castro's takeover of Cuba, where the United States had previously supported the rightist regime.[12] The president had generated refugee policy by a series of executive orders and through the process of "paroling" refugee and asylum seekers into the country under the authority of the Justice Department. Congress passed the 1980 act in order to codify the hodgepodge of executive orders, congressional provisions, and other de facto policy measures. The 1980 Refugee Act also removed the refugee quota provisions from the legal migration preference system established by the 1965 act.

The 1990 act marked a shift in attention to legal migration issue dimensions. While the principle of family reunification still remains a dominant policy image within the immigration policy subsystem, changes in the composition of immigrant streams shifted attention to the recurrent issue of new immigrants as a challenge to American national identity. The overall percentage of immigrant arrivals from Europe from the total number of immigrant arrivals steadily decreased from 29 percent in the period from 1965 through 1974 to 13.4 percent in period from 1975 through 1984 to 11 percent in the period from 1985 through 1994. At the same time, immigrant arrivals from Asia increased from 22 percent in the period from 1965 through 1974 to 43 percent in the period from 1975 through 1984 and then decreased to 32 percent in the period from 1985 through 1994 (Immigration and Naturalization Service 1999, 20). The 1990 act increased the upper limits to overall migration but also added a provision called diversity visas that set aside a quota for Irish immigrants in order to increase migration from "old stock" immigrant groups.

However, different issue definitions of immigration emerged on the national agenda (see table 4.1). There was the negative definition of immigrants and immigration as a threat to American national identity, national sovereignty, and democratic values. There was also great concern that migrants would bring subversive communist and socialist ideas into the state (Reimers 1998).

Figure 4.2 displays the shifts in hearings activity in different congressional committees as a response to the emergence of new problem definitions. These new definitions generated more policy making activity. On the whole, changes in policy still fell under the policy image of national sovereignty concerns of entry and exit. While the judiciary committees and their immigration subcommittees remained the dominant location of decision making, these committees were not able to control the emergence of new problem definitions. As new issue dimensions emerged, competition between the judiciary and alternative congressional committees resulted.

While the 1965 act has been often cited as the most significant change in modern immigration policy, each of these amendments brought significant changes to immigration policy. This is surprising. Using the punctuated equilibrium model, we would expect the policy change enacted by the 1965 Hart-Celler Act to be followed by a relatively short period of policy innovation: creation of new agencies, entry of new policy actors, and introduction of new issues on the decision agenda. The policy domain would then settle down into a relatively quiet period governed by negative feedback forces of incrementalism resulting in little policy change.

EXAMINATION OF HOUSE AND SENATE HEARINGS ACTIVITY

Figure 4.3 displays hearings activity in the House and Senate for the 80th through 103d Congresses. Taken together, Senate and House hearings activity roughly parallel each other from the 80th through the 89th Congress. The House showed steeper increases and decreases in the number of hearings held in each Congress than did the Senate. The two chambers diverged in the 91st Congress with the Senate hearings activity rising in comparison to House

FIGURE 4.3 COMPARISON OF HOUSE AND SENATE IMMIGRATION HEARINGS

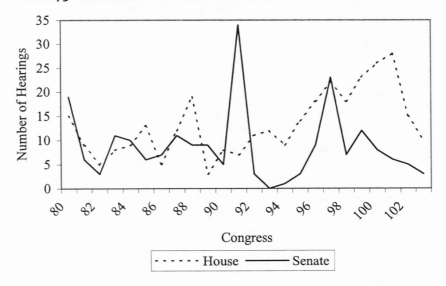

activity. Senate hearings increased sharply from five hearings in the 90th Congress to thirty-four hearings in the 91st Congress; in the House in the same period, the number of hearings declined from eight to seven. This divergence occurred in the congressional year after the landmark 1965 legislation. However, increases in Senate activity were not sustained; the number of Senate hearings fell from thirty-four in the 91st Congress to three in the 92d Congress. The number of hearings in the Senate continued to fluctuate; the chamber held no hearings in the 93d Congress, and the number sharply rose and fell several times from the 94th Congress to the 103d.

In comparison, House activity continued to rise steadily throughout the entire time period with fewer declines than found in Senate activity. House activity began an upward climb after the 1976 act with peaks that coincide with the identified amendment legislation of 1980, 1986, and 1990 before declining sharply after the 101st Congress.

The correlation coefficient for the House and Senate hearings activity (in congressional years) also reveals the independence of the two trends. Pearson's r of $-.055$ (not statistically significant) indicates little or no relationship between the two chambers.

In sum, the data show that immigration policy making within Congress fits the punctuated equilibrium model of long periods of relative quiet and bursts of activity and change. What is different is that the positive feedback forces operate for longer periods than expected.

COMPARISON OF HEARINGS AND PASSED LEGISLATION

When comparing the levels of hearings activity surrounding the major legislative reforms between 1965 and 1990, we see a marked difference in the patterns of the two chambers. With the exception of the 1965 act, the upward trend in House hearings activity corresponds to all the major reform legislation. The Senate hearings activity is more volatile.

During the period around the 1980 Refugee Act (96th Congress), Senate activity increased more than House activity. The number of hearings held in the House increased from eighteen to twenty-two; the number of hearings in the Senate increased from nine in the 96th Congress to twenty-three hearings in the 97th. Following the 1986 act in the 99th Congress, House activity continued to increase while Senate activity decreased.

Research indicates that the House committees were more proactive in initiating immigration reforms. In their recent study of immigration reform for each congressional period, Gimpel and Edwards (1999) find that the House took the lead on all major reforms from 1965 to 1979. This fourteen-year pattern of proactive House/reactive Senate was in no small measure due to the chairmanship of the Senate Judiciary Committee and its immigration subcommittee. Senator James Eastland (D-Miss.) was one of the staunchest adversaries of immigration reform. During his tenure as chair of the Senate Judiciary Committee and the immigration subcommittee, the committee reacted to House reform measures by refusing to release bills. Under the chairmanships of Senator Edward Kennedy (1979–80) and Senator Alan Simpson (1981–86) the Senate immigration subcommittee and the Senate as a whole became a proactive decision making venue.

A comparison of immigration statutes with hearing activity reveals other findings. First, the significant peak in activity in the 91st Congress is not accompanied by major legislation. Second, similar surges in activity did not result in attendant major legislation in the 97th and 98th Congresses. Given that agenda space and attentiveness of congressmembers are scarce (Kingdon 1984; Jones 1994), what would drive so much activity for so little gain?

Analysis of secondary research points to changing issue definitions in Congress. During the 1970s and 1980s two major issue dimensions of illegal immigration were on the decision agenda: "out-of-control borders" and the concern for preventing employers from hiring undocumented workers. During the

1970s, Congress, the executive branch, and the nation turned their attention to the plight of people dislocated from their homelands due to wars in Indochina and Central America. The United States felt an obligation to provide refugee assistance to its political allies from these regions. Although the national security concern of controlling the U.S. border was (and is) a fundamental issue in immigration, illegal migration of peoples across the Mexican and Canadian borders was still an issue with low salience on the public agenda. Indeed, the federal government's bracero program (1946 to 1964) supported the migration of Mexican workers seeking employment in labor-hungry agricultural business in the west and southwest. The cessation of the bracero program in 1964 led to an increase in undocumented labor, a development that drew congressional attention to the issue of illegal migration (Calavita 1992). However, agribusiness interests were able to keep illegal migration off the decision agenda in the congressional judiciary committees.

After 1980, the issue dimension of illegal migration became especially salient. When attention shifted from refugee migration to redefining the cause and solution for legal and illegal immigration, legislative activity became quite contentious in Congress. Rhetoric and activity around how to address illegal immigration began to heat up in both the House and Senate. It is during this period that we see more congressional committee competition over defining immigration and determining which committee venue had legitimate property rights over policy decision making.

EXAMINATION OF ISSUE REDEFINITION EFFORTS IN HEARINGS ACTIVITY

Peaks in congressional hearings activity provide clues to redefinition efforts. The most notable spikes in hearings activity in both chambers occur during the 91st and 97th Congresses. An analysis of the content of the hearings and the location of the hearings activity helps clarify how issues were redefined.

The House experienced a positive feedback cycle during the redefinition period around refugee status and handling of illegal migration flows. The period 1976 to 1980 saw a positive surge where attention focused on the refugee and refugee resettlement question. Even after these new reforms were enacted, immigration still remained an important topic on the governmental agenda. The surge peaked in the 97th Congress with no new significant legislation (see figures 4.1 and 4.2). This surge is particularly interesting because both the House and the Senate had dramatic increases in attentiveness to immigration. A return to the legislative history reveals what was happening. The surge in hearings activity for both chambers marked heightened controversy around the Simpson-Mazzoli-initiated efforts to curb illegal migration flows and to establish sanctions for the hiring of undocumented workers. The Simpson-Mazzoli measures involved a major redefinition effort on the part of restrictionists both inside and outside Congress. The efforts sparked much controversy that cut across partisan lines and engaged minority, labor, and agribusiness interests.

Each chamber harbored different dominant policy definitions. The Simpson-Mazzolli legislation initiated a protracted and highly contentious fight about whether to characterize the immigration problem as one curtailing illegal migration flows through border control measures or as an issue of reducing migration incentives by sanctioning employers who knowingly hire undocumented workers. Agribusiness and western growers' preference for a cheap, uninterrupted flow of labor, which had been successful in keeping a low public profile for decades, was now in the open and subject to scrutiny and vigorous counterclaims.

Alan Simpson's chairmanship of the Senate immigration subcommittee ushered in a new challenge to the prevailing definition of immigration as border control of legal migration flows. Simpson's position was that illegal immigration was a problem of employer accountability. With this new perception of the problem, Simpson and his House counterpart, Romano Mazzoli (D-Ky.), introduced legislation calling for sanctions against employers who knowingly hired undocumented workers. There were two significant implications. First, this essentially nullified the Texas proviso, the long-standing legislative loophole that made it legal for employers to hire undocumented workers. Second, employer sanctions marked a shift in perception of appropriate policy solutions (e.g., fines and jail sentences).[13] These policy solutions were vehemently opposed in both chambers.

DISCUSSION

Preliminary findings of hearings activity suggest that after 1965, as immigration received more overall congressional agenda attention, the House and the Senate agendas diverged in terms of policy making activity. Overall, the House seemed to give more agenda space to immigration hearings activity than the Senate for the forty-eight-year period. Nonetheless, a close reading of legislative history and research conducted by immigration scholars indicates that immigration was a very salient issue in the Senate. Senate leaders used the tactic of keeping immigration reform off the decision agenda. As a result, 1965 to 1993 was a prolonged period of mobilization and countermobilization between and within the two chambers. The Senate, in its efforts to keep immigration reform measures off the decision agenda, used several institutional processes. Reform bills were allowed to die in committee, and at times the chair of the immigration subcommittee refused to hold hearings on immigration (LeMay 1994; Gimpel and Edwards 1999). The Senate's reactive approach to immigration reform provides some explanation for the dramatic upward and downward surges.

Congressional actors and other policy advocates (particularly agricultural and textile interests) resisted efforts to redefine illegal migration as connected to demand-pull efforts of employers who needed a steady cheap labor supply. Labor groups resisted IRCA's amnesty provisions on the grounds that amnesty of large numbers of undocumented workers would drive down wages and destabilize the labor market. However, this new wave of redefinitions finally resulted in policy solutions that granted amnesty to undocumented aliens who had resided in the United States since 1982. Employer sanctions involved a compromise where the law was drafted around knowingly hiring illegal aliens.

CONCLUSION

This study of U.S. immigration policy reform demonstrates that the multidimensionality of issues not only creates opportunities for major policy punctuations within a policy subsystem, but subissues also can also cause shifts in attentiveness resulting in further changes. Newly emergent issues also create opportunities for challenges from competing policy venues. The data support the punctuated equilibrium thesis that the interplay of issues and venues can lead to significant changes not only in the policy outputs but also in the structure of the policy venues. While there has been some recent research on interinstitutional agenda dynamics (Flemming, Bohte, and Wood 1997; Flemming, Wood, and Bohte 1999; Baird 1998), more studies need to examine the linkages between the agendas of different institutions and the influence of these linkages on the policy process.

A second and equally important goal of this essay was to demonstrate the utility of the Policy Agendas Project databases on policy activity in conducting exploratory analysis of long-term changes in a policy domain. By comparing trends in hearings activity between the House and Senate, one can examine how different policy venues react to issue salience and to the redefinition efforts of policy actors both inside and outside the respective committees. By comparing trends in hearings activity to actual passed legislation, one can discern where issue salience and entrepreneurial activity of congressional actors shaped changes in the policy process (the structure of the committee system) and in policy outcomes (the composition of the public statutes).

NOTES

1. Kitty Calavita does take an approach oriented toward long-term policy in her researches on U.S. immigration reform. In an essay on policy responses and changes in immigration (1994), Calavita argues that a series of "paired oppositions" govern the way policy makers perceive immigration. She contends that the "inability of Congress to respond effectively has less to do with the difficulties of finding a solution than it does with arriving at a consensus of what is the problem" (1994, 77).

2. For research on the issue evolution of pesticides from a "wonder product" facilitating a vibrant domestic agriculture industry to an environmental and health hazard, see Bosso 1987. For a detailed study on the fractured nature of health care policy making in Congress, see Baumgartner, Jones, and MacLeod 1997.

3. The congressional battles around IRCA are legendary. Senator Alan K. Simpson (R.-Wyo.) and Congressmen Romano Mazzoli (D-Ky.) and Peter Rodino (D-N.J.) engaged in several skirmishes, victories, and reversals in their respective chambers on immigration reform since the mid-1970s.

4. The INS, with the assistance of local police authorities within the border states, developed several paramilitary border patrol policies. In addition to Operation Wetback and Operation Hold-the-Line, the INS instituted Operation Gatekeeper (begun in 1994) to "secure" the border at San Diego, California, and Operation Denial (begun in 2000) to target airports and smuggler "drop houses" in Arizona and Nevada.

5. Undocumented labor from Mexico was vital to U.S. agriculture. Fuchs reports that undocumented labor during the 1960s may have made up to 10 percent of the labor force in the border areas (Fuchs 1990, 126).

6. Due to the constraints of the data series, the period from 1994 to 2000 is not examined in this study. The period after 1993 experienced another major policy change in the 1996 Illegal Immigration Reform and Immigration Responsibility Act (IIRIRA). This policy change occurred in the wake of the controversial passage of California's Proposition 187 of 1994, which called for denial of social, health, and educational services to undocumented migrants and their children. IIRIRA focused on illegal migration flows in similar ways: limiting access to welfare and social benefits and focus on border control and deportation.

7. Each congressional side in a policy debate has its own cadre of supporters who are

often called upon to provide witness testimony at hearings. For a study on the role of congressional witnesses in hearings activity, see Talbert, Jones, and Baumgartner 1995.

8. Kingdon (1984) and Baumgartner and Jones (1993) define these high-profile events as "focusing events." For an interesting account of natural disasters as focusing events that influence the national policy agenda, see Birkland 1997.

9. For a detailed analysis of the congressional politics around IRCA, see Gimpel and Edwards 1999 and LeMay 1994.

10. It should be noted that the 1924 National Origins Quota Act first introduced the family unification preference. The 1965 act made the principle of family reunification the centerpiece of U.S. immigration policy.

11. Immigration to the United States has always been linked to labor. During the earliest period of the nation, America recognized its need for migrants to settle the "uninhabited" frontiers and to work in its newly emerging industrial enterprises. During the middle to late nineteenth century, American industries used Chinese immigrant laborers to build western railroads and Irish immigrants to build southern cities and work in coal mines.

12. The United States policy toward Cuban migrants as political refugees is a direct reflection of evaluating and using refugee policy as a foreign policy tool rather than as a domestic policy. For an excellent review of the evolution of U.S. refugee policy see Haines 1996.

13. Few employers were ever fined or jailed.

5

MULTIPLE TOPICS, MULTIPLE TARGETS, MULTIPLE GOALS, AND MULTIPLE DECISION MAKERS: CONGRESSIONAL CONSIDERATION OF COMPREHENSIVE HEALTH CARE REFORM

JOHN W. HARDIN

INTRODUCTION

Committees serve as one of the most important institutional components of Congress. In an average session, congressional committees receive thousands of bills to consider, yet they discharge only about 10 percent of those bills to their parent chambers for further consideration (Nickels 1994).[1] Central, therefore, to the study of congressional committees are questions about committee information: How extensive is the information committees use when considering policy? What is the nature of that information (i.e., is it biased or balanced)? Is that information acquired in an efficient manner? Does that information facilitate or hinder policy making?

When addressing these questions, many studies take a cross-sectional approach, assuming two things: (1) that committee jurisdictions remain static over time and (2) that committees hold monopolistic control over issues in their jurisdictions. Based on these assumptions, those studies often focus their theoretical and empirical analyses on certain *structural* features of the committee system: the committee assignment process, the ideological/policy preferences of committee members, the rules by which committees receive, consider, mark up, and report legislation, and the rules governing floor consideration of committee legislation.[2] This focus, in turn, rests on a third, deeper assumption: (3) that structure serves as the primary determinant of function (i.e., institutions are considered to be exogenous to the policy process). Together, these assumptions have caused much of the research on congressional committees to virtually ignore the policy making *process*. Hence, while we know a great deal about committee structures and information at particular points in time, we know far less (in a coherent, systematic sense) about how those structures and that information change over time or how they interact with the policy making process.

As discussed in the introductory chapter, an emerging body of longitudinal, process-focused research has begun to question the common cross-sectional, structural approach. It offers instead a more dynamic approach and understanding to congressional committees and the positive and negative feedback processes influencing the ways they acquire and consider information (e.g., Baumgartner and Jones 1993; Baumgartner, Jones, and Rosenstiehl 1997; Jones, Baumgartner, and Talbert 1993; Baumgartner, Jones, and Mac-Leod 2000; Hardin 1998a; Jones and Strahan 1985; King 1994, 1997; Talbert, Jones, and Baumgartner 1995). This research highlights how committee jurisdictions can be quite dynamic, both causing and responding to political changes as old issues become redefined in the political process or as new issues arise on the political agenda. Such changes will likely have a dramatic influence on the nature and extent of the information committees acquire. Thus analyses focusing on committee information must explicitly consider the coevolution of issues and structures.

In this chapter, I adopt a longitudinal, process-focused approach to examine how committee jurisdictions have changed over time and influenced the nature and extent of committee information surrounding an important issue in American political history: comprehensive health care reform. I first discuss the nature of committee information and outline three dimensions influencing the nature and extent of that information: (1) the topics of hearings, (2) the target groups providing the context of hearings, and (3) the witnesses providing input at hearings. I then examine how each of these dimensions differs across the 468 referral and nonreferral hearings on comprehensive health care reform between 1947 and 1993.[3] I find that the number of hearings, particularly nonreferral hearings, has increased dramatically over time, most notably during the 1970s and early 1990s. A wide variety of committees lacking formal jurisdiction over comprehensive health care reform held the majority of these hearings, causing a corresponding increase in the degree of jurisdictional overlap surrounding the issue. This increasing overlap highlights how the topics, target groups, and witness types differ significantly across time, committees, and type of hearing. These differences, which highlight a positive feedback process driving the coevolution of issues and structures, can be observed only with a long-term, process-focused analytical perspective.

THE NATURE OF COMMITTEE INFORMATION

As a central organizational unit of Congress, the committee system divides and assigns policy making responsibility to jurisdiction-specific work groups. Primarily through acquiring information about policies in their jurisdiction and then conveying that information to their respective chambers, committees serve as early-stage legislative linchpins in the policy making process. Hence, if committees acquire incomplete, inaccurate, or biased information regarding policies in their jurisdiction, subsequent legislative decisions based on that information may manifest those deficiencies. Such behavior would be consistent with the long-standing "distributive" theory of committee power, which assumes that committees have monopolistic jurisdictions, thus allowing them to serve primarily as means to "distribute" specialized, private policy benefits to their constituents (Fiorina 1974; Shepsle and Weingast 1987). If, however, committees acquire more complete, accurate, and unbiased information regarding policies in their jurisdictions, subsequent legislative decisions based on that information should manifest those strengths. Behavior along these lines would be consistent with the more recent "informational" theory of committee power (Krehbiel 1991), which assumes that committees, due partly to their potential to have conflictual and overlapping jurisdictions (Hardin 1998a; King 1997), serve primarily as a means to "inform" the parent chamber accurately regarding policies and their outcomes.

ROLES AND TYPES OF HEARINGS

Although committees have several ways of acquiring information about issues in their jurisdiction, holding hearings serves as a principal means. Through hearings, committees primarily receive policy input from witnesses: administrative officials, interest groups, independent experts, constituents, etc. Interest groups in particular consider hearings a crucial forum for providing information and expressing their viewpoints; 99 percent of the interest groups lobbying Congress testify at hearings (Schlozman and Tierney 1986). While hearings ostensibly serve as fact-finding exercises, they may also serve as means to publicize an issue, assess the intensity of support or opposition to a bill, allow citizens or interest groups to express their views, provide publicity to politically ambitious committee chairs and members, or investigate new problems or issues (Oleszek 1996, 109–12).

Committee hearings come in two basic types: referral and nonreferral. Referral hearings are those in which a committee considers bills referred to it by the parliamentarians, who make referral decisions on behalf of the congressional leadership. Committees are under no obligation to hold hearings on bills referred to them by the parliamentarians, and so the decision to hold hearings is a crucial point in the life of a bill, signaling that the committee views the bill as worthy of consideration. Moreover, those members not on a committee look to that committee's referral hearings to provide a record of the committee's scrutiny and views of a bill. Without first being the subject of hearings, a bill considered by the chamber is likely to come under sharp criticism from members of Congress. Referral hearings shape the fate of bills directly by providing a visible indicator of committee activity on a bill.

Nonreferral hearings, in contrast, are those in which committees initiate investigatory or oversight hearings on issues for which they have not received a bill referral. Such hearings can be on issues either within or outside of a committee's jurisdiction. More often than with referral hearings, committees use nonreferral hearings entrepreneurially to establish a "track record" or to gain expertise on issues, which in turn might increase their standing with several audiences: congressional colleagues, the parliamentarians, bureaucrats, interest groups, constituents, or the media. This increased standing helps committees justify future claims for jurisdiction over issues they wish to consider (Talbert, Jones, and Baumgartner 1995). Nonreferral hearings shape policy indirectly, since committees holding such hearings can help define issues not in their jurisdiction and ultimately help determine how those issues are considered by the committee(s) having jurisdiction over the issues in question. Consequently, the information acquired in nonreferral hearings, especially those held by committees lacking formal jurisdiction over an issue, is likely to differ from that acquired in referral hearings.

THE MULTIPLE DIMENSIONS OF HEARINGS INFORMATION
Regardless of whether a hearing is referral or nonreferral, three dimensions in particular influence the nature and extent of information acquired at that hearing: (1) the specific *topic* of the hearing, (2) the *target group(s)* providing the context of the hearing, and (3) the *types of witnesses* testifying at that hearing.

For example, a hearing addressing the topic of comprehensive health care reform potentially could focus on several narrower topics within that issue: costs of medical care, quality of medical care, access to/availability of medical care, fraud in medical care, etc. Moreover, that same hearing potentially could consider how its topics relate to one or more target groups, since those topics impact a variety of groups in American society: health personnel, health facilities, citizen groups (e.g., the aged, the poor, women, disease groups), businesses, labor, government programs (e.g., Medicare, Medicaid, public health programs), etc. Finally, when considering how topics impact various target groups, a committee potentially could ask several types of witnesses to provide input at its hearing: physicians, allied health personnel, hospitals/ health facilities representatives, labor groups, government officials, citizens, businesses, experts/academics, etc.

With three dimensions of hearings information, minor changes along each of the dimensions can greatly influence a committee's views, decisions, and recommendations. And since more than one committee has the potential to consider a given issue at a given time and to different extents across the three dimensions, the nature and extent of committee information has the potential to differ considerably.

IMPLICATIONS FOR EMPIRICAL ANALYSES

Given the multidimensional nature of information acquisition in hearings, empirically examining the nature and extent of committee information regarding an issue requires examining two factors: (1) how many committees acquire information about that issue at any given time and (2) the nature and extent of the information committees acquire along each of the three dimensions discussed above. Because recent research (Jones, Baumgartner, and Talbert 1993; Baumgartner, Jones, and MacLeod 1999b; Hardin 1998a; King 1997) illustrates that committee jurisdictions change over time, and because information values along each of the three dimensions are also likely to differ across time, committees, and type of hearing (referral or nonreferral), examining both of the factors just noted requires a longitudinal approach that explicitly considers how information acquisition along the three information dimensions varies across time, committees, and type of hearing. The following sections provide one example of such an analysis, highlighting the dynamic coevolution of an issue and the congressional committee system.

ANALYZING COMMITTEE HEARINGS INFORMATION

DATA

To illustrate the value of an analysis examining differences along the three information dimensions across time, committees, and type of hearing, I focus my analysis on congressional hearings addressing the comprehensive health care reform issue. Several factors make this issue particularly valuable for studying issue-institution coevolution and changes in information acquisition. First, public debate regarding the issue has persisted for more than seventy years, and the issue has received congressional attention for nearly fifty. Second, since the time comprehensive health care reform first appeared on the congressional agenda, several important exogenous events have helped redefine and highlight various dimensions of the issue: rapidly rising medical costs, decreasing insurance coverage, numerous congressional elections, and major congressional reforms. Third, throughout this period the natures of public opinion and interest group activity have undergone significant and meaningful change. And finally, committee jurisdictions surrounding this issue show considerably more overlap than do jurisdictions surrounding most other issues (Baumgartner, Jones, and MacLeod 1999a). These factors, I argue, have greatly influenced the nature and extent of information acquired at hearings on the issue.

METHODS

To measure the nature and extent of information acquisition at congressional hearings on comprehensive health care reform, I adopt an approach similar to that used by Baumgartner and Jones (1993). Paying particular attention to committee hearings activity, I follow the comprehensive health care issue over time, highlighting both dynamic and cross-sectional differences in committee information acquisition. Specifically, I focus my analysis on five factors pertaining to each of the 468 hearings on that issue from 1947 to 1993: (1) the committee holding the hearing, (2) the type of hearing (i.e., referral or nonreferral), (3) the specific topic(s) of the hearing, (4) the target group(s) of the hearing, and (5) the interest affiliation of witnesses testifying (i.e., providing input) at the hearing.

I obtained my population of hearings from the Policy Agendas Project congressional hearings data set.[4] This data set contains the majority of variables necessary for this analysis (e.g., which committees held which hearings, type of hearing, date of hearing, etc.). It does not, however, contain variables addressing the specific topics of hearings, the target groups of hearings, or witnesses testifying at hearings. Thus I added those variables after reading summaries of each hearing in the *Congressional Information Service Abstracts* (CIS annual) and using an extensive coding procedure.[5]

To classify the specific focus of a hearing, I coded each hearing as focusing on one or more of the following six topics: (1) access to/availability of care, (2) cost of delivering/insuring care, (3) allocation of financial resources (among services, and between services and administration), (4) administrative burden imposed on providers and patients, (5) quality of medical care, and (6) fraud/malpractice. As we will see below, some hearings focus on few topics, while others focus on several. Next, to classify the target groups of each hearing, I coded each hearing as targeting one or more of the following nine groups: (1) physicians, (2) allied health,[6] (3) hospitals/health facilities, (4) labor, (5) business, (6) federal government programs, (7) state and local government programs, (8) citizens, and (9) insurance. As with topics, some hearings target a narrow range of groups while others target a much broader range. Finally, to classify witnesses by their interest affiliation, I coded each witness as representing one of the following ten categories: (1) physicians, (2) allied health, (3) hospitals/health facilities, (4) labor, (5) business, (6) federal government, (7) state and local government, (8) citizens, (9) insurance, and (10) experts/academics.[7] The findings below illustrate that hearings differ considerably in the types and range of witnesses they invite.

EMPIRICAL FINDINGS

In this section I present summary findings illustrating how information acquired along each of the three dimensions discussed above varies across time, committees, and type of hearing. Before doing so, however, I first briefly review the political history of comprehensive health care reform and present findings illustrating how the number and types of committee hearings have changed over time. The over-time patterns suggest that the multidimensional nature of comprehensive health care reform has caused it to experience two distinct periods of positive feedback processes involving the coevolution of the issue and the congressional committee system considering it.

HISTORY AND LONGITUDINAL PATTERNS OF COMMITTEE HEARINGS
Although comprehensive health care reform appeared on the national agenda two times during the early part of this century — during the Progressive Era and the New Deal administration — Congress did not begin to hold hearings on the issue until the late 1940s. Specifically, Congress first held hearings on comprehensive health care reform after President Truman revived the idea and spurred the introduction of the Wagner-Murray-Dingell bills in 1945, 1947, and 1949 (Marmor 1994; Starr 1982, bk. 2, chap. 1). During the forty-six years from 1947 to 1993, twenty-nine committees held 468 hearings for a total of 902 days and heard testimony from 7,686 witnesses. Four committees held the majority of these hearings: House Commerce (formerly Energy and Commerce), House Ways and Means, Senate Finance, and Senate Labor and Human

FIGURE 5.1 DAYS OF REFERRAL AND NONREFERRAL HEARINGS ON COMPREHENSIVE HEALTH CARE REFORM

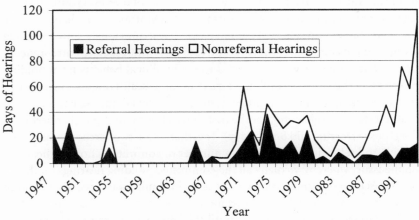

Year

Note: Total number of referral hearing days = 347; total number of nonreferral hearing days = 555.

Resources (formerly Labor and Public Welfare).[8] These committees are the ones having primary formal jurisdiction to authorize changes in the structure of the U.S. health care financing system.

Figure 5.1 displays the total number of days devoted per year to referral and nonreferral hearings on comprehensive health care reform from 1947 to 1993. The overall pattern of the activity reflects the issue's rise and fall from the political agenda and illustrates the dramatically increasing proportion of nonreferral hearings over time.[9] Between 1947 and 1954, only four committees — House Commerce, House Education and the Workforce (formerly Education and Labor), House Government Reform and Oversight (formerly Government Operations), and Senate Labor and Human Resources — held hearings on the issue, the vast majority of which involved a bill referral. The lack of hearings in the 1950s and 1960s reflects the fact that attention shifted away from comprehensive health care reform and toward less comprehensive proposals such as Medicare and Medicaid.[10] The 1970s mark the period when debate shifted away from Medicare and Medicaid and back toward more comprehensive health care reform, with both Presidents Nixon and Carter backing comprehensive reform proposals. This decade saw increasing competition among several proponents of reform, making it the first period of dramatic, self-reinforcing changes in committees' level of activity regarding the issue.

Throughout the 1970s, a greater number and variety of committees began to hold hearings on comprehensive health care reform. These changes came from two sources. First, the 1970s saw a wider array of interest groups increase their activity on the health care reform debate (Morone 1990, chap. 7; Peterson 1993, 1994; Starr 1982, bk. 2, chap. 4). These previously unrepresented groups sought committees more receptive to their interests, and entrepreneurial committees also saw the potential to reap political benefits from holding hearings on the issue. Second, the 1970s saw large-scale congressional reform that decentralized the committee system, broadened the Senate's existing multiple-referral rules, and, for the first time, allowed multiple bill referrals in the House (Deering and Smith 1997). Together, these two forces caused an explosive and self-reinforcing trend in number of committees holding hearings on the issue, whereby virtually all the committees holding hearings on the issue focused on new dimensions of the issue in similar ways (see discussion of figures 5.2–5.4 below). Despite this increased activity no legislation resulted, and congressional activity waned until the latter part of the 1980s and early 1990s, when it increased a second time, even more explosively than during the 1970s. The most notable feature from figure 5.1 is that the majority of this increased activity came from nonreferral hearings. Although figure 5.1 does not display which committees held these hearings, a more in-depth analysis of the data (available at the Policy Agendas web site) indicates that committees other than the four primary authorizing committees held most of these hearings. Examples of key players among these other committees include the Bipartisan Commission on Comprehensive Health Care (i.e., the Pepper Commission), the House and Senate Select/Special Aging committees, the House Education and Labor Committee, the Senate Judiciary Committee, and the Senate Small Business Committee. Like firms rushing in to capture new shares of emerging markets, these committees held hearings in hopes of capitalizing on or creating new understandings of a multidimensional issue.

To assess the influence these jurisdictional encroachments had on the overall jurisdictional situation, I constructed Herfindahl indexes (available at the Policy Agendas web site) to serve as measures of jurisdictional overlap during selected periods between 1947 and 1993.[11] The indexes (which, in theory, range from a high of 100, indicating a monopoly, to a low near zero, indicating considerable overlap) indicate that for both types of hearings, jurisdictional overlap increased considerably over time.[12] The increase in overlap is greater and more consistent for nonreferral hearings than for referral hearings, reflecting the greater freedom committees have when holding nonreferral hearings. For referral hearings, the index ranges from a high of 89.6 in the 1960s, when committees focused their legislative attention more on Medicare and Medicaid, to a low of 41.1 in the 1980s. For nonreferral hearings, the index ranges from a high of 100 in the 1950s to a low of 15.0 in the early 1990s. Clearly, committees lacking legislative jurisdiction over comprehensive health care reform increasingly have desired to influence the nature and extent of information acquired surrounding the issue. The following sections illustrate the ways in which they have done so.

TOPICS

As noted above, within an issue area such as comprehensive health care reform, committees may choose to focus their hearings on a variety of more specific topics. Tables 5.1 and 5.2, respectively, display the range of attention to six topics across referral and nonreferral hearings during the 1970–93 period.[13] In both tables, the committees with primary authorization power in each chamber are listed first, followed by the remaining committees holding hearings. Committees with limited activity are grouped together.

Looking first at the topic total column in each table, we see that two topics combined (cost of delivery system; access to care) account for over 60 percent of the total committee attention. Four additional topics (allocation of resources; administrative burden; quality of care; fraud/malpractice) share the remainder of the total committee attention. For referral hearings, as summarized in table 5.1, the two committees with primary authorization power in each chamber account for the vast majority of committee attention; joint committees account for none of the activity. The differences in attention across committees and topics are not large enough to ensure that they did not arise from mere chance, and it is clear that there are few dramatic differences in attention across committees; committees typically focused their referral hearings on the same topics. Of the differences that do appear, however, most notable is that in the House the eight other committees focus 36.4 percent of their attention on access topics, while the two lead committees (Commerce, and Ways and Means) focus 29.6 and 26.7 percent of their attention, respectively, on access topics. In addition, those eight other committees focus noticeably less of their attention (0 percent) on resource allocation topics than do the two lead committees (9.9 and 10.5 percent, respectively). In the Senate, the most notable difference arises when comparing the attention of the two lead committees (Labor, and Finance) to the attention of the four other committees. Though the number of observations is quite small for the four other committees, it appears that those committees prefer to focus much more of their attention on cost and access issues (85.8 percent for the two topics

TABLE 5.1 Topics Discussed at Referral Hearings on Comprehensive Health Care Reform, 1970–93 (by percentage)

Topic	House Committee			Senate Committee			Joint Committee	Topic Total	(N)
	Commerce	Ways and Means	Eight Other	Labor	Finance	Four Other	None		
Cost of delivery system	31.0	32.6	36.4	28.6	34.1	42.9	—	32.6	(102)
Access to care	29.6	26.7	36.4	38.1	31.8	42.9	—	31.3	(98)
Allocation of resources	9.9	10.5	0.0	7.1	9.4	14.3	—	8.9	(28)
Administrative burden	12.7	17.4	9.1	14.3	8.2	0.0	—	12.5	(39)
Quality of care	12.7	8.1	9.1	11.9	15.3	0.0	—	11.5	(36)
Fraud/malpractice	4.2	4.7	9.1	0.0	1.2	0.0	—	3.1	(10)
Committee total	100.1	100.0	100.1	100.0	100.0	100.1	—	100.0	—
(N)	(71)	(86)	(22)	(42)	(85)	(7)	—		(313)

Note: Because hearings may focus on more than one topic, the total number of topics (313) is greater than the total number of hearings (121). An additional three hearings were uncodable by topic and are not included here. Chi-squared (25 d.f.) = 17.9 ($p < .85$).

TABLE 5.2 Topics Discussed at Nonreferral Hearings on Comprehensive Health Care Reform, 1970–93 (by percentage)

Topic	House Committee				Senate Committee					Joint Committee		Topic Total	(N)
	Commerce	Ways and Means	Aging	Ten Other	Labor	Finance	Aging	Judiciary	Nine Other	Pepper	Two Other		
Cost of delivery system	30.9	35.9	34.7	36.1	31.3	45.5	38.5	25.0	28.3	42.9	34.6	34.9	(238)
Access to care	24.5	28.9	33.3	33.7	30.0	36.4	50.0	21.4	34.8	52.4	23.1	31.4	(216)
Allocation of resources	9.6	5.6	2.8	4.8	12.5	4.5	7.7	7.1	6.5	0.0	15.4	7.1	(47)
Administrative burden	13.8	16.2	9.7	12.0	7.5	6.1	0.0	28.6	15.2	0.0	7.7	11.7	(80)
Quality of care	16.0	12.0	13.9	12.0	15.0	4.5	3.8	10.7	8.7	4.8	15.4	11.6	(80)
Fraud/malpractice	5.3	1.4	5.6	1.2	3.8	3.0	0.0	7.1	6.5	0.0	3.8	3.3	(23)
Committee total	100.1	100.0	100.0	99.8	100.1	100.0	100.0	99.9	100.0	100.1	100.0	100.0	
(N)	(94)	(142)	(72)	(83)	(80)	(66)	(26)	(28)	(46)	(21)	(26)		(684)

Note: Because hearings may focus on more than one topic, the total number of topics (684) is greater than the total number of hearings (301). An additional nineteen hearings were uncodable by topic and are not included here. Chi-squared (50 d.f.) = 63.3 ($p < .10$).

combined) than do the two lead committees (66.7 percent in Labor, 65.9 in Finance).

Turning next to nonreferral hearings in table 5.2, the two committees with primary authorization power in each chamber again account for a majority of the committee attention, but to a much smaller degree than with referral hearings. In addition, three joint committees focus their hearings activity on comprehensive health care reform topics. Unlike referral hearings, the differences in attention across committees and topics are large enough to suggest that they did not arise from mere chance, and more notable differences in attention appear across the committees. When not constrained by bill consideration, committees vary more in the types of topics they consider. For example, in the Senate, the Finance Committee focused 45.5 percent of its attention on cost topics, while the remaining Senate committees focused, on average, approximately 30 percent of their attention on cost topics. The Senate Aging Committee is also notable, focusing 50 percent of its hearings attention on access issues (primarily targeted on elderly groups) and 38.5 percent of its attention on cost topics (also primarily targeted on the elderly groups). One particularly notable finding is that the Judiciary Committee focused a plurality of its attention (28.6 percent) on administrative burden topics (primarily related to the legal aspects of regulations), while no other Senate committee focused more than 15.2 percent of its attention on that topic. Among the joint committees, the Pepper Commission focused the vast majority of its attention on cost and access topics (95.3 percent for the two topics combined), which is notably more than did any other committee in either chamber.

To illustrate how the focus of committee attention to comprehensive health care reform topics has varied over time, figure 5.2 displays the proportion per year that two topics combined — cost and access — represent of total referral and nonreferral hearings attention from 1970 to 1993. The figure illustrates a noticeable increase in the amount of committee attention focused on cost and access topics. In the 1970s, committees, on average, focused their hearings (referral and nonreferral) on three topics, most often cost, access, and quality. In the 1980s and 90s, however, committees focused most of their hearings (referral and nonreferral) on only two topics, most often cost and access (the third most common topic was administrative burden).[14] Thus, throughout the 1970–93 period, the overall focus of committee hearings on comprehensive health care reform narrowed, aimed increasingly more on two topics (cost and access), and shifted unsystematically in emphasis among the remaining four topics. These trends, combined with the findings in tables 5.1 and 5.2, suggest that while committee focus depends partly on changing issue

FIGURE 5.2 COST AND ACCESS AS PROPORTION OF TOTAL TOPICS DISCUSSED AT REFERRAL AND NONREFERRAL HEARINGS ON COMPREHENSIVE HEALTH CARE REFORM

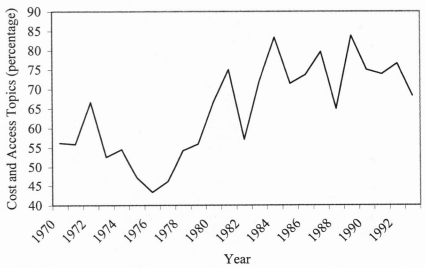

Note: Topics were uncodable for pre-1970 hearings.

definitions (i.e., the focus of referral hearings changes over time despite the fact that the same four committees held the majority of those hearings), committees such as Senate Aging, Senate Judiciary, and Joint Pepper, through their nonreferral hearings, also played a pivotal, driving role in shaping the overall focus of committee hearings on comprehensive health care reform (potentially through redefining the issue and causing committees with primary jurisdiction to shift their focus). Because these changes in focus occurred in both referral and nonreferral hearings held by both the primary authorizing committees and other committees, it suggests a self-reinforcing, overarching positive feedback process.

TARGET GROUPS

To better evaluate the above findings concerning hearings topics, it is useful to consider patterns in the target groups discussed at hearings. Tables 5.3 and 5.4, respectively, present this information for referral and nonreferral hearings. In both tables, the committees with primary authorization power in each chamber are listed first, followed by the remaining committees holding hearings. Committees with limited activity are grouped together.

TABLE 5.3 Target Groups Discussed at Referral Hearings on Comprehensive Health Care Reform, 1970–93 (by percentage)

Target group	House Committee			Senate Committee			Joint Committee		Target Group Total	(N)
	Commerce	Ways and Means	Eight Other	Labor	Finance	Four Other	Pepper	Two Other		
Physician	5.0	7.5	2.4	8.4	5.6	5.6	–	–	6.6	(39)
Allied health	8.4	7.5	0.0	8.4	4.5	11.1	–	–	7.1	(42)
Hospitals/facilities	18.5	11.2	9.8	13.3	10.1	11.1	–	–	13.0	(77)
Labor	5.9	8.1	12.2	7.8	6.7	5.6	–	–	7.6	(45)
Business	8.4	11.2	9.8	7.8	11.2	5.6	–	–	9.4	(56)
Federal govt.	18.5	16.8	22.0	16.9	20.2	11.1	–	–	17.8	(106)
State and local govt.	11.8	12.4	14.6	11.4	11.2	11.1	–	–	12.0	(71)
Citizen	16.8	11.8	19.5	16.9	18.0	16.7	–	–	15.8	(94)
Insurance	6.7	13.7	9.8	9.0	12.4	22.2	–	–	10.8	(64)
Committee total	100	100	100	100	100	100	–	–	100	–
(N)	(119)	(161)	(41)	(166)	(89)	(18)	–	–	–	(594)

Note: Because hearings may have more than one target group, the total number of target groups (594) is greater than the total number of hearings (124). Chi-squared (40 d.f.) = 25.5 ($p < .97$).

TABLE 5.4 Target Groups Discussed at Nonreferral Hearings on Comprehensive Health Care Reform, 1970–93 (by percentage)

Target Group	House Committee				Senate Committee					Joint Committee		Target Group Total	(N)
	Commerce	Ways and Means	Aging	Ten Other	Labor	Finance	Aging	Judiciary	Nine Other	Pepper	Two Other		
Physician	9.5	9.4	1.9	5.4	5.6	7.3	7.5	12.8	4.4	13.2	2.6	7.1	(83)
Allied health	5.7	7.8	8.3	2.7	6.3	4.0	12.5	7.7	10.0	5.3	5.1	6.5	(76)
Hospitals/facilities	12.7	14.7	12.0	14.1	13.4	9.7	17.5	15.4	10.0	13.2	7.7	12.9	(151)
Labor	5.1	5.7	0.9	10.1	4.9	4.0	0.0	2.6	2.2	2.6	10.3	4.9	(58)
Business	7.6	8.6	1.9	10.1	9.2	8.9	2.5	0.0	8.9	10.5	15.4	7.9	(93)
Federal govt.	19.0	16.7	23.1	17.4	17.6	19.4	12.5	12.8	22.2	15.8	15.4	18.2	(213)
State and local govt.	14.6	11.8	15.7	16.8	9.2	12.1	20.0	17.9	11.1	10.5	7.7	13.1	(154)
Citizens	15.2	13.1	24.1	14.8	20.4	21.0	17.5	15.4	22.2	10.5	23.1	17.5	(205)
Insurance	10.8	12.2	12.0	8.7	13.4	13.7	10.0	15.4	8.9	18.4	12.8	11.9	(139)
Committee total	100	100	100	100	100	100	100	100	100	100	100	100	—
(N)	(158)	(245)	(108)	(149)	(142)	(124)	(40)	(39)	(90)	(38)	(39)	—	(1,172)

Note: Because hearings may have more than one target group, the total number of target groups (1,172) is greater than the total number of hearings (313). An additional seven hearings were uncodable by target group and are not included here. Chi-squared (80 d.f.) = 88.9 ($p < .25$).

Looking first at the target group total column in both tables, we see that no single target group dominates and the spread of groups does not differ dramatically across the two types of hearings. In both tables, the federal government (due largely to discussion of the six topic categories in the context of various proposed federally funded and administered health programs) comprises the largest single target group (17.8 percent and 18.2 percent respectively), while each of four other categories (hospitals/facilities; state and local government; citizens; insurance) comprises over 10 percent of the target groups. In both tables, each of the remaining four target groups comprises less than 10 percent of the total.

For referral hearings, summarized in table 5.3, the two committees with primary authorization power in each chamber account for the vast majority of committee activity. As with topics for referral hearings, the differences in attention across target groups and committees are not large enough to ensure that they did not arise by chance. Moreover, the minor differences that do appear are even smaller in magnitude than the differences for topics. Together, these findings suggest that the small number of committees holding referral hearings tend to focus on roughly the same topics related to roughly the same target groups.

The situation is somewhat more varied, however, for nonreferral hearings, which are displayed in table 5.4. As with topics for nonreferral hearings, the two committees with primary authorization power in each chamber account for a majority of the committee attention, but to a much smaller degree than with referral hearings. In addition, three joint committees targeted their hearings activity on target groups. Although the differences in target groups across committees are not strongly statistically significant, there is a greater than 75 percent chance they did not arise from chance, and some notable patterns appear. As with topics, when not constrained by bill consideration, committees vary more in the types of groups they target.

In the House, for example, the Aging Committee is the main outlier in terms of the types of groups it targets for its discussions on topics such as cost and access. It targets groups such as physicians (1.9 percent), labor (0.9 percent), and business (1.9 percent) much less than do the other House committees, but it targets groups such as the federal government (23.1 percent) and citizens (24.1 percent) much more than do other House committees. In the Senate too, the Aging Committee is the main outlier, with much less of its attention targeted on groups such as labor (0.0 percent) and business (2.5 percent), and much more targeted on groups such as hospitals/facilities (17.5 percent) and state and local government (20.0 percent). Among joint committees,

FIGURE 5.3 HEALTH CARE PROVIDERS AS PROPORTION OF TOTAL TARGET GROUPS DISCUSSED AT REFERRAL AND NONREFERRAL HEARINGS ON COMPREHENSIVE HEALTH CARE REFORM

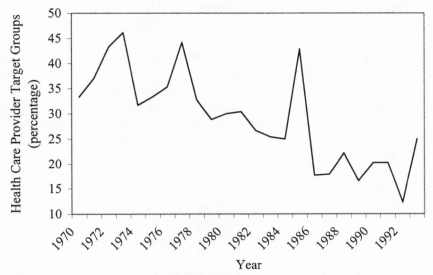

Note: Target groups were uncodable for pre-1970 hearings.

the Pepper Commission tends to target groups such as physicians (13.2 percent) and insurance (18.4 percent) more than do the other committees, but it tends to target citizens (10.5 percent) less than do most of the other committees. Although these differences across committees and target groups are bigger than they were for referral hearings, taken together the findings suggest that the committees do not differ greatly in the types of groups they target when considering comprehensive health care reform topics.

To illustrate how the target groups of comprehensive health care reform hearings have varied over time, figure 5.3 displays the proportion per year that one broad type of target group — health care providers (physician + allied health + hospitals/facilities) — represents of total referral and nonreferral hearings attention from 1970 to 1993. The figure illustrates a noticeable decrease in the amount of committee attention targeted on health care providers. In the 1970s, committees, on average, targeted 35 percent their hearings (referral and nonreferral) on health care providers. In the 1980s and 90s, however, committees targeted only 20 percent of their hearings (referral and nonreferral) on health care providers. The spread of the remaining six target groups remained fairly constant over time, meaning those groups absorbed fairly equally the shift in attention away from health care providers. These trends, combined with the findings in tables 5.3 and 5.4, suggest that while the groups committees target depends partly on changing group mobilizations and issue definitions (i.e., the target groups of referral hearings change over time despite the fact that the same four committees held the majority of those hearings), committees such as Senate Aging, Senate Judiciary, and Joint Pepper, through their nonreferral hearings, also played a pivotal role in shaping the overall range of groups targeted in committee hearings on comprehensive health care reform (potentially though mobilizing groups, redefining the issue, or causing committees with primary jurisdiction to target different groups). Much like the changes occurring with respect to topics, because these changes in target groups occurred in both referral and nonreferral hearings held by both the primary authorizing committees and other committees, it suggests a self-reinforcing, overarching positive feedback process. Congress as a whole, not just a single committee or a small group of committees, reacted to the shifting focus and target populations over time.

WITNESS TYPES

The preceding findings concerning hearings topics and target groups prove even more interesting when judged in the light of patterns for witness types testifying at hearings. Tables 5.5 and 5.6, respectively, present this information for referral and nonreferral hearings. In both tables, the committees with primary authorization power in each chamber are listed first, followed by the remaining committees holding hearings. Committees receiving testimony from a small number of witnesses are grouped together.

Looking first at the witness total column in both tables, we see that no single type of witness dominates, and the spread of witnesses does not differ dramatically across the two types of hearings. In both tables, citizens comprise the largest single witness category (17.6 and 20.1 percent respectively), while three other categories (physician; hospitals/facilities; federal government) each comprise over 10 percent of the total witnesses testifying. In both tables, each of the remaining six witness types comprises less than 10 percent of the total witnesses.

For referral hearings in table 5.5, the two committees with primary authorization power in each chamber heard testimony from the vast majority of the witnesses. The differences in witness presence across committees are strongly statistically significant, however, and many of those differences are notable. The House Commerce Committee, for example, received 23.6 percent of its testimony from witnesses representing hospitals/health facilities. This compares to a hospitals/facilities witness appearance rate of 11.9 percent for the Ways and Means Committee and 6.9 percent for eight other House committees combined. Testimony rates across committees also differ considerably for witnesses representing the federal government. In the Commerce Committee and the eight other House committees, federal government witnesses comprise 16.9 and 16.4 percent of the total witnesses, respectively, while they comprise only 5.6 percent of the total witnesses in the Ways and Means Committee. The testimony rate of citizens also varies considerably across committees, with citizens comprising 8.6 percent of total witnesses in the Commerce Committee, but 24.4 percent in the Ways and Means Committee and 25.9 percent in the eight other House committees combined. Finally, the eight other Housecommittees received a much larger proportion of their testimony from expert/academic witnesses (17.2 percent) than did either the Commerce Committee (4.6 percent) or the Ways and Means Committee (3.4 percent).

In the Senate, the cross-committee differences are less dramatic, but three are notable. First, the two committees with primary authorization power (Labor, and Finance) received a much larger proportion of their testimony from physicians (16.6 percent and 17.1 percent, respectively) than did the four other Senate committees (2.4 percent). Second, this pattern reverses for the next witness type, allied health, where the Labor and Finance committees received 8.2 percent and 7.8 percent of their testimony from allied health witnesses, but the four other Senate committees combined received 16.7 percent of their testimony from allied health witnesses. Finally, the Labor and Finance committees, respectively, received 14.2 percent and 19.3 percent of their testimony from citizens, whereas the four other Senate committees received 7.1 percent of their testimony from citizens.

Turning next to nonreferral hearings in table 5.6, the two committees with primary authorization power in each chamber again account for a majority of the committee attention, but to a much smaller degree than with referral hearings. In addition, three joint committees received testimony from witnesses. As with referral hearings, the differences in witness testimony rates across committees are strongly statistically significant, but the cross-committee differences are starker than for referral hearings. Although several differences deserve note, I highlight only the most significant.

In the House, for example, allied health witnesses comprise as much as 12.8 percent of the total witnesses in the Ways and Means Committee, but as little as 2.6 percent of the total witnesses in the Aging Committee. Similarly, whereas citizens (primarily the elderly) comprise 30.0 percent of the

TABLE 5.5 Witnesses at Referral Hearings on Comprehensive Health Care Reform, 1947–93 (by percentage)

Type of Witness	House Committee			Senate Committee			Joint Committee	Witness	
	Commerce	Ways and Means	Eight Other	Labor	Finance	Four Other	None	Total	(N)
Physician	10.6	13.4	14.7	16.6	17.1	2.4	—	14.0	(362)
Allied health	10.2	12.6	0.9	8.2	7.8	16.7	—	9.9	(257)
Hospitals/facilities	23.6	11.9	6.9	15.6	14.3	14.3	—	15.4	(399)
Labor	5.9	7.6	8.6	6.0	5.6	2.4	—	6.6	(170)
Business	3.7	6.1	4.3	6.6	6.5	9.5	—	5.8	(149)
Federal govt.	16.9	5.6	16.4	16.2	12.7	11.9	—	12.2	(315)
State and local govt.	6.7	6.9	0.9	5.2	7.8	11.9	—	6.3	(164)
Citizen	8.6	24.4	25.9	14.2	19.3	7.1	—	17.6	(457)
Insurance	9.1	8.1	4.3	4.0	8.1	14.3	—	7.2	(186)
Expert/academic	4.6	3.4	17.2	7.2	0.9	9.5	—	5.1	(131)
Committee total	100	100	100	100	100	100	—	100	—
(N)	(538)	(905)	(116)	(667)	(322)	(42)	—		(2,590)

Note: An additional 110 witnesses were uncodable and are not included here. Chi-squared (45 d.f.) = 281.7 ($p < .001$).

TABLE 5.6 Witnesses at Nonreferral Hearings on Comprehensive Health Care Reform, 1947–93 (by percentage)

Type of Witness	House Committee					Senate Committee					Joint Committee		Witness Total	(N)
	Com-merce	Ways and Means	Aging	Ten Other	Labor	Finance	Aging	Agri-culture	Small Busi-ness	Eight Other	Pepper	Two Other		
Physician	13.4	15.4	9.9	7.5	14.1	14.2	5.7	16.8	2.9	10.6	4.7	6.7	12.2	(584)
Allied health	3.9	12.8	2.6	3.4	6.9	5.7	8.9	18.1	8.8	7.3	8.2	1.7	7.7	(368)
Hospitals/facilities	13.3	11.5	15.7	17.0	7.9	14.6	13.0	27.7	6.5	21.2	8.2	11.2	13.2	(632)
Labor	5.7	4.0	2.2	3.2	4.2	2.6	1.6	0.6	0.6	1.2	3.5	1.7	3.4	(161)
Business	5.0	6.2	4.2	13.4	3.8	9.4	5.7	1.3	54.1	3.0	10.5	7.9	8.0	(384)
Federal govt.	17.8	14.5	13.1	14.4	5.6	12.3	4.1	2.6	1.8	7.3	4.1	16.9	11.4	(549)
State and local govt.	7.6	6.7	12.5	14.4	4.9	13.4	15.4	11.6	5.9	13.6	7.0	8.4	9.1	(437)
Citizen	11.7	14.8	30.0	13.6	43.2	8.5	25.2	16.1	5.3	17.9	42.7	14.6	20.1	(965)
Insurance	10.0	6.6	6.1	6.3	5.2	8.3	4.1	3.9	7.6	9.4	5.8	6.2	7.0	(335)
Expert/academic	11.7	7.4	3.8	6.8	4.0	11.1	16.3	1.3	6.5	8.5	5.3	24.2	8.1	(389)
Committee total	100	100	100	100	100	100	100	100	100	100	100	100	100	—
(N)	(618)	(1,204)	(313)	(411)	(708)	(424)	(123)	(155)	(170)	(330)	(171)	(178)	—	(4,804)

Note: An additional 182 witnesses were uncodable and are not included here. Chi-squared (108 d.f.) = 1441.8 ($p < .001$).

total witnesses testifying at Aging Committee hearings, they comprise only 11.7 percent of the witnesses testifying at Commerce Committee hearings. In the Senate, the Agriculture Committee received 27.7 percent of its testimony from hospitals/facilities representatives (primarily rural hospitals and facilities), while the Labor Committee received as little as 7.9 percent of its testimony from this same type of witness. Of particular note are the testimony rates of citizens in Senate committees. While the Labor Committee received 43.2 percent of its testimony from citizens, and the Aging Committee received 25.2 percent of its testimony from citizens, the Small Business Committee received only 5.3 percent of its testimony from citizens (it received 54.1 percent of its testimony from business witnesses, 44.7 percentage points more than the next closest Senate committee).[15] Finally, among the joint committees, the Pepper Commission received 42.7 percent of its testimony from citizens, a proportion considerably higher than for most other committees and surpassed only by the Senate Labor Committee.

To illustrate how the types of witnesses testifying at comprehensive health care reform hearings has varied over time, figure 5.4 displays the proportion per year that one broad witness type — health care providers (physician + allied health + hospitals/facilities) — represents of total referral and non-referral hearings attention from 1947 to 1993. The figure illustrates an overall decrease in the proportion of total testimony accounted for by health care providers over time. In the period between 1947 and 1970, health care providers accounted for 42 percent of all the witnesses testifying at referral hearings and 39 percent of all the witnesses testifying at nonreferral hearings.[16] In the 1970s, those percentages increased to 45 percent for referral hearings and 41 percent for nonreferral hearings. The 1980s saw a noticeable decrease in the presence of health care providers as, on average, they accounted for 29 percent of witnesses at referral hearings and 31 percent of witnesses at nonreferral hearings. Their presence decreased even further in the early 1990s, dropping to 25 percent for referral hearings and 28 percent for nonreferral hearings.[17] These trends, combined with the findings in tables 5.5 and 5.6, suggest that while the types of witnesses committees invite to testify depends largely on changing group mobilizations and issue definitions (i.e., the proportion of witnesses testifying at referral hearings changes over time despite the fact that the same four committees held the majority of the hearings), committees such as House Aging, Senate Aging, Senate Small Business, and Joint Pepper, through their nonreferral hearings, also played a pivotal role in shaping the overall distribution of witnesses testifying at committee hearings on comprehensive health care reform (potentially through mobilizing groups, redefin-

**FIGURE 5.4 HEALTH CARE PROVIDERS AS PROPORTION OF TOTAL WITNESSES AT
REFERRAL AND NONREFERRAL HEARINGS ON COMPREHENSIVE HEALTH CARE REFORM**

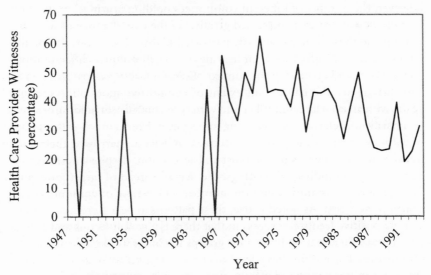

Year

Note: Years without data are those in which Congress held no hearings on comprehensive health care reform.

ing the issue, or causing committees with primary jurisdiction to seek testimony from different witness types). Again, like the changes occurring with respect to topics and target groups, because these changes in witness types occurred in both referral and nonreferral hearings held by both the primary authorizing committees and other committees, it suggests a self-reinforcing, overarching positive feedback process. Taken together, the longitudinal changes across all three dimensions illustrate broad, and sometimes dramatic, changes in the way Congress considered the comprehensive health care reform issue in the postwar period.

CONCLUSION

Clearly, the nature and extent of committee information regarding a given issue can differ considerably across time, across committees, and within committees. With respect to the comprehensive health care reform issue, my analysis showed how between 1947 and 1970, a small number of committees held

hearings (referral and nonreferral) on the issue and received a large proportion of their information from health care providers. Beginning in the 1970s,
however, the number of different committees holding hearings (particularly
nonreferral) on the issue increased greatly, yet the overall range of witnesses
testifying at those hearings actually narrowed slightly. Moreover, during that
decade, committees focused their hearings primarily on three different topics
(cost, access, and quality) in the context of several target groups. In the 1980s
and early 1990s, the nature and extent of committee information changed
again, with an even larger number and variety of committees holding hearings
(primarily nonreferral) and receiving information from a much wider variety
of witnesses than in the past. Committees, in general, narrowed their focus
to two topics during this period (cost and access), but despite a narrowing of
target groups in individual hearings, the overall spread of target groups remained fairly constant because the number and variety of committees and
hearings increased. As noted above, these patterns appear to reflect an overarching positive feedback process in that there is a simultaneous and consistent increase in attention by various groups in Congress to particular health
care themes. Beyond this basic level of consistency, however, several notable
cross-committee patterns in information acquisition appear along each of the
three information dimensions.

These patterns are not as stark or punctuated as those found for other
issue areas (e.g., pesticides, tobacco, civilian nuclear power, and drug abuse)
by other researchers (Baumgartner and Jones 1993; Jones, Baumgartner, and
Talbert 1993), suggesting that the coevolution of issues and institutions takes
different forms for different issues. Whereas highly salient, complex, multidimensional, broad-scope issues such as comprehensive health care reform
may interest several committees but offer few opportunities for committees to
acquire incomplete or biased information, less salient, less complex, one-
dimensional, narrow-scope issues such as agricultural subsidies may interest
few committees but offer more opportunities for committees to acquire incomplete or biased information. Similar studies on a wider range of issues
are required to make definitive judgments along these lines, but the patterns
emerging suggest that committees differ, particularly in their nonreferral
hearings, in the nature and extent of information they acquire. In the case of
comprehensive health care reform, the congressional committee system accurately reflected the complexity of the issue — committees fought for jurisdiction, focused on a variety of topics and targets, heard from a wide variety
of witnesses, and then, faced with this bewildering array of facts, choices, and

interests, ultimately could not reach a consensus. The politics of comprehensive health care reform reflects both the triumph of information gathering and the potential for (and realization of) stalemate.

So what do these findings regarding information acquisition surrounding one issue suggest about the broader question of issue-institution coevolution and hence the even more basic analytical approaches political scientists should adopt to understand the policy making process? I offer three brief answers here.

First, my analysis and findings suggest that issues and institutions are not independent; understanding one requires understanding the other. Thus, to the extent that the two are related, and to the extent that analyses focus on one to the exclusion of the other, those analyses will be incomplete and potentially misleading. Future analyses on the committee system (as well as on other institutional structures) should devote more attention to the ways in which issues and institutions interrelate.

Second, such a shift in attention/approach will require political scientists to devote much more effort to designing and building large, comprehensive, longitudinal data sets capable of addressing coevolution questions. The congressional hearings data set, which my analysis supplements with more detailed codes, is one such example, and the larger Policy Agendas Project of which it is a part provides the type of breadth and depth necessary to provide a foundation for addressing several other questions important to political scientists and others. Without more data sets of this type, political science will remain overly fragmented and incapable of thoroughly explaining the complex political phenomena it addresses.

Third, becoming less fragmented and more comprehensive will require political scientists to collaborate more. Compared to more mature scientific disciplines, particularly those in the natural sciences (e.g., biology, chemistry, physics), political science exhibits very little intradiscipline collaboration. Whereas scientific publications in physics journals, for example, average five major contributing authors, scientific publications in political science journals average just over one major contributing author (McDonald 1995; Memory et al. 1985). Although substantive differences across the disciplines (e.g., complexity of research questions, the amount of technology needed to addresses those questions) at least partly explain the differing rates of collaboration, other reasons include discipline norms, promotion criteria, and communication barriers. The former have little room for change, but the latter have considerably more room for change. Thus, to the extent that political scientists see fit to exploit new communication technologies and provide more incentives for collaboration, political science has the potential to become a more unified, coherent discipline.

NOTES

I owe special thanks to Nancy Edwards and Corine Norman. Without their considerable data collection and coding assistance, I could not have written this chapter.

1. This statistic represents only bills and joint resolutions. Simple resolutions, concurrent resolutions, and private bills are excluded.

2. For a comprehensive review of this literature, see Shepsle and Weingast 1995.

3. Data for 1994 regarding comprehensive health care reform were incomplete at the time this chapter was written.

4. The Policy Agendas Project congressional hearings data set contains 416 hearings on the topic of comprehensive health care reform. However, because that data set assigns only one topic code (the topic that predominates) to each hearing, it potentially understates the number of hearings focusing on aspects of comprehensive health care reform. I therefore supplemented my data set with fifty-two additional hearings that focus on aspects of comprehensive health care reform but are coded in other, related health topic categories in the Policy Agendas data set. These additional hearings derive from previous analyses I conducted regarding comprehensive health care reform (Hardin 1994, 1998b).

5. Eleven hearings (three referral, eight nonreferral) were held jointly by two committees. To avoid double counting data for these hearings, I recorded topic, target group, and witness data for only the primary committee holding each of these hearings.

6. The allied health category includes those health care personnel that could not be coded in the physicians category.

7. Detailed definitions for each of these coding categories are available at the Policy Agendas web site. To establish my coding categories and procedures and to help ensure their validity, I consulted selected literature on health policy and also had several conversations with colleagues regarding the proper way to divide up each of the three dimensions. To test and improve the reliability of the coding procedures, I took random samples of the coded hearings along each dimension and had a second person code those hearings using the same categories. I then compared the correspondence between my coding and the second person's coding, identified the cases in which we differed, and attempted to resolve the differences in a consensual manner. After approximately three rounds of coding and recoding for each of the dimensions, we arrived at a coding structure and process that yielded an intercoder reliability level equal to or greater than 95 percent.

8. For simplicity, I use the current names of committees even though some had different names during much of the time period under study.

9. I computed similar figures using the number of witnesses testifying at hearings and the number of document pages produced at the hearings. The data for each of these figures were over 95 percent correlated. For simplicity I present only days of committee hearings over time.

10. The Policy Agendas Project coding structure contains a separate category for Medicare and Medicaid.

11. The Herfindahl index (a measure of market concentration used by economists) is simply the sum of the squared proportion each committee's hearings represent of all hearings on a given issue within a given period. Calculating the index involves the following steps: (1) determining the proportion that each committee's hearings activity represents of a hearings type (referral, nonreferral), (2) squaring each committee's proportion, and (3) summing the resulting amounts.

12. See Baumgartner, Jones, and McLeod 2000 for a fuller explanation of jurisdictional overlap.

13. Due to limited descriptions provided by the *Congressional Information Service Abstracts* (CIS annual), topics were uncodable for pre-1970 hearings.

14. Graphs (available at the Policy Agendas web site) of the average number of topics per year illustrate that the average number of topics declines dramatically over time for both referral and nonreferral hearings. Some of the early years averaged five or six topics, while some of the later years averaged one or two topics. In addition, graphs (available at the Policy Agendas web site) of the proportion of total hearings focused on different numbers of topics illustrate that, over time, the proportion of hearings focused on two or fewer topics increased greatly for both referral and nonreferral hearings. In the early years 30 to 40 percent of the hearings focused on two or fewer topics, while in the later years 70 to 80 percent of hearings focused on two or fewer topics. Finally, I computed Herfindahl indexes (not shown here) to measure the concentration of topics over time. The indexes corroborate the graphical analyses by illustrating that the concentration of topics increases over time.

15. The noticeably large citizen presence at Labor and Human Resource hearings results primarily from two large sets of hearings that committee held in 1978. These hearings took place not in Washington, D.C., but rather in various U.S. cities.

16. The percentages cited here derive from actual witness counts. Thus, they may differ somewhat from figure 5.4, which does not display the actual counts generating the percentages.

17. Detailed graphical analyses (not shown here) displaying each of the witness categories over time indicate that the relative proportions of each witness type within each

of the two broad witness type groupings (health care providers; all other) become more equal over time. Due to their complexity, these graphs are not presented here. In addition, I computed Herfindahl indexes (not shown here) to measure the concentration of witness types over time. While also complex and difficult to interpret, the indexes corroborate the graphical analyses by illustrating that the concentration of witness types decreases over time.

6

THE MULTIPLE GOALS OF SCIENCE
AND TECHNOLOGY POLICY

T. JENS FEELEY

INTRODUCTION

Forged in the crucible of the Cold War, modern science and technology policy has undergone both dramatic change and unusual continuity in the post–
World War II era. The specific issues, definitions, and institutions of government concerned with this policy area have changed over time. This area
involves diverse constituencies and interest groups and has been associated at
different times with various underlying policy goals or dimensions. As such,
science and technology policy represents an excellent opportunity to explore
the concept of multiple goals or multidimensionality in public policy.

The constituency groups involved in science and technology policy included universities, corporations, national laboratories, advocacy groups, and
the general public, to name just a few. Universities and national laboratories
are involved as the recipients of government funding and as the main incuba-
tors of scientific ideas from the drawing board through development. Business concerns, especially aerospace companies, have important stakes in science and technology policy, as government contracts for their services are a
major source of corporate revenue and income. Advocacy groups and the
general public also play significant roles in decisions about science and technology policy, especially in periods when these issues are actively under consideration on the governmental agenda.[1] In different circumstances these individual constituencies can be rallied in different combinations to bolster the
prospects for, or against, individual science and technology issues, policies, or
programs.

The ability to rally different constituencies depends on the ability of policy
entrepreneurs to interject policy goals or policy dimensions that are relevant
to these independent groups. Different policy goals appeal to different groups

in different ways. A successful policy entrepreneur is able to correctly assess which goals will be most attractive to the constituency groups she is targeting and will adjust her tactics accordingly to maximize her chances for success. Being able to alter the dimensions of the debate is often the difference between political success and political failure.

The underlying policy goals associated with science and technology policy include military, commercial, and environmental goals and the advancement of knowledge, among others. Savvy policy entrepreneurs work to associate science and technology programs with these underlying policy goals as each becomes more salient to the debates of the day. For example, during a period of military confrontation, supporters of science and technology policies can focus on the military competition or national prestige goals, and during a later period of relative peace, these same supporters may stress the commercial or pioneering spirit goals.

The multidimensional nature of science and technology policy and its diverse constituency groups make possible strategic and tactical maneuvering by policy entrepreneurs interested in this area of policy; as such, these factors should help us understand the different periods of rapid change and relative stability in science and technology policy during the post–World War II period. In certain periods, a single dimension can dominate (to the near-total exclusion of others) and lead to a virtual policy monopoly in science and technology policy. The dominance of one dimension, and with it of one group or small number of groups, can lead to the establishment of negative feedback mechanisms that dampen change. As other groups are successful in reintroducing other dimensions, the policy monopoly begins to break down and the prospects for more dramatic change increase (Baumgartner and Jones 1993).

This chapter explores changes that have occurred in U.S. science and technology policy from 1947 to 1992. This analysis is divided into several parts. The first part defines science and technology policy. The second part contains a historical analysis of science and technology policy, with a particular focus on the post–World War II period. Based on this historical analysis, the third part lays out a number of theoretical hypotheses about the role of political factors in influencing the funding levels for science and technology programs. The fourth part tests these hypotheses using ordinary least squares (OLS) regression. The chapter concludes with a brief set of conclusions and some suggestions for further study.

DEFINITIONS AND DATA

DEFINING SCIENCE AND TECHNOLOGY

For the purpose of this chapter, science and technology policy is defined as all issues and programs related to nonagricultural, nonmedical, and non-communications-related civilian activities of a scientific or technological nature. That's a mouthful. What it means is that this chapter will deal with U.S. research and development programs and technological issues associated with basic science, computers, education, energy, the environment, geology/weather, civilian space, commercial space, international cooperation in science and technology, and general science (including issues that cross over two or more of the other topics).

This chapter will *not* deal with medical science and medical technology (commonly referred to as biotechnology or bioscience); these health-related issues are covered in chapter five. Likewise, telecommunications and other communications technologies are largely covered in chapter three. I have also chosen to exclude overtly agriculture- and defense-related research and development issues. However, as discussed later, even the overtly civilian scientific endeavors of the U.S. Government were often conceived of (and associated with) national security goals.

USING THE POLICY AGENDAS PROJECT DATA SETS

In this chapter, the Policy Agendas Project hearings data set was the primary source for the analysis. Specifically, all hearings coded using subtopics that directly relate to the working definition of science and technology were isolated.[2] In addition, each entry in the hearings data set includes a short, textual description of the content of the hearing. This topic description field was used to isolate additional hearings of interest. A number of hearings important to the analysis were coded under general government regulation codes (2000–2099); where possible, I have isolated select hearings within the 2000 series based on their topic description, analysis of the original source materials, or a combination of both. Data from the Policy Agendas Project budget data set are combined with these hearings data to explore whether congressional competitive issue salience affects funding levels for science and technology programs. The resulting working data set constitutes the basis for the rest of the analysis in this chapter.[3]

SELECT HISTORY

EARLY HISTORY

From its earliest days, federal involvement in science and technology policy has reflected the inherent multidimensionality of these issues. In particular, the military and nonmilitary goals of science and technology have waxed and waned over the last 210 years. In some periods, the military goals of science and technology have predominated; at other points in our nation's history, the nonmilitary goals have dominated. Furthermore, during periods where the nonmilitary goals have been at the forefront, there has been considerable variation in which nonmilitary goals (commercial, pioneering spirit, etc.), were the most prominent.

For example, the first federal science agency created by Congress was the U.S. Coast and Geodetic Survey (USC&GS). Its primary objective was to systematically survey the territorial shores of the United States to more clearly map our new nation's territorial borders and to make possible the production of more accurate maritime maps. Both of these goals further served to promote commerce during a period when most trade was conducted using ships.[4] Over the ensuing 190 years, the USC&GS has adapted well to changes in science and technology policy. For example, during certain historical periods the functions and employees of USC&GS were highly focused on military pursuits; at other times, both its functions and employees were focused on nonmilitary pursuits. In fact, during certain periods the employees of this agency were explicitly required by law to be members of the armed forces, were limited to civilian pursuits and employees, or were required to be a mixture of military and civilians.[5]

RECENT HISTORY

World War II, and the Cold War that followed, helped to alter the focus of federal involvement in science and technology. The success of the Manhattan Project in developing the atom bomb by 1945 served as an example of the value of science for military goals. The cojoining of university and military scientists to develop atomic weapons is an example of how during World War II the predominant dimension in science and technology policy was the military dimension. Science and technology programs were largely judged on how well they contributed to the war effort.

Just a few years later, however, the explosion of an atomic bomb by the Soviet Union helped escalate the emerging Cold War. While there remained some attention to the military dimension of science and technology, during the following years, U.S. support for science and technology quickly became defined in terms of government support for "peaceful uses," as the underlying dimension started to shift. In part, this was the result of a conscious strategy of some to contrast U.S. policies from the "militaristic" goals of Soviet efforts in science and technology.

For example, in September 1945 President Truman first proposed the creation of a civilian-led federal agency for scientific coordination and support. Along with several influential members of Congress, he hoped to establish a permanent peacetime equivalent of the Office of Scientific Research and Development, which was responsible for science and technology coordination during World War II and oversaw the Manhattan Project. House committees with jurisdictions over both military and commercial affairs debated the proposed agency and sought control over its future direction. Finally in 1950, after several bills were considered, amended, and discarded, the National Science Foundation was established as a civilian agency and oversight for it was granted to the civilian-focused committees.

During the 1950s, this trend away from a focus on the military goals of science and technology continued. President Eisenhower's Atoms for Peace initiative was intended to expand international cooperation through the peaceful uses of nuclear power. In his speech before the United Nations General Assembly on December 8, 1953, President Eisenhower proposed that a new international agency be created to

> devise methods whereby this fissionable material would be allocated to serve the peaceful pursuits of mankind. Experts would be mobilized to apply atomic energy to the needs of agriculture, medicine and other peaceful activities. A special purpose would be to provide abundant electrical energy on the power-starved areas of the world. Thus the contributing powers [i.e. the United States, the United Kingdom, France, and the Soviet Union] would be dedicating some of their strength to serve the needs rather than the fears of mankind. (Eisenhower 1953)

His later decision to establish the National Aeronautics and Space Administration (NASA) as a strictly civilian agency is further evidence of this emerging focus on science for its nonmilitary purposes. As President Eisenhower noted in a statement released April 2, 1958, he was recommending

> that aeronautical and space science activities sponsored by the United States be conducted under the direction of a civilian agency, except for

those projects primarily associated with military requirements. I have reached this conclusion because space exploration holds promise of adding importantly to our knowledge of the earth, the solar system and the universe, and because it is of great importance to have the fullest cooperation of the scientific community at home and abroad in moving forward in the fields of space science and technology. Moreover, a civilian setting for the administration of space function will emphasize the concern of our Nation that outer space be devoted to peaceful and scientific purposes. (Congressional Quarterly 1958, 599)

Eisenhower's statement referred to four factors that gave urgency to his request: man's interest in exploring the unknown, the military potential for space, the effect on national prestige, and finally, the increase in scientific knowledge that would result (Congressional Quarterly 1958). His statement is further evidence that science and technology policy has several underlying dimensions, of which the military uses or goals are just one.

LEGISLATIVE ROLE OF COMMITTEES

As was the case with the formation of the National Science Foundation, committee hearings are often a major hurdle for legislation to overcome before it can become law. Under the standing rules of the House, the House speaker (or the House parliamentarian) refers all legislative bills to a committee or committees for review shortly after they are introduced.[6] The procedure is somewhat similar in the Senate.[7] While there are other procedural mechanisms for bills to reach the floor of either chamber, these other mechanisms are used sparingly, especially in the House. The vast majority of bills follow the normal process of being considered in committee before reaching the floor, especially during the bulk of the period covered in this analysis.

In this regard, congressional committees fulfill a vital role, whittling down the torrent of bills into a more manageable flow of legislation. Of the large number of bills introduced in any given year, only a small fraction become law (Schiller 1995), in large part because of the role of committees. For example, of the 2,924 bills introduced in the U.S. Senate during the 100th Congress, only 498 (17.0 percent) received a hearing before a committee, and only 474 (16.2 percent) were reported out of committee. In all, only 303 (10.4 percent) of the bills introduced became law (Wilkerson et al. 1999a, 1999b). Clearly, congressional committees are active players in filtering what bills make it to the floor for debate and formal passage. Since not all committees have the same outlook or approach on a given issue area, savvy policy entrepreneurs can increase their likelihood of success by steering legislation they support to committees that are receptive to their positions; alternatively, they can try to steer legislation they oppose to committees that can delay, alter, or even kill the legislation. This concept is referred to as "venue shopping"; policy entrepreneurs will shop around until they find a receptive committee and then work to have policy decisions made in that venue. For some scholars, it is increasingly clear that jurisdictional battles between and among committees are becoming more common (Baumgartner and Jones 1993; Baumgartner, Jones, and MacLeod 2000; King 1994, 1997), which suggests enhanced opportunities for venue shopping.

As conflict among congressional committees over policy areas grows, the possibilities for major shifts in policy increase. Conflicting approaches and attributes will emerge as the monopoly of one committee comes under attack from other committees attempting to carve out a role for themselves in a particular policy area. Committees are increasingly becoming the arenas in which these conflicting approaches are played out before the issue reaches the floor.

So, which are the main congressional actors setting national science and technology policy? How have these players changed over time? This chapter explores two different ways of answering these questions: (1) an aggregate analysis of all hearings across the House and Senate,[8] and (2) a more focused analysis of nonreferral hearings in the House.

AGGREGATE ANALYSIS ACROSS CHAMBERS

As displayed in figure 6.1, if one looks at all hearings for the 80th through 102d Congresses (calendar years 1947–92), one would see that science and technology policy appears to be largely dominated by five committees: (1) House Science; (2) Senate Commerce, Science, and Transportation, (3) Senate Aeronautical and Space Sciences, (4) House Appropriations; and, (5) Senate Appropriations (listed in descending order of the total number of hearings held). In all, these five committees were responsible for 74.1 percent of all science and technology hearings during this forty-six-year period (1,174 of 1,584 total hearings). These committees dominated the statutory responsibility for science and technology authorization and appropriations throughout this period; it is not surprising, then, that they held more hearings than all other committees combined.

FIGURE 6.1 HOUSE AND SENATE COMMITTEES INVOLVED IN SCIENCE AND TECHNOLOGY POLICY

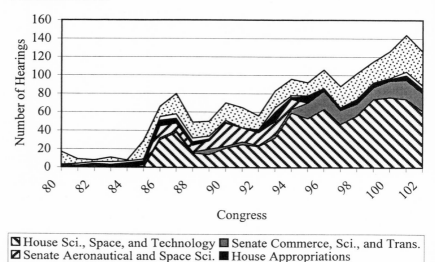

However, a significant portion of what congressional committees do is routine, repetitive actions such as authorizations and appropriations that are referred to the same committees on an annual basis. These activities must be completed each year (or every other year in some cases) to just maintain the current level of federal participation in a specific area; therefore, they are often task driven rather than policy driven. These hearings are normally tied to specific legislation that is under consideration and are, therefore, mostly referral hearings. Therefore, to explore where committees might be competing for control over a topic area, it makes more sense to focus on nonreferral hearings, those that are not tied to specific legislation and are called at the discretion of the committee or subcommittee chair.

As shown in table 6.1, a significant proportion of all hearings are nonreferral hearings. Across the House and Senate for the 80th through 102d Congresses, some 32,220 hearings (or 51.54 percent) were nonreferral hearings. That means that more than half of all hearings during this period were determined not by statutory jurisdictions or parliamentary precedence, but rather solely by the interests of the respective chairs of the committee or subcommittee calling the hearing. This suggests that there is ample opportunity for entrepreneurial members to explore topics beyond their statutory jurisdiction

TABLE 6.1 Comparison of Referral to Nonreferral Hearings (80th–102nd Congresses)

Hearing Type	All House and Senate	Per-cent	S&T House and Senate	Per-cent	S&T House	Per-cent	S&T Senate	Percent
Referral	30,293	48.46	532	33.59	310	28.78	222	43.79
Nonreferral	32,220	51.54	1,052	66.41	767	71.22	285	56.21
Total	62,513	100.00	1,584	100.00	1,077	100.00	507	100.00

S&T = science and technology hearings.

and attempt to expand their influence onto issues nominally beyond their control. The percentage of nonreferral science and technology hearings is highest in the House, where a total of 71.22 percent are nonreferrals; it makes sense, therefore, to focus on House nonreferral hearings as evidence of competition between committees for control of science and technology policy.

NONREFERRAL HEARINGS IN THE HOUSE

The committees with the broadest statutory jurisdiction for science and technology issues are the House Appropriations Committee and the House Science Committee. The House Appropriations Committee's statutory jurisdiction has changed little in the last fifty years. It retains responsibility for appropriations bills, including those that fund the various science and technology agencies within the federal government. By tradition, appropriation bills usually begin in the House.

The purview of House Science Committee, on the other hand, has been revised a number of times since the end of World War II. Originally formed in March 1958 as the House Select Committee on Science and Astronautics, this committee has changed names and jurisdictional responsibilities over the years. In January 1959, it was formally established as a standing committee of the House, the first standing committee added in the House since the Legislative Reorganization Act of 1946 drastically reduced the number of standing committees from forty-eight to nineteen (Committee on Science and Technology 1980). The Committee on Science and Astronautics became the Committee on Science and Technology in January 1975, was renamed the Committee on Science, Space, and Technology in January 1987, and acquired its current name of House Science Committee in January 1995.

When focusing on nonreferral hearings, it appears that these two committees have dominated much of the discussion of science and technology issues since the end of World War II. A full 82.4 percent of the all nonreferral science and technology hearings in the House between 1947 and 1992 were conducted by these two committees. Broadly speaking, this suggests that these two committees continue to dominate areas where they have statutory responsibility even in nonreferral hearings, where there is the greatest opportunity for encroachment by other committees. It is possible, however, that other committees are attempting to gain control over specific subtopics and are concentrating their efforts in select areas. Examining the subtopics within science and technology should identify areas where the other committees are exerting disproportionate influence as measured by the number of hearings they hold. As shown in table 6.2, there are areas where certain committees exert a near monopoly on discussions, while in other areas they have a noticeably smaller share of the discussions.

In particular, education research and development, other science, government oversight of science and technology, and government procurement related to science and technology are areas where other committees played a dominant role in discussions. These other committees also played above-average roles in geology and weather, commercial space, computers, and science cooperation.

In contrast, the House Science and Appropriations committees held all the nonreferral hearings during this period in three subtopics: government property, science appropriations, and transportation research and development. These two committees also exerted a near monopoly over discussions in several other areas, including energy research and development, environmental research and development, civilian space, general science, and science research and development.

These differences suggest that there is some opportunity for political entrepreneurs to explore venue shopping. The evidence suggests that some areas of science and technology policy are strongly influenced by committees without statutory authority for those issues. However, there remain questions about the degree of venue shopping and, more importantly, whether it has any impact on political or budgetary outcomes.

CONGRESSIONAL ATTENTION TO SCIENCE AND TECHNOLOGY ISSUES
The specifics of congressional attention can help map the changing content of science and technology policy in the United States in the post–World War II era. Within the working definition of science and technology used here, there are more than fifteen subtopics that can be discussed in some detail. As shown

TABLE 6.2 House Committee Control over Science and Technology Subtopics (Non-referral Hearings, 80th–102nd Congresses)

Agendas Code	Subtopic	House Science and Appropriations Committees	Percent	Other House Committees	Percent
698	Education R&D	0	0	10	100.0
1799	Other science	0	0	1	100.0
2002	Government oversight	1	14.3	6	85.7
2007	Government procurement	1	33.3	2	66.7
1708	Geology and weather	44	59.5	30	40.5
1704	Commercial space	30	69.8	13	30.2
1709	Computers	17	77.3	5	22.7
1705	Science cooperation	69	78.4	19	21.6
—	— Mean across all subtopics —	632	82.4	135	17.6
1798	Science R&D	94	83.9	18	16.1
1700	General science	57	89.1	7	10.9
1701	Civilian space	218	91.6	20	8.4
798	Environmental R&D	31	93.1	2	6.1
898	Energy R&D	36	94.7	2	5.3
1098	Transportation R&D	12	100.0	0	0.0
2000	Science appropriations	21	100.0	0	0.0
2008	Government property	1	100.0	0	0.0

in figure 6.2, the amount of attention paid to the general area of science and technology (including all subtopics) has increased substantially over the last five decades. During the immediate post–World War II period (80th–84th Congresses or 1947–56) the total number of hearings focused on science and technology was quite small, averaging just 10.4 hearings per congressional term across all committees in both chambers. The number of hearings starts to rise noticeably during the 85th Congress (1957–58) and maintains a generally upward trend throughout the rest of the study period. For the last decade studied (98th–102d Congresses or 1983–92), the average number of hearings per congressional term had risen to 121.6, more than an elevenfold increase.

The focus of science and technology discussions has changed over time. Some issue areas, such as science research and development (R&D) and geology/weather, have remained the focus of significant congressional attention[9]

FIGURE 6.2 CHANGING TOPICS OF SCIENCE AND TECHNOLOGY HEARINGS

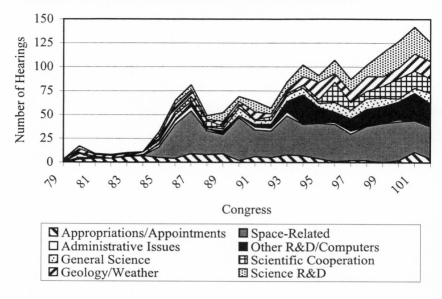

throughout this period. Others, such as civilian space and commercial space, emerged in the late 1950s. Still others (education R&D, energy R&D, environmental R&D, transportation R&D, and computers) have only recently become the focus of significant congressional attention. As the military dimension has faded, the commercial dimension, national prestige dimension, and advancement of knowledge dimension have become more prevalent, and different issues areas have garnered more attention.

This is evident from the analysis of all congressional hearings from 1947 to 1992. As shown in table 6.3, the data suggest the existence of four distinct historical periods in which different policy goals and policy topics emerged in the congressional debates concerning science and technology issues. In the first period (1947–56), nonmilitary goals emerge in the immediate post–World War II period as the Cold War begins. The second period (roughly 1957–66) is marked by the reemergence of the scientific achievement and commercial goals, especially as they apply to space research. The emergence of these two types of goals helps spawn a period of rapid growth in nonmilitary space activities. The third historical period (the early to mid-1970s) is characterized by the emergence of environmental goals. The final period (post-1976) includes the emergence of other goals in computers and education research.

Throughout the post–World War II period, four issue areas within the gen-

TABLE 6.3 Emergence of Science and Technology Goals over Time (House and Senate, 80th–102nd Congresses)

Agendas Code	Subtopic	1st Congress with Significant Congressional Attention	Number of Total Hearings	Percent of All S&T Hearings
Nonmilitary goals emerge				
1798	Science R&D	80	217	13.7
1708	Geology/weather	80	172	10.9
1700	General science	80	106	6.7
2000	Science appropriations	80	77	4.9
Advancement of knowledge and commercial goals emerge				
1701	Civilian space	85	517	32.6
1705	Science cooperation	86	143	9.0
1704	Commercial space	87	78	4.9
2002	Government oversight	87	20	1.3
2005	Nominations	89	36	2.3
Environmental goal emerges				
898	Energy R&D	93	72	4.5
798	Environmental R&D	94	50	3.2
Other goals emerge				
1709	Computers	97	47	3.0
698	Education R&D	102	12	0.8
1098	Transportation R&D	#	14	0.9
Several	Other	n/a	23	1.5
	Totals		1584	100.2

Notes: # = Did not have three hearings in any one Congress; n/a = not applicable; R&D = research and development; S&T = science and technology.

eral field of science and technology have garnered measurable attention and prominence in Congress: (1) science appropriations, (2) science R&D, (3) geology/weather, and, (4) general science.[10] Five other issue areas first emerged in the 85th through 89th Congresses: civilian space, science cooperation, commercial space, government oversight, and nominations/appointments. The International Geophysical Year (which ran from July 1, 1957, to December 31, 1958) helped prompt congressional interest in international cooperation in science and technology. As mentioned earlier, the undertone of peaceful scientific cooperation in the West as a response to military cooperation in the East was quite evident during this period.

The launch of *Sputnik,* the first man-made satellite, by the Soviet Union on October 4, 1957, had far-reaching impacts on the direction and speed of U.S. efforts in space. It also contributed directly to reshaping both the executive and legislative branches of the U.S. government. It spawned the establishment of both NASA and the National Aeronautics and Space Board in the executive branch. It also directly led to the creation of two new standing committees in Congress, the Senate Committee on Aeronautical and Space Sciences (later absorbed into the Senate Commerce, Science, and Transportation Committee) and the House Committee on Science and Astronautics (later the House Science Committee).

Other issue areas within science and technology emerged even later. Energy R&D emerged in the 93d Congress and environmental R&D followed in the 94th. This timing suggests that the environmental dimension of science and technology policy started to emerge during this four-year period. Computers gained prominence in the 97th Congress and education R&D followed in the 102d Congress. As shown in table 6.3, transportation R&D was the focus of almost 1 percent of all science and technology hearings in the post–World War II era, yet it never achieved much prominence in any single congressional term.

In general, these results support the idea that different policy goals and policy dimensions emerged over time in science and technology policy. This phased emergence of policy goals relative to science and technology policy also appears to coincide with periods of dramatic change, especially in relation to space research activities.

THEORY AND HYPOTHESES

GENERAL THEORY

So far, this historical analysis suggests that science and technology policy is characterized by (1) competition between congressional committees in some subtopic areas, and (2) the phased emergence of new goals or policy dimensions in the post–World War II era. Another question of interest is whether the two major parties (Democrats and Republicans) have any significant differences when it comes to science and technology policy. If committees are important and agenda control is crucial to success, the influence of these political variables on annual budget changes in science and technology programs should be measurable. The next part of this chapter examines whether issue salience (how prominent an issue becomes), jurisdictional competition among congressional committees, and party control systematically influence federal budgets for science- and technology-related activities.

In general terms, the basic theory being evaluated in this part of the chapter is as follows:

$$\Delta budgets = f(politics + budget + economics + history + error)$$

HYPOTHESES

Several hypotheses flow from this general theory; three distinct hypotheses have been constructed for testing the political variables. Descriptions of the dependent and independent variables used to test each hypothesis are provided below.

Hypothesis 1: Budget authority levels for of science- and technology-related activities will be systematically influenced by changes in the levels of issue salience for lawmakers.

This hypothesis suggests that as the issue of science and technology funding becomes more salient to the members of the House (vis-à-vis all other issues), nonincremental changes in overall funding levels for science and technology will be more likely. As the issue becomes more visible, and members devote greater attention to it, their divergent policy goals and policy preferences should become more evident in policy outcomes. Under such a scenario, conditions are ripe for policy entrepreneurs to attach new goals or dimensions to the issues under debate and control funding decisions in the near term.

Hypothesis 2: Budget authority levels for science- and technology-related activities will be systematically influenced by changes in the levels of committee competition over time.

This hypothesis holds that as more members are drawn into the debate over science and technology funding, nonincremental changes in the amount and distribution of science and technology funding become more likely. This should be particularly true in cases where the absence of committee competition is rapidly replaced with considerable committee competition. Different committees are likely to have different preferences, and as one committee's traditional dominance over this issue area starts to come under attack, differences in committee preference will eventually affect the distribution of power across the issue area. Over time, these preference differences will be played out in the legislative area and their results should be evident in changes to the annual budgets for federal science and technology programs. This should be true even if the competition between committees is indirect, focusing on aspects of science and technology policy other than appropriations and budgets.

Hypothesis 3: Budget authority levels for of science- and technology-related activities will be systematically influenced by changes in the levels of party control across both chambers of Congress.

An underlying assumption behind this hypothesis is that there are systematic differences between the Democratic and Republican parties in their support for science and technology vis-à-vis other policy areas. As the partisan distribution of seats changes over time, one would expect to see systematic shifts in the funding levels for science and technology activities. During periods of relatively equal distribution of seats between the two main parties (close to 50 percent for each) more bipartisanship is likely on all issues. This is likely because even a small defection of members of the majority party can defeat legislation, which makes the majority leadership more inclined to compromise to ensure some minority party support to overcome any defections from within the majority party.

Conversely, when the proportion of representation is more unbalanced, the majority party can accept a larger level of defection from its own members and still get legislation enacted. In this situation, there should be less of an incentive to accommodate the minority party's wishes in the hopes of ensuring passage because the potential need for minority support is reduced. As a result, the systematic differences between the parties should be more evident as the size of the majority increases.

DEPENDENT VARIABLES

The budget authority data set developed by the Policy Agendas Project (and adapted for this study) contains detailed estimates of congressional budget authority at the Office of Management and Budget (OMB) function and subfunction level. All of these data were organized in a consistent manner across time by adjusting the budget authority data for fiscal years (FY) 1947 through 1997 to be consistent with OMB subfunctions as defined in the FY 1995 Budget for the Federal Government. In all, eighteen OMB functions and sixty-two subfunctions are used in this budget-coding scheme.[11]

The dependent variables used in this part of the chapter are measured in terms of the proportional change in U.S. science and technology budget authority for General Science and Basic Research (OMB budget subfunction 251; hereafter "general science") and Space Flight, Research, and Supporting Activities (OMB budget subfunction 252; hereafter "space research"); all values reported are in terms of budget authority. Subfunction 251 is composed of

National Science Foundation (NSF) programs in the physical, biological, chemical, and social sciences, as well as high-energy and nuclear physics research of the Department of Energy and the Superconducting Super Collider. Subfunction 252 is composed of the nonaeronautical programs of NASA; in earlier budgets this category consisted of government support to NASA's predecessor agency (the National Advisory Committee on Aeronautics, or NACA).

These two budget categories were run through four versions of the model individually. There is significant anecdotal evidence to suggest that the funding process for the NSF (the largest component of subfunction 251) and for NASA (the largest component of subfunction 252) may be handled differently in Congress. In any event, determining whether or not there are systematic differences in the way the two subfunctions have been handled appears to be a worthwhile research objective.

The raw budget levels for the dependent variables in this analysis were taken directly from the Policy Agendas Project budget authority data set; the inflation adjusted figures (in constant FY 1997 dollars) were used. As such, the effects of inflation already have been controlled in this model. For ease of use in regression analysis, absolute funding levels for each of these two budget categories were converted into measures of proportional change from the previous fiscal year:

$$\Delta B = (B_y - B_{y-1})/B_{y-1}$$

where ΔB = proportional change in budget authority, B_y = budget authority in the current fiscal year, and B_{y-1} = budget authority in the previous fiscal year.

INDEPENDENT VARIABLES

The independent variables utilized in this chapter are divided into four subcategories: (1) political factors (issue salience, committee competition, and party control); (2) budgetary trends (total discretionary spending and total budget authority); (3) economic trends (changes in gross domestic product, or GDP); and, (4) unique historical events (the Cold War and space race).

Issue Salience

One assumption in this approach is that attention matters. In contemporary America, decision makers are confronted with an almost unlimited number of potential issues on a daily basis. Given an ever growing number of political activists, decision makers at all levels face increasing demands for their attention. Attention, therefore, has become a crucial commodity (Jones 1994).

The salience values used here attempt to measure the extent of attention directed toward science and technology as a proportion of the total attention being directed toward all issues during each fiscal year. These indices for issue salience were computed using the Policy Agendas Project hearing data set. The number of hearings on a particular topic (across all committees) was divided by the total number of hearings in the House during that fiscal year. This proportion was then squared and the resulting indexed values measure the squared proportion of all House hearings for a given fiscal year that were concerned with science and technology.

Committee Competition in the House

One independent variable is an indexed measure of intercommittee competition within the House of Representatives. This variable consists of a Herfindhal index that measures the openness of debate in a policy area within the House of Representatives. This type of index was originally developed as a measure of market concentration and has been used widely in economics; however, it has only recently been introduced in political science (Hardin 1998a; Baumgartner, Jones, and MacLeod 2000). It is used in this study to measure the extent to which committees compete for control over science and technology policy and budgets.

Constructing Indices

The total number of hearings held on science and technology policy in each committee was summed for each fiscal year.[12] The total number of hearings on science and technology across all committees in the House for that fiscal year was also computed. Each committee's total for the year was then divided by the total; the resulting quotient is the proportion of all House hearings on science and technology that were held by a particular committee during that fiscal year. This proportion was then squared, and the squared totals were then summed to give us a single index value, across all committees, for each fiscal year for FYs 1949–93.[13]

To facilitate the analysis, the committee competition index was further transformed for this chapter. Each year's value for committee competition was subtracted from 1 (the theoretical maximum) so that the values reported here would be more intrinsically understandable. With this transformation, a committee competition index score of 0 translates into the absence of any competition among committees (evidence of an issue monopoly). Conversely, committee competition index values just below 1 would suggest a high degree of competition. In that case, hearings on science and technology would have been dispersed across numerous committees, with no one committee (or even a few committees) dominating the discussion on this topic for the year in question.

Party Control

Another assumption inherent in this approach is that parties matter. Party control has been a major factor in national legislative decision making for nearly two hundred years. It is quite possible that party control could explain at least part of the variation observed in the dependent variables:

> Once elected, officeholders remain partisans. Congress is organized by parties. Party-line votes elect its leadership, determine what its committees will be, assign members to them, and select their chairs. Party caucuses remain a staple of congressional life, and they and other forms of party organization in Congress have become stronger in recent years. Party voting in committee and on the floor of both houses, though far less common in the United States than in many democracies, nonetheless remains the first and most important standard for understanding congressional voting behavior, and it too has grown stronger, in this case much stronger, in recent years. (Aldrich 1995, 15; citations deleted)

If there are significant policy differences between the two major parties in the Congress, then policy outcomes (in the form of budgets) should be affected by changes in the partisan distributions across both chambers. To test this idea the proportion of seats controlled by the Democratic Party in *both* the House and Senate was calculated. This measure is designed to recognize that there may be differences of control between chambers during a particular congressional session. Using this measure will allow exploration of how party control across chambers can impact funding decisions that require passage in both to become law. Democratic percentages were used because the Democratic Party controlled the House for most of the time covered by this study.[14] One of the strengths of this measure is that it captures both party control and the extent of that control.

Nonpolitical Factors

When attempting to understand the influence of political factors on science and technology budgets, it is necessary to isolate the independent effects of these factors from competing possibilities. What else might be causing the observed variation in the dependent variables? What other factors might be masked if this analysis focused exclusively on these three political factors to the exclusion of other factors? To answer those questions, I constructed several additional control variables. These control variables fall into three general areas: general budgetary factors, general economic factors, and special historical events.

The first category, general budgetary factors, introduces two controls. The first is the level of domestic discretionary budget authority.[15] If there are large increases in the availability of domestic discretionary funding (of which science and technology programs are a part), then individual domestic discretionary spending accounts should increase as well, all other factors remaining constant. The second control is the level of total budget authority; it consists of the summed total of all spending, whether mandatory or discretionary, defense or domestic. The logic here is similar; if total spending increases, then science and technology spending should, all other factors being equal, increase as well.

In the case of economic factors, this chapter focuses on annual changes in inflation-adjusted GDP, using chained FY 1992 data. If the U.S. economy is growing, there should be more resources available for federal spending on science and technology programs, all other things being equal. Of course, this economic factor is more distant on the possible chain of causality than discretionary or total funding levels mentioned above. Nevertheless, it is possible that general economic trends can help explain some of the variation observed in science and technology funding levels. Perhaps the rising tide of economic prosperity can help lift the boat of science and technology funding. Perhaps the two are joined in the minds of the public or lawmakers. This control variable is used to further isolate the impact of the primary political factors mentioned above.

It is also possible that the annual variation observed in these budget categories is being affected by historical events that are only peripherally related to the political variables under study. The most obvious candidates for this type of event are the Cold War and the related space race. Perhaps U.S. funding for science and technology programs was largely driven by competition between the United States and the Soviet Union during the period of this study. Perhaps science and technology programs were conceived simply as adjunct investments to more directly defense-related programs. It is possible that a significant amount of the variation observed in the dependent variables could be explained in Cold War or space race terms alone.

For the purpose of this study, the Cold War dummy variable is set at 1 for FY 1949 through 1990 (the fall of the Iron Curtain and the collapse of the Soviet Union) and 0 for fiscal years 1991 through 1993. Likewise, the space race dummy variable is set to 1 for FY 1961 through 1973 and 0 for all other years. This definition of the space race period includes the ten months of fiscal year 1961 leading up to President Kennedy's famous May 1961 speech in which he expressed the goal of "put[ting] a man on the Moon and return[ing] him safely to Earth" and extends several months after the completion of the final Apollo lunar mission in December 1972.[16]

STATISTICAL ANALYSIS

The science and technology issue salience and committee competition values computed for this chapter (averaged for the two-year congressional term) are displayed in figure 6.3 and the exact annual values for these indexes[17] are detailed in table 6.4. Figure 6.3 uses two y-axes. The left axis measures the values for the salience and committee competition indexes (which are displayed as dotted lines with open markers). It varies from 0 to 0.7. The right axis measures the amount of budget authority for two major science and technology budget categories (which are displayed with solid lines and closed markers); it varies from $0 to $25 billion (FY97). The data are displayed here in terms of the average level for each two-year congressional term.

The similar shapes of the curves displayed in figure 6.3 suggest that there may be some relationship between the committee competition and space research funding variables, especially for the period after the 86th Congress. Likewise, the similarities between the curves for issue salience and general science funding suggests that there may be a relationship between these two variables.

However, these visual representations are not conclusive. Additional analysis is necessary to explore whether these apparent relationships or associations are in fact systematic; the ordinary least squares regression results reported below will directly address the presence or absence of systematic relationships between the variables in this study. Nevertheless, these shapes also suggest that there may be different processes at work in determining general science funding from those involved in determining space research funding.

BRIEF BUDGET HISTORY

The funding histories of these two budget categories are significantly different. The budget authority levels for space research and general science are presented in figure 6.4.[18] Space research is characterized by very obvious large-scale changes over relatively short periods of time. Funding for this budget function increased fivefold from the start of the space race in FY 1961 to its peak just

TABLE 6.4 Index Values for Issue Salience and Committee Competition

Fiscal Year	Science and Technology Issue Salience	Science and Technology Committee Competition
1947	.004	.444
1948	.011	.446
1949	.005	.667
1950	.002	.000
1951	.006	.667
1952	.001	.000
1953	.004	.500
1954	.006	.625
1955	.002	.000
1956	.006	.320
1957	.005	.444
1958	.016	.828
1959	.038	.499
1960	.051	.480
1961	.075	.442
1962	.053	.607
1963	.070	.524
1964	.045	.753
1965	.035	.611
1966	.030	.639
1967	.036	.245
1968	.031	.560
1969	.027	.580
1970	.036	.420
1971	.038	.580
1972	.024	.347
1973	.024	.703
1974	.047	.479
1975	.042	.250
1976	.031	.230
1977	.025	.306
1978	.038	.301
1979	.030	.230
1980	.034	.195
1981	.029	.433
1982	.028	.405
1983	.039	.449
1984	.032	.384
1985	.044	.325
1986	.042	.332
1987	.041	.409
1988	.045	.392
1989	.049	.533
1990	.038	.463
1991	.045	.435
1992	.030	.560
1993	.002	.440

**FIGURE 6.3 COMPARING POLITICAL FACTORS AND BUDGET AUTHORITY (BA) FOR
SCIENCE AND TECHNOLOGY PROGRAMS**

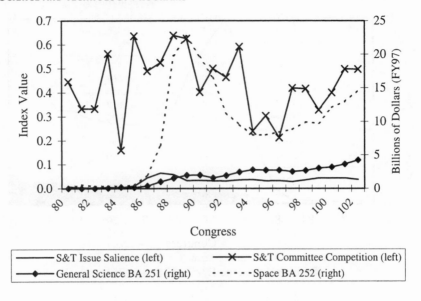

four years later in FY 1965 (from $4.6 billion to $23.8 billion). It then declined
by nearly two-thirds (to $8.4 billion) by FY 1974.

The funding levels for general science are small in comparison. One of the
disadvantages of displaying both budget categories in the same figure is that
the degree of changes in general science are largely hidden in this format.
Budget levels for general science doubled from FY 1961 to FY 1965 (from $842
million to $1.9 billion); it had increased by over 450 percent from its 1961 level
by the time it peaked in FY 1992 (at $4.65 billion).

OLS REGRESSION RESULTS

In this study the use of ordinary least squares regression uncovers several interesting relationships among these variables. First and foremost, a clear distinction emerges relative to the role of various factors in explaining space research budgets and general science budgets. While this general conclusion is
consistent with previous research in this area (see Feeley 1999a, 1999b), the
particulars are unique to the expanded model and the refined data set used
here. Each of these budgetary categories will be discussed in turn. As shown
in tables 6.5 and 6.6, the independent variables were added in groups to the

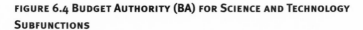

FIGURE 6.4 BUDGET AUTHORITY (BA) FOR SCIENCE AND TECHNOLOGY SUBFUNCTIONS

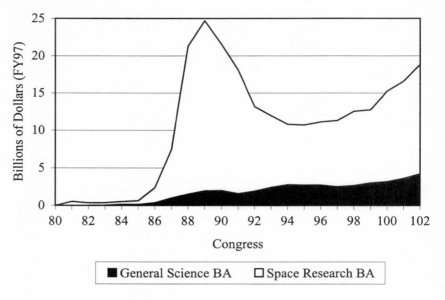

regression equations. Models 1 through 3 are intermediate results of individual regression equations leading to model 4, which is the fully developed model.

Space Research

The regression results suggest that annual fluctuations in space research funding are driven in part by three factors: committee competition, levels of total discretionary funding, and changes in real GDP. There appears to be a positive relationship between space research funding and both committee competition and issue salience. This suggests that when the issue of space becomes more salient, and committees compete for attention in this area, that funding will tend to increase. The coefficients for committee competition are positive and statistically significant at conventional levels. The lone exception is the coefficient in model 3, which while positive is just beyond the convention for statistical significance ($p = .058$). The coefficients for issue salience are all positive; however, only the one in model 3 is statistically significant.

These relationships remain even after including the control variables for economic, budgetary, and historical factors. It is also clear that both budgetary and economic factors play important roles in determining budgetary decisions for this category. Both total discretionary spending and changes in GDP

TABLE 6.5 Regression Results for Space Research

	Model 1	Model 2	Model 3	Model 4
Political Factors				
Issue salience	4.422	6.181	6.412*	6.078
	(3.978)	(3.736)	(3.459)	(4.039)
Committee competition	.733*	.593*	.473	.610*
	(.338)	(.314)	(.294)	(.310)
Party control	−.022*	−.009	−.007	.001
	(.012)	(.012)	(.011)	(.013)
Budgetary Factors				
Total domestic discretionary	—	>−.001*	>−.001**	>−.001**
	—	(<.001)	(<.001)	(<.001)
Total budget authority	—	<.001	<.001	<.001
	—	(<.001)	(<.001)	(<.001)
Economic Factors				
Changes in GDP	—	—	−5.601**	−5.462**
	—	—	(2.044)	(2.148)
Historical Factors				
Cold War	—	—	—	.346
	—	—	—	(.315)
Space race	—	—	—	−.154
	—	—	—	(.207)
Constant	.985	.870	1.110	.389
F-test	2.958*	4.057**	5.197**	4.204**
Adjusted R^2	.118	.258	.364	.368
Standard error of the estimate	.4119	.3778	.3498	.3486
Number of observations	44	44	44	44

Notes: Values in parentheses are standard errors.
*$p < .05$; **$p < .01$ (one-tailed tests).

are statistically significant in the models that include them; however, the coefficients for these two factors are consistently negative. This suggests that space research funding tends to run counter to trends in both domestic discretionary spending and growth in GDP, decreasing when these other indicators are increasing and vice versa. One possible explanation for this phenomenon is that spending on space research is conceived of as an investment in the technological and economic interests of the country. It is conceivable that during bad times (when spending is decreasing and GDP is declining) informed

TABLE 6.6 Regression Results for General Science

	Model 1	Model 2	Model 3	Model 4
Political Factors				
Issue salience	−2.720	−1.314	−1.376	1.380
	(4.779)	(4.769)	(4.845)	(5.722)
Committee competition	−.150	−.274	−.270	−.332
	(.433)	(.429)	(.436)	(.491)
Party control	−.040**	−.037*	−.037*	−.037*
	(.016)	(.016)	(.017)	(.021)
Budgetary Factors#				
Total domestic discretionary	—	<.001	<.001	<.001
	—	(.000)	(.000)	(.000)
Total budget authority	—	<.001	>−.001	>−.001
	—	(.000)	(.000)	(.000)
Economic Factors				
Changes in GDP	—	—	.567	1.261
	—	—	(2.997)	(3.283)
Historical Factors				
Cold War	—	—	—	−.451
	—	—	—	(.444)
Space race	—	—	—	−.095
	—	—	—	(.308)
Constant	2.695**	2.781**	2.757**	3.060*
F-test	2.996*	2.583*	2.101	1.663
Adjusted R^2	.127	.162	.139	.115
Standard error of the estimate	.4679	.4586	.4648	.4713
Number of observations	41	41	41	41

Notes: Values in parentheses are standard errors.
$*p < .05; **p < .01$ (one-tailed tests).

legislators would increase funding in countercyclical accounts like space research as a hedge against economic and budgetary downturns. It also suggests
that when times are good (discretionary funding is increasing and GDP is improving), legislators shift to more consumption-related activities and abandon their investments in space research. Additional research needs to be done
to more fully understand these somewhat surprising findings.

There does not appear to be any systematic association between space
research funding and party control, total budget authority, or either of our

historical factors, the Cold War and the space race. All of these factors fail to reach the conventional levels for statistical significance once the nonpolitical factors are added to the models (although party control is statistically significant in model 1 before the other factors are added).

General Science

A different set of relationships appears to exist between the political factors being studied and general science programs. Funding levels for general science appear to be largely driven by changes in party control as measured by the proportion of seats in both chambers controlled by the Democratic Party. It is the only factor that is statistically significant at conventional levels; all other factors fail to reach statistical significance in even one of the four models.

Party control is negatively correlated with general science spending. This strongly suggests that the two major parties have different priorities for spending when it comes to basic science. The negative coefficients for party control in these regression models means that funding for general science should systematically decline as the size of the Democratic coalition grows. Conversely, funding for science research should increase as the number of seats held by Democrats declines.

One possible explanation of this finding is that Democratic members of Congress are more interested in other topic areas and are more interested in funding nonscience activities. Increased numbers of Democrats in the Congress should shift the institutional focus of Congress toward issues of greater importance to Democrats and impact funding decisions accordingly. Under this scenario, a larger Democratic caucus in Congress should be more free to express its funding preferences, and therefore, more willing to reduce science funding, all other factors being equal.

Committee competition and issue salience both appear to be negatively associated with science funding, although none of the coefficients are statistically significant. All of the other factors also fail to achieve statistical significance, although the direction of their coefficients is consistent. Total domestic discretionary funding and changes in GDP produce positive coefficients, while the Cold War and space race dummy variables yield negative coefficients.

CONCLUSIONS AND FUTURE RESEARCH

The historical analysis presented in this chapter provides some evidence that political factors (along with other factors) explain changes in science and technology policy over an extended period. It provides anecdotal evidence that modern science and technology policy is systematically influenced by the phased emergence of policy goals, that these changing policy goals make possible venue shopping by policy entrepreneurs, and that venue shopping (in turn) helps foster competition among committees in the House.

In select cases, the statistical models used in this study also provide information about how political factors in Congress (along with budgetary and economic factors) influence funding levels for federal programs in science and technology. While it is logical to assume that the influence of these factors should be evident in policy outcomes (i.e., budget levels for science and technology projects), the statistical results reported here only partially support that assumption.

This analysis also reveals some underlying associations between variables that appear ripe for future research. Specifically, it appears that there are important differences between the two budget functions analyzed, with space research being determined in large part by one set of political and economic forces (committee competition, total domestic discretionary funding, and GDP), while general science is solely influenced by party control. This suggests that the processes at work in each subfield of science and technology are largely independent of each other in spite of the fact that the institutional structures for determining these budgets are largely the same (in terms of statutory jurisdictions). Both categories are largely controlled in the authorization and appropriations processes by the same committees (and often the same subcommittees) in the House.[19]

Finally, while the amount of variance explained by the statistical models is not insignificant (adjusted R^2 values were .115 and .368 for the complete models), there is ample opportunity for exploring additional causal relationships. Additional research directed toward determining other important explanatory variables seems warranted. Until then, this preliminary analysis has provided a good starting point for future research.

NOTES

1. Here the governmental agenda refers to items that are immediately before a governmental decision-making group, whether it be in the legislative or executive branch of the U.S. federal government.

2. These include subtopics 698 (Education Research and Development), 798 (Environmental R&D), 898 (Energy R&D), 1098 (Transportation R&D), 1700 (General Science), 1701 (Civilian Space), 1704 (Commercial Space), 1705 (Science Cooperation), 1708

(Geology/Weather), 1709 (Computers), 1798 (Science R&D), and 1799 (Other Science) in their entirety.

3. Select hearings were included from these additional subtopics: 2000 (General Government, includes Science Appropriations), 2002 (Government Oversight), 2004 (Civil Service), 2005 (Nominations), 2006 (Commemorative Coins), 2007 (Government Procurement); 2008 (Government Property Management), 2011 (Branch Relations and Administrative Issues); the working data set for this study is available at the policy agendas web site.

4. For the debate concerning the creation of this new agency, and the reasons for its creation, see *Annals of Congress* (1806); for the text of the law see "An act to provide for surveying the coasts of the United States" (1807).

5. From 1807 until 1818, the president was authorized to use his judgment in selecting "proper and intelligent people" to conduct the surveys of the U.S. coasts; during this period no explicit reference to the military or civilian status of these persons was included in the authorizing legislation; see "An Act to Provide for Surveying the Coasts of the United States" (1807). From 1818 to 1844, only military personnel could be employees of the USC&GS; see "An Act to repeal part of the act, entitled 'An act to provide for surveying the coasts of the United States'" (1818). In 1844, Congress again allowed some civilians to participate, including a provision in law to ensure that officers of the U.S. Army and U.S. Navy would be employed "as far as practicable" in the coastal surveys; see the coast survey proviso contained in "An Act making appropriations for the civil and diplomatic expenses of Government for the fiscal year ending the thirtieth day of June, eighteen hundred and forty-five, and for other purposes" (1844). Eventually, the functions of the USC&GS were transferred to what is now a component of the wholly civilian National Oceanic and Atmospheric Administration (NOAA).

6. For the current procedure in the House, see clause 2 of House Rule 12, available on-line at http://www.house.gov/rules/RXII.htm.

7. For the current procedure in the Senate, see Senate Rule 17, available on-line at http://rules.senate.gov/senaterules/rule17.htm.

8. All joint committee hearings were excluded from this analysis; there were a total of twenty-three science- and technology-related hearings held by joint committees during the period of this study.

9. Defined as at least three hearings across the House and Senate during a single two-year congressional term; hearings before joint committees were not counted.

10. Shortened titles are used throughout this chapter; some of the figures use combined titles to improve their presentation. For full titles of the Policy Agendas Project topics and subtopics, as well as detailed examples of what is contained in each category, see appendix 1.

11. A detailed description of the functional categories and terms used in the budget authority data set is available in appendix 2.

12. This approach avoids a potential lag in the data. The hearing data were available only on a calendar basis, whereas the budgetary data were available only on a fiscal year basis. To use both without converting to a common fiscal year basis would have been somewhat problematic. The U.S. government shifted the term of the fiscal year by three months near the middle of the period covered by this study. Without this conversion, some of the data would have been lagged by six months while the rest would have been lagged by three months, potentially biasing the analysis (especially if the number of hearings is disproportionately distributed across the year). By converting all of the data to fiscal year basis, this potential bias is minimized.

13. All data from the "transition quarter" (July 1–September 30, 1976) were excluded from this part of the analysis.

14. The Democrats controlled the House throughout the period of this study except for January 3, 1953–January 5, 1955; the Democrats controlled the Senate throughout these years except January 3, 1953–January 5, 1955 and January 5, 1981–January 6, 1987. Substituting Republican proportions should make no significant difference in the analysis since the proportions are basically reciprocal; the only difference would be the small number of seats held by independents or third-party members.

15. This category of budget authority is usually called out in annual appropriations acts and excludes mandatory spending. The domestic discretionary category is composed of the budget subfunctions that remain after mandatory, national security, and financial subfunctions are accounted for.

16. For excerpts from President Kennedy's speech see Logsdon 1995, 453–54. For detailed information about the budgetary history of the Mercury, Gemini, and Apollo manned missions to the moon, see Nimmen and Bruno 1988.

17. These indices are some of the first for the Policy Agendas Project data set to be computed using fiscal years. Previously published indices were all computed in calendar years; this should explain any differences between the values reported here and those found in other studies.

18. All funding levels reported here are in constant FY 1997 U.S. dollars.

19. In statutory terms, the House Appropriations Subcommittee on Veterans Affairs, Housing and Urban Development, and Independent Agencies (VA-HUD-IA) is responsible for most of the appropriations covered by both 252 and 251, while the authorizations for both of these categories are largely controlled by the House Science Committee.

7

THE CHANGING FOCUS OF NATIONAL SECURITY POLICY

JAMES L. TRUE

Over the years, various theories and studies have produced many efforts to discover the root causes of government spending for defense. But beyond the fact that wars are expensive, there has been surprisingly little agreement among scholars about what has actually influenced U.S. security policy and defense spending. In this chapter three traditional perspectives on national defense policy are compared and tested empirically with that of punctuated equilibrium theory.

This analysis indicates that United States security policies and the resource allocations to support them have not been driven by a single logic across the entire period since World War II. Despite the continuity of the Cold War containment policy during most of the postwar years, U.S. security policy and resource decisions have sprung from different frames of reference and followed different logics in different eras. Consequently, theories that use a single logic have yet to provide adequate explanations of U.S. national security policy or of U.S. defense spending.

From the first traditional perspective, government is seen as essentially an adaptive machine responding to the currents of a few important pressures. Scholars using this approach assume that government is well studied as a "black box" whose outputs vary almost entirely depending upon changes in the inputs. Those who make this assumption may be called the cybernetic school.[1] Some of these scholars earlier concluded that election cycles cause a surge in military spending while others found no significant relationship. Similar contrary findings have emerged about nearly automatic effects from arms races and domestic unemployment rates. Again some scholars found these to be important influences on defense spending while other equally serious scholars did not.[2]

A second group of scholars (usually called incrementalists) maintained that internal decision rules and marginal adjustments made inertia the only important determinant of defense spending. From an incrementalist perspective, acceptance of a large portion of the previous year's budget focuses attention on marginal adjustments, and such acceptance creates an "own inertia" factor in defense budgets. These scholars agreed that internal processes were critically important, but they disagreed about the significance of external influences.[3]

Third, some practitioners described the Defense Department planning, programming, and budgeting processes as an essentially rational system for balancing missions, threats, and force structure. From the perspective of program budgeting (and later performance-based budgeting), the major internal influence on U.S. defense spending would be U.S. interests, goals, and missions; and the major external influence would be the military capabilities of those who oppose them.[4]

The upshot is that there is little consensus about the calculus of influences on resource allocations for defense and national security — although these policy areas have clearly made significant claims on the treasury for a number of years. At its high point at the end of World War II, U.S. national defense spending commanded 38 percent of the nation's gross domestic product (GDP) and 90 percent of the total outlays of the entire national government. The estimates for FY 2000 constitute the low point since World War II; national defense accounts for only 3 percent of GDP and 15.5 percent of national government outlays. Nonetheless, the $268 billion in budget authority estimated for national defense in FY 2000 amounts to 48 percent of all discretionary spending for that year (*The Budget of the U.S. Government, Fiscal Year 2000,* hereafter *FY 2000 Budget*). Obviously, the budget for national defense remains an important part of government priorities, and it would be to our advantage to have clearer ideas of what does and does not influence it and when.

This chapter presents evidence that one important reason for contradictory findings from traditional studies in this area is that the relationships among the variables have changed over time. If influences on national security spending are episodic rather than continuous, then most of our analyses have aspired to timeless generalization in an inappropriate way. If such were the case, it would be advantageous to deal explicitly with temporally changing relationships.

This analysis offers aid to such a project in two ways. First, it uses punctuated equilibrium theory to approach defense spending from both continuous and episodic perspectives, and second it uses a more comprehensive data set than has been previously available to test for changing relationships empirically.

AN EPISODIC PERSPECTIVE ON DEFENSE . . .
AND ITS PREDECESSORS

Rather than assuming all foreign and defense policy decisions have been dominated by a single logic for the last fifty years, punctuated equilibrium theory assumes that they probably have not, and it is not alone in that assumption about government policy making. Twenty years ago John Kingdon saw the need for more fluid metaphors that could handle the complex and probabilistic nature of the policy making he observed in Washington. His resulting multiple streams theory posits that problems, policies, and politics often flow largely independently. Each stream may have its own logic and rhythms, yet structures such as national mood, budget constraints, political culture, and government institutions act as river banks to restrain the moving streams until there is a flood (Kingdon 1995, 1997; cf. Carpenter 1996). Even more generally, social scientists are coming to appreciate the global stability and local unpredictability found in complexity and chaos theories (Kiel and Elliott 1996).

The value of punctuated equilibrium theory to this analysis of national security policy is its emphasis on attention-driven shifts in what would otherwise be largely incremental processes. This theory links shifts in image and attention with political mobilizations, with positive feedback processes, and with shifts in the institutional responsibility for deciding. Such shifts in venue can have important policy and budgetary effects. The relationships among variables can be changed by shifting attention from one aspect of the situation to another and by shifting decision making from one set of institutions to another. Cybernetic theory, in contrast, calls for continuing organizational attention to the same few key aspects of the environment. For punctuated equilibrium theory, a shift from one frame of reference (and its inherent logic) to a new one can radically redirect what would otherwise be a negative feedback process of generally agreed-upon marginal adjustments (Baumgartner and Jones 1993; Jones 1994; Jones, Baumgartner, and True 1998; Worsham 1998; and True, Jones, and Baumgartner 1999).

This new theory is founded on two premises — the first based upon boundedly rational decision making and the second based upon appreciating government as a complex, interactive system. The first premise concerns the process of individual political decision making, and the second relates to the processes by which political institutions aggregate those choices. The first postulates a serial-processing model of decision making and extends the seminal work of Herbert Simon (1983) and John Padgett (1980).

The second premise is that U.S. political institutions amplify this tendency toward decisional stability interspersed with abrupt changes. New mobilizations of interests and macropolitical attention are necessary to overcome the inertia of entrenched interests and policy monopolies. But — once an issue is in the hands of the full Congress and the public presidency — these macropolitical institutions may cause major shifts in policy decisions and resource allocations. The result is institutionally induced stability episodically broken by major shifts in attention, venue, and policy outputs.

In terms of national security policy, punctuated equilibrium theory expects relationships to be stable for a time then to change dramatically. It assumes policy making responds to shifts in macropolitical attention to a particular aspect of the security environment, rather than to changes in the environment itself. Often policy making will be left to government subsystems like the Department of Defense and its particularly interested groups and congressional members or the Department of State and its interested groups. Subsystems typically favor little or no change to entrenched arrangements, yet macropolitical attention to an issue area may result in disjunctive shifts in frames of reference and large-scale changes, rather than continuous adaptation. From this perspective, attention can focus on a specific logic for defense spending during certain times, but that can change over the decades. Episodic shifts in high-level attention to national security issues make possible major departures from previous policy, which in turn create lurches and redirections in defense budgets. The premises of punctuated equilibrium theory are tested herein as the "episodic attention hypothesis."

On the other hand, the traditional approaches to national security policy making call for output changes driven by essentially unchanging relationships between the organization and its environment. If relationships were unchanging and if the cybernetic assumptions were correct, then close organizational attention to a few important variables and the use of standardized responses should allow the nation to adapt to important changes and to survive. From this perspective, changes in the domestic economy and presidential election pressures would have affected defense allocations. In the analyses in this chapter, cybernetic assumptions underlie what are called the "domestic economy hypothesis" and the "election cycle hypothesis."[5]

If relationships were unchanging, and if the incrementalist assumptions were correct, then most important adaptations to the environment are embodieds in the existing arrangements and the current budgets. Government could most usefully focus attention on marginal adjustments to the existing arrangements — first, in order to safeguard the "base" of previous accommodations and, second, in order to adapt, one increment at a time, to new constraints in the external environment. From this perspective, limits on time, intelligence, and cost prevent policy makers from identifying the full range of alternatives and their consequences. Yet governments and nations survive by accepting the legitimacy of previous choices and concentrating on "fair share" decisions about the next adjustment. The incrementalist assumptions will be found below as the "inertia hypothesis."

Conversely, if relationships were unchanging and the rationalist assumptions were correct, then defense spending would have responded consistently to external military threats. From this perspective, national interests are the driving motive of policy, and its method is logical analysis. Interests are relatively stable, but threats will vary. These threats may come in many forms as self-interested nations vie with one another to maximize their power within an anarchic international system. Yet careful gathering of foreign intelligence, support for new technologies, and balanced military programs should allow the government to safeguard national interests despite international challenges to its security.[6] The rationalist assumptions underlie both the "Soviet influence hypothesis" and the "coordinated policy hypothesis," which are tested below.

Hypothesized relations are also tested by using a more comprehensive data set that includes both military spending and nonmilitary spending for national security. One can thus explore whether U.S. military spending was part of a larger national response to international threats and domestic pressures. Another part of that response may have been what the U.S. spent on support for other nations, either to arm them as in the Nixon program of Vietnamization or to support them in other ways as was done during the Marshall Plan. This combination of U.S. defense spending and other-nation support is referred to as national security spending. It seems important to explore both elements of these potential national responses. And it is necessary to do so, if one is to provide a fair test of the rational coordination hypothesis.

These data, analyses, and new theory allow answers to these questions:

1. What has significantly influenced national defense budgets?
2. How much have they responded to continuous internal or external influences?
3. How much have they responded to episodic influences?

ATTENTION AND INERTIA IN NATIONAL
SECURITY DECISION MAKING

Punctuated equilibrium theory posits that external circumstances and internal attentiveness can combine to create "tipping points" in every issue area, but it cannot predict ex ante what those specific points will be for every area of government. Consequently, one must ask two questions of the national security literature. What was the nature of the subsystem context? That is to say, what was the nature of routine budget decision making for national security? And, equally importantly, what events attracted macropolitical attention and thus may have triggered a policy punctuation?

AN INCREMENTAL SUBSYSTEM ASPIRING TO RATIONALITY

The subsystem context for U.S. national security policy making was largely created by the National Security Act of 1947 and its amendments and practices. The act envisioned a rational coordination of various policy instruments — all aimed at securing U.S. interests in a potentially hostile world. During World War II, the U.S. government had conducted its foreign and defense policy making, after the British model, through interagency and joint-service committees and through ad hoc arrangements among the office of the president and the Departments of State, War, and Navy. After the war, the National Security Act sought to institutionalize wartime coordination into a more formal and more nearly unified organization (Trager 1977). The immediate result for the U.S. armed services was "federalization rather than unification" (Futrell 1974, 98), but the results for overall coordination of national security policies have taken longer to become visible.

A major impetus in the adoption of the 1947 act was a belief that foreign policy, defense policy, and intelligence gathering could be rationalized, not as separate concerns, but as a coordinated whole. The National Security Council, with the president as its head, would be responsible for formulating and implementing national security policy while Congress would continue its Constitutional responsibilities "to declare war, . . . to raise and support Armies, [and] . . . to provide and maintain a Navy." Such an executive-led integration of policies and resources for national security received not only the legal support of the 1947 act but also recurring declaratory support from the executive branch (NSC-68 1950 [1975]; NSC-162 1953 [1971]; Kissinger 1979;

Vance 1980; and Haig 1981). A major goal of the national security subsystem was rational coordination of policies.

While coordinating foreign, defense, and intelligence policies was the job of the National Security Council — rationalizing and coordinating the various elements of defense policy and resources was the job of the Department of Defense. Since 1961, a central feature of DOD's efforts to support policy with resources has been the Planning, Programming, and Budgeting System (PPBS) (Hitch and McKean 1960), and PPBS continues as the framework for performance budgeting in DOD today (Melese 1999).

Yet punctuated equilibrium theory suggests that neither PPBS nor other program-based or performance-based budgeting can be a comprehensively rational process for reaching actual decisions. In practice, high-level attention must be selective. Selective attention means that not all strategies, plans, programs, and budget items can receive senior-level attention during a year, nor can anyone examine and understand all alternatives and consequences for each decision. Among the uncertainties and competing values of defense policy, comprehensive rationality sets too high a standard for continuous attainment.

While a punctuated equilibrium theorist would not expect the unbroken integration of foreign policy and defense policy, many rational theorists would. Rational analysts anticipate optimization, that is to say goal maximization across domains as well as within them. If the language of PPBS and the 1947 act were examined for details on the preferences to be maximized, both policy and instrument integration would appear. Policy integration would coordinate the intermediate goals of both foreign and defense policies. The rational integration of instruments would coordinate support for other nations with support for the U.S. military. Those who accepted a goal of policy integration would not only hypothesize that defense budgets respond to changes in the capabilities of adversaries, but they would also hypothesize that budgets for U.S. defenses and budgets for other-nation support would be coordinated with one another in responding to changing international threats.

In contrast, incrementalist scholars expect budgets to be driven primarily by an internal logic of "base" and "fair share" adjustments. To a lesser extent, if at all, incremental budgets would respond to external factors such as international threats or factors, such as domestic politics, which are internal to the nation but presumably external to organizational decision making. Incrementalists, therefore, have no theoretical expectation or explanation for large-scale lurches and redirections in budgets. Acceptance of incrementalist norms creates an "own inertia" factor that appears in budget aggregates (Ostrom 1977;

Majeski 1983; Wildavsky 1992; Correa and Kim 1992). Incrementalists would hypothesize that the main influence is inertia, which is operationalized below by including last year's budget as an independent cause of the current one. The incrementalist perspective on defense budgets contrasts sharply with the PPBS-oriented explanations put forward by senior DOD executives, but it does seem an apt description of much of the decision making in defense budgets.

COMPLICATIONS FROM SHIFTS IN GOVERNMENT ATTENTION

Although the U.S. government may have sought to coordinate U.S. foreign and defense instruments into a single policy, punctuated equilibrium theory indicates such continuous coordination will be difficult to achieve routinely. Coordination between these two conceivably separate aspects of security policy is more likely to be complicated by attention-driven shifts — both shifts between these two aspects of national security and shifts between them and a host of domestic concerns. As senior decision makers in the executive and legislative branches attend to first one aspect or evaluative dimension and then another, the relationship between spending for support for other nations and spending for support of U.S. military should change over time. Nonetheless, most political scientists who have empirically investigated defense spending in the United States have focused on U.S. military spending alone and largely ignored arms and support for other nations.[7]

National security decision makers may consider foreign, defense, and intelligence policies as separate dimensions or attributes of a vexingly complex problem or as separate problems altogether. Different conceptual dimensions may be expected to embody different values, evoke different frames of reference, produce different institutional subsystems, and often result in different policy decisions. Those circumstances seem to be an appropriate description of national security policy making in the hands of our fragmented national government institutions despite the coordination sought in the 1947 National Security Act.

Punctuated equilibrium theorists expect national security policies and budgets will exhibit both periods of large-scale changes and periods of incrementalism. Large-scale changes are driven by serial shifts in attention and exacerbated by overlapping institutions. Incremental changes are driven by accepted frames of reference and made even more marginal by institutional inertia and standardized responses. Thus — while punctuated equilibrium theorists must depend upon detailed analyses of an issue area to anticipate specific local-level "tipping points" or policy punctuations — they have the advantage of a system-level theory that can be tested empirically.

The framework of this new theory is bounded rationality, rather than comprehensive rationality. Its framework does not, in the case of national security policy making, focus only on national states whose methods are solely analytical and whose motives are solely power and interests. Instead, the new theory asserts that understanding the characteristics of the decision makers is necessary to understanding policy decisions, and those characteristics include serial shifts in attention from one area or frame of reference to another.

PREDICTING LURCHES AND STABILITY
IN GOVERNMENT BUDGETING

The systems-level predictions of punctuated equilibrium theory can be distinguished from the predictions of rationalist, incrementalist, and cybernetic models. Comprehensive rationalists (such as PPBS proponents and performance budgeting enthusiasts) would forecast continuous adaptation to changing circumstances as well as ongoing coordination among policy instruments. Punctuated equilibrium theory predicts periods of very incremental stability punctuated by large changes as well as on-again, off-again coordination among instruments. Pure incrementalists would forecast continuous marginal changes driven primarily by internal logic with little reference to external circumstances. Punctuated equilibrium theorists predict that budget punctuations will follow policy punctuations, which in turn have responded to changes in issue definitions, political mobilizations, and attention-riveting external events. Cybernetic models such as Davis, Dempster, and Wildavsky 1974 would forecast basically continuous incremental adjustment with nonincremental shift points driven solely by external events (either from the domestic economy or from the international system). Punctuation theory forecasts very stable "budgeting as normal" with episodic punctuations driven by the interactions of external events, continuing external circumstances, and internal attentiveness. These theories and predictions lead to the following hypotheses that will be tested here.

Hypothesis 1 (domestic economic hypothesis): U.S. government decision makers used increases in defense spending to counter economic downturns, and defense budgets should respond to domestic unemployment.

Hypothesis 2 (election cycle hypothesis): Incumbent U.S. presidents used defense spending to garner additional political support in the year they ran for reelection, and defense budgets should show increases in those years.

Hypothesis 3 (Soviet influence hypothesis): U.S. defense budgets should respond positively to Soviet defense spending as the government sought to safeguard long-term U.S. interests against the changing military capability of its primary adversary.

Hypothesis 4 (inertia hypothesis): U.S. defense budgets should respond primarily to internal rhythms and decision rules with little or no influence from external influences, i.e., the prior-year budget largely determines the current defense budget.

Hypothesis 5 (coordination hypothesis): National security policy makers have coordinated both support for U.S. military defenses and support for other-nation security and development, and the two budgets should roughly parallel each other.

Hypothesis 6 (episodic attention hypothesis): Since two separate processes produced the budgets for national security, U.S. national security spending should be driven by organizational inertia when decisions are left to foreign and defense policy subsystems. But attention-riveting international events should have created tipping points after which macropolitical participants made nonincremental policy decisions that should have produced major changes in the U.S. defense budget.

DATA AND METHODOLOGY

Empirical tests of the above hypotheses are presented in two stages. First, there are tests for continuous influences on defense budget authority after controlling for episodic U.S. war involvement. The tested continuous influences are (a) estimates of Soviet defense spending (the Soviet influence hypothesis), (b) budget authority for U.S. security support for other nations (the coordination hypothesis), and (c) U.S. annual unemployment rates (the domestic economic hypothesis). At the same time, a dummy variable is used to test for defense spending increases associated with the U.S. presidential election cycle (= 1 when the incumbent president is running for reelection, else = 0). The dependent variable is budget authority for U.S. spending for national defense (budget function 050) portrayed in millions of constant FY 1998 dollars (i.e., the implicit GDP deflator for each fiscal year was used to control the effects of inflation before accomplishing the analyses).[8]

Soviet military spending is represented by the U.S. government estimate of what it would cost to replicate Soviet military forces in the U.S. It is based on the CIA estimates that were available or should have been available to Congress at the time of U.S. defense budget deliberations, rather than later retrospective estimates. Arms Control and Disarmament Agency (ACDA) publications were used to extend the Soviet expenditure data in Marra and Ostrom 1992 so that the displayed series runs from FY 1964 through FY 1995.[9] The defense estimates for FY 1992 through 1995 are for Russia alone. The fact that U.S. government estimates of Soviet military expenditures were not systematically available before 1964 is both an indicator and a problem. A lack of formal U.S. government monitoring of Soviet expenditures before 1964 suggests that they were not per se a systematic part of long-term government attention before then. But that same lack creates an analytical problem by limiting the period for meaningful tests of influences on U.S. government defense decisions from 1964 to the dissolution of USSR in 1991. Since the original CIA estimates were denominated in current-year U.S. dollars, they too have been adjusted for inflation using the implicit GDP deflator for the U.S.

Second, there are tests for episodic changes in the relationship between spending for U.S. military spending and spending for international security assistance and between U.S. military spending and Soviet military spending. Political history provides for delineating periods of greater and lesser attention to the Soviet military threat. Attention to Soviet military capabilities is assumed to be higher during the height of the Cold War (1950–64) and after the 1979 Soviet invasion of Afghanistan (1979–91) than during the Vietnam and post-Vietnam period (1964–79). Episodic attention to the Soviet threat may have resulted in periods when U.S. defense spending decisions responded to changes in Soviet defense spending and periods when they did not. Similarly, government efforts at rational coordination of the national and international components of U.S. national security policy may have been continuous, or they may have been episodic.

There are two final points to make about defense budget data. Aggregations of them are not normally distributed, and the series are autoregressive. The two conditions together raise serious questions about appropriate statistical tests and inferences, and they may account for some of the previous contradictory findings. Both conditions arise from the nature of budgetary decision making. Many separate policy and program decisions occur throughout the year, but they are represented by a single annual figure. There are often more likely causes than there are effects. For budget equations to be solved, some potential decision influences must be omitted, even though omitting a relevant variable may bias OLS estimates. In addition, budget aggregations are lepto-kurtotically distributed, not normally distributed. They have more outliers than a normal distribution. Tests that depend upon normally distributed disturbances, like the Chow test for a change in parameters, are not appropriate for nonnormal data (Gujarati 1988; Kennedy 1992). Appropriate controls and a modest amount of skepticism would seem to be called for in dealing with annual budget data.

A POLITICAL HISTORY OF MILITARY SPENDING

Studies of national security are hampered by the fact that important decisions are often made in secret and are not authoritatively analyzed for many years. Measuring actual presidential and congressional attention and accessing decision details about national security are extraordinarily difficult. The original documents and discussions often are classified, and cover stories can be disseminated to the public. Consequently, the public record may not accurately reflect high-level attention to security issues. Constructing an authoritative direct measure of macropolitical attention that would cover from 1946 through 1998 will not be possible until recent decisions and documents are available and have been thoroughly analyzed. Even then, practical difficulties may prove to be insurmountable.

Instead of directly measuring macropolitical attention, the analyses in this chapter use a proxy. Punctuated equilibrium theory suggests that episodic attention-focusing events can generate tipping points wherein issues are viewed with alarm or borne up on waves of enthusiasm. Policy images may then be challenged, and issues redefined with radical policy results. Edwards and Wood's (1999) analysis of the *Public Papers of the President* indicates that events, inertia, and media attention are important influences on the amount of presidential public statements about foreign policy issues (1999, 342). Although there are clearly differences between the public and secret agendas for national security, attention-focusing events may provide a reasonable ex post facto proxy for increased macropolitical attention.

Political history allows for a variety of categorizations of important national security policies and events. The list used in this analysis began in the National Security Department of the Air War College as a study of what were then called policy "watersheds" or turning points. In this chapter, such events are assumed to have involved high-level government attention, and as such they can be tested as episodic, rather than continuous, influences on defense budgets.

The complete history of U.S. national security policy making may never be written, but earlier decisions are more available for study than recent ones. Case studies of the start of the Cold War and those of the war in Vietnam support the inclusion of the events listed below. In short, although there is some agreement on the importance of the events in this list,[10] other lists of important events are clearly possible. The events and policies are as follow:

1. Postwar Soviet influence in Europe, Truman Doctrine, and Marshall Plan (1947– 49)[11]
2. Korean War and rearmament for the containment policy (1950 –53)[12]
3. Berlin and Cuban crises, and Kennedy defense buildup (1961– 63)[13]
4. Vietnam War Americanization phase (1964 – 68)[14]
5. Vietnam War Vietnamization phase (1969 –73)[15]
6. Afghanistan invasion and Reagan defense buildup (1979 – 85)[16]
7. Dissolution of the Soviet Union and Gulf War (1990 –91).[17]

From punctuated equilibrium theory, one would expect these vivid external events to have shifted government policy making out of the national security subsystems (defense and foreign affairs) and into the spotlight of the public presidency and the full Congress. As such, these events appear to have focused macropolitical attention on defense and produced tipping points wherein old policy images and issue definitions are challenged and changed. In short, rather than continuous adaptation to changes in the international environment, these mobilizing events may have engendered episodic shifts or punctuations in policy and budgets.

GRAPHIC AND STATISTICAL ANALYSES

We look first for a direct influence of Soviet defense spending on U.S. budget decisions. A visual comparison of U.S. defense spending from FY 1946 through FY 1998 and estimates of Soviet defense spending from FY 1964 thorough FY 1995 as appear in figure 7.1. All figures were converted to billions of constant FY 1998 dollars to control for the effects of inflation.

The U.S. budget series begins with FY 1946, which included the last three months of World War II. Its features include postwar demobilization through FY 1950; an FY 1951–53 peak for the Korean War; a small bulge in FY 1962 – 64; another bulge for the Vietnam War, peaking in FY 1968; the Reagan buildup, peaking in FY 1985; and a one-year spike in FY 1991 for the Persian Gulf War. On the other hand, the Soviet series starts in FY 1964 and features fairly steady

FIGURE 7.1 U.S. AND SOVIET DEFENSE SPENDING

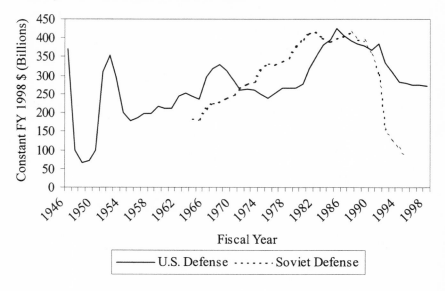

increases from FY 1965 through FY 1982, a relatively level period through FY 1989, steep decreases through FY 1991, and a precipitate drop thereafter, ending with figures that reflect estimates for Russia alone in FY 1992–95.

Coefficients are estimated for the following equation for the period FY 1965–92 when annual estimates of Soviet defense spending were available and may have influenced U.S. budgets:

$$Def_t = Def_{t-1} + Intl\ Sup_t + Vietnam + Gulf + Election +$$
$$Unemp_{t-1} + Buildup + Sov_{t-1} + E_t$$

where Def_t is budget authority for U.S. defenses (budget function 050) at year t converted to millions of constant FY 1998 dollars; Def_{t-1} is the prior-year U.S. defense budget authority in millions of constant FY 1998 dollars; Intl Sup_t is budget authority for international security support (the sum of subfunctions 151 and 152) at year t converted to millions of constant FY 1998 dollars; Vietnam is a dummy variable (= 1 for FY 1966–72; else = 0); Gulf is dummy variable (= 1 for FY 1991; else = 0); Election is a dummy variable (= 1 when incumbent president is running for reelection; else = 0); $Unemp_{t-1}$ is the annual unemployment rate for the prior year; Buildup is a dummy variable (= 1 for FY 1981–85; else = 0); Sov_{t-1} is estimated Soviet defense spending available when Congress deliberated about the forthcoming defense budget in millions of constant FY 1998 dollars, e.g., the estimate of Soviet defense spending in FY 1991 presumably influenced decisions for the U.S. defense budget for FY 1992; and E_t is the error term.

Table 7.1 portrays the results of ordinary least squares (OLS) regressions as well as estimated generalized least squares models with autocorrelated errors (AUTO). The OLS models capture prior-year spending by using a one-year lag of the dependent variable as an independent variable. The AUTO models capture the effects of prior-year spending (and other autoregressive processes) by estimating an autocorrelation parameter (rho) that assumes first-order autoregression in the error term (White 1997, 139). The regressions were conducted first with the variables represented as levels and second as annual changes (first differences). The diagnostic statistics indicate that more reliance may be placed on estimates from the models of first differences.

There is little evidence in table 7.1 of a continuous direct influence from Soviet defense spending. The intelligence estimates available to Congress when they considered U.S. defense budgets produced a statistically significant influence on U.S. defense in only the first OLS model, and its diagnostic statistics provide good reasons for challenging the reliability of that model. When some of the statistical problems were controlled, Soviet spending did not produce a statistically significant influence on U.S. defense spending in any of the remaining models.[18] The time series of levels of estimated Soviet spending is not demonstrably stationary, and diagnostic statistics for the first two models indicate problems with residual autocorrelation, which could bias estimates (Kennedy 1992; Greene 1993). Changes in Soviet spending did not have any statistically significant influence on changes in U.S. defense spending, whether modeled with or without the other potential continuous influences.

There is a possibility that including the post-Afghanistan Reagan buildup as an independent variable masks the statistical significance of Soviet defense spending, but these regression analyses suggest otherwise. The buildup (modeled as a dummy variable = 1 from FY 1980 through FY 1985) and Soviet spending changes have a slight negative correlation with each other. More to the point, the last three models in table 7.1 indicate that the Reagan buildup is statistically significant with or without Soviet spending, but changes in Soviet spending do not provide a statistically significant direct influence on U.S. defense spending whether modeled with or without the Reagan buildup. The question of a more complex relationship is addressed later, but here one can conclude that Soviet military spending did not have a large enough continuous influence on U.S. defense spending to be counted as a direct factor in U.S. defense budgets.[19]

TABLE 7.1 Regressions of U.S. Defense Spending on Support for Other Nations, Wars, Election Cycles, Unemployment, Reagan Buildup, and Soviet Military Spending, FY 1965–92

MODEL	OLS	AUTO	OLS^a	AUTO^a	AUTO^a	AUTO^a
			First Differences	First Differences	First Differences	First Differences
Variables	RDBA	RDBA	in RDBA	in RDBA	in RDBA	in RDBA
Prior spending[b]	.80***	.94***	.55***	.59***	.61***	.58***
	(11.99)	(14.03)	(3.71)	(3.82)	(4.04)	(3.68)
International	1.28**	−0.06	0.38	—	—	—
support	(2.31)	(−0.09)	(0.76)			
Vietnam War	31755**	35839**	37422***	18847*	17704*	18690*
	(2.42)	(2.39)	(3.26)	(1.90)	(1.86)	(1.70)
Gulf War	33790*	27478*	34716***	32472***	32596***	32632***
	(2.02)	(1.83)	(3.00)	(4.07)	(4.22)	(3.68)
Presidential	−12296	−7125	−6552	—	—	—
election	(−1.35)	(−0.79)	(−0.94)			
Unemployment	1841	313	1091	—	—	—
percentage$_{t-1}$	(0.63)	(0.07)	(0.32)			
Reagan	27335**	24169	27415**	22719**	22107**	—
buildup	(2.40)	(1.49)	(2.21)	(2.47)	(2.50)	
Soviet	0.20*	0.30	0.21	0.08	—	−0.03
spending$_{t-1}$	(2.05)	(1.53)	(1.37)	(0.41)		(0.12)
Constant	−47391	212910***	—	—	—	—
	(−1.17)	(2.85)				
R^2	.95	.92	.68	.63	.63	.53
Adj R^2	.93	.89	.57	.58	.60	.49
DW stat	1.24^c	1.1^c	1.70^c	1.41^c	1.39^c	1.56^c
DH stat	2.14^d	2.23^d	0.47	1.37	1.33	0.96
Residual rho^e	0.38	0.39	0.06	0.16	0.16	0.11
Runs normal	−0.93	−0.36	−0.83	−1.76	−0.93	−0.93

Note: *T*-ratios are in parentheses; SHAZAM OLS and AUTO estimates. RDBA = Real Defense Budget Authority.

*Significant at the .10 level; **significant at the .05 level; ***significant at the .01 level (two-tailed tests).

[a] All variables have been differenced once.

[b] In OLS models prior spending is real defense budget authority or differences in real defense budget authority lagged one year and used as an independent variable; in AUTO models, this is rho, an estimate of the first-order autoregressive process in the error term using Cochrane-Orcutt procedures in SHAZAM.

[c] Evidence from the Durbin-Watson statistic of residual first-order autocorrelation.

[d] Evidence from the Durbin *h* statistic of remaining higher-order autocorrelation.

[e] An estimate of the first-order autocorrelation remaining in regression residuals.

On the other hand, prior U.S. defense spending remains a key factor even after first differences are taken. The estimates of the influence of inertia in these models range from .80 to .94 for levels of spending and from .58 to .61 for first differences. Here is some evidence for attributing much of current U.S. defense spending and about half of the current-year changes to the prior-year figures. There is a tide in defense affairs. Even after controlling for event-related elevated spending with dummy variables for the Vietnam War, the Reagan buildup, and the Gulf War — an increase (or decrease) in U.S. defense spending in one year was likely to be followed by succeeding increases (or decreases). Prior-year spending retains an impressive influence over present budgets in all of the tested models.

The presidential election cycle and the unemployment rate were not statistically significant influences in any of the models. Considering those variables as well as Soviet defense spending, one finds little support here for the Soviet influence hypothesis, for the domestic economy hypothesis, or for the presidential election hypothesis.

The statistically insignificant estimate for international support (in all but the first OLS model) is troubling for the coordination hypothesis as well. If government decision makers have uniformly responded in a coordinated way to changing international challenges, one would expect to find evidence of a long-term positive correlation between the budget records of the military and those for international support as both instruments respond to relatively fixed security objectives and changing international threats — although it is possible that coordination might also include a sequence of first one instrument and then another. Figure 7.2 provides a more detailed picture of the budgets for these two policy instruments. Please note that two different scales are portrayed so that the greatly larger military component can be compared graphically with the smaller support for other nations.

Figure 7.2 suggests that there may have been a rough positive relationship between spending for U.S. defenses and spending for other nations, at least for some time periods. The Marshall Plan (European Recovery Program) generated an early peak in support for others. It was followed shortly by the defense peak for the Korean War and U.S. rearmament for the Cold War. The two variables followed slowly increasing trajectories during the ensuing Cold War years, until an apparent change in FY 1965. During the "Americanization" of the Vietnam War, military spending went up while spending for others was markedly decreased. Then, after FY 1969, during the "Vietnamization" of the Vietnam War under the Nixon doctrine, U.S. military spending went down

FIGURE 7.2 U.S. DEFENSE VS. INTERNATIONAL SECURITY SUPPORT SPENDING

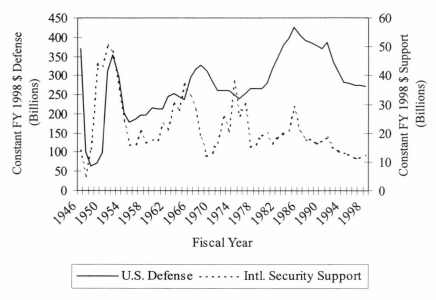

Fiscal Year

———— U.S. Defense · · · · · · · Intl. Security Support

while spending for other nations was sharply increased. After the later peaks in FY 1985, both series are generally declining.

By substituting a dummy variable for the Cold War (FY 1951–89) in place of Soviet defense spending, one can expand the period of coverage to include all fifty-three years of data for broader tests for influences on U.S. defense spending. The Cold War dummy variable provides a crude measure of what the literature describes as an important policy influence on U.S. defense spending. Two additional dummy variables are included in the period covered by these regressions: (1) Korean War (= 1 for FY 1951–53, else = 0) and (2) Berlin crisis/Cuban missile crisis/flexible response/Kennedy defense buildup (= 1 for FY 1962–64, else = 0). The results of those regressions appear in table 7.2.

The analysis indicates ceteris paribus that U.S. defense budgets during the Cold War period (FY 1951 through FY 1989) were about $45 billion a year higher (in FY 1998 dollars) than at other times. This crude measure of U.S. Cold War policy was statistically significant while the continuous measure of Soviet military spending in table 7.1 was not. In short, American Cold War policy appears to have had a strong effect on U.S. defense budgets, but there was little or no direct effect from annual estimates of Soviet military spending themselves.

TABLE 7.2 Regressions of U.S. Defense Spending on Support for Other Nations, Wars, Election Cycles, Unemployment, Reagan Buildup, and the Cold War, FY 1946–98

MODEL	OLS	AUTO	OLS[a]	AUTO[a]	AUTO[a]
			First Differences	First Differences	First Differences
Variables	RDBA	RDBA	in RDBA	in RDBA	in RDBA
Prior spending[b]	.68***	.96***	0.19***	0.30**	0.22
	(8.33)	(24.03)	(3.23)	(2.21)	(1.60)
International support	0.98	0.20	0.54	0.35	—
	(1.23)	(0.43)	(1.27)	(0.80)	
Korean War	82547***	128430***	117440***	109300***	116100***
	(2.56)	(6.53)	(6.62)	(6.14)	(6.53)
Kennedy buildup	384	24909	22953	30264*	21952
	(0.02)	(1.45)	(1.52)	(1.88)	(1.42)
Vietnam War	47693**	33019*	32953**	25688	25462*
	(2.49)	(1.96)	(2.21)	(1.62)	(1.65)
Gulf War	77596*	28909*	32467**	21665	27442**
	(1.84)	(1.71)	(2.71)	(1.55)	(1.95)
Presidential election	−11841	−5953	−3864	−5259	—
	(−0.78)	(−1.00)	(−0.73)	(−1.05)	
Unemployment percentage$_{t-1}$	20272***	−883	1365	−1847	—
	(3.98)	(−0.28)	(0.47)	(−0.63)	
Reagan buildup	9710	26700	26091*	20454	25836*
	(0.41)	(1.55)	(1.72)	(1.29)	(1.68)
Cold War	18903	47119**	48487***	44134**	44501**
	(1.28)	(2.48)	(2.87)	(2.49)	(2.49)
Constant	−76718*	206630***	—	—	—
	(−1.95)	(3.48)			
R^2	.82	.94	.78	.74	.72
Adj R^2	.77	.92	.73	.68	.69
DW stat	1.03[c]	1.27[c]	1.91	1.88	1.94
DH stat	2.49[d]	1.46	0.32	0.82	0.05
Residual rho[e]	0.28	0.19	0.04	0.03	0.00
Runs normal statistic	−3.08[f]	1.12	−0.68	−0.87	−0.29

Note: T-ratios are in parentheses; SHAZAM OLS and AUTO estimates. RDBA = Real Defense Budget Authority.
*Significant at the .10 level; **significant at the .05 level; ***significant at the .01 level (two-tailed tests).
a. All variables have been differenced once.
b. In OLS models prior spending is real defense budget authority or differences in real defense budget authority lagged one year and used as an independent variable; in AUTO models, this is rho, an estimate of the first-order autoregressive process in the error term using Cochrane-Orcutt procedures in SHAZAM.
c. Evidence from the Durbin-Watson statistic of residual autocorrelation.
d. Evidence from the Durbin h statistic of remaining higher-order autocorrelation.
e. An estimate of the first-order autocorrelation remaining in regression residuals.
f. Evidence from a normalized runs test of nonrandom residuals.

The variable for a presidential election cycle is still not statistically significant in any of the models, nor are changes in U.S. spending for international
support. Unemployment appears to have a significant influence in the first
OLS model, but when that model's statistical problems are controlled with
generalized least squares or with differencing its significance disappears. Indeed, prior-year spending, wars (hot and cold), and the Reagan buildup are
all that are consistently significant in this longer-period test.

It is arguable that the Cold War and the Reagan buildup are both policy responses to tipping points, i.e., international events that made security circumstances urgent and demanding of government attention. The Korean War
solidified Truman administration deliberations about U.S. rearmament and a
Soviet containment policy, and the Afghanistan invasion galvanized interest
and actions from both the Carter and Reagan administrations. U.S. defense
budgets clearly are affected by hot wars, but their responses to the Cold War
and Reagan buildup are generally supportive of episodic macropolitical atten-
stion to national security affairs.

The relationship between U.S. defense spending and support for other nations also appears to be a complicated one. Note that the OLS model in the
previous table 7.1 indicated a positive, statistically significant relationship between international support and U.S. defense spending. Such a relationship
would support the coordination hypothesis of using both the military and
nonmilitary components of national security policy. However, there was no
statistically significant relationship between these two variables found over the
longer period in table 7.2. More tests of potential relationships are desirable,
for punctuated equilibrium theory suggests that relationships may change
from one era to another, as we examine in the next section.

EPISODIC ATTENTION TO DIFFERENT
ASPECTS OF THE ENVIRONMENT

Punctuated equilibrium theory predicts that U.S. government attention to international problems will be episodic, rather than continuous. In times of
peace, the primary goals of the nation typically would be prosperity and internal stability, and national security decisions would be largely left to the
defense and foreign affairs subsystems. When external threats to security are
perceived, the security goal may again dominate the high-level government
agenda (cf. Danziger 1998). As a consequence, one may expect that U.S. policy and budgets have responded episodically, rather than continuously, to the

independent variables (Jones, Baumgartner, and True 1998; True, Jones, and Baumgartner 1999).

A CHANGE OF FOCUS

From the Americanization of the Vietnam War in 1965 until the Soviet invasion of Afghanistan in 1979, there appears to have been reduced American attention to Soviet military capabilities. The Johnson administration focused on a potential budget competition between the Great Society and the war in Vietnam. The elections of 1968 and 1972 centered on crime, civil rights, civil disorders, and the war in Vietnam. The Nixon administration focused on getting the U.S. out of Vietnam, opening relations with China, and on many domestic political concerns — culminating in the Watergate scandal and the resignation of the president. The Ford administration was concerned with protecting the legitimacy of the presidency, controlling domestic inflation, and a hostage rescue offshore from Cambodia. The Carter administration evaluated U.S. relations with the Soviet Union and decided early on that the U.S. could focus more usefully on limiting nuclear weapons and on adding human relations concerns to its international dealings. However, that undertaking was seriously challenged, first by the taking of U.S. diplomatic hostages in Iran and then by the Soviet invasion of Afghanistan. The Iran hostage situation and the failure of a U.S. raid to rescue the hostages drew attention to the capabilities and limitations of U.S. military forces, and the Soviet invasion of Afghanistan drew attention to the bellicosity and military capabilities of the Soviet Union. Countering Soviet military capabilities returned to the U.S. macropolitical agenda (Carter 1980; Reagan 1981, 1982).

This reading of political history suggests that, from FY 1966 through FY 1980, U.S. attention to Soviet military spending and capabilities was lower and more sporadic than it was during the early days of the Cold War and lower than it became after FY 1980. We can use this presumed change in focus to sharpen the previous analyses. Assuming that Soviet spending was not a large factor in U.S. defense spending decisions during the Vietnam War and during the early focus of the Carter administration, we can break these series into two epochs. We divide the series into before and after the 1979 (FY 1980) Soviet invasion of Afghanistan (recall that government estimates of Soviet defense spending were not formally available before 1964). The results of testing the two periods separately appear in table 7.3.

Regressions by attention eras indicate little or no relationship between

TABLE 7.3 Regressions of Changes in Defense Spending on Support for Other Nations, Wars, Election Cycles, Unemployment, Reagan Buildup, and Soviet Military Spending by Eras of Attention, FY 1966–79 and FY 1980–92

	FY 1966–79		FY 1980–92		OVERALL FY 1966–92	
MODEL	OLS[a]	AUTO[a]	OLS[a]	AUTO[a]	OLS[a]	AUTO[a]
Variables	First Differences in RDBA	First Differences in RDBA	First Differences in RDBA	First Differences in RDBA	First Differences in RDBA	First Differences in RDBA
Prior spending[b]	.34	.42	.71***	.87***	.58***	.59***
	(1.33)	(1.73)	(11.25)	(6.38)	(4.02)	(3.82)
International support	−0.36	−0.47	1.94***	1.41**	0.14	−0.09
	(−0.58)	(−1.01)	(5.32)	(2.54)	(0.30)	(−0.24)
Vietnam War	31700**	24490*	—	—	32801***	19602*
	(2.45)	(2.03)			(3.12)	(1.85)
Gulf War	—	—	35139***	28914***	23852	32666***
			(10.00)	(5.72)	(1.44)	(3.99)
Reagan buildup	—	—	27768***	16228**	33124***	23016**
			(7.94)	(2.66)	(3.13)	(2.43)
Soviet spending$_{t-1}$	−0.02	−0.08	0.34***	0.03	0.06	0.07
	(−0.05)	(−0.23)	(5.92)	(0.20)	(0.31)	(0.38)
R^2	.47	.49	.98	.88	.67	.63
Adj R^2	.31	.40	.97	.83	.59	.56
DW stat	1.28[c]	1.26[c]	2.41[c]	1.22[c]	1.67[c]	1.42[c]
DH stat	2.68[d]	1.91[d]	−0.80	1.39	0.48	1.38
Residual rho[e]	0.24	0.21	−0.22	0.33	0.06	0.16
Runs normal statistic	−0.56	−0.56	−0.85	−0.85	−0.83	−1.76

Note: *T*-ratios in parentheses. RDBA = Real Defense Budget Authority.
*Significant at .10 level; **significant at .05 level; ***significant at .01 level.
[a]All variables have been differenced once.
[b]In OLS models prior spending is differences in real defense budget authority lagged one year and used as an independent variable; in AUTO models, this is rho, an estimate of the first-order autoregressive process in the error term using Cochrane-Orcutt procedures in SHAZAM.
[c]Evidence from the Durbin-Watson statistic of residual autocorrelation.
[d]Evidence from the Durbin *h* statistic of remaining higher order autocorrelation.

Soviet and U.S. defense spending during the Vietnam era versus a possibly significant relationship from FY 1980 to FY 1991. During the period of greater attention after Afghanistan, U.S. spending may have followed U.S. attentiveness with positive influences from changes in Soviet defense spending and from the Reagan buildup, although the AUTO model for that period did not find Soviet spending was significantly influential. If we had limited this analysis solely to the overall period of FY 1964 to FY 1991, we would have seen little reason for concluding that Soviet military capabilities had ever influenced U.S. defense spending. Except for the Reagan buildup and U.S. Cold War policy, the overall analysis produced an estimate of the Soviet influence that was insignificant (that is to say it was statistically indistinguishable from zero or no relationship). Cutting the longer period into theoretically relevant epochs yielded a more complete picture of the influence of Soviet defenses on U.S. defense spending.

The relationship between Soviet capabilities and U.S. defense spending was a complicated one, and it appears to have been episodic. The OLS regression estimate for the post-Afghanistan period indicates that changes in Soviet defense spending may have had a positive relationship on the annual changes in U.S. defense spending. Their estimated influence was an increase (or decrease) of $340 million in U.S. defense spending for every $1 billion increase (or decrease) in Soviet spending — in addition to annual increases associated with the Reagan buildup.[20] On the other hand, when attention was focused on the war in Vietnam and its aftermath, Soviet defense spending does not appear to have had any direct influence on U.S. defense spending in either the OLS or the AUTO models. At some times Soviet spending may have been important to U.S. budget decision making, and at other times it was not.

A substantial measure of caution is in order in extracting meaning from only fourteen data points (fiscal years) in the first period and thirteen data points in the second. Even after these series have been differenced, changes in prior-year spending have a statistically significant influence on the current changes — at least in the latter period. The diagnostic statistics and large changes in estimates between two models of the same period should caution us against overconfidence in drawing conclusions from them. However, the record suggests that macropolitical attentiveness may have been an important intervening factor between changes in Soviet defense spending and those in the U.S. In short, Soviet military capabilities may have been important to U.S. defense budgets only for times when Congress and the president were likely to have been paying attention to them.

COORDINATING THE INSTRUMENTS OF U.S. NATIONAL SECURITY

Table 7.2 provides little evidence of a potentially important relationship between spending for U.S. defenses and spending for other nations. On the other hand, table 7.3 indicates that this relationship was also episodic, rather than continuous. Table 7.3 provides evidence that the relationship between U.S. defense spending and spending for other-nation support was a positive one after Afghanistan and a negative one before that. Estimates for the overall period alone would have found no statistically significant support for the hypothesis of rational coordination. Yet, when attentiveness is crudely taken into account by breaking the time series into epochs, coordination appears to have been strong and positive at one time but not at another.

There are, of course, many other influences on support spending besides those reflected directly in U.S. defense spending;[21] however, after the Afghanistan invasion, spending for these two instruments of national security policy seems to have moved together or in tandem. During the years from FY 1965 to 1980, they acted against each other. The hypothesis of rational coordination of these two instruments of security policy was supported for some periods and not for others.

FINDINGS

What has and has not influenced U.S. spending for national defense? Inertia was the only continuous direct influence that was strongly supported by these analyses although episodic attention to external factors also seems to have been important. Both the inertia hypothesis from incrementalism and the episodic attention hypothesis from punctuated equilibrium theory were supported. Some typically cybernetic factors did not fare well. There was no evidence of direct influence from a presidential election cycle and virtually no evidence of direct influence from the unemployment rate. The fiscal years when an incumbent president was running for reelection were not statistically or graphically different from any other year in these regressions, nor was there any consistent evidence of an effect from annual unemployment rates or changes in unemployment rates. This analysis did not support the domestic economic hypothesis that defense spending was used to counter downturns in the domestic economy, nor did it support the election cycle hypothesis of presidential increases in defense during a reelection year.[22]

Inertia wielded an important continuous influence on U.S. defense spending since World War II. Beneath the episodes of war and changing attentiveness, there was evidence of steady incremental processes and the heavy hand of history. Prior-year spending was a statistically significant feature in most of the models in these analyses. Indeed, whenever the period of analysis included the years of the Reagan defense buildup and subsequent build-down, there was a statistically significant influence of prior-year changes on current-year changes. The presence of effects from both inertia and shifts in attention supports punctuated equilibrium theory's notion of incremental stability when subsystems are left to their own devices and large-scale redirections when macropolitics takes charge.

The Soviet influence hypothesis proved to be too simplistic a representation of U.S.-Soviet relations. Overall, Soviet military spending had no significant continuous influence on U.S. defense spending. Rather, the U.S. government budgeted about $45 billion a year (in FY 1998 dollars) more for defense during each year of the Cold War than it did for other periods. And, after the tipping event of the Soviet invasion of Afghanistan, the Reagan buildup added another $20 to $30 billion a year in addition to the Cold War increment.

Government attention to the threat posed by the former Soviet Union and its essentially rational efforts to coordinate policy instruments were episodic rather than continuous influences on U.S. defenses. During and after the Korean War, U.S. Cold War policy appears to have employed a measure of coordination between U.S. defenses and support for other nations. During and after the Vietnam War, the relationship between these two components of security policy appears to have been one of competition or instrument substitution, rather than coordination. During and after the Afghanistan invasion, that relationship was again apparently one of positive coordination — a relationship that seems to be continuing even after the dissolution of the Soviet Union. Thus the coordination hypothesis was supported to a degree, but its influence appears to have been episodic.

To what degree are other influences on defense spending continuous and to what degree are they episodic? All of the external influences on U.S. defense spending appear to have been episodic. Attention to Soviet defense spending may have had an episodic influence, but that influence was clearly not continuous. Wars are clearly episodic occurrences as was the Reagan defense buildup. Indeed, the internal factors of organizational inertia and U.S. Cold War policy (while it lasted) were the only significant continuous influences in most of the models.

Nonetheless, pure incrementalism did not fare well in these graphic and statistical analyses. Clearly, there were periods when incremental decision making and marginal changes dominated defense budgeting, but there were also times when they did not. And the nature of the incremental results varied by period. Episodic attention to external influences was also important and provided statistically significant influences during some periods but not in others. There were large-scale changes and redirections of defense spending evident in these analyses. In short, one must go beyond pure incrementalism to understand both incremental and nonincremental influences on U.S. national security spending.

Similarly, the idea of defense budgeting as a rational response to changing external threats found only the modest support of the aforementioned periods of apparent coordination between U.S. defenses and support for other nations. There was no evidence of continuous adaptation to changing external circumstances. Instead there were periods of little change interrupted by episodic redirections. The essentially rational assumptions of PPBS, zero-based budgeting, or performance-based budgeting require some sort of continuous adaptation, but this analysis found no evidence that such has occurred. Adaptation seems to be more a matter of episodic redirections, rather than continuous adjustments.

Punctuated equilibrium theory provides a better approach to explaining U.S. defense spending than that of cybernetic, incremental, or rational analytic theories. Cybernetic theory misses episodic attention, "underreactions" from clinging to extant decision designs, and "overreactions" as frames of reference shift. Pure incrementalism misses the attention- and agenda-driven shifts in perspective and concomitant lurches in policy and budgets. Rational budgeting approaches miss the democratic politics of multiple motives and decisional shortcuts as well as the policy results from first ignoring then "overreacting" to changed environments. None of its predecessors seem to do as well as punctuated equilibrium theory in relating both incremental changes and large-scale redirections to their decisional and institutional foundations.

In understanding national security and in explaining policy decisions over time, no one logic and no single frame of reference lasts forever. That is because high-level government attention not only is selective, but it also shifts among perspectives and objects of attention. Any one perspective is always an incomplete representation of a complex, important, and changing environment. Some aspects of the domestic and international environments must be emphasized and some ignored. A single logic may do well for a time, but eventually it will be caught up in its own successes and failures. And there is always a chance that the environment will produce an important surprise. Since government policy and budget processes are necessarily incomplete in information and perspective, our theories of them would do well to account for both organizational inertia and macropolitical shifts in attention.

NOTES

1. See Steinbruner 1974 for an explanation of the cybernetic paradigm. The analytic paradigm and public choice theory often also focus on changes in the environment as the key determinant of output changes (Steinbruner 1974; Simon 1985). What makes the above analytical tradition cybernetic, rather than comprehensively rational or system analytic, is the limitation of input channels to one or a few important aspects of the environment.

2. Those finding election cycle effects on defense spending include Nincic and Cusack (1979) and Cusack and Ward (1981). Those finding no significant effect from election cycles include Zuk and Woodbury (1986) and Kamlet and Mowery (1987). Concerning unemployment, Griffin, Devine, and Wallace (1982); Cusack (1992); and Su, Kamlet, and Mowery (1993) found a statistically significant influence on defense spending while Majeski (1992) and Kiewiet and McCubbins (1991, 201–2) did not. Concerning arms race effects, those who concluded that U.S. and USSR defense spending responded primarily to their own inertia include Ostrom (1977) and Correa and Kim (1992). Yet later, Ostrom (1978) and Ostrom and Marra (1986) found that the two defense budgets did respond significantly to each other in some form of an arms race.

3. Those who specifically focused on inertia as a cause of defense spending include Ostrom (1977); Majeski (1983); and Correa and Kim (1992).

4. For explications of the rationality of planning, programming, and budgeting, see Hitch and McKean 1960, Schick 1966, and Lyden and Miller 1967. For reviews of new performance budgeting, see Osborne and Gaebler 1993, General Accounting Office 1996, Smith 1999, and Willand 1998. For analysis of relatively stable U.S. interests, see Morgenthau 1951 and Nuechterlein 1978.

5. Of course, a key cybernetic variable might have been Soviet military spending. That variable is tested herein as the "Soviet influence hypothesis."

6. This rational perspective is related with the traditional realism thesis of international relations (Mintz 1992, 1–8; Kegley 1995). But the rational perspective entered defense budgeting most strongly through the introduction of the planning-programming-budgeting system. Indeed, PPBS was held to be the "very model of rational budgeting" (Axelrod 1988, 283).

7. Similarly, other scholars have sought to explain U.S. support for other nations without dealing with defense spending. However, there are notable exceptions. Meernick, Krueger, and Poe concluded their analysis of foreign aid with a call to expand the study to include the use of military force, defense budgets, and foreign investment (1998,

81). Those who examined both domestic and security policies over time often found interactions between them. Kinsella concluded that superpower arms transfer policy was complicated by the "vicissitudes" of internal policies over time (1994, 578); and Ward, Davis, and Lofdahl found that tradeoffs between defense spending and economic growth "change dramatically in scope and direction over time" (1995, 45).

8. Most scholarly studies of resource allocations for national security have focused on either appropriations or outlays for the military services. However, this chapter is based on budget authority, a more comprehensive measure than appropriations and a more timely link to congressional decision making than outlays. Outlays for defense lag congressional decision making and defense budget authority in lengthy and complicated ways (True 1995). Appropriations can confuse the timing of contract decisions (Schick 1995b). Budget authority (formerly called new obligating authority) includes contract authority granted in advance of appropriations, and it is a more timely measure of decision making than outlays. This series extends the policy agendas data set to FY 1946 and FY 1998, and it adjusts the 1990, 1991, and 1992 figures for estimated transfers to defense from the Persian Gulf Defense Fund (see note 17).

9. Marra and Ostrom (1992) discuss the ambiguities and complexities in unraveling what would superficially seem to be relatively straightforward data choices. They refer to the ACDA/CIA approach used in this chapter as meeting the Howard Baker standard. That is to say, these estimates portray what was formally available to U.S. decision makers at the time of decision, rather than earlier forecasts or later revisions.

10. For example, see Hartmann and Wendzel 1985; Spanier 1988; and to a lesser degree Schulzinger 1984.

11. See Kennan 1947; Truman 1948; and National Security Council (NSC) 20/1 1948.

12. U.S. rearmament for the Cold War began in FY 1951 with the start of the Korean War (NSC-68 1950; Schilling, Hammond, and Snyder 1962; Wells 1979). Cold War containment was institutionalized in 1953 under a strategy of "massive retaliation" (NSC-162 1953; Dulles 1954; Huntington 1961; Schilling, Hammond, and Snyder 1962; and True 1997, 188–201). Jones, Baumgartner, and True (1998) discuss the impact on U.S. domestic budgets of what they term Eisenhower's "bombs and highways" (cf. Dodd 1994). However, the Soviets' first ICBM test in 1957 and subsequent public launch of *Sputnik* appear to have confirmed the "massive retaliation" reasoning of NSC-162 for some as well as energizing a reexamination that resulted later in the "flexible response" strategy of the Kennedy administration (Taylor 1959).

13. See Taylor 1959, Kennedy 1962, Allison 1971, Weigley 1973, and Kahan 1975 for continuation of Cold War containment under a new strategy of "flexible response."

14. See Berman 1982, Moise 1996, and Gittenger 1997 regarding U.S. entry into the war in Indochina.

15. See Nixon 1970, Kissinger 1979, and Spanier 1988 for the Vietnamization of the war under the Nixon Guam Doctrine and the shift of Cold War containment to détente.

16. See Carter 1980, Vance 1980, Korb and Laird 1981, Reagan 1981, and Reagan 1982 for pre- and post-Afghanistan U.S. policy toward the USSR. The Reagan defense buildup is a convenient but not entirely accurate term to refer to U.S. defense policy after the failed U.S. attempt to rescue hostages in Iran and the Soviet military invasion of Afghanistan in 1979. For the purposes of these analyses these two events (coupled with the 1980 election) constituted a tipping point and a major policy redirection, but that policy change began in the last year of the Carter presidency. President Reagan and Secretary Weinberger asked Congress for sweeping commitments to larger and more modern military forces and received them for the next four years. This set of policies across two administrations is referred to herein as the Reagan defense buildup.

17. See Bush and Scowcroft 1998; True 1995; and Meernick, Krueger, and Poe 1998 regarding U.S. foreign and defense policies after the dissolution of the Soviet Union and the Iraqi invasion of Kuwait. Defense budget authority figures in this chapter include credit entries in historical defense spending records from what appear to be transfers from the Persian Gulf Defense Fund (*FY2000 Budget,* table 5-1 and the *New York Times,* September 7–8, 1990).

18. Nor was there any statistically significant coefficient for levels or differences in Soviet spending lagged two years.

19. There was weak evidence of a contemporaneous relationship between Soviet defense spending at time *t* and U.S. defense spending at time *t*, but when AUTO models were employed or when first differences were taken, it disappeared.

20. However, the AUTO model did not confirm the statistical significance in the OLS model for the same period. Thus there is a possibility that the OLS relationship is spurious with decreases in Soviet spending acting here as a proxy of U.S. deficit concerns after FY 1985.

21. Meernick, Krueger, and Poe (1998, 75), for example, confirmed that Egypt and Israel accounted for the lion's share of foreign aid during the period of their study (1977–94).

22. Note, however, that Mayer (1992) found evidence of a biennial acceleration of defense contract awards, and he saw such changes in the timing of contract awards as evidence of an electoral cycle.

PART THREE

THE COEVOLUTION OF
THE ISSUES AND STRUCTURES
OF AMERICAN POLITICS

As political leaders and members of the public shift their attention from issue to issue and from dimension to dimension of the same issue, inevitably institutional changes occur as well. As new issues rise on the agenda, new government institutions are sometimes formed to help deal with them. For example, as health care has become an increasing part of the public agenda, a variety of new federal, state, and local institutions have been created in order to deal with different elements of it. It is important to remember that just after World War II, when our data series begin, there was no Medicare or Medicaid program, and federal health care spending, like federal activities in the areas of transportation, energy, environmental protection, education, and social welfare, was minimal by today's standards. As new issues have risen to the public agenda, one important institutional response has been the creation and growth of a great variety of new government agencies that did not exist, or existed only in limited forms, before 1940.

The coevolution of issues and structures that we refer to in the title of this section is not limited to the establishment and growth of new agencies as new issues are discovered, though the process does seem to begin there. Issues and institutions continue to change over time, and they change in tight synchronization with each other. As we discussed in part two, almost all issues of public policy are inherently multidimensional. Typically, complex social problems cannot be solved by focusing on only one element of the issue, but institutions usually have limited mandates. Further, as one problem is solved (say, producing electricity and delivering it across rural America — truly a great accomplishment of the twentieth century), other problems can be created (for example, issues of radioactive waste disposal, mine safety issues, or other byproducts of electrical production). As attention shifts from one dimension to another, or as new problems continually arise, institutions change as well.

They either alter their focus or they enter into competition or symbiosis with other institutions in government that deal with a different element of the same policy or with the new problems that were created by the activities of the old institutions. Institutions are not purely reactive in this process either; rather, institutional changes such as shifts in the memberships of various committees in Congress or changes in the personnel of government that stem from new elections can influence how policies are considered and which dimensions are given attention and which are ignored. In this part, we focus on the tight interactions between issues and structures of government. As one changes, so the other must adapt. As adaptations are made, so further changes can be required as institutions affect each other. The result can be a series of changes in both the institutional structures of government and the problems with which they deal.

The chapters included in this section share a focus on institutional change over time. They focus less than the chapters of the previous section on the development of public policies in a single issue area, but rather aim their attention at the institutional dynamics of the federal government. Jeffery Talbert and Matthew Potoski show the dramatic changes that have taken place over the postwar period in the structure and complexity of the public and governmental agenda. These changes have had many institutional impacts, and Glen Krutz discusses one of the more important ones in Congress. Congress increasingly deals with legislation in enormous pieces of "omnibus" bills, often running into thousands of pages, covering multiple issue areas, and leading to important changes in how average members of Congress can participate in the legislative process. John Wilkerson and colleagues discuss more changes in congressional behavior and the incentives to introduce legislation.

Scott Adler focuses on the tight interactions between changing foci of attention within two House committees and resulting changes in membership in those committees. If, as many congressional scholars have argued, members select certain committees because of their interest in the subject matter, then one might observe changes in membership as the focus of the committee shifts over time. Adler shows quite neatly how member recruitment onto House committees stems from, but then later reinforces, changes in the focus of attention of those committees. As one changes, so the other changes. As one remains stable, so the other will be stable. Issues and structures both react to the same changes, and to each other as well.

Congress has reacted to the rise in new issues in a number of ways; however, these are not the only possible ways in which government institutions could adapt. Frank Baumgartner and Jamie Gold compare the congressional agenda with that of the Supreme Court. While both national institutions have had to react to the increasing social and economic complexities of American society in the past fifty years, their institutional designs allow and force them to react to this development differently. Congress, with its diverse and decentralized power centers, has multiplied its activities, gained greater staff, and diversified its work tremendously over the past fifty years. The Supreme Court has done nothing of the kind. Though a great variety of different issues have been thrust on the Court just as has occurred with Congress, the two institutions could not have reacted in more contrasting ways. This comparison demonstrates clearly how institutions are not forced to react to the rise of new issues in the same way. Their internal structures also play important roles in determining their reactions to new issues. Considering institutional structure without paying attention to the changing set of public issues over time would be just as misleading as considering the changing set of public issues without looking at the particular institutional designs and behaviors of affected government agencies. Baumgartner and Gold show the independence and the contrasting reactions of two branches of government, both affected by a similar onslaught of new issues over the postwar period.

Government is larger now than it was when our data series begin. More importantly, government is more diverse. A great variety of different issues are simultaneously attended to every day in various institutions of government. As the mix of public issues has expanded and changed over the decades, it should be no wonder that institutional design, procedures, and interrelations have changed as well. These chapters show the tight links between the issues and structures of American politics.

8

THE CHANGING PUBLIC AGENDA
OVER THE POSTWAR PERIOD

JEFFERY C. TALBERT AND

MATTHEW POTOSKI

There are many issues that at least some people believe are problems worthy of Congress's attention. People believe that Congress should resolve funding inequities among schools, combat teenage pregnancy, increase the strength of the armed services, or stabilize the price of health care. While many issues such as these compete for Congress's attention at any one moment, space on the congressional agenda is limited. During most legislative sessions only a few major problems receive serious attention from Congress. During the 106th Congress the most pressing problems were the Clinton impeachment trial, preserving social security and Medicare, and deciding how to spend the projected budget surplus. These issues rose to the surface from among many competing problems to win a place in congressional hearings and perhaps become targets of proposed legislation.

Of course the remaining issues — those not winning a spot on the legislative agenda — do not simply go away. Issue advocates within Congress and without believe the government should focus more on cleaning the environment, pacifying the Middle East, getting tough with China, improving health care for the poor, or building a strategic missile defense system, and they would like to see Congress take some or more action in these areas. But Congress is not able to attend to all publicly salient issues or even to all the issues that are important to its members. As we show in this chapter, the congressional agenda has a limited capacity — Congress can address only a relatively small number of issues at any time. Just as individuals only focus on a portion of the many projects facing them during a day at work, Congress can focus on only a few of the potential issues that clamor for legislative attention. The organization of Congress and the limits of human cognitive abilities mean that only a small number of issues can find a place on the legislative agenda.

But this agenda capacity of Congress can change, particularly if legislative institutions are adapted to improve information processing. To investigate these dynamics, we adapt theories of agenda setting and legislative institutions to help understand how individuals and institutions divide their attention among competing issues. The central purposes of this chapter are to describe the capacity, complexity, and volatility of the congressional agenda and investigate how these agenda features have changed over time in response to changes in the institutional structure of Congress.

Describing the congressional agenda is important not only for understanding congressional behavior in general, but also for understanding the institutional context of other important political theories. The congressional agenda — the amount of information Congress can process during a legislative session — defines the parameters in which feedback (positive and negative) and serial shifts occur. In fact, understanding the dynamics of the congressional agenda can help link such theories with theories of legislative organization and behavior.

We begin with a brief survey of literature on individual, aggregate, and institutional information processing. Next, we explore how the organization of Congress may structure the capacity of its legislative and nonlegislative agendas. Third, we present evidence gauging the size and diversity of the congressional agenda since the post–World War II period. Finally, we offer some discussion and conclusions about the institutional capacity of Congress and its ability to respond to new issues and problems.

AGENDAS: ISSUES, INDIVIDUALS, AND INSTITUTIONS

We can study agenda dynamics across three levels of analysis. First, an individual issue agenda is the set of problems that a person believes merit government attention. An aggregate issue agenda is a collection of individual issue agendas. Finally, an institutional agenda refers to the issues and problems that a group of people is working on *as part of their formal or informal roles in an organization.*

INDIVIDUAL AGENDAS

At the individual level, a person's agenda is the group of issues she considers worthy of government attention. Some people have only a few issues they consider important, while others may focus their attention more broadly on many public issues. Of course, different people also think different issues are worthy of a place on the government's agenda. For example a student may have several issues she believes are important: government funding for higher education, protecting the environment, and perhaps abortion issues. The student may prioritize these issues, ranking one over the others in terms of how important, or salient, it is to her. Later, after the student graduates and enters the workforce, she may add other issues to her agenda, such as taxes or fair employment laws, and she may drop other issues (higher education funding) because they are less relevant to her daily life.

This idea of an individual agenda extends to formal political contexts as well. As Hall's (1996) work on participation in Congress shows, members are bound by time and resource constraints so that they cannot address all problems that interest them. Instead, they must focus their attention and decide where to invest their limited resources. Members of Congress, like the general public, have limited space on their issue agendas.

Consider, for example, the case of Representative Mike Andrews (D-Tex.), a fairly typical member of Congress during the summer of 1994. After an unsuccessful bid for a Senate seat earlier that year, the Houston Democrat was looking to end his twelve-year career in the House of Representatives on a positive note. Representative Andrews maintained an active position in Congress by focusing on issues that were either related to his constituency, such as health care and the energy industry, or reflected his own personal interests. He divided his attention and legislative staff accordingly, with the lion's share focused on health issues such as an alternative to President Clinton's health reforms, and the remainder dispersed among a smaller subset of salient issues. With the national attention focused on the Clinton health care reform movement, health issues were clearly the most important issues to the country, and in Representative Andrew's congressional office.

But during that summer, another unexpected issue came to the forefront and caught Representative Andrew's attention. In the late spring of 1994, The Walt Disney Company announced plans to construct a new theme park called "America" near Civil War battlefields in Manassas, Virginia. Although many in his constituency may not have even heard of Manassas, Representative Andrews had a keen personal interest in Civil War history and he generally opposed the commercialization of important Civil War sites such as Manassas. In response to the Disney initiative, Representative Andrews immediately shifted his attention away from health care reform and focused on the Manassas issue. During the few weeks that the "stop Disney" movement was at the top of his agenda, Andrews devoted much of his time to lobbying other members, initiating industry support, and holding a press conference on the Capitol steps. Thus, Andrews focused almost exclusively on the Disney project while paying much less attention to the other issues on his agenda.

As countless studies of human behavior demonstrate, individuals have limited cognitive ability to process information, and this translates into a limited ability to be actively involved in multiple issues. At the simplest level, individuals have a limited number of hours in the day to focus on problems, and thus are unable to be experts on all topics. Another explanation (Jones 1994) argues that a change in focus such as Andrews's is commonplace in decision making, reflecting a process where individual attentiveness may shift rapidly in response to external stimuli. Such rapid changes in focus are called "serial shifts" because they reflect the fact that individuals process information serially. In other words, each individual's attention to issues is a zero-sum game in which no one can be involved in all issues. Rather, people must choose which issues are most important to them while leaving the remainder for others or other times. Hall (1997) highlights this limitation in his work on participation by members of Congress. Time and staff limitations force members of Congress to focus on a few select issues. For Representative Andrews, this meant he had to sacrifice his focus on health reforms in order to redirect his attention to the Manassas controversy. Once the controversy subsided, Andrews renewed his earlier focus on health reforms.

THE PUBLIC AGENDA

The public's agenda is the aggregation of individuals' agendas. The public agenda measures the issues that are salient to the general public and reflects what is on the mind of the country, or the most important problems that people think about. Communication scholars have studied issues and their salience extensively for the public agenda, finding that the public agenda is usually composed of from five to seven issues at any given time (Shaw and McCombs 1977). Individual agendas are finite so that as new issues come about, individuals shift their attention from old topics to new ones. Zhu (1992) formalized this relationship, finding that new and old issues continually compete for saliency, where an increase in saliency for one issue leads to a decrease for some other issues. This zero-sum game for agenda status suggests a finite capacity for individuals and the public to engage in issues.

INSTITUTIONAL AGENDAS:
THE U.S. HOUSE OF REPRESENTATIVES

The Andrews-Disney example illustrates the finite agenda capacity at the individual level, and McCombs and Zhu (1995) have identified similar constraints operating on the public agenda. Both individual and aggregate agendas have finite capacity, resulting in a zero-sum game among issues competing for agenda space. Does a similar situation apply at the institutional level? The question becomes, what is the issue carrying capacity of Congress and how has it changed in the modern era? This chapter takes this issue head on and investigates the carrying capacity of the U.S. House agenda and whether its capacity changes over time. Specifically, the chapter investigates how much information Congress is able to process in a legislative session and how much complexity the legislative agenda can hold. Tracing the capacity and complexity of the congressional agenda between 1945 and 1994, this chapter shows how the shape of the legislative agenda was altered with the exponential growth in the professionalization of Congress and with the institutional changes of the 1974 reforms.

Moving to the more formal institutional agenda, we find dynamics similar to those for individuals and public agendas. The congressional agenda is the list of subjects or problems that legislators (or their staff) pay serious attention to over any given time period, as part of their formal and informal roles as members of an organization.[1] A look at a recent Congress illustrates the size and diversity of the issues that congress considers each legislative session. To match our Andrews-Disney case, we highlight the 103d Congress.

The 103d Congress had several legislative successes in the first session, but was more gridlocked during the second session. The 103d Congress was the first unified Democratic congressional-presidential government in decades. President Clinton offered a broad and sweeping agenda as the session began. The president's agenda included providing aid to the former Soviet republics, deficit reduction, family and medical leave, gays in the military, NAFTA, motor voter legislation, the Brady bill gun control legislation, and national service legislation. Yet many of his issues failed to attain broad support from established Democratic Party leaders, the Democratic rank and file, or the Republican opposition.

Priorities for the second session focused on health care reform, a crime reduction program, conservation legislation for the California desert, campaign finance reform, a balanced budget, Superfund reauthorization, safe drinking water legislation, and telecommunications legislation. The second session offered fewer successes for President Clinton's issues as health reform proved costly in terms of time and political resources. The president invested a great deal of resources into the health initiative, and Congress responded by placing health reform at the top of the agenda. For example, eight House full committees were involved in some aspect of health reform legislation, although in the end there was no presidential signature enacting a major health reform law. The attention focused on health reform may have contributed to Congress's inability to pass other major legislation, such as campaign finance and lobbying reform. Did health care reform displace issues such as these on the legislative agenda? How many major policy problems can Congress address at once? Our next section addresses this question by developing a set of theoretical questions that focus on the capacity of the legislative agenda.

CAPACITY, COMPLEXITY, AND VOLATILITY

Following other agenda scholars (McCombs and Zhu 1995) we describe the House agenda along three evaluative dimensions: capacity, complexity, and volatility. These are general agenda characteristics that can be used to describe not only institutional agendas, such as the House agenda, but also individual and aggregate agendas. Each dimension is discussed in turn below. While these dimensions may be fixed in a zero-sum game at the individual and aggregate levels, institutions may be altered in ways that expand their agenda capacity.

First, the capacity of the House agenda is the amount of information that the House can process in a specified time period, a two-year congressional term for the purposes of this chapter. Just as people have a natural limit to what they can accomplish — there are only so many hours in a day — Congress may also have an institutional carrying capacity that governs how much attention it can devote to items on its agenda. Congressional attention may be spread thinly over many issues, or it may be focused on just a few important problems. In either case, the capacity of the agenda, the amount of policy information that the House can process, has an inherent upper limit that is governed by the amount of information the institution can process during a session.

Second, the complexity of the House agenda is the diversity of the issues that the legislature addresses in a specified time, again a two-year session in this chapter. Diversity reflects the number of issues on the agenda so that more issues means a more diverse (complex) legislative agenda. Diversity also reflects the distribution of attention among the issues on the agenda so that a more

diverse agenda has a more equal distribution of attention among agenda issues. Consider a simple example illustrating this concept of diversity: three
issues are on the House agenda in two sessions. In the first session, the House
spends ninety percent of its attention on issue A and only five percent each on
issues B and C. In the second session, the House's attention is equally divided
among the three issues. According to our theory, the House agenda is more
diverse in the second session where the Congress's attention is more evenly
divided among the topics. This conceptualization of diversity was originally
developed to study market concentration and competition within and among
industries, as well as for communications theory to describe the entropy
of signals. The concept has also proved useful in studies of the diversity of
the *public's* issue agenda (McCombs and Zhu 1995) and other agenda arenas
(Baumgartner, Jones, and MacLeod 1998; Culbertson 1992; Chaffee and Wilson 1977).

Third, the volatility of the House agenda is the "life span" of issues on the
House agenda. Some items take longer to process through the agenda. For example, during the 106th Congress, the House devoted many days to hearings
on President Clinton's impeachment, creating a stable agenda item. In contrast, some issues require only a single day of hearings. If issues come and go
more rapidly, then they are considered or debated for shorter periods, which
may reduce the effectiveness of legislative decisions. In our theory, the House
agenda is more volatile when the House devotes less time to each item on its
agenda.

These three dimensions of the House agenda — capacity, diversity, and
volatility — may not be permanently fixed as they generally are for individuals. Rather, changing institutional structures over time may affect how much
attention the House can focus on its agenda and how many issues the agenda
can hold. The agenda is the amount of information the House is processing at
any given point in time. Therefore, to understand the evolution of the House
agenda we need to look toward those institutions that shape the House's ability to process information. Two institutions stand out in this regard: House
committees and professional legislative staff.

COMMITTEES

The study of committees and their relationship to policy outputs has consumed much of the research on Congress. At the simplest level, committees
were created to divide the workload through specialized issue areas where
efficiency and expertise could flourish. Regardless of the institutional flavor

on why committees exist, most "legislative work" — bill construction and debate, legislative markup, investigations and oversight, conferences between chambers — occurs during committee meetings. If at least part of the purpose of legislative committees is to process information for the parent chamber (Krehbiel 1991), then the number of committees and subcommittees should be positively related to the capacity, complexity, and stability of the House agenda. In 1974 the House reformed its committee system and expanded the number of committees and subcommittees, granted subcommittees new importance under the subcommittee "bill of rights," limited the number of leadership positions members could hold, and allowed legislation to be referred to multiple committees (Deering and Smith 1997). The 1974 committee reforms therefore should have increased the House's agenda capacity, diversity, and volatility.

PROFESSIONAL STAFF

Professional staff carry out much of the heavy lifting of legislative work — answering constituent mail, researching problems, scheduling hearings, drafting legislation, and so on. Thus, professional staff can grease the wheels of legislative production, freeing members to focus on making policy. Over the last fifty years, the House professional staff has grown substantially, from 1,440 in 1947 to 7,569 in 1989. This growth expanded the House's institutional potential and according to our theory the capacity, complexity, and volatility of its agenda.

Thus we expect the capacity, complexity, and volatility of the House agenda to change in response to the chamber's evolving institutional features. Specifically, the growth in the House's professional staff during the 1960s and early 1970s should have expanded the amount of attention the House can devote to issues on its agenda, the complexity of its agenda issues, and their volatility on the agenda. Likewise, we expect the 1974 House committee reforms also to expand the capacity, complexity, and volatility of the House agenda. Finally, we expect the House agenda to remain relatively stable in the post–committee reform period between 1974 and 1992, reflecting the relative stability of the House staffing and committee system during this period.

MEASURES AND FINDINGS

Our theory identifies three dimensions of the legislative agenda. The capacity of the agenda is the amount of information the U.S. House can process in a legislative session. The complexity of the legislative agenda is the diversity of the topics on the agenda. The volatility of the agenda is the amount of attention the House devotes to each specific issue on its agenda. To measure these dimensions, we draw on the Policy Agenda Project data covering the universe of congressional hearings between 1947 and 1993 (Baumgartner, Jones, and MacLeod 1998).

We separate our analyses into two parts. The legislative agenda consists of issues for which the U.S. House is considering proposed bills. The nonlegislative agenda consists of issues that the House is investigating or considering without proposed legislation. Thus, we report each of our measures dividing the hearings into legislative and nonlegislative types. Previous research finds that nonlegislative hearings are used to make claims over committee jurisdictional boundaries and to perform oversight and investigative functions (Talbert, Jones, and Baumgartner 1995).

The capacity of the House agenda is simply the number of legislative and nonlegislative hearings in each session from the 79th (1947– 48) through the 102d (1991–93) Congresses. More hearings means that the House can process more items on its agenda or can devote more attention to a narrower range of issues.

To measure the diversity of the legislative agenda, we employ an entropy measure borrowed from communications theory and used to gauge diversity in other agenda studies (McCombs and Zhu 1995; Culbertson 1992; Chaffee and Wilson 1977). Entropy (also called the H-statistic or Theil coefficient) is calculated from the proportion of hearings held in each minor topic category. More specifically, entropy is calculated as

$$E = \sum_{i=1}^{n} p_i \log(p_i)$$

Where p is the proportion of hearings in the ith category for each legislative session. Thus E is zero when all the hearings are in one category and grows with the number of categories (i) and as the p's become more uniform. This entropy measure captures the two dimensions of agenda complexity: the number of issues on the agenda (the number of i's) and the equality of the distribution of hearings among topic categories, as recorded in the Policy Agenda Project data. We calculated entropy scores for legislative and nonlegislative hearings for each Congress from the 79th to the 102d.

The volatility of the House agenda is the amount of time the House devotes to each issue on its agenda. To gauge this volatility, we use the average length

FIGURE 8.1 HOUSE STAFF LEVELS

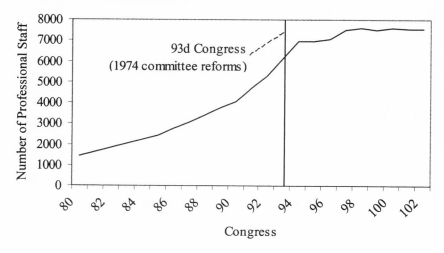

(in days) of hearings for each Congress from the 79th to the 102d. Shorter hearings in our theory mean a more volatile House agenda. The entropy, capacity, and volatility measures all parallel measures from previous empirical studies that used a similar theoretical framework to study the dynamics of the public's agenda (McCombs and Zhu 1995).

Our theory posits that the capacity, complexity, and volatility of the House legislative and nonlegislative agenda have expanded in response to changes in the institutional structure of Congress. The first institutional change is the expansion of congressional staffing. The number of House staff for each year as reported in *Vital Statistics on Congress* (Ornstein, Mann, and Malbin 1992) is shown in figure 8.1. The second institutional change is simply the 1974 congressional reforms.

To evaluate our theory, we present a series of simple figures comparing the House agenda capacity, diversity, and volatility with the amount of professional staffing in the House and the 1974 House committee reforms.

THE CAPACITY OF THE HOUSE AGENDA

Figure 8.2 shows the capacity of the House agenda for legislative and nonlegislative hearings from the 79th through the 102d Congresses. The left *y*-axis represents the number of hearings in each Congress and the *x*-axis represents time. Legislative hearings significantly outnumbered nonlegislative hearings during the early Congresses through the 92d Congresses. During the first eight congresses, the House legislative agenda capacity averaged about one

FIGURE 8.2 THE CAPACITY OF THE HOUSE AGENDA, NUMBER OF HEARINGS

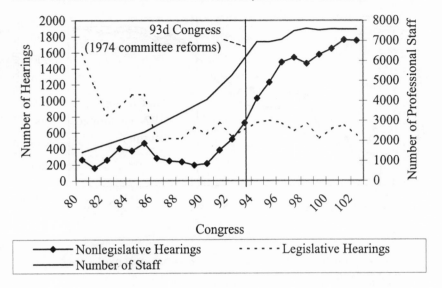

thousand hearings in each session, while the nonlegislative agenda averaged only around three hundred hearings per session.

As shown in figure 8.2, starting around the 91st Congress the capacity of the House nonlegislative agenda expanded dramatically; it rose from about two hundred hearings in the 91st Congress to over seven hundred during the 93d Congress following the 1974 committee reforms. Meanwhile, the capacity of the House legislative agenda held constant, averaging about six hundred hearings from the 88th through the 102d Congresses. Consistent with our theory, the growth in the capacity of the House nonlegislative agenda parallels the expansion of the House staff, although it preceded to some extent the 1974 committee reforms. As the House staff and committee system grew during the 1960s and 1970s, so to did the capacity of the House agenda.

However, the dynamics in the capacity of the House legislative agenda remain a bit of an anomaly. First, according to the results presented in figure 8.2, the legislative capacity declined substantially from the 80th to the 86th Congress, without any apparent change in the House's institutional capacity. Second, the capacity of the legislative agenda remained constant when our theory predicts that it would increase; legislative capacity should have expanded during the 1960s and 1970s (the 86th through the 96th Congresses), while figure 8.2 shows that it held steady.

FIGURE 8.3 THE COMPLEXITY OF THE HOUSE AGENDA, ENTROPY SCORES

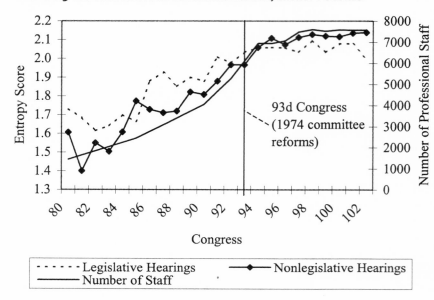

THE COMPLEXITY OF THE HOUSE AGENDA

Figure 8.3 shows the complexity of the House agenda between the 80th and 102nd congresses. The left y-axis represents the diversity of the agenda as measured by the entropy of the hearing topics, and the x-axis represents time. The dashed line represents the entropy of legislative hearings and the solid line represents nonlegislative hearing entropy. Overall, the complexity of the House agenda also shows a substantial increase between the 80th and 102nd Congresses. Over this period, the legislative and nonlegislative hearing entropy increased from 1.7 to 2.0 and 1.6 to 2.1, respectively.

The growth in the complexity of the House agenda coincided with substantial growth in House legislative staff and committee systems. The large staff, in this context, allowed the House to devote attention to a broader, more diverse range of legislative and nonlegislative topics. The 1974 House committee reforms also coincided with an increasingly complex House agenda. According to figure 8.2, the reforms coincided with an increase in the entropy of legislative and nonlegislative hearings. However, following the reforms, the complexity of the House agenda stayed fairly constant, hovering around 2.05 for the legislative agenda and 2.10 for the nonlegislative agenda. This leveling off in the growth of House agenda complexity occurred against a backdrop of relatively stable House staffing levels and relatively few (and minor) institutional changes to the committee and staff systems.

While the complexity of both the legislative and nonlegislative agenda increased dramatically from the 80th through the 94th Congresses, the nonlegislative agenda became more complex at a faster rate, as shown in figure 8.3. In the early Congresses, the legislative agenda was generally more complex than the nonlegislative agenda. However, after the 1974 committee reforms, the situation was reversed and the House's nonlegislative agenda was consistently more complex than its legislative agenda.

THE VOLATILITY OF THE HOUSE AGENDA

Figure 8.4 shows the volatility of the House legislative and nonlegislative agendas from the 80th through the 102d Congresses. Overall, the results show that the House agenda has become significantly more volatile over time, with agenda items in the modern Congress receiving lower levels of debate than those in earlier periods. In particular, the volatility score of the legislative agenda declined from an average of around four days per hearing during the 80th through 90th Congresses to fewer than two days per hearing during the 102d Congress. The volatility of the House nonlegislative agenda followed a somewhat similar path, although its initial volatility (about two days per hearing prior to the 85th Congress) was much lower than the legislative agenda's. By the mid-1960s, however, the volatility of the nonlegislative agenda was comparable to the legislative agenda volatility and the two experienced a near identical decline from the 90th through the 102d Congresses.

Again, these changes in the volatility of the House agendas trace important institutional changes. Agenda volatility increased as the House institutional capacity expanded with the growth in staff through the 1960s and 1980s and the 1974 committee reform. This volatility may reflect an agenda where issues are more demanding and complex and may be a consequence of the competition for attention from a substantially more complex issue agenda. A more complex agenda may mean that the House has less time to focus on every individual item.

In sum, the House's legislative and nonlegislative agendas are not infinite. Not every issue can receive legislative attention or be the subject of congressional hearings. Nor are these agendas static. Clearly, as others in this volume have shown, the mix of issues on the House agenda changes over time as attention to different problems waxes and wanes. This chapter has shown that

FIGURE 8.4 THE VOLATILITY OF THE HOUSE AGENDA, AVERAGE LENGTH OF HEARING

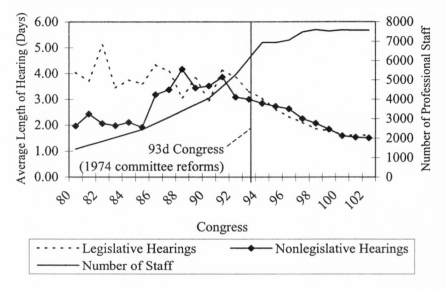

the House agenda is dynamic in another sense as well. The dimensions of the House agenda, its capacity, complexity, and volatility, have evolved over time, largely in response to changing institutional features in the House. The expansion of the House committee system in 1974 and the growth in its professional staff during the 1960s and 1970s has allowed House to conduct more hearings, to consider a more complex mix of issues, and to process the issues more quickly.

DISCUSSION AND CONCLUSION

Nobody cares equally about every issue. Some people focus more on the environment, others on taxes or foreign affairs. Likewise, some people are politically active and care about many policy issues, while others are more apathetic and care only about one or two issues. In any case, no one can become actively involved in every issue because our natural cognitive limitations and the number of available work hours bound our ability to process information. This applies within politics as well. Members of Congress can devote attention to only a few of the many issues that compete for their attention.

This chapter has shown the House as an institution has a finite issue agenda. The House can divert attention to only a few of the many issues that are important to its members. Using the measures of capacity, complexity, and volatility, Congress appears to process an increasingly complex agenda along with more demands to consider additional issues. In response to the changing issue system, Congress has responded as an institution by reforming its organization and expanding its professional staff. These changes have allowed the institution to consider more issues, but the increased capacity comes at a cost of shorter review of issues.

The idea of a finite but evolving House agenda is important because it defines the context for many political and policy process theories. Entrepreneurs competing for political attention can win a place on the agenda only by promoting their issue against attention potentially given to other issues. A serial shift (Jones 1994), or any less dramatic change in attention toward an issue, comes at the expense of other issues currently enjoying the congressional spotlight, although institutional changes that expand the House's agenda capacity can mitigate this zero-sum game. In the context of Kingdon's (1984) policy streams and garbage can model, the finite capacity of the House agenda limits at any given time the potential for joining policy problems with policy solutions to those issues on the congressional agenda.

Of course this chapter raises more questions than it answers. Future research in this area should investigate more closely the determinants of the capacity, complexity, and volatility of the House agenda. Beyond the role of committees and staff discussed above, other institutional features may structure the House agenda. For example, stronger parties may expand the agenda by allowing members to devote more of their attention to a broader range of issues. Informal institutions may influence the agenda as well, such as the caucus system or demands placed by interest groups. In addition to institutions, the broader social and political context may play a role in shaping the House agenda. The agenda may be narrower under divided government as heightened party competition drains attention and energy from solving public problems. Or, just as the issues within the agenda change because the public's attention shifts, the capacity of the House agenda may also change as the public devotes its attention to a larger or smaller number of issues.

Finally, additional research should investigate how the structure of the House agenda — its capacity, complexity, and volatility — shapes how the House performs its functions. For example, does the House conduct more effective bureaucratic oversight when its agenda is more complex or simpler? How does the capacity of the House's agenda shape its ability to pass laws or address important national problems? In short, does a larger, more complex, or more volatile agenda mean a more effective House? Such ties to effective legislative governance may place the House agenda near the heart of political scholarship.

NOTE

1. Our definition of the House agenda closely follows that proposed by Kingdon (1984, 3). "The *agenda,* as I conceive it, is the list of subjects or problems to which government officials, and people outside of government closely associated with those officials, are paying some serious attention at any given time" (italics in original). We limit our definition to members of the House and their staff, reflecting the focus of this chapter.

9

OMNIBUS LEGISLATION: AN INSTITUTIONAL REACTION TO THE RISE OF NEW ISSUES

GLEN S. KRUTZ

Omnibus legislating is the controversial practice of combining numerous measures from disparate policy areas in one massive bill. This technique has proliferated on Capitol Hill across the post–World War II period and it alters the lawmaking process in important ways. Omnibus packages are considered "must-pass" bills because they typically contain a nucleus that has widespread support in Congress (Sinclair 1992, 668). The interesting part, however, and where the power exists for congressional leaders, is deciding what gets folded in along with the nucleus. Bills that have become overly controversial, have had too much attention paid to them, and therefore are likely to fail alone, can be tucked away in an omnibus bill. Therein, the controversy and attention paid to the items suffocates under the massive nucleus of the omnibus measure. Once assembled, the nucleus is what is debated, not the attachments. Members-at-large, busy people with too much to do (Hall 1996; Kingdon 1981), pay attention to the main part of the bill as it is processed through Congress and are seldom aware of the minutiae of omnibus packages (Oleszek 1989; Smith 1989). When asked about the contents of a recent omnibus package, Senator Robert Byrd replied, "Do I know what's in this bill? Are you kidding? No. Only God knows what's in this monstrosity" (Hager 1998).

Bryan Jones asks the important question: "how do the structure and organization of democratic institutions direct the attention of policymakers to issues?" (1994, 7). Shifting attentiveness can dramatically affect political choices and outcomes. Omnibus legislating is just such a technique for directing the attention of policy makers to certain things and away from others. Members do not pay attention to the attachments, which are safe in the friendly confines of an omnibus bill. The omnibus strategy affects outcomes because omnibus bills (consisting of the nucleus plus previously controversial attachments) are a different set of outputs than what would be achieved if all the bills were processed sequentially.

Yet, while institutional mechanisms like the omnibus method affect how political issues are attended to and thus subsequent political outcomes, understanding that is only half of the theoretical picture. Institutions are not simple ex ante bargains struck before the game begins (Binder 1997; Dion 1997). Institutions change and develop dynamically; that is, they are partly endogenous (their change may be explained by other factors) and partly exogenous (they help explain change in other phenomena). When institutions are studied across time, we gain important and interesting insights into the nature of congressional change more broadly (Baumgartner and Jones 1993; Baumgartner, Jones, and MacLeod 1998b; Binder 1997; Bosso 1987; Cooper and Young 1989; Gamm and Shepsle 1989; Jenkins 1998; Jones, Baumgartner, and Talbert 1993; King 1997; Schickler 1998).

In the case of omnibus legislating, the technique affects the policy process and outcomes presently, but how did we get here? Why did Congress move to omnibus bills across the post–World War II period? In this paper, I argue that the omnibus method, while appearing overtly political in any one circumstance, is an example of congressional institutions adapting to tough governing circumstances. Chief among these tough circumstances, yet receiving little previous attention from scholars and political pundits, is the rise of new issues and the redefinition of old issues pressed upon a committee system that was designed for the most part in the 1940s. Alongside this increasing issue complexity and committee system fragmentation, I consider several other important environmental factors that have been discussed by legislative scholars, like increased instance of divided party government and ballooning deficits.

I also provide a strategic actor-level perspective that captures how the omnibus change carried out in reality. The main development at that endogenous level of analysis was that, in the aforementioned environment of increasing issue complexity, members found it necessary to delegate more authority in lawmaking to party leaders (who bundle the omnibus bills). The environmental (exogenous) factors and the endogenous ones are indeed self-reinforcing. New issues arise, making the governing context more complex. Leaders accrue more power so that laws can actually be made (via the omnibus technique for example). This increased leader power changes the relative powers of members and leaders. Leaders, with the omnibus technique, find it easier to introduce new issues. This process, like many others covered in this book, is a positive feedback process. Changes in the environment have had interactive effects when combined with the internal balance of power in Congress.

Hence, two main points of this chapter are, first, that institutions are inherently dynamic and, second, that any theory of institutional change must capture that dynamism. The move to omnibus legislating is an example of a large-scale change in lawmaking carried out over time that is reflective of the general movement of power from committee chairs to central party leaders.

The remainder of the chapter proceeds as follows. I begin by discussing in more detail the omnibus concept. Next, a theoretical framework is developed for why omnibus bills are employed, including micro- and macro-level incentives. I present an original definition of omnibus bill in the subsequent section. The findings of a longitudinal analysis of aggregate omnibus use per Congress from 1949 to 1994 are then presented. I conclude the chapter by discussing the dynamic interplay of issues and institutions suggested by the rise and impact of omnibus legislation.

THE CONCEPT OF OMNIBUS LEGISLATION

Several scholars have concluded that a major recent change in the legislative process is the development of omnibus legislation (Baumgartner et al. 1997; Browne 1995; Cameron et al. 1997; Davidson and Oleszek 1994, 1998; Mayhew 1991; Oleszek 1989; Sinclair 1992, 1995, 1997; Smith 1989). Scholars studying lawmaking outputs note an increase in omnibus use (Baumgartner et al. 1997; Cameron et al. 1997; Mayhew 1991; Sinclair 1992, 1995, 1997), a decrease in the numbers of bills reaching chamber floors (Smith 1989), and a decrease in public laws enacted (Baumgartner et al. 1997; Ornstein, Mann, and Malbin 1996). The move to omnibus legislating is particularly important because these packages present a viable alternative route for policy entrepreneurs pushing legislation. Omnibus packages almost invariably succeed. In a study of prominent failures, Edwards, Barrett, and Peake (1997) did not come across many omnibus bills. That they did not find any is not surprising because omnibus bills almost always succeed. Hence, measures that become attached to them almost always become law. In contrast, the overwhelming majority of standard bills fail at some point in the legislative process (Ornstein, Mann, and Malbin 1996).

Omnibus bills also alter the time-honored legislative process. This technique affects democratic deliberation; omnibus bills are often fast-tracked through committees with less consideration than typical bills. Once assembled by leaders in the prefloor process, omnibus packages are treated as one piece of legislation, thus seriously restricting the choices available to members on the floor. Members-at-large must take it or leave it and are seldom aware of the details contained in omnibus bills (Sinclair 1992, 1995, 1997; Smith 1989). Leaders, on the other hand, possess the critical and complex information on these measures and are strengthened by omnibus bills. "These are must-pass bills and only the party leadership possess the coordination capacity required to put together and pass such legislation" (Sinclair 1992, 668; see also Cox and McCubbins 1993, 248–49).

An agenda control and coalition-building tool, omnibus bills are typically assembled in order to get something passed. The big bill has its own locus of attention and is more likely to have support from the important players in the legislative process. By focusing on one part of an omnibus bill that enjoys widespread support, party leaders (who assemble the bills) take attention away from controversial items of certain substantive policy areas. The controversial items if considered alone are thought to face opposition within Congress or at the president's desk. Omnibus bills provide a way to get by the Congress and/ or the president in enacting such policies; they provide greater certainty (Bach and Smith 1988). Two brief case examples illustrate the strategy involved in omnibus bills.

GETTING THROUGH CONGRESS

In 1982, several members and leaders sought to revive a dormant airport development program that had failed to be reauthorized in the previous Congress. The previous act expired in 1980. Lawmakers had failed in numerous prior attempts to bring the airport improvement act to the floor for two reasons. First, members disagreed over the future direction of the program (Sarasohn 1982). Second, if considered alone, the bill was required to take a circuitous route because five House and four Senate committees had to be coordinated to secure such an airport development program. To get the bill through the legislative process, Senate Majority Leader Robert Dole (R-Kan.) together with Commerce Committee Chairman Robert Packwood (R-Ore.) attached the measure to an omnibus tax bill with widespread support making its way through Congress.

GETTING BY THE PRESIDENT

In the 99th Congress (1985–86), health care policy featured a strong disagreement between congressional leaders and the president. President Reagan promised vetoes of several individual bills related to child vaccinations and the Medicare program, while favoring other established programs in the health care policy domain that were being considered in the legislative process. To get the programs by the president, leaders packaged numerous bills into a large and complex omnibus health measure. Expressing major reservations about provisions in the bill, the president nevertheless signed it (Congressional Quarterly 1987).

In summary, these case examples illustrate how omnibus bills provide a way to enact policies whose outcome in one or both of the lawmaking steps (passing the Congress and president) is doubtful or unclear. That is, the mechanism provides a way to manage uncertainty in the legislative process (Bach and Smith 1988; Browne 1995; Oleszek 1989; Smith 1989). Moreover, in addition to showing the coalition-building uses of omnibus packaging, these illustrations also suggest dual motives that may underpin omnibus usage.

The airport development program was bundled with the tax bill to squelch controversy. However, the tactic also was a way around having to have nine different committees in two different chambers weigh in on it. The first rationale suggests politics, the second efficiency. The health care omnibus bill was indeed a way to get by the president — again politics. Health care, though, is the most fragmented of issues on Capitol Hill with scores of committees having a claim to jurisdiction (Baumgartner, Jones, and MacLeod 1997). Bundling health care policies together centrally and moving them to the floor suggests an efficient alternative to jurisdictional wrangling. These differing political and efficiency rationales exemplify two schools of thought that have developed on the nature of congressional change and legislative organization, one emphasizing efficiency and the other politics.

STUDYING INSTITUTIONAL DYNAMICS

The study of institutional arrangements and mechanisms in Congress has been an on-again/off-again enterprise (Binder 1997). Several studies early in the development of the discipline examined institutional change: McConachie's (1898) work on committees, Harlow's (1917) work on legislative methods, and Hasbrouck's (1927) research on party government. An "off-again" period began after World War II in which political scientists became more interested in explaining individual-level political behavior than institutions.

The last few decades are an "on-again" period, beginning with Polsby's (1968) study of the institutionalization of the House (Baumgartner, Jones, and MacLeod 1998b; Binder 1997; Cooper 1977; Cooper and Young 1989; Gamm and Shepsle 1989; Jones, Baumgartner, and Talbert 1993; Katz and Sala 1996; King 1997; Sinclair 1997; Wright 1997). However, studies of institutions still pale in comparison to the volumes of research on individual member behavior. While scholars generally consider them to be important determinants of policy outcomes, institutional arrangements are portrayed in two vastly different lights. To some, institutional arrangements are exogenous factors to congressional decision making determined a priori (e.g., Krehbiel 1991; Shepsle 1979; Shepsle and Weingast 1987).

In contrast, I follow here the lead of recent research that considers institutional arrangements and mechanisms — while not easily changed — themselves as endogenous potential objects of choice, indeed not something we should assume to have been set in advance and immune from change. This literature asks why we have the institutional arrangements that we do and how they change (e.g., Baumgartner, Jones, and MacLeod 1998b; Binder 1995, 1996, 1997; Cooper 1977; Cooper and Young 1989; Gamm and Shepsle 1989; Jenkins 1998; Jones, Baumgartner, and Talbert 1993; Katz and Sala 1996; King 1994, 1997; Schickler 1998; Sinclair 1997).

To illustrate the distinction between these two views of institutional arrangements, the "purely exogenous institutions" proponents consider committee jurisdictions as rigid determinants of policy outcomes. In contrast, King (1994, 1997) conceives of jurisdictions as "turbulent battle grounds on which policy entrepreneurs seek to expand their turf" and "heavy with policy consequence" (1994, 48). In a study that directly pertains to the topic of omnibus legislation, Sinclair (1997) finds that many successful bills do not follow the textbook bill-becomes-a-law diagram, emphasizing the increasing importance of special rules and procedures, what she calls "unorthodox lawmaking." If institutional arrangements were entirely exogenous, then all bills would be treated the same way once the legislative game begins. Sinclair shows that this is increasingly not the case.

ALTERNATIVE EXPLANATIONS OF INSTITUTIONAL DEVELOPMENT

Among those studying the emergence of congressional institutions, two schools of thought have developed. In one approach, change is based on institutional concerns; in the other, changes bubble up from the political actions of goal-oriented actors. One of these approaches — the efficiency theory of institutional change — holds that changes are driven by institutional concerns (Cooper 1977; Cooper and Young 1989; Polsby 1968). To illustrate, Cooper and Young (1989) posit that the House gradually changed rules pertaining to bill introductions in the nineteenth century largely in response to changes in the size and complexity of the House agenda. Polsby (1968) argues that as the responsibilities of the national government increased and as career paths led to longer terms of service, the House developed an organizational structure that emphasized a division of labor, routine modes of procedure, and respect of seniority.

A second school of thought — the redistributive theory of institutional change — holds that institutions are designed to allocate power and resources to certain actors over others (Binder 1995, 1996, 1997; Gamm and Shepsle 1989; Katz and Sala 1996; Mayhew 1974). For example, Binder (1996) finds that short-term partisan goals — not secular trends as suggested by many (Cooper 1977) — shaped both the creation and suppression of rights for partisan and political minorities in the House from 1789 to 1990. Gamm and Shepsle (1989) argue that Speaker Henry Clay worked for the development of a standing committee system in the House in an effort to hold together a coalition after the War of 1812.

Some scholars find support for both approaches in examining particular institutional developments. King (1997) finds a mix of efficiency considerations (parliamentarians using the criterion of the "weight of the bill") and policy entrepreneurial activity in explaining day-to-day bill referrals to committees. Hardin (1998a) studies aggregate-level jurisdictional concentration for health care policy across time and finds that jurisdictions are both a way for committees to promote certainty and a mechanism for members to fish for constituents.

Which rationale (efficiency or politics) characterizes the omnibus change? I next build a theoretical framework for understanding why and when omnibus bills are employed. This framework, like the research of King (1997) and Hardin (1998a), suggests a role for both explanations of institutional change.

THEORETICAL FRAMEWORK: WHY OMNIBUS LEGISLATION?

I described above two processes, interaction among leaders and members and between Congress and the president, that reflect the two major steps that bills must clear to be enacted into law. Omnibus bills provide a technique to clear both hurdles. To provide logic for why Congress increasingly utilized omnibus bills, I develop explanations of omnibus usage based on these two steps and environmental factors.

One dynamic exists between congressional leaders and members-at-large. A second dynamic involves the Congress and president. How does omnibus lawmaking help these strategic actors in achieving their goals? Further, and particularly pertinent to our examination of the rise of omnibus legislation, these two dynamics play out within unique governing contexts that may change across time. Certain contexts place strain on congressional institutions and make it more likely that actors will rely on nontraditional means of

FIGURE 9.1 THEORETICAL FRAMEWORK

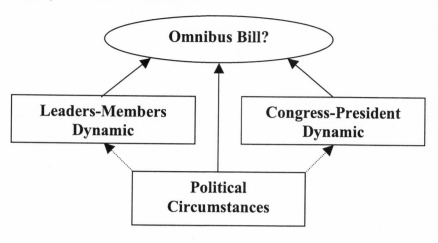

policy making such as omnibus legislating. Figure 9.1 presents a graphical outline of the basic framework.

LEADERS-MEMBERS

I focus first on the relationship between those with the resources to package
bills (party leaders) and members-at-large. What do leaders and members
have to gain from omnibus legislation? How are their goals advanced? Leaders gain more power with omnibus bills (Sinclair 1992, 1995, 1997) and, because
they assemble omnibus bills, are afforded the opportunity to advance party
agenda items. Both of these (more power and pushing an agenda) are principal goals of party leaders (Bader 1997; Cox and McCubbins 1993; Davidson
and Oleszek 1998; Sinclair 1995).

Why do members allow leaders to package bills? Members surrender the
right to consider items one at a time so leaders can get legislative items passed
that face uncertainty in the regular legislative process. In allowing packaging
to occur, members are disadvantaged in three ways. First, they are giving the
leaders a potent source of power to enact items. Second, in allowing leaders to
package bills, members are giving up traditional channels of deliberation. On
omnibus items, rank-and-file members seldom are included in the minutiae
of lawmaking (Smith 1989) and have a severe informational disadvantage on
the floor (Oleszek 1989; Smith 1989; Sinclair 1997). Third, omnibus bills are so
vast, election opponents may potentially pick whatever part of an omnibus
bill they want to hammer the incumbent with in a campaign.

What do members gain while they are disadvantaged? After all, a bargain suggests that both sides benefit; what incentives do members have to allow omnibus packaging by leaders? Members are driven by many goals, but primarily by reelection (Fenno 1973; Hall 1996; Mayhew 1974) and the desire to enact their policy preferences (Fenno 1973; Hall 1996). In exchange for allowing packaged bills by leaders, members get two major benefits that aid in achieving these overarching goals of reelection and making public policy. These benefits help us to see why members accept the costs associated with omnibus use.

First, omnibus bills potentially aid the members' reelection chances. Mayhew (1974), Fiorina (1977), and Arnold (1979) discuss the many features of congressional institutions that contribute to reelection of incumbents. The omnibus mechanism in part serves the needs of incumbents through the use of distributive or pork-barrel politics. Members may put up with omnibus bills if the mechanism provides some distributive benefit that will aid reelection. Because omnibus bills nearly always succeed, members get a surefire way to get distributive items incorporated into omnibus bills that might be opposed if pursued sequentially.

Second, through the omnibus bill attachment process, members also get a potential vehicle for enacting policies they care about. Among other things (position taking and credit claiming; see Mayhew 1974), members want to get their bills passed. In institutions with large continuing agendas and therefore a scarcity of attention, members find it difficult to get their bills noticed and moved forward. The overwhelming majority of bills fail before getting a hearing (Ornstein, Mann, and Malbin 1996). One way to get around the traditional and extremely challenging typical legislative channels is to get your provision included in an omnibus bill. Leaders help in this regard because if members are reelected, then their party retains majority status, a principal goal of leaders.

If both sides of this bargain get benefits, why not use omnibus bills all the time? A main goal of leaders is to stay leaders, that is to not be thrown out of their leadership posts by members-at-large. The rise and fall of Speaker Newt Gingrich illustrates all too well that legislative leadership power is tenuous. Therefore, leaders will avoid abuse of the omnibus technique. There likely exists some threshold above which omnibus use will lead to retaliation by members. Therefore, leaders cannot use this technique all the time.

CONGRESS-PRESIDENT

A second omnibus bargain occurs between Congress and the president (really between congressional leaders and the president). What does the president gain? After all, one expectation is that omnibus bills will include measures that the president opposes and yet will not veto as part of the package. Why does the president even participate in omnibus bargains? Why hold his nose and sign these measures into law? Why not just veto everything?

Presidents, too, want to enact their policy preferences, an assumption presidential-congressional relations scholars typically employ (e.g., Bond and Fleisher 1990; Edwards 1989). Beyond that assumption, the motivations of presidents in policy making are less focused upon than the much-discussed motivations of members of Congress. First-term presidents surely want to get reelected. Getting something done in policy making may aid a president's reelection prospects (in the case of first-term presidents). There is also some indication that presidents care about their historical legacy. Enacting policies they prefer and promises they make may lead to a favorable historical rating of their presidency.

Presidents understand that our legislative institutions were designed to block items rather than enact policy. One important thing presidents can gain from omnibus bills is the possibility of having their own agenda items folded in as attachments to omnibus bills. This alternate route gets the president around having his bills go it alone in the legislative process and perhaps getting blocked. The president, like members of Congress, faces a presumption of failure for bills introduced in Congress (Krutz, Fleisher, and Bond 1998). While more likely to succeed in the legislative process than a typical member of Congress, only one-fourth of presidential proposals are enacted into law in a form still recognizable to the president (Peterson 1990). In congressional committees, presidential drafts are less likely to move forward than legislation pushed by the given committee and subcommittee leaders (Larocca 1995). Presidents, therefore, have something potentially very helpful to gain in omnibus bargains. Congress (in the form of the leaders and the members), on the other hand, is willing on occasion to incorporate the president's legislative items in order to avert a veto of items the Congress wants that are contained in omnibus bills.

GOVERNING CIRCUMSTANCES

Party leaders, members-at-large, and the president operate under political circumstances, some of which complicate the legislative process. In such scenarios it becomes particularly necessary to find a way to bring certainty, and omnibus use is more likely. Circumstances that challenge the capabilities of our legislative institutions include deficit politics, divided party control, ripe conditions for minority obstructionism, issue complexity and committee fragmentation, and burgeoning congressional workloads. These five factors break up nicely into political explanations (divided government, ripe conditions for minority obstructionism), efficiency explanations (issue complexity and workload), and a hybrid of the two (deficit politics).

Divided government. A challenging contextual circumstance for lawmaking arises from divided government. When the president is from the opposition party in Congress, it is likely that the president (who typically comes from the ideological mainstream of his party; see Bond and Fleisher 1990) will oppose many of the initiatives forwarded from the majority party and veto them. Moreover, presidential items will more likely be blocked in Congress since the opposition party controls the institutional levers of power. This predicament presents a particularly heightened sense of uncertainty for both branches and increases the likelihood that omnibus bargains will be struck. Therefore, omnibus use is expected to be higher in divided than in unified government.

Ripe conditions for minority obstructionism. Minority obstructionism provides a challenging governing situation for legislative institutions. Certain governing conditions are riper for minority obstructionism than others. The most ideal conditions for the majority party are its majority is large and party unity is high, as is the case during realignments (Brady 1988). Under such circumstances, the majority party can use traditional legislative channels to push through its favored policies. In contrast, a more daunting legislative task faces the majority party when it has a narrow majority and its unity is low, and the minority party is cohesive. It is in these times that we expect the majority party to look for special legislative procedures for moving its agenda past a noisome minority. Hence, omnibus use is more likely when majority party has a small majority and its unity is low than when it has a large majority and party unity is high.

Issue complexity. Deficit politics, divided government, and partisanship are topics discussed by political pundits and scholars alike. The increasing complexity of the national policy agenda is a less studied and understood phenomenon. Issue complexity refers to the degree of concentration of congressional attention to particular issues. An issue agenda is more complex when attention is dispersed across many issues and less complex when attention is devoted to a few main issues.

In their study of congressional hearings, Baumgartner, Jones, and Rosenstiehl (1997) displayed the increase in issue complexity that has occurred in Congress since 1947. "Legislative activity was concentrated in a smaller number of issue-areas in the early post-war period. Increasingly, congressional attention has become spread thinner among a wider range of topics than in the past, suggesting greater competition for access to the congressional agenda" (Baumgartner, Jones, and Rosenstiehl 1997, 13). In a study of legislative production, they also show an increase in omnibus use across the same time period. They suggest that the increasing complexity of the issue agenda since World War II is related to the rise of omnibus usage. "Omnibus bills provide a way to get things done in an increasingly complex issue environment" (Baumgartner, Jones, and Rosenstiehl 1997, 1).

Increased issue complexity manifests itself in committee fragmentation. The setup of the congressional committee system was developed in the 1946 reorganization of Congress when, as Baumgartner, Jones, and MacLeod (1998b) show, just a few main issues were on the agenda. Since that time, several new issues that do not fit into one committee's jurisdiction have risen on the agenda. These issues include health care and environmental policy. As a result, issues have increasingly been considered in more than one principal committee. Issues increasingly "spill over" into several committees. This jurisdictional fragmentation becomes a structural strain on the institution. While sharing issues among committees allows institutions the flexibility to address new and expanding issues (Baumgartner and Jones 1993; King 1997; Jones, Baumgartner, and Talbert 1993), it also makes coordination a big challenge. In a highly fragmented committee system, omnibus bills are a way to make policy because they centralize authority with party leaders.

Congressional workload. A contextual strain forwarded by organizational theorists as important to understanding institutional change is workload (Cooper 1977; Cooper and Young 1989). When workload increases, pressure is placed on an institution with finite time and resources. In this scenario, a legislative technique is needed to make lawmaking more efficient. Omnibus bills are larger and processed more quickly than traditional bills, and may thus provide an efficient way to conduct legislative business. According to this logic, we expect higher levels of omnibus use when the congressional workload increases. I suspect, however, that an alternative response of congressional institutions to increased workload would be to simply increase staff size where needed. Therefore, this contextual strain may not have the impact of the other political contexts.

Deficit politics. At the top of almost everyone's list as a cause of the omnibus revolution is budget deficit politics (Davidson and Oleszek 1998; Oleszek 1989; Sinclair 1997; Smith 1989). Deficit politics, the argument goes, severely constrains lawmaking and makes it harder to get anything new done (Brady and Volden 1998; Sinclair 1995, 1997; Wright 1997). One way for the players to conduct business in such a challenging environment is to utilize omnibus bills. "The need for omnibus measures in the first place is the result of a spending policy gridlock and highly constrained spending choices" (Smith 1989, 57). Hence, omnibus use should increase when the budget deficit increases. Is this a political or efficiency explanation of omnibus use? I believe it could be either. Using omnibus bills in a period of high deficits may be a way to make tough choices about spending (Oleszek 1989). Alternatively, omnibus use in deficit periods provides a way to forge distributive logrolls that may "unravel" if bills are considered sequentially.

WHAT IS AN OMNIBUS BILL?

Studying omnibus legislation in a systematic fashion requires an operational definition and measure of omnibus legislation. No such definition currently exists. What are the options for defining an omnibus bill? One option is to use the name of the bill. However, this is problematic. The term "omnibus" may potentially be used arbitrarily. At the introduction stage of the process, members of Congress may call a bill whatever they choose. They may simply label a bill "omnibus" to make it sound more important. Moreover, several omnibus bills do not have the word "omnibus" in their title, like certain budget reconciliation bills and continuing appropriations measures.

This state of affairs poses a challenge. Relying on political observers to identify omnibus legislation could lead to substantial error, since they report what the bill was called rather than relying on a precise definition. It also points to the need for the development of a reliable measure of omnibus legislation.

I choose to take an alternative route to simply using the name of the bill. I seek to provide a behavioral definition of omnibus that follows from the concept. Omnibus bills differ from typical major bills in their *scope* (number of substantive policy areas spanned), in their *size,* and, following from scope and size, in their *complexity.* My definition captures the key attributes of scope and size.

Omnibus bill: any piece of major legislation that (1) spans three or more major topic policy areas *or* ten or more subtopic policy areas, *and* (2) is greater than the mean plus one standard deviation of major bills in size.

This definition requires further explanation of major legislation, major-topic policy area, subtopic policy area, and size. Defining *major legislation* provides a group of bills from which to isolate the omnibus bills. Defining *major topic and subtopic policy area* provides one of the tools to distinguish omnibus bills from other major bills by ascertaining how many policy areas they span. The other tool for distinguishing omnibus bills from other major bills is the *size* of the bill.

MAJOR LEGISLATION

Omnibus bills are quite prominent. Hence, we expect to find them in the list of important bills compiled regularly in *Congressional Quarterly Weekly Report* and to receive prominent coverage in annual editions of *CQ Almanac.* Several scholars have utilized these sources to identify samples of important bills for analysis (Baumgartner et al. 1997; Cameron et al. 1997; Edwards, Barrett, and Peake 1997; Sinclair 1997; Taylor 1998). The *CQ Almanac* has featured consistent coverage since 1948 (Baumgartner et al. 1997; Cameron et al. 1997). *CQ Weekly Report,* on the other hand, has varied in title and length.

I use a two-pronged approach to get a list of major bills from which to classify omnibus bills. First, I utilize the top 10 percent of covered bills in *CQ Almanac* from the Baumgartner and Jones dataset. Second, I check that list of bills against the same list from *CQ Weekly Report* that Sinclair (1997) used to identify major bills in her study of unorthodox lawmaking (about fifty per Congress). If *CQ Weekly* contains bills not in the top 10 percent of *CQ Almanac* bills, I also include those bills (only a few such cases). This procedure yields 1,180 major bills from 1949 to 1994 (an average of fifty-one per Congress).

MAJOR-TOPIC AND SUBTOPIC POLICY AREA

I utilize the topic coding scheme described in chapter 2, which proceeds by substance, rather than by typology of policy "types." In discussing the omnibus change conceptually, scholars have been consistent in arguing that a major difference of these bills from typical bills is that they span numerous substantive policy areas. Therefore, the substantive policy scheme of Baumgartner and Jones provides a good fit. In studying the major bills to identify those that are omnibus measures (which consisted of reading legislative summaries and histories of each), I looked for the number of different substantive major policy areas and subtopic areas they spanned. Those spanning three or more major policy areas *or* ten or more subtopic policy areas met one of the necessary conditions to be included in my population of omnibus bills.

SIZE

The second condition to be met for omnibus classification is size. I measured size as the number of words in each of the bills from LEGI-SLATE, publications of Congressional Quarterly, or the relevant sections of the *United States Code* for those major bills becoming law. Major bills clearing one standard deviation

FIGURE 9.2 NUMBER OF STATUTES PER CONGRESS

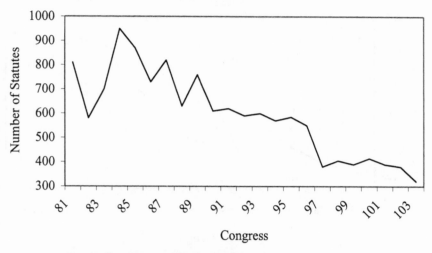

FIGURE 9.3 NUMBER OF OMNIBUS BILLS PER CONGRESS

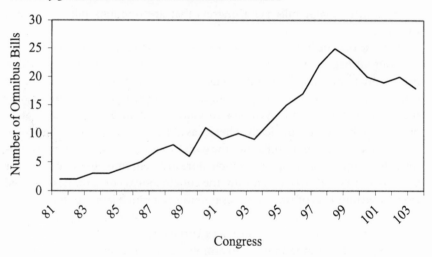

above the mean length of major bills met the size requirement. This procedure yielded 242 omnibus bills of the 1,180 major bills from 1949 to 1994.[1]

Figures 9.2 through 9.4 demonstrate the move to omnibus legislating across the post–World War II period. Figure 9.2 shows the number of
public laws per two-year Congress from 1949 to 1994. Figure 9.3 displays the
number of omnibus bills per Congress from 1949 to 1994. Figure 9.4 shows the

FIGURE 9.4 OMNIBUS PROPORTION OF MAJOR BILLS

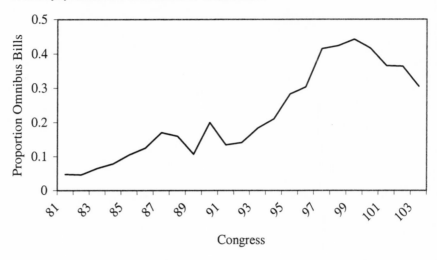

Congress

proportion of major bills per Congress that are omnibus bills from 1949 to 1994.

As these data bear out, there has been a decrease in raw numbers of statutory output beginning after the Great Society juxtaposed with an increased propensity to pass larger, bundled bills into law. The first modern use of the omnibus procedure was in 1950 (Congressional Quarterly 1951) and the omnibus technique was employed on a regular, increasing basis until the 1980s, when use increased dramatically. There was a slight decline and leveling off in raw numbers of omnibus bills after the 99th Congress (1985–86), but the omnibus technique is still employed much more in recent times than earlier in the post–World War II period.[2] In sum, the congressional currency has changed from large numbers of small statutes to fewer but much larger public laws.

OMNIBUS ATTACHMENTS

How many bills become attached to omnibus bills? To answer this question, it is necessary to isolate a group of bills with enough consideration that they might become attached to omnibus bills.

What is the proper population of bills that are candidates for attachment to omnibus packages? Most bills are never seriously pushed or considered in Congress (Davidson and Oleszek 1998; Oleszek 1989). Including all of the thousands of bills introduced in a Congress in the sample of potential omnibus attachments will distort the results. On the other hand, considering only the most major of bills (such as the 1,180 major bills from 1949 to 1994 studied above to isolate the omnibus bills) misses many of the bills that are attached to omnibus bills. What is needed is a subset of bills that are "seriously considered" and hence are potential candidates for inclusion as an attachment on an omnibus bill.

Fortunately, Congressional Quarterly has identified in its annual editions of the *Almanac* a subset of seriously considered bills from which potential omnibus attachments will emerge. From 1949 to 1994, Congressional Quarterly had over twelve thousand write-ups on legislation and other congressional matters in the *Almanacs* (Baumgartner et al. 1997). As I mentioned above, several scholars have utilized CQ to focus on different subsets of bills that receive serious consideration in Congress (Bader 1997; Baumgartner et al. 1997; Cameron et al. 1997; Edwards, Barrett, and Peake 1997; Sinclair 1992, 1995, 1997; Taylor 1998).

My first coding task, which I describe above, was to determine which major bills qualified as omnibus bills (required to meet a dual threshold of scope and size). Sorting out which bills were attached to these omnibus bills was the next task and required me to "unpack" the omnibus bills. To determine which bills were attached to the omnibus bills, I looked in two places. First, for each of the CQ-covered bills from 1979 to 1994, I reviewed the written summary or summaries to determine whether the measure was attached to an omnibus bill or not. Second, I also studied the provisions of the omnibus bills to make certain I had each of the attachments in my population of "seriously considered" legislation. Looking in detail at the omnibus bill summary for attachments was important because some of the bills attached to an omnibus bill did not receive a separate write-up in the *Almanac*. For the period from 1979 to 1994, this process yielded 3,190 seriously considered bills.

To illustrate this attachment coding process, let us consider the 1992 Urban Aid Tax Bill. I found in initial coding of this bill along with the other 1,180 major bills from 1949 to 1994 that the bill met the size requirement and spanned five major policy areas and twenty-nine subtopic policy areas within those five major areas. To code attachments for that Congress, I read summaries of every CQ-covered bill and found that four bills covered in separate CQ write-ups were incorporated into the Urban Aid Tax Bill. I then looked in detail at the summary of the Urban Aid Tax Bill and found two other bills that became attached. In total, six attachments exist in the dataset for the Urban Aid Tax Bill.

Table 9.1 shows the breakdown on bill attachments to omnibus bills from 1979 to 1994. We see that about 16 percent of 3,190 bills considered got to "hitch a ride on the omnibus." Because omnibus bills typically succeed, 98 percent of

TABLE 9.1 Bills Hitching a Ride on the Omnibus, 1979–94

Attached to Omnibus		Unattached		Total Bills	
N	%	N	%	N	%
511	16	2,679	84	3,190	100

bills attached to omnibus bills became law. It appears that omnibus bills provide a viable and important alternative route to enactment for bills introduced in Congress. This finding is important because entrepreneurs pushing the other 86 percent of bills have to overcome a presumption of failure for bills introduced (Krutz, Fleisher, and Bond 1998). The vast majority of these bills will not survive the legislative gauntlet; only 28 percent become law.

A LONGITUDINAL ANALYSIS OF OMNIBUS USE, 1949–94

I conduct separate analyses for the House and Senate. Table 9.2 presents the results of the analyses that seek explanations of aggregate omnibus usage per Congress from 1949 to 1994. Several of the contextual factors that we expect to affect omnibus lawmaking receive support, including the *budget deficit, divided government, chamber potential for minority obstructionism,* and *issue complexity.* These findings suggest that both redistributive rationales (those in which change is a means of distributing power and political resources) and efficiency rationales (those benefiting the operation of the institution) underpin the move to omnibus legislating.

Issue complexity had a strong contextual coefficient in both of the longitudinal regression models. As the complexity of House and Senate issue agendas increase, omnibus bills are more likely to be utilized. This finding is consistent with Baumgartner et al.'s (1997) argument that the rise of omnibus legislation is related to the increasing issue complexity facing Congress in the post–World War II era.[3]

As many legislative scholars have argued (Davidson and Oleszek 1998; Oleszek 1989; Sinclair 1997; Smith 1989), the specter of deficit politics appears to be part of the answer to the "why omnibus?" question. As deficits climb, so too does omnibus use.

The legislative potential for minority obstructionism variables are also significant. The more challenging the coalitional circumstances for the majority

TABLE 9.2 Models of House and Senate Omnibus Usage per Congress, 1949–94

Independent Variables	Expected Direction	House		Senate	
		B	t	B	t
Budget deficit	−	−.378**	−2.496	−.374**	−2.561
Divided government	+	.126*	1.959	.110*	1.924
Legislative potential for minority obstructionism	−	−.384**	2.671	−.262*	2.234
Issue complexity	+	.365**	2.504	.395**	2.795
Workload	+	.131*	2.406	.118	1.528
(Constant)	−	−.227*	−2.176	−.194*	−2.276
R^2		.871		.846	
Adj. R^2		.858		.818	
F-statistic		24.438***		23.097***	
N of cases		23		23	

$*p < = .05; **p < = .01; ***p < = .001$. The dependent variable in both models is the proportion of major bills per Congress that are omnibus bills. Models estimated with maximum-likelihood iterated generalized least squares.

party (i.e., a narrow and/or heterogeneous majority governing against a large and/or cohesive minority), the more likely omnibus bills are to be used as a way to get things done. This finding was stronger for the House than the minority rights–oriented Senate. This difference may result from the fact that obstructionism in the Senate is less dependent on coalition size (any senator may filibuster) than in the House.

Statistically speaking, divided government is significantly more likely to result in omnibus use than unified government. However, the low values of the coefficients suggest the substantive effect is marginal; higher values are typically expected for a dichotomous variable. Finally, the congressional *workload* variable is significant in the House model, but not in the Senate model. This finding makes sense because the House has more members and a larger institution than the Senate. Various workload pressures — bill introductions, committee hearings, recorded roll call votes — are greater in the House than in the Senate (Ornstein, Mann, and Malbin 1996).

In summary, the findings support the contextual expectations of the theoretical framework. Omnibus bill use is related to several of the challenging contextual circumstances, and political as well as efficiency rationales for the change are supported. As several such governing circumstances have confronted Congress, the political actors have found omnibus bills to be a useful tool for getting things done.

As scholars suspected, deficit politics, divided government, and increased potential for minority obstructionism are all related to aggregate omnibus use. Issue complexity also exhibited a strong relationship with omnibus use. This finding, together with the strong issue fragmentation finding in the "hitching a ride" model (Krutz 2001), suggests that the increasing issue complexity of the congressional agenda is a strong undercurrent of omnibus legislating.

DISCUSSION

Omnibus legislating is a powerful legislative technique that has proliferated on Capitol Hill in the post–World War II era. Several scholars argue that the rise of omnibus legislation is one of the most important changes in recent decades. Much major lawmaking is undertaken with this method and a significant proportion of legislative initiatives in Congress see the light at the end of the legislative process because they become attached to omnibus bills. Omnibus bills alter the traditional lawmaking process in many ways, affect the processing of issues, and alter the set of policy outcomes produced. Yet we know little about this legislative method. The purpose of this paper was to explain the move across time to omnibus legislating. I presented a theoretical framework of omnibus employment that helps explain why and when omnibus bills are used. An original definition and measure of omnibus legislation was developed. The findings of a longitudinal test support the framework and suggest dual motives driving omnibus use: politics and efficiency. Where does this leave us?

I think if we ponder in chronological order the unfolding of the omnibus change and the effects of that change to issue processing in Congress, a strong argument may be made for the coevolution of issues and institutional structures (Baumgartner, Jones, and MacLeod 1998b). Institutional structures are not entirely exogenous and issues are not just endogenous. They impact one another in a relationship that unfolds across time.

Issue complexity and the resulting issue fragmentation that resulted when new issues and redefined old ones were forced again and again onto a committee system that was developed in the 1940s (Baumgartner, Jones, and Rosenstiehl 1997) creates a governing challenge for political actors in Congress. Omnibus legislation provides one way to more efficiently process legislation centrally with the party leaders rather than leaving some matters to be settled by scores of committee barons. That the issue complexity variable was strongly significant in the longitudinal analysis should not surprise.

The second step is also consistent with the coevolution of issues and structures framework. Once adopted as a viable institutional mechanism, the omnibus method dramatically affects the processing of issues. Issues that have become too controversial and stand no chance in the legislative process may be veto-proofed in an omnibus bill. This changes the composition of policy outcomes from what would be produced if bills were processed sequentially.

Next in the temporal sequence, the entrenched new technique affects the balance of power in Congress, which becomes the third step in the coevolutionary sequence of issues and structures. The omnibus technique empowers party leaders. In the ability to bundle bills, party leaders possess a powerful policy tool. They can push through their most treasured policy goals and introduce new issues.

Omnibus lawmaking is detrimental to the power of committee chairs. Omnibus bills rarely go through authorizing committees. Hence, the committee chairs never see omnibus provisions of policy that are pertinent to their committees' jurisdiction. Put another way, the tough governing circumstances increasingly present across the post–World War II period created institutional conditions where stronger central authority was needed from party leaders. One of the tools needed to exercise this authority is omnibus legislating.[4] Finally, omnibus legislating also helps the Congress by veto-proofing items the president opposes. Legislation that is headed for a veto stands a better chance in an omnibus bill alongside main items the president supports.

In conclusion, this chapter examined a major change in the lawmaking process in Congress, the move to omnibus legislating. It showed the importance of envisioning institutions as dynamic entities. The chapter also demonstrated the interaction of environmental or exogenous factors (issue complexity) and internal or endogenous factors (party leaders). The increase of issue complexity in Congress increased the need for central leader power, which in turn affects the introduction of new issues. This is clear example of a positive feedback process that led to a major change in the legislative process.

This chapter also shows how someone can utilize the Policy Agendas Project as an empirical starting point for an ambitious scholarly project. Many other professors and graduate students can benefit from these excellent data sets. I used and adapted both the hearings and CQ stories data sets in this project. Having these publicly available data to use as a starting point allowed me to cover much more ground empirically than I would have had I started from scratch.[5]

To code omnibus bills, I needed a sample of all major bills from which to select omnibus bills. I decided to rely on the impartial editors at Congressional Quarterly to focus on major bills the most in their coverage. Accordingly, I utilized the top 10 percent most-covered bills by CQ as my sample of major bills. The Policy Agendas Project data sets made this very doable. One of the variables in the CQ stories data sets is the number of column lines per story, my indicator of amount of coverage per bill. Some significant recoding was necessary, however. The CQ stories data set is annual and the unit of analysis is the story. I needed a time increment of two-year periods (or Congresses) and bills as the unit of analysis. Therefore, I worked through the CQ stories data to eliminate duplications in coverage from the first and second sessions (years) of a Congress and to purge stories not related to legislation.

Once I had a list of the 10 percent of stories that were most covered, I used the topic coding system described in chapter 2 to revisit the CQ stories about each of the bills (which were easier to find using the numbers of headlines and/or numbers of pages provided as variables in the CQ stories data sets). I read the CQ summary of each major bill (and consulted CIS Congressional Universe as well) to determine how many major topic and subtopic areas the bills covered in a significant manner. The hearings data set was helpful in constructing measures of issue complexity of the congressional agenda. Other legislative and policy scholars (especially graduate students) should take advantage of these datasets to carry out important projects.

MEASURES

DIVIDED GOVERNMENT

Unified government occurs when the houses of Congress and the president are controlled by the same political party. Divided government exists otherwise and is measured as a dummy variable (1 = divided, 0 = unified). To clarify, when the president's party controls one of the chambers of Congress, this case is coded as divided. When the House, Senate, and president are not controlled by the same party, there will be an incentive to use omnibus packages to get things through.

LEGISLATIVE POTENTIAL FOR MINORITY OBSTRUCTIONISM

To measure the potential for minority obstructionism, I utilize a measure developed by Hurley, Brady, and Cooper (1977) for both the House and Senate. Hurley, Brady, and Cooper produced a statistical measure of "legislative potential for policy change," which takes account of the size and cohesion of the majority and minority parties. Party size is measured in percent of members in the chamber. Cohesion is average party unity on party votes (votes on which a majority of one party opposes a majority of the other party). The measure is

$$(\text{majority size} \times \text{majority cohesion}) - (\text{minority size} \times \text{minority cohesion})$$

The measure assumes a high value when the majority is large and cohesive and the minority is small and heterogeneous. Such conditions are ripe for policy change by the majority party. In contrast, when the majority is narrow and less unified, and the minority is larger and unified, it is more likely the majority party will have policy items blocked. I expect higher omnibus use in the latter case as a way of surmounting gridlock and uncertainty. Therefore, the lower the value of the variable, the more likely omnibus bills are to be used (negative relationship).

ISSUE COMPLEXITY

Issue complexity refers to the degree of concentration of congressional attention to particular issues. Using the Policy Agendas Project topic categories, a measure of issue concentration by Congress can be computed based on all congressional hearings, which provides the measure for issue complexity in the longitudinal analysis. Each congressional hearing is coded into a major issue topic category. The measure of topic concentration is a Herfindahl score (see Hardin 1998a), based on the sum of squares of the proportions of statutes or stories or column lines in each topic area. A high score reflects congressional attention dedicated to a few topics, as was the case just after World War II. A low score indicates congressional attention spread more evenly across all topics. I subtract these values from 100 so that high scores reflect greater issue complexity.

WORKLOAD

It is indeed a challenge to identify a measure that fully taps the workload of Congress. Binder (1995, 1996, 1997) was particularly hindered in trying to develop a measure of size of the agenda for the entire history of the Congress, 1789–1990. She produced a measure that tapped into the number of days in the session and the number of public laws produced. Counting public laws in recent times understates the actual workload because Congress has resorted to passing fewer but larger bills into law. Additionally, counting laws does not capture the oversight activities that take up a great deal of the agenda

(Aberbach 1990). Luckily, much better measures exist in the postwar period in which omnibus use started and then proliferated. A better measure of workload would tap committee activity as well as floor activity, since committees are the workshops of Congress. The chief way that committees accomplish their consideration of policy is through committee hearings. Hence, I measure the House and Senate workload separately with a composite measure of committee and floor activity.

The measure ranges from 0 to 1. Floor activity and committee activity can each take a value from 0 to .5; the measure is the sum of the two values. Floor activity is measured as the number of floor votes in the House or Senate per Congress (Ornstein, Mann, and Malbin 1996). Committee activity is measured as the number of committee hearings in a particular Congress in each chamber from the Policy Agendas Project hearings data set. The Congress in the covered period with the largest number of floor votes receives a value of .5 for floor votes. The number of floor votes from each of the other twenty-two Congresses is divided by the number of floor votes in the Congress with the largest number, yielding a quotient ranging from 0 to 1. This proportion is then divided in half. The same procedure is used for committee hearings. The two scores for each Congress are added to produce the final value of the variable.

BUDGET DEFICIT

I measure the budgetary situation as the average budget deficit or surplus as a percentage of outlays for the two fiscal years of each Congress from the *Statistical Abstract of the United States, 1996* (U.S. Bureau of the Census 1996). Others have used a similar measure (Edwards, Barrett, and Peake 1997; Mayhew 1991). Another measure of this variable is the deficit percentage of gross domestic product. The outlays version of the measure and the GDP version are highly correlated and both measures produce similar results.

NOTES

1. How are regular appropriations bills treated? Congress is required to complete action each year on thirteen regular appropriations bills to formally enact the budget. Many of these bills include budgets for programs and areas that span many topical areas. However, these bills in their regular form do not represent a change in lawmaking that I am attempting to explain through definition of omnibus bills. Still, there is the potential that leaders will incorporate major policy enactments in regular appropriations bills, therefore reflecting a change along the lines of omnibus legislation. While this is more common on reconciliation and continuing appropriations bills than on the thirteen regular

appropriations bills, I also examined in detail the regular appropriations bills, and if policy attachments distinct from the budget aspects met the "span" requirement and the entire bill met the size requirement, then the bill was designated omnibus. This occurred on certain defense appropriations bills in the 1980s and energy and water development appropriations bills in the 1990s.

2. This slight decline and leveling off in raw numbers is somewhat misleading. Omnibus bills are indeed even larger after the mid-1980s than before.

3. In an analysis of why some bills may "hitch a ride on the omnibus" while most must go it alone (Krutz 1999) in which the theoretical framework is tested most fully, bills from fragmented issue areas are more likely to be attached than other bills. This represents one of the strongest findings in the model.

4. This case illustrates well the theory of conditional party government forwarded by Rohde (1991). Across time, stronger party leadership is needed under certain conditions more than others.

5. For more information on precisely how I revised the data sets and what I added, please see Krutz 2001. In addition to the longitudinal analysis presented here, I also devised a system, again with the help of Policy Agendas Project data, for identifying omnibus riders for an analysis of the omnibus attachment process.

10

NEW ISSUES, NEW MEMBERS: COMMITTEE COMPOSITION AND THE TRANSFORMATION OF ISSUE AGENDAS ON THE HOUSE BANKING AND PUBLIC WORKS COMMITTEES

E. SCOTT ADLER

The process of governing in America is "continually swept by policy change, change that alternates between incremental drift and rapid alterations of existing arrangements" (Baumgartner and Jones 1993, 236). This fundamental finding of Baumgartner and Jones's study of issue agendas and policy making was probably not new to any scholar who has followed a public policy issue over time. It is no surprise to learn that long periods of policy equilibrium in any one issue area can be interrupted by short bursts of innovation. However, Baumgartner and Jones's advance was the identification of a number of wide-ranging systemic factors that commonly explain the ebb and flow in policy development. In tracing the fluctuations of congressional attention to specific policy issues, Baumgartner and Jones tracked the type, frequency, length, and institutional location of congressional hearings devoted to a political topic. This "commonsense" approach (Bosso 1994) not only provides them with a simple accounting of congressional attention to specific issues but also reveals a tremendous amount about the biases and diffusion of that attention across varied actors or structures within Congress (see also Baumgartner, Jones, and Rosenstiehl 1997).

Perhaps most importantly, Baumgartner and Jones reinforced for scholars of Congress the fact that there is a strong bond between the structure of the congressional policy process and an issue area's political evolution. Scholars have long understood that activities in Congress's principal policy-making structure — the congressional committee — are heavily influenced by the external forces bearing down on it (Fenno 1973; Hall and Wayman 1990; Price 1979). Conversely, researchers have also revealed that legislators' goals combined with a committee's policy agenda can influence the types of outside groups or actors that are accepted into policy decision–making circles (Evans 1994). Baumgartner and Jones were able to uncover the details of this relationship over a number of policy arenas and across long periods of time.

Thus, this association between the years of acquired knowledge about congressional structure and the inferences about the development of issue areas raises a number of valuable questions. Most importantly, how does the knowledge of political agendas imparted by Baumgartner and Jones (and other scholars) comport with what we already know about committee composition and the structure of the process of issue deliberation? Congressional scholars have revealed a tremendous amount about the makeup, leadership, and proceedings of committees. However, can our understanding of the evolution of issues in Congress help us to further comprehend why congressional committees are composed and structured as they are or, vice versa, is it possible that our knowledge of committee structure can help to inform us about the progression of policy issues in the legislature and beyond? With respect to the themes raised in this volume, can the relationship between congressional structure and agendas be seen as part of a system of negative or positive feedbacks?

I approach these questions with reference to the subject of committee composition and its relationship to committee work on specific issues. I examine the evolution of policy making in two issue areas that fall within the purview of two standing House committees between the early 1960s and early 1990s — federal aid to urban areas for the Banking, Finance, and Urban Affairs Committee and transportation policy for the Public Works and Transportation Committee.[1] I track how these panels addressed each policy matter, but specifically inquire as to the relationship between issue evolution and changes in the composition of the panels' memberships, if any at all. Ultimately, this study will help to provide some insight into our understanding of the role that members' constituency concerns play in the direction of their committee agendas.

COMMITTEE COMPOSITION AND ITS
POTENTIAL EFFECTS ON LEGISLATIVE WORK

Research on the membership of congressional committees has for a number of years been fertile ground for questions concerning the structure of our legislative system (see works as varied as McConachie 1898 and Deering and Smith 1997). Over the last decade or so, scholars have examined the characteristics of members on specific panels for evidence in support of their theories of congressional structure (Cox and McCubbins 1993; Groseclose 1994; Krehbiel 1991). This literature on committee composition includes research that utilizes new data and statistical techniques to reintroduce the notion of distributive politics to the subject of committee assignments. The basic concept about panel membership, articulated by Rundquist and Ferejohn, is that "when the districts of committee members are compared with those of other congressmen, the committees will be found to overrepresent constituencies with a stake in their subject matter" (1975, 88). As Mayhew might assert, the overrepresentation of constituency interests on certain congressional committees is due to the "electoral connection" (Mayhew 1974). That is, representatives seek particular committee assignments in order to protect or garner outlays from federal programs of special interest to their districts. The assumption is that such behavior should be beneficial to one's electoral prospects (Alvarez and Saving 1997; Levitt and Snyder 1997; Stein and Bickers 1994). Recent work on the temporal dimension of this relationship has uncovered evidence that certain committees have for a long time attracted members with disproportionate constituency interests in the subject matter under their purview. Adler and Lapinski find that this is not only the case for a number of committees traditionally perceived as "constituency-oriented," but also for several panels thought to be more "policy-oriented" (Adler and Lapinski 1997; see also Canon and Sweet 1998).

The findings regarding the constituency orientation of committee membership suggest that there may be a strong and constant relationship between the policy agendas of specific congressional committees and the type of members who seek or have assignment to those panels. Members with similar constituency characteristics are persistently attracted to certain committees, and seemingly those panels spend much of their time deliberating on policy areas of common interest to those constituency groups. The important question is the direction of this causal relationship: do the reelection/constituency needs of committee members drive the policy focus and legislative agenda of a committee, or does the issue direction a congressional panel adopts eventually shape the type of legislators attracted to it? Alternatively, is it the null hypothesis that prevails? That is, does the distributive approach completely mischaracterize the functioning and composition of congressional committees, which would mean that there is no relationship at all between legislators' constituency needs and the policy direction their assigned committees take?

To address the link between member characteristics and the ebb and flow of committee attention to specific policy issues I return to the data on committee hearings. I examine the workload of two committees on issues commonly perceived to be sizable portions of their policy domain. Using Baumgartner and Jones's coding of the CIS congressional hearings index, I track for a thirty-two-year period the evolution of Banking Committee hearings on community development and urban mass transit issues and Public Works Committee hearings on transportation matters, specifically highway construction and airline and surface transportation regulation issues. To measure the degree of each committee's attention to these policy areas I determine the proportion of their work devoted to each subject. For this I calculate the number of hearing days per year on each subject (rather than simply the numbers of hearings), and calculate them as a percentage of the total days of hearings for that committee in that year.

The two committees provide contrasts that help to broaden the implications for the analysis beyond just the issues and the panels examined. First, these committees are frequently perceived as serving different roles in the legislature and therefore as attracting members with different motivations. Banking is often seen as a committee that attracts members with specific policy goals, while Public Works is seen to be more constituency oriented (Bullock 1976; Deering and Smith 1997, 64; Murphy 1974).[2] Second, public salience on issues falling within the purview of the two committees significantly changed in opposing directions during the period examined. Deering and Smith's study of the national news coverage devoted to topics under each panel's jurisdiction demonstrates that while Banking's public exposure dramatically decreased between 1969 and 1994, news reporting on topics contained within Public Works' jurisdiction increased almost as drastically (1997, 92).

HYPOTHESES OF CONSTITUENCY
RELATIONSHIP TO COMMITTEE AGENDAS

If a distributive theory of committee composition and agendas is correct then one of two things should occur with respect to changes in committee work:

Hypothesis 1: Alterations in committee agendas *are preceded by* corresponding alterations in committee composition. A committee takes on a new policy issue after legislators with similar district interests in a specific issue area congregate on that particular panel. Conversely, the abandonment of an issue area by a panel should be preceded by the disappearance of a collection of members with strong constituency interests in that policy matter. The inference from this hypothesis is that, at least in part, the variation in the attention a committee paid to particular issue areas is propelled the composition of its membership.

Hypothesis 2: Alterations in committee agendas *result in* corresponding alterations in committee composition. As a committee expands its jurisdictional boundaries to include an issue area over which it did not previously have authority, it will subsequently attract legislators with a profound district interest in this issue. On the other hand, as a committee reduces its association or control in a specific issue area, eventually it loses its attractiveness to members with extreme district interests in that issue. The conclusion from this proposition is that committee orientation toward specific policy issues is determined by factors beyond mere panel membership but nevertheless has an effect on the type of representatives attracted to that committee.

If a distributive theory of legislative organization does not correctly characterize the relationship between committee work and panel membership, then agenda changes should follow a third hypothesis:

Hypothesis 3: Alterations in committee agendas *neither precede nor result in* alterations in committee composition. No relationship whatsoever exists between the type of members attracted or belonging to a specific committee and the work orientation of that panel. Changes in committee composition and committee issue agendas vary in unrelated ways. The inference is that distributive theory tells us little about variation in committee issue agendas.

To study the changing composition of House panels during this period, I examine a number of relevant district characteristics for all 435 members of Congress in each congressional term. Similar to previous studies of committee composition that rely upon ideology and vote cohesion scores (Groseclose 1994; Maltzman 1997; Peterson and Wrighton 1998), I test whether the median member of either committee is significantly different from the chamber median on the district characteristic(s) relevant to the subject matter at hand. For example, in the policy area of federal urban aid I utilize three constituency characteristics to measure interest in urban legislative issues — percentage of constituency living in urban areas, whether or not the district is located in one of the fifty largest central cities of that decade (a dichotomous measure), and the district's median family income. These variables highlight not just urban populations but specifically poor, inner-city congressional districts. I also employ three measures to contrast highway construction with other transportation interests: percentage of constituency employed in construction, percentage unemployed, and percentage employed in transportation.[3] The first two transportation measures capture an interest in securing funds for high-way construction[4] and the third highlights district concern for other trans-portation issues, like subsidies and regulation.

For district interests in urban and highway construction issues it was nec-essary to create a single measure of need that combined the two or three rele-vant dimensions into one score. This was done to ensure that members who rank high on all possible measures register a greater level of "demand" for the policy benefits provided by that committee than a member who ranks high on only one of the measures. I constructed the combined measure by standard-izing all component measures (a mean of zero and a standard deviation of one) and then summing them.[5] For example, the measure of "urban demand" is an additive scale of standardized measures for the percent urban, a central city dummy variable, and an inverted median family income.[6] For interests in general transportation subsidies and regulation I use just the percentage em-ployed in transportation.

In testing committee composition I utilize demand score *medians* rather than *means* for two reasons: (1) medians are less susceptible to the tendency of outliers to bias the results of a difference tests in one direction or another, and (2) medians have more theoretical appeal when exploring the central ten-dency of decision-making bodies like congressional committees (Black 1958; Shepsle 1979). I employ a nonparametric Monte Carlo simulation technique to test the difference of medians between the committees and the entire chamber.[7] Simply put, I create a computer program that constructs ten thou-sand "sample" committees of randomly selected members from the entire House membership for each real committee and report their medians. These "sample" committees are of the same size as the actual committee in each con-gressional term. Using the sample committees as a distribution we may then determine how much more extreme (a higher demand score) the actual panel is from the central tendency of the chamber. Like the convention for statisti-cal inference, the standard for Monte Carlo median tests of this type has been to utilize a significance level of .05. Therefore, the null hypothesis, that com-mittees are "representative" of the chamber as a whole, is rejected if less than 5 percent of the sample committee medians are as extreme as the actual com-mittee median.[8]

Results from the tests of the changing composition are then compared with the swings in the focus of committee work to see if there is any correspon-dence. For instance, if increases in the median constituency demand for a pol-icy among committee members occurs before an escalation in their work on that policy we might infer that panel composition influences the committee agenda. Conversely, if the decline of work on an issue by a committee precedes the departure of numerous representatives from districts with high need for its policy output, this may indicate that agenda affects panel composition.

URBAN PROBLEMS AND THE BANKING, FINANCE, AND URBAN AFFAIRS COMMITTEE

BANKING COMMITTEE HEARINGS AND THE FEDERAL URBAN AGENDA

Not surprisingly, the attention that the Banking, Finance, and Urban Affairs Committee (hereafter, Banking) paid to urban issues from the early 1960s to the 1990s tracks closely the fate of governmental programs addressing the problems of inner cities. The trend of Banking hearings directed at urban matters during this era is not all that different from the overall trend of urban-oriented hearings in Congress as a whole (Baumgartner and Jones 1993, chap. 7). As part of the agendas of the Kennedy, Johnson, and Nixon administrations, the federal government initiated and implemented programs to improve urban housing, to renew neglected inner-city neighborhoods, to expand metropolitan mass transit, and finally to inject badly needed dollars into city treasuries. The House and Senate Banking committees were the primary congressional setting to debate these issues, write the legislation and dole out the funds. Among the more important legislation the Banking committees considered were numerous housing acts (1961, 1965, 1968, 1971, etc.), the Area Redevelopment Act of 1961, the Urban Mass Transit Act of 1964, and the Demonstration Cities Program enacted in 1966.

As can be seen in figure 10.1, Banking hearings on community development and urban mass transit issues during this period were a very large part of the committee workload. From 1961 to 1972, hearings addressing community development or urban mass transit subjects made up 31 percent of the total Banking work and in many years constituted between 35–65 percent of the panel's hearing days (1961, 1963, 1968, 1969, 1970, and 1972).[9] For the most part these hearings covered topics like redevelopment of blighted urban areas, housing for the poor and elderly, grants for urban mass transit, and creation and funding for the Department of Housing and Urban Development.

However, by the mid- to late 1970s the federal government had taken a new approach to urban problems. Decline in federal aid to cities began with the redefinition of the federal role in revitalization of urban areas under the Nixon administration. President Nixon attempted to shift responsibility for urban

FIGURE 10.1 PERCENTAGE OF HEARINGS BY THE HOUSE BANKING, FINANCE, AND URBAN AFFAIRS COMMITTEE DEVOTED TO URBAN ISSUES (DAYS OF HEARINGS)

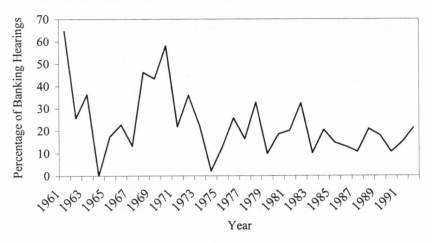

problems back to the cities and states through his partially successful efforts at consolidation of federal grant programs to individuals and groups into block grants to city governments and his establishment of general revenue sharing (Conlan 1998). Funds for state and local governments hit their peak in 1978, but before President Carter left office Congress had eliminated a large part of general revenue sharing along with a range of other urban assistance programs. Urban areas took their biggest hit during the Reagan and Bush administrations, where broad cuts in community and economic development programs and the eventual elimination of general revenue sharing and urban development action grants took place (Caraley 1992; Conlan 1998, 146–47).

As various administrations turned their backs on the problems in our nation's cities, so did Banking. Starting with the dramatic drop in urban-oriented hearings in 1974, work on Banking directed at the troubles of cities never returned to earlier levels. Only 17 percent of Banking hearing days after 1972 are related to urban issues and in many years it drops close to or below 10 percent. This occurs even though the percentage of total congressional hearing days devoted to urban issues that were held by Banking barely changed (about half the total urban-oriented hearing days in Congress both before and after 1972 were held by this panel). The relative decrease in urban-oriented hearings by Banking during this period is in some ways understandable — there was simply less to do. Presidents Carter, Reagan, and Bush were rarely initiating new programs to help the inner cities, and a large part of Reagan's domestic agenda was specifically devoted to dismantling the federal infrastructure serving America's cities (Caraley 1992).

If we are to believe the distributive description of committee composition — members gravitate to committees that can help them provide for the economic and social needs of their districts — then the behavior of the Banking Committee is quite puzzling. If Banking should be composed of a disproportionate number of members with needs related to the issue areas under its jurisdiction, presumably members from urban areas, then why did it simply abandon the subject of urban problems, particularly when successive presidential administrations were dismantling the programs essential to their home districts? Indeed, Baumgartner and Jones (1993) ask this very question (on a broader level) in their treatment of urban problems: "why did the collapse of the urban initiative occur without provoking more congressional attention? One might expect that increased conflict associated with the dramatic downsizing of the urban grant system would be reflected in congressional hearing activity, but our evidence indicates otherwise" (144).

They argue that congressional indifference to the urban initiative is a result of partisan conflicts over the definition of urban problems and the proposed solutions. Republicans, led by their long-serving conservative presidents Nixon and Reagan, were simply much more successful in redefining how the public conceived of urban problems and governmental approaches — "solving local problems without national bureaucratic interferences" (Baumgartner and Jones 1993, 144 – 48).

While this redefining of the problem may be a sufficient answer for the lack of *public outcry* on the issue of urban decay, it still does not fully explain why fairly liberal Democratic-dominated Congresses fiddled while the pillars of their urban support system burned. The Democratic caucuses both in the House and Senate during this period were among the more left-leaning in the postwar period and were considerably more liberal than the party caucus had been during the 1960s (Groseclose, Levitt, and Snyder 1999; Poole and Rosenthal 1997), when most of the urban programs were established. Moreover, Wolman and Marckini note that in the mid-1970s central-city congressional districts constituted the single largest category of district types (central-city, suburban, and nonmetro) in the Democratic House contingent and was the highest percentage (37.5 percent) it would be in the entire period between the early 1960s and early 1990s (Wolman and Marckini 1998, 299). If

FIGURE 10.2 HEARINGS ON URBAN MATTERS AND CONSTITUENCY CHARACTERISTICS FOR MEMBERS OF THE HOUSE BANKING, FINANCE, AND URBAN AFFAIRS COMMITTEE

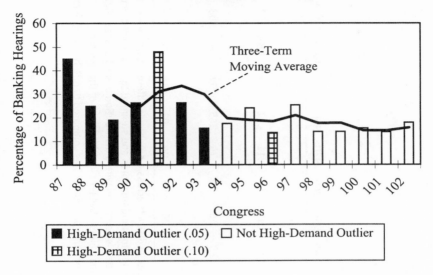

anything, the Democratic Party in the 1970s should have been more urban focused than ever.

One possible answer to the question of congressional inactivity in the face of the dismantling of urban-aid programs is that the House Banking Committee was simply lacking its earlier urban contingent. The evidence of this can be seen in figure 10.2. I have aggregated into congressional terms the yearly data on urban hearings held by the Banking Committee (with a moving average for emphasis) and added information as to the urban orientation of panel members' congressional districts. The shaded bars represent congressional terms when the median demand score of members of Banking meets the .05 level of significance to identify it as an outlier as compared to the chamber using my measure of poor inner-city congressional districts. The cross-hatched bars represent those committees that are outliers at the .10 level, and the unshaded bars represent those that are not considered outliers at either level of significance. (Actual p-values appear in table 10.1.)

The Banking Committee was consistently attractive to representatives from these needy urban districts during the New Frontier and Great Society eras of the Kennedy and Johnson administrations, and even during part of Nixon's New Federalism. The committee's membership was an outlier with respect to poor, urban districts for every congressional term from the 87th Congress

TABLE 10.1 *P*-values for Median Tests of Congressional Committee Outliers

Committee / Constituency Measures	87th	88th	89th	90th	91st	92d	93d	94th	95th	96th	97th	98th	99th	100th	101st	102d
Banking / *Urban, central city, income*	.00	.04	.04	.01	.06	.02	.01	.22	.31	.07	.11	.12	.29	.18	.32	.41
Public works / *Construction jobs, unemployment*	.20	.30	.01	.00	.00	.00	.00	.27	.26	.26	.25	.45	.09	.06	.08	.13
Public works / *Transport employment*	.10	.03	.20	.32	.50	.16	.01	.06	.06	.06	.04	.01	.01	.09	.03	.26

Note: The above tests employ data on the characteristics of all congressional districts across a number of different categories (percentage unemployed, percentage urban, etc.). These data are converted to standard scores and summed to create a committee "demand" score for each district. The *median* score for the actual committee is compared with a distribution of medians for 10,000 randomly assembled committees each term to see if it is more extreme than ninety-five (or ninety) percent of the random committees. A score of .00 would mean the actual committee was more extreme, an "outlier," as compared to one-hundred percent of the random committees.

(1961–62) to the 93d Congress (1973–74).[10] However once the federal government signaled a change in approach to solving the problems of America's cities — shifting responsibility back to the cities and states — legislators from poor urban areas were significantly less attracted to the committee that had been responsible for devising many such programs. The dramatic shift occurred after the enormous Democratic landslide in the post-Watergate election of 1974. In the transition from the 93d (1973–74) to the 94th (1975–76) Congress, the Banking Committee lost a fair number of its members from relatively high-demand urban districts — Frank Brasco and Ed Koch (New York City), Joe Moakley (Boston), Fortney Stark (Oakland), and Andrew Young (Atlanta).[11] But unlike previous terms, when such losses were fairly common due to retirement and transfer to more influential panels, these members were generally not replaced by legislators from similar districts. Among the newcomers to the panel only a few were from urban areas, and they were from significantly smaller cities such as Indianapolis, Cincinnati, Buffalo, and Memphis and (with the exception of Harold Ford from Memphis) districts with much lower poverty rates (U.S. Bureau of the Census 1973). Moreover, this phenomenon was occurring as the relative proportion of the Democratic contingent on the committee was expanding (from 60 percent of the membership to 66 percent) due to a decrease in the size of the Republican Party chamberwide, and central-city districts made up a more significant percentage of the Democratic contingent. In short, Banking never regained its appeal to legislators from poor inner-city districts after presidential agendas started to exclude urban renewal as a priority.

The evidence presented here shows a distinct distributive connection between the constituency needs of committee members and the focus of the panel's policy agenda. Depending on one's perspective, this evidence can support either hypothesis 1 or hypothesis 2. If we see Banking's urban agenda as determined by outside factors, primarily the policy program of presidential administrations, then the shift in the federal agenda that transformed the work of Banking away from programs to aid distressed inner-city regions *subsequently* resulted in urban members no longer gravitating to the committee (hypothesis 2). Alternatively, the fact that Banking did not take up arms in struggle against the dismantling of urban-aid programs is likely a result of the fact that such policies were not all that important to a committee that was no longer composed of a large contingent of members representing needy cities (hypothesis 1). The combination of factors interacting around the urban agenda is reflective of a positive feedback mechanism. Either way, it is not difficult to refute the contention that there is no relationship at all between the work orientation of the Banking panel and the district concerns of its members (hypothesis 3).

CHANGES IN TRANSPORTATION POLICY AND
THE PUBLIC WORKS AND TRANSPORTATION COMMITTEE

THE SHIFT FROM HIGHWAY CONSTRUCTION
TO TRANSPORTATION REGULATIONS

The agenda of the Public Works and Transportation Committee (hereafter, Public Works) changed at about the same time as the transformation of the Banking Committee, but for very different reasons. To a certain extent, Public Works had been involved in transportation issues since its creation in 1946, but the transportation focus of the panel until the early 1970s was largely highway construction. Federal involvement in a nationwide system of high-speed roadways to link major American cities began with the Federal-Aid Highway Act of 1944. After its initial proposal it was more than a decade before passage of the Interstate Highway Act of 1956 resolved many of the major provisions of the highway system's planning and financing, including establishment of the Highway Trust Fund. Two more decades would pass before completion of the actual construction of the National System of Interstate Highways (Lieb 1981, 53; Rose 1990). However, conflicts and oversight of the highway program hardly ended with the agreements achieved in 1956. Harper (1982, 395) and Rose (1990, 102) contend that between 1956 and the early 1980s there were a number of political issues to be resolved, including route selection and expansion (around or through cities, etc.), environmental and beautification concerns, relocation assistance, and financial matters.

It was these concerns over the construction of the interstate highway system that consumed a large portion of the efforts of Public Works, and nearly its entire transportation focus for many years. Figure 10.3 shows the extent to which the committee's agenda was devoted to highway construction. Over 32 percent of the yearly committee hearing days between 1961 and 1972 were concerned solely with highway construction, and for several years at least half of the panel's agenda was consumed with highway matters. Figure 10.4 focuses only on Public Works' transportation hearings [12] and it shows that until about 1972 the panel concentrated almost exclusively on the highway program when considering transportation issues.

By the early to mid-1970s the nation's transportation agenda began to change from highway construction to other issues — namely promotion and

FIGURE 10.3 PERCENTAGE OF HEARINGS BY THE HOUSE PUBLIC WORKS AND TRANSPORTATION COMMITTEE DEVOTED TO HIGHWAY CONSTRUCTION (NUMBER OF DAYS)

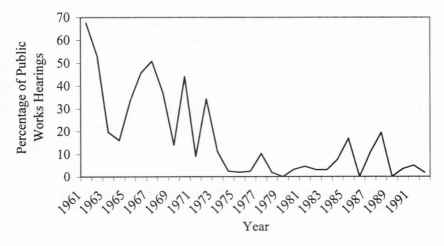

FIGURE 10.4 PERCENTAGE OF HEARINGS BY THE HOUSE PUBLIC WORKS AND TRANSPORTATION COMMITTEE DEVOTED TO HIGHWAYS AS OPPOSED TO AIRLINE AND MOTOR CARRIER REGULATION AND SUBSIDIES

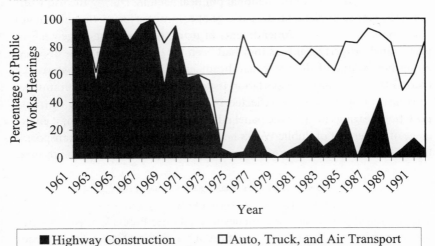

regulation of transportation industries that had seen little federal intervention since the 1930s and early 1940s. The beginning of the transformation occurred with the enactment of the Airport-Airway Development Act of 1970, which served to greatly expand federal financing of the civil aviation industry and the construction of airports (Lieb 1981, 99). Simultaneously, calls for radical reforms in transportation policy arose because existing laws protected inefficient operators, promoted unreasonably high rates, and generally fostered a misallocation of transportation resources. Starting in 1971, the newly created Department of Transportation regularly sponsored legislation to change the system of regulation and subsidies to the railroad, motor carrier, and airline industries (Lieb 1981, 231–32). This effort led to a series of deregulation statutes in all major transporstation industries: the Railroad Revitalization and Regulatory Reform Act of 1976, the 1977 Amendments to the Federal Aviation Act (concerning deregulation of air cargo transportation), the Airline Deregulation Act of 1978, the Motor Carrier Act of 1980, and the Staggers Rail Act of 1980.

The shift in the nation's transportation focus is evident in the efforts of the Public Works Committee. Figure 10.4 shows the stark conversion of the panel's transportation focus from highway issues prior to the mid-1970s to an almost exclusive focus on airline and motor carrier regulation and subsidy concerns after 1974. This shift in the panel's agenda, however, was not entirely driven by a new focus in the national political agenda. During the 93d Congress, the House implemented a package of committee jurisdictional changes (the Committee Reform Amendments of 1974) that, in effect, largely left in place panel property rights as they had been for the previous three decades. Nevertheless, one of the more significant jurisdictional alterations was the consolidation of most transportation issues in the Public Works Committee. This institutional change is reflected in the increased proportion of transportation hearings held by the panel after the reform. Starting in 1975, an average of 50 percent of Public Works hearing days were devoted to transportation issues, a 10 percent increase over the average for the period 1961 to 1974.

CONSTITUENCY CONCERNS AND THE
CHANGING TRANSPORTATION AGENDA

The relationship between constituency interests and Public Works' legislative agenda can be seen through examination of the shifting transportation focus of the panel. Figure 10.5 aggregates to congressional terms the yearly data on highway construction hearings held by the Public Works panel, with additional information about the district characteristics of committee members

FIGURE 10.5 HEARINGS ON HIGHWAY CONSTRUCTION AND CONSTITUENCY CHARACTERISTICS FOR MEMBERS OF THE HOUSE PUBLIC WORKS AND TRANSPORTATION COMMITTEE

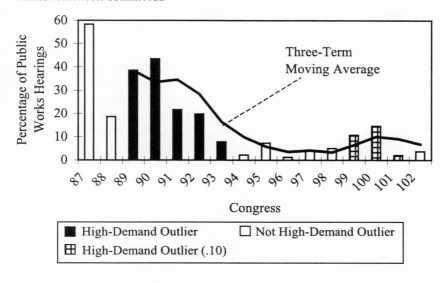

(see table 10.1, above, for the p-values related to this figure). For much of the period examined in which highway construction was the bulk of the panel's transportation concerns, the committee was disproportionately composed of representatives from districts with elevated need for highway construction funds (districts with high employment in construction and high unemployment). In five of the seven congressional terms prior to the 94th Congress the committee was a significant outlier on the highway need measure.[13] This attraction is understandable given that "[e]xpenditures for the Interstate [would] ultimately exceed $100 billion, making it the largest peacetime public works program in our country's history" (Lieb 1981, 53). As highway construction slowed in the mid-1970s and committee attention to the subject diminished, members with these constituency needs were no longer crowding seats on Public Works. Like the fading of federal urban-aid programs that prompted the flight of legislators from poor inner-city districts away from the Banking Committee, the decrease in members representing districts with interests in the highway program can be read as partly a result of changes in external political agendas affecting the committee's attractiveness to certain types of members (hypothesis 2).

The shift of the committee's focus to regulation of transportation industries, however, does not embody the same reactive relationship between constituency needs and committee work. As noted earlier, the committee reforms instituted in the 93d Congress (1973–74) were partially responsible for the altered panel agenda. Debate over consolidation of transportation issues under the purview of the Public Works Committee was among the most heated during that period, with supporters of consolidation largely coming from districts with high levels of public-transportation usage and opponents representing constituencies with high levels of employment in transportation. Adler (forthcoming) demonstrates that transportation industry interests wished to maintain the existing fragmented jurisdiction so as not to disrupt long-standing relationships with influential legislators and committees,[14] while representatives of constituencies dependent upon public transportation felt that a single committee for consideration of transportation policy would create a more coherent and focused policy of planning, subsidies, and regulation. However, the one group of legislators with high district transportation employment that *did support* consolidation were those who were already members of the Public Works Committee. In fact, among the nine most vocal supports of this jurisdictional change were five Public Works members, including three who belonged to its Transportation Subcommittee (Adler forthcoming).

As Figure 10.6 illustrates, the committee was already an outlier with respect to district employment in transportation by the 93d Congress. Not surprisingly, when this jurisdictional change came up for a floor vote on October 2, 1974, all but two members of the Public Works panel voted in favor of consolidation. The committee for many years after its jurisdictional change and shift in agenda toward transportation regulation issues remained attractive to members with high transportation interests in their home districts. The committee is an outlier on the transportation measure, at the .05 level, for five congressional terms from the 93d Congress on, and an outlier for an additional four terms if measured at the .10 level.

Similar to urban issues treated by the Banking Committee, transportation policy considered by the Public Works panel exhibits many of the attributes of an issue area whose agenda is closely tied to the constituency needs of the committee's membership. However, the changing dimensions of this policy agenda over time provide evidence to support both the contention that alterations in committee work subsequently lead to changes in the characteristics of committee members (hypothesis 2) *and* the claim that alterations in the type of members belonging to a panel can consequently modify the committee's agenda (hypothesis 1).

FIGURE 10.6 HEARINGS ON AUTO, TRUCK, AND AIR TRANSPORT REGULATION AND SUBSIDIES AND CONSTITUENCY CHARACTERISTICS FOR MEMBERS OF THE HOUSE PUBLIC WORKS AND TRANSPORTATION COMMITTEE

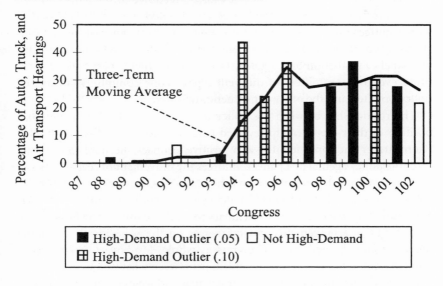

DISCUSSION AND CONCLUSION

Scholars of congressional structure have occasionally speculated about the issue agendas of congressional committees (see, for example, Sinclair 1986), but without sufficient data it has heretofore been very difficult to adequately study these trends in committee work. Using Baumgartner and Jones's data on congressional hearings, I have been able to examine the changing focus of two committees over an extended period. The concept of punctuated equilibriums in issue agendas may be quite helpful to congressional scholars in the further development and refinement of their theories of legislative structure.

Other scholars have suggested that propositions from their theories of congressional organization have implications for understanding changes in committee issue agendas. For example, works by Cox and McCubbins (1993), Aldrich and Rohde (1997), and Rohde (1992) have all stressed the powers of political parties in shaping the policy focus of congressional committees in one way or another. However, this research rarely applies its theoretical conjectures to data on committee work over long periods of time.

I have provided two hypotheses as to how members' constituency and reelection needs should manifest themselves in the work of their committees and shown that, at least for the issues and committees under consideration, such a relationship seems to exist. The causal direction of this relationship can vary — for two policy issues committee agenda changes preceded alterations in committee composition and for one policy a convergence of similar constituency characteristics of committee members helped to formally change the panel's jurisdiction and agenda. Furthermore, these shared experiences occur even on committees of different types — one commonly considered policy oriented and the other constituency oriented.

The relationship between the policy focus of committees and the composition of their membership revealed here is reasonably reflective of what Baumgartner and Jones identify as a positive feedback mechanism. In some cases the policy agenda of a panel reinforces the movement of certain types of legislators on or off a committee, in other cases it is the transfer of particular types of members that ends up influencing issue agendas. Ultimately, this evidence should serve to encourage scholars to further consider the importance of distributive arrangements and influences on the behavior of individual members and the actions of Congress as whole. Moreover, congressional scholars should not ignore the possible link between what we can learn about policy making in the research on issue agendas and what we are trying to discover about the effects of institutional arrangements in legislatures.

NOTES

1. I employ the titles of all congressional committees as they were in the last Congress considered here, the 102d Congress.

2. Adler and Lapinski (1997) and Bullock (1976) argue that many policy committees may have a constituency element to their workload, and find that Banking's attention to urban problems is one instance of this.

3. All information is taken from the decennial U.S. Censuses.

4. Highway construction funds were not seen simply as a lucrative federal construction program, but more broadly as means of increasing employment. Rose states that "those planning for postwar road building thought mainly in terms of employment. Highway building, both in the minds of public and private leaders, would create needed jobs" (Rose 1990, 16). Not surprisingly, much of the initial planning for the interstate highway system came from the National Resources Planning Board — an office established by President Roosevelt in 1938 (Rose 1990, 17).

5. In one case, median family income, "lowest" values on the measure were considered to be the "highest" demanders. For this measure the standardized scores were multiplied by -1 to reverse their effect on the additive scales.

6. This technique makes an important assumption that the component measures have "equal" effect on a legislator's sense of "need" for the benefits provided by a specific subcommittee. For example, this would mean that the percentage in a district employed in construction is *as important* in measuring demand for highway construction benefits as the percentage unemployed. While this is not always the case, there is no obvious means of determining proper weights for each component.

7. See Groseclose (1994) and Adler and Lapinski (1997) for descriptions as to why this particular technique is well suited to tests of preferences on congressional committees.

8. Since there is some variance of opinion on the appropriate significance level for tests of these types, I provide the *p*-values for each simulation so that the reader may make her own judgment.

9. In one year, 1964, Banking held no hearings on urban issues (according to the Baumgartner and Jones data), although this had followed a flurry of activity the previous year, including the hearings for a large mass transit authorization bill that passed in 1964.

10. For one term, the 91st Congress, the committee only met the .10 threshold for outliers.

11. Wolman and Marckini date the transformation of the Banking Committee later — some time between the early 1980s and 1990s (1998, 303). However, their measure of legislators' urban orientation only examines whether or not the district was in a central city and does not include the income element that helps to identify the neediest districts with respect to federal aid.

12. These include categories such as, highway construction; airports, airlines and air traffic safety; railroad transportation; truck and automobile transportation; etc.

13. Note that the committee also ranks as an outlier on this measure (at the .10 level) in the mid- and late 1980s (the 99th through 101st Congresses) as hearings on highway construction increase slightly.

14. Prior to the reforms, transportation jurisdiction was originally divided among the Commerce, Banking, Merchant Marine, Science, and Public Works committees.

11

USING BILLS AND HEARINGS TO TRACE ATTENTION IN CONGRESS: POLICY WINDOWS IN HEALTH CARE LEGISLATING

JOHN D. WILKERSON, T. JENS FEELEY,

NICOLE S. SCHIERECK, AND CHRISTINA SUE

INTRODUCTION

A central theme of this volume is that policy making over time is characterized by long periods of relative stability punctuated with occasional rapid changes. The periods of stability reflect policy environments where efforts to promote change are strongly resisted by those who would be adversely affected by those changes. Major policy shifts occur when this balance of competing forces is disrupted such that the forces supporting change overwhelm the forces opposing it. Change is most likely when a positive feedback system develops where even those who resist change may conclude that it is inevitable and as a result are compelled to participate in the change process.

This perspective on policy change is also emphasized in John Kingdon's *Agendas, Alternatives, and Public Policies* (1984). Kingdon takes issue with a traditional policy making perspective that portrays decision makers as searching for important problems to solve and designing solutions to those problems. Kingdon has famously argued that it is more useful to conceive of the policy making process as solution driven, rather than problem driven. Opportunities for major policy change, what Kingdon calls "policy windows," do not come along very often. Policy entrepreneurs take advantage of these windows to promote their pet policies. A spike in energy prices compels politicians to *do something*. Environmentalists propose more subsidies for developing alternative and renewable energy sources. Petroleum interests propose opening up the Arctic National Wildlife Refuge to oil and gas exploration. Social welfare advocates propose energy subsidies for the poor. Windows can close as quickly as they open, giving policy entrepreneurs with preexisting solutions an advantage: "If you're not ready to paddle when the big wave comes along, you're not going to ride it in" (Kingdon 1984, 173).

A policy window opens as policy makers' beliefs shift from thinking that change is highly unlikely to thinking that change is probably inevitable. Objective conditions matter, but because policy makers are strategic, perceptions are critical. If a policy is going nowhere, most will see little reason to give it much attention. As one congressional staffer put it, "we concentrate on issues that we think are going to be productive. If they're not productive, then we don't have unlimited time here, and we're not going to go into them" (Kingdon 1984, 176). When changes in objective circumstances signal possibilities for real change, this mindset shifts, and policy makers "become more flexible, bargaining from their previously rigid positions, compromising in order to be in the game" (Kingdon 1984, 176). Even opponents may alter their positions in order to avoid being excluded from the decision making process.

Thus the policy window metaphor closely parallels the concept of a positive feedback system. Changing perceptions alter behavior, further increasing the prospects for policy change. At the same time, Kingdon offers a rich description of how policy windows (positive feedback systems) come about, as well as how the opening of a policy window can alter policy making down the road. The "solutions looking for a problem" perspective emphasizes the role of policy entrepreneurs, who are distinguished by their commitment to a particular solution and their willingness to push it even when its prospects of success are dim. Entrepreneurs can also play a central role in facilitating the opening of a policy window. The right solution can resolve many of the stalemates that have prevented policy change in the past. Kingdon also argues that the increased attention that a problem receives when a window opens can alter the policy landscape and increase "the probability that a window will open for another similar subject" (Kingdon 1984, 200).

One criticism of Kingdon's work, as well as much of the work on public policy formation, is that a phenomenon like a policy window is difficult to study systematically. In this chapter, we begin to investigate whether policy windows and their effects can be studied quantitatively. Policy windows are not simply products of changing perceptions. They are catalyzed by changing objective conditions, and they generate changes in behavior. So while we may find it difficult to study perceptions, we may be able to systematically study the *effects* of changing perceptions.

HEALTH LEGISLATION

Health policy making in the United States is a fruitful area for investigating agenda setting processes. The first serious effort to provide all Americans with health insurance coverage in the United States was initiated in the 1930s but was left out of FDR's New Deal social welfare package (Starr 1982). Since then there have been numerous attempts to establish a universal health care system in various forms. Some significant reforms have become law. During the 1940s and 1950s a growing number of corporations began to offer health insurance policies as a tax-deductible employee benefit. The Medicare and Medicaid programs were established in 1965. During the 1990s, new programs increased coverage for children in families that did not qualify for Medicaid, and new rules and tax incentives were created to make it easier for individuals to change jobs without losing their coverage. Nevertheless, seventy years after the New Deal, more than forty million Americans (15 percent) still do not have health insurance, and this number is growing rather than shrinking.

The forces resisting change are well documented. Doctors, insurance companies, and drug manufacturers have traditionally opposed efforts to "socialize" medicine through government-provided health insurance. These interests do not oppose expanding coverage per se. They anticipate (correctly it seems) that governments that pay for health care will try to regulate how much providers can charge for their services.

Governments (federal, state, and local) have also resisted expansions of health care coverage. A health care entitlement is expensive. The Medicare and Medicaid programs alone consume 19 percent of the annual federal budget (estimated at $350 billion in 2001). This is serious money that is not available for other purposes, and the share of the budget that is devoted to these programs grows every year. Not surprisingly, many politicians resist efforts to spend more of a limited budget pie on new health benefit programs.

Public support can provide the incentive for elected officials to resist special-interest opposition, but experience demonstrates that the public can be fickle on the question of extending health care coverage (Skocpol 1997). Although opinion polls indicate widespread support for universal coverage, politicians have learned that championing the issue can be risky. Most Americans, and especially politically active wealthier Americans, already have health insurance. Widespread public support for universal coverage does not always translate to widespread support for specific policy proposals where the costs of reform are more apparent. On more than one occasion, groups already benefiting from government-provided health insurance programs have forced politicians to backtrack on efforts to extend coverage to new groups. Indeed, Medicare's status as an electoral issue seems to be approaching the "third rail" status of social security — touch it and you die!

Nonetheless, the health policy area also offers some fine examples of policy windows in action. Medicare's enactment is an example of a solution looking for a problem. The solution in this case was universal health care coverage, which had encountered serious opposition from the American Medical Association during the Eisenhower administration and had gone nowhere under the Kennedy administration (Starr 1982). A series of events in the early 1960s helped to lay the groundwork for Medicare. Studies released in the early 1960s reported that one-third of elderly Americans were financially impoverished. Part of the explanation was the fact that half did not have health insurance.

Proponents of universal health care coverage, already a feature of most advanced nations, calculated that passing legislation to protect the deserving elderly would soften up Congress to the idea of guaranteeing health care coverage for all Americans (Ball 1995). Medicare was an attempt to get an old solution's nose under the tent rather than a new policy developed in response to a newly perceived problem. The Democratic landslide election of 1964 and President Johnson's Great Society program provided the policy window. Even legislators and interests that had stymied reform efforts in the past felt compelled to participate in the change process — or risk losing influence altogether. Marmor (1970) describes how House Ways and Means Committee chairman Wilbur Mills became an unexpected advocate for reform, and how the American Medical Association switched from obstruction to working with Mills and others to include coverage for physicians' services in the new program.

The 1993–94 health care reform effort, on the other hand, seems to demonstrate how quickly a policy window can close. Some observers would argue that the window never opened. President Clinton made health care reform a central feature of his 1992 campaign, but he was elected with 43 percent of the vote at a time when polls indicated that health care reform was low on the list of "most important problems" for most Americans.[1] But there are also indications that reformers missed a legitimate window of opportunity. Early on, there seemed to be a shared sense that something *was* going to happen. Congressional committee chairmen fought over which committees would mark up and report on Clinton's proposal (Evans 1995). House minority leader Robert Michel actively promoted an insurance reform package as an alternative to the Clinton plan, at least until it became clear that Republicans would be shut out of the process. Many states considered (and several passed) legislation mandating that employers provide health insurance for their employees. Anticipation of major change also seems to have contributed to rapid mergers in the health insurance industry and to a political split between firms that would be expected to benefit from the alliance system and those that would not.

But if there was a widespread perception that reform was likely, why did the window close without any policy change? According to Kingdon, "there is no irresistible momentum that builds for a given initiative" (1984, 177). An initial perception of inevitability can fade with inaction because the sense of impending crisis fades, the complexities and costs of addressing a problem become more apparent, and new issues compete for the attention of policy makers and the public (Downs 1972). Among other things, the Clinton administration did not build on the momentum of the election. The Health Security Act was introduced more than nine months after Clinton took office. This by itself did not cause the plan's defeat, but it made the objective of a comprehensive costly reform more difficult to achieve. The delay reduced the sense of urgency and inevitability. As time progressed, it became increasingly likely that legislators and the public would become interested in other issues. Initial ally Senator Daniel Patrick Moynihan (D-N.Y.) groused that health care reform was beginning to get in the way of the issue he really cared about, welfare reform (Schauffler and Wilkerson 1997). Opponents who had been caught off guard by initial events regrouped and developed effective counterstrategies, including the Harry and Louise ads of the Health Insurance Industry Association, which focused media attention on the costs of reform. Republican opponents began to perceive that with just a year remaining in the Congress, obstructionist tactics might actually kill the effort outright (Hacker 1997).

Finally, it is also worth noting that the 1993–94 debate, although it did not result in a universal health care system, had important spillover consequences. Major changes in the private health care system were driven in part by the restructurings that occurred in anticipation of reform. Health care costs did not rise as quickly for several years. And a new wave of more modest reforms making health insurance more portable and providing coverage for children followed.

A QUANTITATIVE APPROACH TO STUDYING POLICY WINDOWS

In this chapter, we investigate a single health care issue — insurance coverage for catastrophic costs — to illustrate how policy windows can be studied systematically. Our approach is to use introduced bills to trace attention to this issue over time. Ten thousand bills are introduced in a typical Congress. Less than 15 percent of these bills will emerge from congressional committees, and even fewer will be enacted into law. A common explanation for why so many bills are introduced despite their small probability of success has been that most are introduced for symbolic purposes. That is, legislators introduce bills not because they hope to influence policy, but because introducing a bill is an easy way to express agreement or sympathy with the concerns of one's constituents (Mayhew 1974).

More recent research by congressional scholars indicates that patterns in bill introductions can also shed light on more substantive questions. Schiller (1995) studied bill introductions in the Senate and found that members of the referral committee introduced half. The congressional staff she interviewed said that many of these bills were introduced for the purpose of shaping the committee's agenda. Similarly, Wawro (2000), in his study of entrepreneurship in the House of Representatives, found that representatives introduce bills to stake a claim to issues in the chamber. Richard Armey (R-Tex.) developed his reputation as an effective legislator by championing the issue of military base closings. While he was not well positioned to promote his pet cause as a junior legislator, Armey's bills attracted the attention of legislators who were.

Schiller, Wawro, and others who have studied bill introductions have focused on the individual legislator as their unit of observation. While many interesting questions remain to be explored in this area of research (for an example see Krutz 2000), bill introductions can also be used to study policy dynamics. Instead of comparing the activities of individuals, the focus here is on collective activities and their impact on the policy making process.

We have proposed using bill introductions to study agenda setting processes and have received National Science Foundation support to collect extensive information on all bills introduced for the period 1946–2000 (approximately 250,000 bills).[2] As is often pointed out in the public policy literature, resources are scarce and institutions have limited capacities. These institutions must set priorities, and the priorities they choose can tell us something about the character of democratic systems. Among other things, we are coding these bills for policy content, with the intention of comparing bill activity in a policy area to committee hearings activity.

Our working assumption is that bill activity is a more sensitive indicator of legislative interest in a policy topic than hearings activity. Legislators can introduce as many bills as they please, on any subject they desire. In contrast, committees have limited capacity and must decide where they will focus their limited attention. A lot of theories have been proposed and examined in this regard (e.g., Shepsle and Weingast 1987; Krehbiel 1991; Cox and McCubbins 1993; King 1997). Our reading of this literature indicates that much of the empirical research is misdirected. It has focused on the composition of committees (comparing the membership of committees to the chamber as a whole) instead of on what committees do (Hall and Grofman 1990; Maltzman 1997; Adler and Lapinski 1997). Perhaps most importantly, this research does not directly investigate the gatekeeping role that committees play in keeping 85 percent of the bills that members introduce off the floor.

We are immersed in this data collection project as we are writing this chapter, and have few results to report. Our purpose here is to illustrate how bill introductions can be used to study questions that interest public policy scholars as well as legislative scholars. At the same time, we will draw attention to some of the complications and limitations of using bills to trace the salience of policy issues within the Congress.

A POLICY WINDOW OPENS—
THE MEDICARE CATASTROPHIC COVERAGE ACT OF 1988

Half of the elderly lacked health insurance coverage before Medicare was created. Private health insurance, when it was available, was often unaffordable. As a result, a serious illness could mean financial disaster for many elderly persons and their families. Medicare reduced this risk but did not completely eliminate it. Even today, Medicare's benefits are quite limited when compared to the private insurance policies that most people receive through their employers. For example, in 1999 Medicare Part A paid all of the costs of the first sixty days of hospital care (after a $768 deductible). After the ninetieth day, the patient was responsible for *all* costs, although each beneficiary also had a "lifetime reserve" of sixty days of care where the patient pays $384 per day. For physician services, Medicare usually pays only 80 percent of the amount of what the government says those services are worth. In addition, Medicare does not cover many services. It pays half the costs of mental health services; it does not pay for prescription drugs or dental or vision care, and it does not pay for long-term convalescent care.

To help bridge the gaps in Medicare's coverage, many seniors purchase private "Medigap" insurance policies. For a monthly premium, these policies reduce out-of-pocket costs and the potential risks of a long-term hospital stay. Federal law requires that all private Medigap insurance policies cover the 20 percent copayments Medicare requires for physician services, and 100 percent of the costs of 365 additional lifetime days of hospital care. However, most Medigap policies fall short in several important respects. Most do not cover the costs of prescription drugs or long-term care services. As a result, Medicare beneficiaries who purchase Medigap policies are at less risk financially than those who do not, but they are still at risk if they face an extended illness.

Medicare has dramatically improved the health and financial circumstances of millions of seniors. Its central shortcoming continues to be its failure to protect the minority of seniors (10 to 15 percent) who suffer from acute and chronic illnesses that require extended care and/or expensive medicines. Policy advocates and legislators have tried to address this limitation for almost as long as the program has been in existence. Currently, the only option for these individuals is to pay their own costs until they become so poor that they qualify for Medicaid, the government health insurance program for the poor. The reform that is arguably the most defensible — capping out-of-pocket health care expenditures — has yet to be enacted. A major reform *was* enacted in 1988, but it was repealed the following year in response to intense opposition from Medicare beneficiaries.

This is the policy story we investigate. Using data on introduced bills and hearings over a twenty-year period, we trace changing attention to the issue of catastrophic health care. In so doing, we can illustrate the opening and closing of a policy window. In July 1988, President Reagan signed P.L. 100–360, the Medicare Catastrophic Coverage Act (MCCA), which capped the amounts that seniors would have to pay for Medicare covered services and extended Medicare's coverage to include prescription drugs. A year and a half later, Congress repealed the same act following intense opposition from seniors.

The reaction of the elderly was not anticipated. The American Association of Retired Persons (AARP), largest interest group in the nation, had backed the reform but was now being accused of losing touch with its membership. Senior citizens blocked the car of House Ways and Means Committee chairman Dan Rostenkowski (D.-Ill.), "beating it with picket signs and pounding on its windows. A few moments later, a shaken Rostenkowski was forced to flee the scene on foot" (Himelfarb 1995, 74). Across the country, congressmen up for reelection discovered that their attempt to do good had backfired.

The MCCA was a budget-neutral reform. The new benefits were funded by a new monthly premium that was automatically deducted from seniors' social security checks and by new copayments for a patient's first eight days of hospital care in a year. Many seniors interpreted these new charges as another effort to cut Medicare's benefits (Bianco 1994). In fact, the reform provided better coverage than private Medigap plans and at a lower cost (Kosterlitz 1989).

While advocates continued to believe that seniors would come around when they better understood what they were getting for their money, Republican legislators sensed blood and began pressing resistant congressional leaders for a vote on a repeal motion. Late in 1989, House and Senate leaders capitulated and both chambers repealed the act by large margins.

HOW DID THE MCCA GET ON THE AGENDA?

The issue of catastrophic health care costs has been a subject of policy discussions since at least the 1930s. More recently, Presidents Ford, Carter, and Reagan all proposed reforms designed to address the problem. Ford proposed tax incentives to promote private catastrophic insurance coverage. Carter proposed national health insurance, including catastrophic coverage. Reagan eventually proposed expanding Medicare's benefits to include coverage for catastrophic costs.

President Reagan was elected at a time when health care costs were rising at three times the rate of inflation. During the 1980 campaign, Reagan opposed national health insurance, even for catastrophic illnesses (Malbin 1980). The Republican position was clearly spelled out in its platform: "What ails American Medicine is government meddling and the straitjacket of federal programs" (Demkovich 1980, 2124). Carter's effort to control health care costs by putting the squeeze on providers was soundly defeated by strong lobbying by the AMA and other provider interests. Reagan shifted the focus of cost control to the health care consumer. His fiscal 1982 budget required that Medicare beneficiaries pay a larger share of their health care costs on the expressed logic that Medicare recipients would spend their own money more wisely than the government's. Of course, the government would save money in either case.

Reagan's election and the early actions of his administration did not encourage advocates of efforts to expand Medicare's benefits. However, in 1983, Reagan also proposed reforming Medicare to protect seniors from catastrophic costs. It turned out that Reagan's catastrophic coverage initiative was something of a smokescreen designed to sell billions of dollars in additional Medicare cuts (Schneider 1987). While Reagan's proposal went nowhere, his expression of interest in the problem encouraged renewed attention to the issue. Democratic presidential nominee Walter Mondale used the issue against Reagan during the 1984 election campaign. In 1995 Reagan appointed Curtis Bowen, a respected physician, to be his secretary of health and human services. Bowen had chaired a blue-ribbon commission that had recommended expanding Medicare's benefits to include a self-funded catastrophic insurance benefit in 1983. As Reagan's secretary, Bowen continued to promote a catastrophic coverage benefit over strong objections from the Medigap insurance industry (Reports 1987). Around the same time, the American Association of Retired Persons began lobbying legislators and educating the public on the issue.

In his 1986 state of the union address, Reagan once again expressed support for a "private-public partnership" to address the problem of catastrophic costs for the elderly. Secretary Bowen presented the administration's first concrete proposal late in the year. The main feature of the proposal increased the patient's share of the costs of their early days in the hospital in exchange for capping their total annual out of pocket costs. The proposal was immediately criticized as inadequate because it did not cover the costs of prescription drugs or long-term care.

By January 1987, the political climate had changed dramatically. The Senate was Democratic again, Reagan was an unpopular lame duck: "As the [November 1986] election returns came in, the analysts said that the days when Washington was seen as the problem and not the solution were passing into the political twilight" (Rauch 1987, 922). The environment for new Medicare benefits looked better than it had for many years. The president had gone on record as favoring catastrophic coverage. His health secretary could be expected to strongly support a budget-neutral reform. And the Democrats were controlling the reins of Congress for the first time since 1980.

Kingdon argues that "a change of administration is probably the most obvious window in the policy system" because a new administration increases the possibilities for new initiatives (1984, 176). Reagan's election had signaled the death of efforts to expand Medicare's benefits. His opposition to "government meddling" raised the bar for enacting legislation from winning simple majorities in both chambers to requiring two-thirds majorities at a time when Republicans controlled the Senate. Reagan's 1983 state of the union address lowered the bar a little. Reform advocates had reason to believe that their efforts to promote the issue might not be entirely wasted. The reestablishment of Democratic control of Congress in 1987 lowered the bar further by making a veto override a realistic possibility. At the same time, the efforts of interest groups and policy entrepreneurs had helped to pave the way for a solution to the problem that fit the politics of the era. Instead of relying on general revenues, the new program would pay for itself.

Figure 11.1 uses congressional bill introductions to trace congressional attention to the issue of catastrophic health care costs from 1973 to 1998. The numbers behind the figure were obtained by using the Library of Congress's

FIGURE 11.1 NUMBER OF HOUSE AND SENATE BILLS INTRODUCED ON THE SUBJECT OF CATASTROPHIC HEALTH CARE COSTS

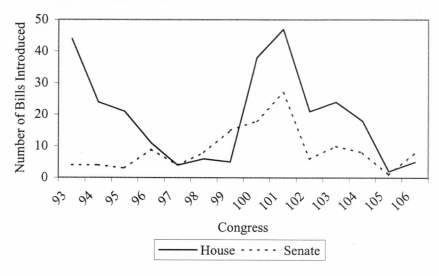

THOMAS website (http://thomas.loc.gov) to search each Congress for bills containing the keywords "catastrophic" and "health." As discussed earlier in this volume (Baumgartner, Jones, and Wilkerson, chapter 2), keyword searches of this kind oversample, because they fail to distinguish bills that are primarily about the subject of interest from bills that include the keywords but have little to do with the subject. Keyword searches of this kind can also undersample if they are about the same subject but use different words to describe it. For example, some legislators may have introduced bills designed to address the problem of high out-of-pocket costs without referring to those costs as "catastrophic."

Both of these limitations are less problematic if our focus is on *relative* interest in a topic. The question then becomes whether our indicator *reliably* captures changing attention, as opposed to capturing actual levels of attention. We addressed the problem of oversampling by excluding those bills that were clearly not health-related from our counts. To address the problem of undersampling, we experimented with several alternative keyword searches before concluding that the "catastrophic" and "health" keyword search did the best job of capturing attention to this issue over a long time period.

Figure 11.1 indicates that interest in the issue has varied over time and across chambers. There has been more activity in the House than in the Senate, and the patterns of activity across chambers have also differed. Interest in the Senate grew slowly until peaking in the 100th–101st Congresses, when Congress passed and subsequently repealed the MCCA. A similar peak in House activity occurs in the 100th–101st Congresses, but there was also more interest in the issue during earlier Congresses. Also noteworthy in the figure is the virtual absence of bills on this subject during Reagan's first two years (97th Congress). Interest increases modestly over the next two Congresses before spiking in 1987. Finally, attention to the issue drops off markedly after the act's repeal in 1989, revives as the 103rd Congress considers the Clinton plan, and then dies completely in the 105th Congress. In this case, the data support the interpretation that Reagan's election contributed to a perception that there was no window of opportunity, while the events of 1985–86 (99th Congress) created a perception that a window might open.

How did bill activity in this area compare with hearings activity? If legislators have incentives to "concentrate on issues that [they] think are going to be productive" we would expect hearings to indicate a higher level of agenda status than the introduction of a bill (Kingdon 1984, 186). Any legislator can introduce a bill. A hearing is a scarce commodity (Talbert and Potoski, chapter 8, this volume). Our approach in this case was to use the hearings abstracts in the Policy Agendas Project database to identify all hearings that addressed issues of patient costs and coverage in the Medicare program. This approach inevitably includes hearings that are not primarily about catastrophic coverage (the oversampling problem), but focusing only on those hearings that are exclusively about catastrophic coverage has a similar downside (the undersampling problem).

To make bill activity and hearings activity more comparable, we report differences from average levels of activity across the entire time period (e.g., negative numbers indicate below-average activity). Figure 11.2 displays these results along with some important dates. The figure indicates two spikes in hearings activity on the subject of Medicare's limited coverage. The first occurs in 1979–80, as the 96th Congress considered Carter's national health insurance proposal. According to one published report, a small number of committee chairs continued to hold hearings on the issue despite a widespread congressional malaise about the prospects for major health reform (Iglehart 1978b). It is worth noting that this spike in hearings activity is not accompanied by a spike in bill introductions. In contrast, we see dramatic increases in both hearing activity and the number of bills introduced in the 100th Congress, suggesting a shared optimism that a policy change was quite possible. Although the results are not presented here, the heterogeneity of bill sponsors

FIGURE 11.2 BILL AND HEARINGS ACTIVITY ON THE SUBJECT OF CATASTROPHIC HEALTH CARE COSTS

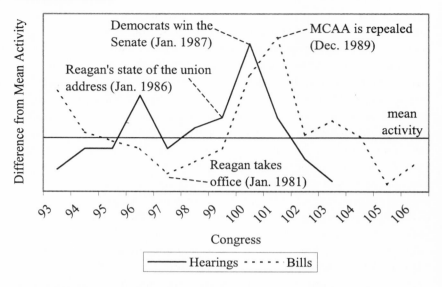

Note: The displayed values represent differences from mean activity. For example, hearings activity on the 93d Congress was below the average number of hearings held on the subject across the different Congresses, while bill activity in the 93d was above average.

also expanded dramatically between the 1970s and the late 1980s. Thus the patterns we observe seem to fit nicely with Kingdon's description of a policy window. After a long period of softening up, a series of exogenous events produced a rapid increase in interest culminating in a major policy change.

SPILLOVERS FROM THE MEDICARE
CATASTROPHIC COVERAGE EFFORT

Policy windows can alter the political landscape even if they do not change policy because "the appearance of a window for one subject often increases the probability that a window will open for another similar subject" (Kingdon 1984, 200). Issues are viewed from new perspectives (Jones 1994; Donovan 1993), policy makers learn (Sabatier 1988), and disruptions in old patterns of behavior pave the way for new ones (Baumgartner, Jones, and Talbert 1993). However, similar subjects face similar constraints. Cost has always been a major constraint in the health care arena. The Medicare Catastrophic Coverage

Act was repealed because Medicare recipients objected to having to pay for the new benefit. Another reform that raised a similar flag would not be expected to fare any better in the shadow of the MCCA. On the other hand, a reform that could address a similar subject without raising the same concerns might stand a better chance of capturing the attention and support of policy makers.

Evidence of a spillover effect is indicated in figure 11.3, which compares catastrophic bill activity to bill activity on two other related subjects, long-term care services and long-term care insurance. As discussed, Medicare has never provided coverage for long-term convalescent care services. Figure 11.3 shows that proposals to provide government-sponsored long-term care services have been a modest but regular feature of congressional bill activity over the past three decades (except for the first two years of Reagan's first term). In 1978, for example, interviews with 50 legislators on health-related committees indicated that long-term care was their top priority (Iglehart 1978a). Legislative interest in long-term care *insurance,* in contrast, seems to be a very recent development. The dramatic increase in interest in this "solution" coincided with increased legislative attention to the problem of catastrophic costs. While the number of bills addressing the issue of catastrophic costs fell off a cliff following the MCCA's repeal, interest in long-term care insurance continued to increase. In 1996, President Clinton signed the Health Insurance Portability and Long-Term Care Act, making private long-term care insurance premiums tax deductible.

Why did the subject of long-term care insurance benefit from a spillover effect but not the subject of long-term care services? We would interpret the patterns as consistent with Kingdon's discussion of the importance of coupling: "If a solution is not available or is not sufficiently compelling, or support is not forthcoming from the political stream — then the subject's place on the agenda is fleeting" (1984, 187). The debates over the MCCA drew attention to the long-term care problem (Shipan 1992; Kosterlitz 1988). However, a new long-term care Medicare benefit was not politically feasible. It would cost tens of billions of dollars per year, and there was little reason to believe that Medicare beneficiaries would be any more willing to pay for it. A tax deduction for the voluntary purchase of long-term care insurance, on the other hand, might do less to address the problem, but it would also have much smaller impact on the budget. The solution of tax deductions for private long-term care insurance coupled policy makers' desire to do something with their desire to "avoid blame" for a visible tax increase (Weaver 1986).

Figure 11.3 also indicates that interest in the long-term care and catastrophic cost issues has returned in recent Congresses. According to one Congress

FIGURE 11.3 CATASTROPHIC COVERAGE, LONG-TERM CARE SERVICES, AND LONG-TERM CARE INSURANCE BILLS

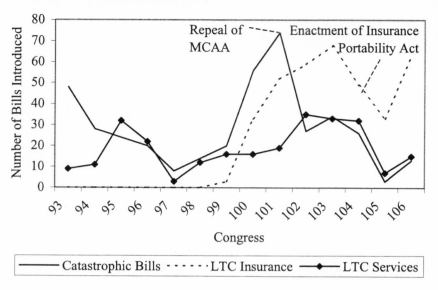

watcher, the "notion of using Medicare to protect the elderly against cata-strophic medical bills — an idea left for dead by Congress a dozen years ago after a revolt by affluent seniors — is back" (Rich 2001, 560). Republicans and Democrats alike have expressed a desire to limit out-of-pocket costs for the elderly. However, the history of the issue tells us that this attention is unlikely to translate into an effective policy response unless someone comes up with a viable solution. Private long-term care insurance is expensive because the people who are most likely to purchase the policies are the ones who are most likely to use them. This "adverse selection" process drives prices up and healthier people out of the insurance pool. Today, most seniors are advised that private long-term care policies are not a good investment. As a result, sev-eral years after the reform, private insurance pays only 7 percent of all long-term care costs.

A government-sponsored program could address the adverse selection problem by distributing the costs of the benefit across a broader population. This would dramatically reduce the costs for those who use the benefit, but it would encounter the same political resistance that confronted the MCCA. Only a small proportion of the paying population would use the services. If the costs are visible, many will once again object to being forced to pay for a new benefit they do not expect to use. Thus while there may be a growing bipartisan consensus for revisiting the issues, the policy window is unlikely to open until a solution is developed that can resolve the elected official's nagging question — who is willing to pay for it?

A BRIEF LOOK AT THE BILL INTRODUCTIONS PROJECT

The case we have examined illustrates how policy scholars might use data on legislative activity to study a subjective concept like Kingdon's policy window. We have found ups and downs in activity on the subject of Medicare's limited benefits, indicating varying levels of attention at different times and in different contexts. The Congress in which the MCCA was enacted is unique in that a range of indicators of attention spike simultaneously. Taken together, these data indicate a dramatic expansion of interest in the subject of catastrophic costs during a very short period of time.

Applying a similar approach to study the *entire* policy agenda of Congress introduces some additional complications. Congress considers thousands of issues, and any individual bill may raise several at the same time. A comparative approach requires a manageable set of topics. The Library of Congress's Legislative Indexing Vocabulary (LIV) includes approximately eighty "top" terms and more than five thousand "subject" terms (http://thomas.loc.gov/bss/abt_bss.html#index). Several subject terms are usually assigned to the same bill, without any indication of which best captures the primary purpose of the bill. The eighty or so top terms are assigned according to relevance, but they have not been applied to congressional hearings and other legislative actions. Finally, to study bills using THOMAS, a researcher must create an entirely new database from text files each time she is interested in tracing attention to a subject.

Our bills project will solve several limitations of the Library of Congress system. We are collecting data on all bills since 1946 whereas THOMAS only provides information about bills introduced since 1973. The data will be released as data tables, ready for analysis. These tables will contain extensive information about each bill, including information about its sponsor and the bill's progress, among other things. We are adopting the methodology of the Policy Agendas Project to allow researchers to compare bill introduction activity directly with other forms of legislative activity. Coding bills has turned out to be more difficult than coding hearings because bills are often more specific in focus. With training, however, our coders are able to approach the intercoder reliability numbers reported for the hearings database (85–90 percent at the major topic level and 75–80 percent at the subtopic level). Finally, researchers who want to develop their own coding schemes will be able to conduct keyword searches using the bills' titles, which will also be included in the database.

WHAT INTERESTS SENATORS?

We have completed this data collection project for the 100th and 101st Senates and can begin to explore how activity on the issue of catastrophic health care costs fits into Congress's larger policy agenda. The approach we adopted earlier in this chapter did not discriminate bills according to relevance. A bill was counted if it was health related and mentioned the issue of catastrophic health care costs. The Policy Agendas Project coding system requires discrimination by relevance. Each bill or hearing receives a single code so that policy activity across subjects can be compared. Thus, the data we present in this section represent the numbers of bills and hearings that are *primarily* about the topics discussed.

What policy topics attracted the greatest amounts of attention in the 100th Senate? We can examine this question at two levels — among health subtopics and across the broader policy agenda. According to figure 11.4, long-term care coverage (a category that includes a broad range of benefits including coverage for catastrophic costs) dominated the Senate's health policy agenda. Thus, it is reassuring that the force coding approach of the Policy Agendas project also points to a policy punctuation in this area during the 100th Senate. We are also struck by the different patterns for bills and hearings. The subjects of health-related bills are quite broadly distributed (many subjects attract similar numbers of bills). Hearings in the 100th Senate, in contrast, are much more focused on long-term care questions (see appendix 1 for explanations of the topic codes). Although these results are far from conclusive, they are consistent with what we would expect if one topic were crowding others off a limited agenda space. The focus on long-term care issues seems to have constrained the Senate's ability to pursue other health topics.

Figure 11.5 compares the Senate's attention to health issues to its attention to other issues. Health issues did not dominate the overall agenda. Environmental, commerce (banking), and defense issues received similar levels of attention, while government operations and public lands issues received considerably more (see appendix 1 for explanations of the topic codes). These patterns raise a lot of interesting questions that we cannot hope to answer without more extensive data. Why are the patterns so different across topics?

FIGURE 11.4 THE CONTENT OF THE SENATE'S HEALTH POLICY AGENDA (100TH CONGRESS)

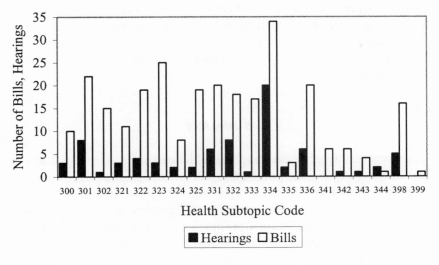

Health Subtopic Code

FIGURE 11.5 THE CONTENT OF THE SENATE'S POLICY AGENDA (100TH CONGRESS)

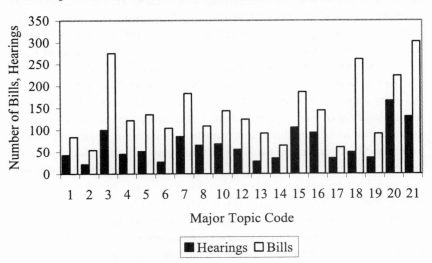

Major Topic Code

For example, why is the ratio of bills to hearings so much higher in some policy areas (health, environment, trade) than in others (defense, government operations)? How do these patterns compare to what one would normally expect? Are the high levels of attention devoted to government operations and public lands characteristic of most Senates, or are they evidence of positive feedback systems in action? We look forward to investigating these questions in the near future.

SUMMARY

The recent history of the catastrophic health care costs issue nicely illustrates the themes of negative and positive feedback systems. Legislative interest in the subject preceded the policy change by decades. The question was never whether catastrophic costs were a legitimate problem. The question was whether there was a politically viable solution to the problem. Prior to 1988, policy advocates including Health Secretary Bowen, the AARP, and members of Congress laid the groundwork for change by documenting the problem, exploring new financing options, and building public support. When the political climate shifted abruptly in 1986 with the election of a Democratic Senate, these advocates moved quickly to translate their earlier efforts into legislation. Other legislators sensed the opportunity and tried to take advantage of the momentum for change to promote their own policy objectives, such as extending Medicare's benefits to include coverage for long-term care.

The key to the MCCA's legislative success was also the cause of its repeal. All of the reform proposals adopted user fee approaches to win the support of an ideologically conservative president. The reformers expected to win political credit for doing something about catastrophic costs and prescription drugs, and they did not expect the backlash that the very visible additional premium generated. Legislators regretted that they had not done a better job of mobilizing public support for a reform that was largely initiated from the inside (Cobb, Ross, and Ross 1976). However, in retrospect it is unclear whether education would have made much difference. Given a choice between the proposed reform with its accompanying costs or no reform at all, many beneficiaries (perhaps most) might well have decided that they were better off under the existing program. The reform addressed a pressing problem, but it was a problem that affected a minority of Medicare beneficiaries. It is not at all clear that most seniors would have supported such a reform, even if they had understood it perfectly.

The policy window approach emphasizes the dynamics of policy making. Preferences are important, but so are expectations and the actions of political entrepreneurs. There may be a consensus that a problem deserves attention, but that consensus is unlikely to result in policy change in the absence of a viable solution. Our analysis of the MCCA indicates that the Policy Agendas Project data can be used to study policy windows more systematically than has been the case in previous research. Kingdon and others propose a list of variables that contribute to the opening of policy windows, including elections, legislative deadlines, budget cycles, national moods, and focusing events, among others. Kingdon and others also hypothesize that reform occurs in cycles where "a burst of reform energy is followed by a period during which the system rests, followed anew by another burst" (Kingdon 1984, 198). The Policy Agendas Project offers a rare opportunity to test the effects of these variables systematically in a comparative context and to explore why reform efforts cycle, if in fact they do.

NOTES

1. The January 19, 1993, Gallup Poll indicated that only 8 percent of respondents considered health care to be the "most important problem facing the nation today," while more than half considered the economy to be the most important problem.

2. "Collaborative Research on Committee Jurisdictions, Gatekeeping and Agenda Setting," E. Scott Adler and John Wilkerson, principal investigators.

12

THE CHANGING AGENDAS OF
CONGRESS AND THE SUPREME COURT

FRANK R. BAUMGARTNER AND
JAMIE K. GOLD

As society has become increasingly complex over the postwar period, govern-ment at all levels has grown larger and more varied, with a multiplication of new programs, agencies, and areas of government involvement. In this chap-ter we focus on the issue agenda of the U.S. Supreme Court, comparing it with Congress's agenda. Like all other institutions of government, the Court has evolved over the postwar period as an ever more complex economy and vari-ous social changes have pushed new issues into its purview. We will note, however, that the Court has reacted to these changes in dramatically different ways than have other institutions of the federal government. Through a de-tailed comparison of the Court with Congress, using new data created espe-cially for this chapter, we show the sharp differences between these institu-tions in the shape of their agendas and how they have changed over the last half century.

Institutional change is not driven only by exogenous social, technological, or economic change. Congress and the Court have been faced with the same such changes over the last fifty years. Their different reactions to these changes show clearly how institutional changes reflect both the impact of outside forces and internal constraints and preferences.

COMPARING THE AGENDAS OF
THE SUPREME COURT AND CONGRESS

Congress's dominant role in the crafting of legislation makes it central to any understanding of governmental policy making more generally. As American society has grown and become more complex over the last fifty years, the number and complexity of issues facing Congress has also increased. As we will show in detail below, these social changes have led to a much more diverse congressional agenda; whereas Congress once focused its attention on a few issues, increasingly its attention has been spread across a multiplicity of issues. (These changes have led to important structural changes within Congress, especially as it relates to the committee system; see Baumgartner, Jones, and MacLeod 2000 for a discussion of these.)

The Supreme Court also plays a crucial policy making role through statutory interpretation and settling questions of constitutionality. However, the Supreme Court differs from Congress in its internal dynamics. Whereas any committee or subcommittee chair in Congress may decide to hold hearings on a particular topic, issues enter the Court's agenda only when four or more of the nine justices agree to take them on. Thus, the Court has more centralized control over the issues on which it will spend its time. These different internal procedures have led the Congress and the Court to adapt to the changing nature of the public agenda in different ways. Whereas the list of items on the congressional agenda has grown larger and more diverse over the decades, reflecting and reinforcing broader economic and social trends, the agenda of the Court has been tightly controlled. Indeed, over the years the diversity of the Court's agenda has been slightly reduced, whereas the diversity of the congressional agenda has increased greatly. To be sure, the content of the Court's agenda has changed: the mix of issues before the Court, like that before Congress, has shifted over time. However, in stark contrast to the situation in Congress, we will show here how the diversity of topics on which the Court has ruled in each period has actually decreased. The Court has a very different agenda now than it did in the middle of the twentieth century, dealing more with discrimination, family, and civil liberties issues and less with economic regulation, transportation, and taxation. In spite of dramatic shifts in the nature of the Supreme Court's agenda, the diversity of that agenda — the number of distinct issues discussed in a given period — has remained steady or slightly decreased. Two institutions facing the same economic, technological, and social changes over a fifty-year period are shown here to have reacted in sharply contrasting ways.

The judicial process affords many opportunities for strategic actors to influence the Court's decisions in order to achieve their policy objectives, including the agenda building stage (Murphy 1964). Cases can reach the Supreme Court in one of five ways (see Perry 1991). First, a case may fall under the Court's original jurisdiction (art. 2, sec. 2 of the Constitution). Second, a case may be technically designated an "appeal." Third, a federal appeals court may certify a case to the Supreme Court to obtain instructions on a question of law. Fourth, the Supreme Court may issue an extraordinary writ to hear a case (Perry 1991). However, these occur very rarely today.

The overwhelming majority of cases come to the Supreme Court seeking a writ of certiorari (referred to as "cert."). Parties wishing to appeal a lower federal court or a state's highest court's decision must petition the Court to issue such a writ. In granting cert., the Supreme Court technically orders the lower court to send the case up for the justices to review. These writs are done completely at the discretion of the justices and are made according to the rule of four. At least four justices must vote to hear the case or else cert. will be denied and the lower court's ruling will be allowed to stand.

Before 1925 the Supreme Court had no control over its agenda because every case properly brought before that tribunal had to receive a hearing. Congress altered this situation by creating the statutory writ of cert. in the Judiciary Act of 1925 (43 Stat. 936). In subsequent terms the Court's docket predominantly consisted of mandatory appeals and discretionary cert. cases. With the passage of time, mandatory appeals occupied a declining proportion of the agenda. In the mid-1980s they made up about 20–25 percent of the docket. At the urging of several justices, in 1988 Congress passed the Act to Improve the Administration of Justice, which greatly restricted the types of cases designated appeals. The result of these changes combined with the rarity of original jurisdiction cases means that today well over 90 percent of the cases the Supreme Court hears are selected by the justices as raising issues worthy of the Court's scarce time (see Baum 1998; Pacelle 1991; Perry 1991; Provine 1980).

Given that the Court now has near complete control over what cases it hears, the justices can potentially render decisions in almost any policy area they choose. The Court differs from other institutions of government, in particular the Congress, in that it is a reactive body: the Court cannot render a decision on a given issue until a case is presented to it. Still, with over five thousand petitions for review every year covering a wide range of issues, the Court has substantial latitude in choosing to avoid or to enter into various issue areas (see Epstein et al. 1996; O'Brien 1993). In spite of the opportunities to rule in a great variety of areas, the Supreme Court has not spread its attention across an increasing number of issue areas. Instead, the Court has focused on a narrower set of issues than Congress, and that focus has narrowed in recent terms.

While the decision on cert. is the single most important step in the case selection process, the procedure works through a series of stages. Once the petitions for appeal come to the Court, they are distributed into the cert. pool.

The cases are reviewed and memos are drafted pointing out the facts and issues under dispute and making an initial assessment of the appeal's cert. worthiness. From the pool memos the chief justice selects a set of cases he deems worthy of further consideration on cert. and places them on the discuss list, which are the cases the justices will look at when making their final cert. decisions. Cases not on the discuss list are automatically denied cert., although any justice may add a case to the list simply by informing the chief justice's office (Perry 1991). The justices then meet in a group to vote on whether to issue a writ of cert. for each case on the discuss list. Following the rule of four, cases that fail to garner the support of four justices are denied cert. and not heard by the Court. Given the vast number of petitions the Court receives every year, the overwhelming presumption is to deny cert. unless there is an especially compelling reason for a case to be heard.

Research has demonstrated that justices, interest groups, lawyers, the solicitor general, and other actors all seek to shape the Supreme Court's issue agenda (see Barker 1967; Caldeira and Wright 1988, 1990; Segal and Spaeth 1993). Models of the factors driving cert. decisions have demonstrated the importance of justices' issue preferences, the presence of lower court conflicts and amicus briefs, and other factors in increasing the likelihood of obtaining cert. (see Schubert 1959 and 1962; Tanenhaus et al. 1963; Epstein and Knight 1998). Interest-group activities include sponsoring test cases, providing financial and legal assistance to litigants, and filing amicus briefs (Bentley 1908; Truman 1951; Peltason 1955; Vose 1959; Hakman 1966; Barker 1967). Amici at the petition stage are evidence to the Court that the case is important and thereby increase the likelihood that the Court will take the case (Stern, Gressman, and Shapiro 1986; Caldeira and Wright 1988).

Conversely, researchers have devoted very little attention to analysis of the overall composition of the Court's agenda and its evolution over time. The most recent is a collection of statistics on the Supreme Court that includes its issue agenda (Epstein et al. 1996). The most prominent exception to this general lack of attention to the Court's agenda is found in the work of Richard Pacelle (1991, 1995). He constructed a data set covering the 1933–88 terms of the Supreme Court. Dividing the agenda space into fourteen issue areas, Pacelle argues that the Supreme Court's agenda has undergone a fundamental change. Economic areas such as internal revenue, state regulation, and ordinary economic legislation went from occupying just over 50 percent of the agenda during the early to mid-1930s to around 10 percent by the late 1980s. Conversely, civil liberties cases, comprising due process, substantive rights, and equity cases, took up more than 50 percent of the Court's agenda by 1987. A factor analysis showed that the change was gradual until the mid-1950s and proceeded more rapidly thereafter. Overall, the Court's agenda, according to Pacelle, has shifted from one concerned with economic matters to one focused on individual rights and liberties.

Pacelle followed this up with an analysis of trends and changes during the Rehnquist Court (1995). The Rehnquist Court continued the decline in the percentage of the agenda space allocated to civil liberties begun in the Burger Court. There was a corresponding rise in agenda space given to tax and economic cases. This has taken place against a backdrop of a dramatic decline in the number of full opinions the Court has been issuing in recent terms. Even though there are now record numbers of filings for review every year, the Court is resolving fewer of them than before and addressing the lowest percentage of them it has faced within the parameters of this data set.

Pacelle's research, however, did not address some important issues. One, he did not show how concentrated the Court's agenda has been. Has the Court focused narrowly on a few issues or spread its focus; has the agenda broadened or become more concentrated over time? Second, he did not systematically compare the Court's agenda with that of the other institutions of the national government. That was not the intention of his book and the data for Congress were not available then. However, this is an important topic to explore, and the Policy Agendas Project now makes this possible.

DATA AND METHODS

This chapter uses data on congressional hearings from the Policy Agendas Project and the U.S. Supreme Court Judicial Database created by Harold Spaeth (see appendix 3). Covering a roughly coterminous time span, these databases enable scholars to study the shape of the agendas of these two institutions and how they have changed over time. The Policy Agendas Project was explained in chapter 2; here we use only the congressional hearings data set, which consists of 67,291 hearings. For the Supreme Court, we created a data set combining data from the original United States Supreme Court Judicial Database (Spaeth 1997), and the Expanded United States Supreme Court Judicial Database (Spaeth 1998). This combined data set consists of information on each of 7,146 cases decided by the Supreme Court from 1946 to 1996. With 246 distinct variables, the data set details the Supreme Court's decisions during this time period (Spaeth 1997). Variables include identification materials, chronological indicators, and a variety of other pieces of information.

For our data set we focused on the major topic addressed by the Court in its decisions, excluding summary decisions and nonsubstantive conference votes. The Spaeth data sets offer several units of analysis, including case citation, docket number, multiple issue case, cases containing multiple legal provisions, split vote case, and case with multiple issues and multiple legal provisions. In the Spaeth data, case citation defines each case by a separate citation. Individual docket numbers are given to cases, even when they are combined with others in a single citation. To illustrate the difference we will use the example of *Brown v. Board of Education*, 347 U.S. 483 (1954). In that decision, the Supreme Court bundled together five separate cases, each with a different docket number, and decided them under one case citation. We chose case citation as our unit of analysis, meaning cases that are decided and reported with a single opinion (Gibson 1997). Therefore, our Supreme Court data set consists of the main issue decided by the Court in each case citation from 1946 to 1996. This is the most compatible with the committee hearing data in the Policy Agendas Project because the Congress data includes the main issue addressed by each committee hearing.

The topic coding system used in the Spaeth data set consists of thirteen major topic categories and 263 subtopic codes. As noted in chapter 2 and presented more fully in appendix 1, the Policy Agendas Project includes 226 subtopic codes. Since the two sources were constructed independently and for different reasons, they do not correspond perfectly. For the purposes of this chapter, where our interest is to compare the nature and the diversity of the agendas of the two institutions, we recombined the subtopics by aggregating them into twenty-one comparable policy areas, as presented in table 12.1. (Appendix 4 gives full details on how we recombined the subtopics in each of the two data sets into a common set of twenty-one policy areas. These topic areas are slightly different from those used in the Policy Agendas project because we want to use a common set of categories for both the Court and the congressional data sets. By recoding the subtopics in consistent ways for both data sets, we were able to construct comparable aggregations of both, thus allowing us to trace trends in attention across the two institutions using a common set of indicators. This is another example of the flexibility of the Policy Agendas Project data sets, and also a reminder of the need to be careful in making use of data from different sources. Substantial work was required to reaggregate the data in consistent ways, as a reader of appendix 4 will note.)

As should be expected, however, using two different sets of data does present some challenges to organizing and presenting the material. Fortunately, the Congress and Court data cover nearly identical time frames. The Congress

TABLE 12.1 Topic Areas for Congress and the Supreme Court

1. Macroeconomics	13. Health
2. Taxes	14 Agriculture
3. Economic regulation	15. Social welfare and family issues
4. Employment and labor issues	16. Indians, immigration, and public
5. Criminal justice	lands and water management
6. Judicial power	17. Community development
7. Civil rights and discrimination	18. Education
8. Civil liberties	19. Foreign trade, international
9. Environmental regulation	affairs, and foreign aid
10. Energy	20. Defense
11. Transportation	21. Federalism, intergovernmental
12. Space, science, technology, and	relations, and government
communications	operations

data extend back to the 79th Congress. The Supreme Court data extend back to 1946, which is the second session of the 79th Congress. So we have full information for the Court back to the 80th Congress. Similarly, the data set for the Supreme Court is complete up to and including the 104th Congress, while we have complete data for Congress up to the 102d. Therefore, our congressional data covers the 79th to 102d Congress, or from 1945 to 1992, whereas the Supreme Court data covers the 80th to 104th Congress, or from 1947 to 1996.

Obviously there are several ways to measure an institution's issue agenda. For Congress we decided to look at the topics covered in hearings. We wanted to cast our net as widely as possible in order to understand all of the areas that Congress spends its resources investigating. As Krehbiel has pointed out, the congressional committee system is conducive to the collection of information by members in areas of interest to them and the diffusion of that information to their colleagues (1995). Given that the universe of issues exceeds Congress's capacity to address them, Congress demonstrates which issues its members deems important by spending time, staff work, and other resources on hearings about them.

Pacelle's work on the Supreme Court analyzed decisions by the Court with written opinions exceeding one page in length (1991). He argued that such cases were more important than those receiving more perfunctory treatment. However, as he and many others have pointed out, the Supreme Court faces an overwhelming number of petitions every year. Since time is such a scarce and valuable resource for the Court, any case occupying even a small part of that time represents valuable agenda space denied other cases. Therefore, we included the major topics decided for all case citations reported in the Spaeth data sets, since this provides the most complete picture of the Court's issue agenda. Decisions on cert. and other summary decisions are not included in our analysis.

Finally, we grouped time periods by Congress rather than by year. Annual presentation of the congressional data shows a dramatic sawtooth pattern, as Congress traditionally holds more hearings in the first year of a two-year term, passing more legislation in the second year; there are no substantial systematic variations in topics of interest across the two years of a term. We aggregate the Court data in the same way, though there is no reason to assume that annual presentation would not be appropriate for the Court. We do so simply to make the data as closely comparable across the two institutions as possible. Therefore, the numbers on the bottom of the figures presented below represent the two-year Congress, ranging from the 79th Congress (1945–46) to the 104th (1995–96).

ANALYSIS

To set the context for our analysis of the diversity and focus of the two agendas, we first present information on the size of the congressional agenda as compared to that of the Court. Figure 12.1 shows the number of congressional hearings (presented on the left-hand scale) and the number of Supreme Court decisions (right-hand scale).

First, one can see that the total number of committee hearings has greatly exceeded the number of Supreme Court decisions over the last fifty years. Congress averages between 2,000 and 4,000 hearings per two-year period, whereas the Court issues only between 150 and 400 decisions. This is not surprising given the 535 members of Congress and the growth in the size of congressional staffs compared to the nine justices of the Court and the small number of staff in their chambers. Also, members are driven to address large numbers of issues by representational and career factors that do not affect the Court.

Second, both institutions show steady growth in their levels of activity throughout most of the period, in both cases reaching a peak during the 1980s. From the 80th to 85th Congress, Congress held a fairly stable number of hearings, except for a drop in the 82d Congress. Following a dramatic decrease in the number of hearings in the 86th Congress, the number of committee hearings increased until peaking in the 96th Congress. Since that time, there has not been a consistent trend in the number of congressional committee hearings.

FIGURE 12.1 TOTAL COMMITTEE HEARINGS AND SUPREME COURT DECISIONS PER CONGRESS

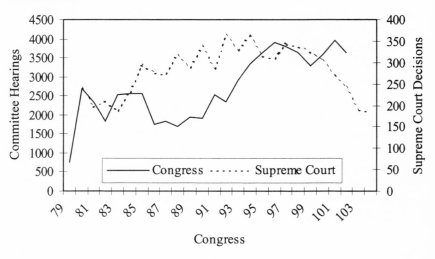

Conversely, the number of Supreme Court decisions rose substantially from the 83d to the 94th Congress. After a decline in the number of decisions in the 95th and 96th Congresses, Supreme Court activity crested in the 97th Congress. Subsequently, the number of decisions rendered by the Court declined slightly until the 99th Congress. Since the 99th Congress, the Court's activity has declined dramatically to 187 decisions in the 104th Congress, the second lowest total in the entire time period.

The drop in the number of cases decided by the Supreme Court is especially dramatic, though others have noted it before. Pacelle (1995) and others explain this change by noting the purposive decision to reduce the Court's agenda made by new members of the Court in the 1980s. This decline commenced shortly after Rehnquist's elevation to chief justice and the appointment of Justice Scalia, and followed by the appointments of Anthony Kennedy, David Souter, and Clarence Thomas. A consensus about decreasing the Court's activity appears to have developed among this group of justices, and with their increasing numbers they were increasingly able to achieve their goal. Chief Justice Rehnquist has often spoken publicly about the need to reduce the burden on what he saw as an overworked judiciary, and he has moved dramatically to reduce the workload of the Court. This is more than merely an efficiency issue, however. Conservative justices have long lamented judicial activism and have argued that more restraint is necessary. With the advent of more conservative members due to the Reagan and Bush appointments, they have a large enough bloc to reduce the number of cases the Court is hearing. Due to the advent of the conservatives, liberal justices also have reasons to restrict the agenda. The Warren and Burger Courts brought about many important precedents. By keeping cases regarding these decisions off the docket, liberals on the Court can protect what they deem to be the advances won in earlier Courts. The confluence of these forces has resulted in a precipitous drop in the number of cases the Court is deciding each year.

These trends are important for two reasons. One, when looking at the changes in proportions of attention devoted to various issue areas, we need to keep in mind whether the total number of decisions is increasing or decreasing. With a growing agenda, a percentage increase for an issue area means the institution is moving actively into it to set policy. An issue with a fairly stable space means the institution is staying involved, but not charting out new areas of activity. A decline in area could mean the institution is moving out of an area, or that it is maintaining a constant amount of activity with the percentage decrease a function of its growing activity in other areas. When the overall size of the agenda is shrinking, as it has most dramatically for the Court since the 99th Congress, changes in space allocation can mean something quite different. A percentage increase could mean that the Court is moving into new areas, or it could be maintaining the same amount of activity so that the rise in agenda space results from the cuts in activity elsewhere. A constant part of the space for a policy area means the institution is cutting its activity at the same rate it is cutting from other areas. Those policy areas with declining proportions of agenda space when the entire space is contracting means the institution has decided to aggressively leave that area of policy making.

We turn next to the percentage share of the agenda for the individual policy areas. First, we note areas of growth and decline in congressional activity, then we show the same for the Court. Both institutions show dramatic shifts not only in their overall activity levels, as we saw in figure 12.1, but they have each changed dramatically in the mix of issues to which they pay attention.

As shown in figure 12.2, three issues have gone from dominating nearly 70 percent of Congress's agenda space to constituting less than 30 percent. Defense experienced the sharpest decline, from 32.6 percent of all congressional hearings in the 79th Congress to only 6.0 percent in the 102d Congress. Federalism, intergovernmental relations, and government operations has also decreased from 22.5 percent to 11.6 percent of the agenda space. Finally, Congress gave a steady amount of attention to Indian affairs, immigration, and public lands and water management from the 80th to 85th Congress,

FIGURE 12.2 THE DECLINE OF OLD ISSUES IN CONGRESS

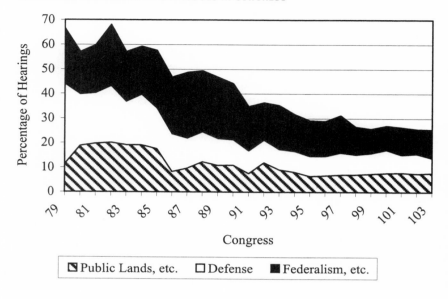

Public Lands, etc.   □ Defense   ■ Federalism, etc.

around 19 percent of the agenda space. This dropped to below 10 percent in the 86th Congress, and while fluctuating somewhat during the middle Congresses of this time period, has stayed around 9–10 percent since the 94th Congress. This dominance of the agenda space by these three areas at the start of this time period explains why the index of topic concentration presented later in the chapter was at its highest in the 79th Congress.

Conversely, as shown in figure 12.3, four policy areas have dramatically increased their share of Congress's agenda space over the postwar period. These consist of health policy, environmental regulation, economic regulation, and foreign trade, international affairs, and foreign aid. Together these have risen from around 13 percent of the agenda space to close to 40 percent of Congress's agenda in the 103d Congress.

Whereas figures 12.2 and 12.3 show the most dramatic gains and declines in congressional attention, a great number of other issue areas also showed more modest gains in the proportion of attention that Congress paid to each. Of the twenty-one issue areas presented in table 12.1 above, only seven are represented in these figures. The remaining fourteen issues increased from about 22 percent of the agenda to around 36 percent by the 102d Congress. The most dramatic growth took place from the 79th to the 87th Congress, which corresponds with a drop in the proportion of attention to the three dominant

FIGURE 12.3 THE RISE OF NEW ISSUES IN CONGRESS

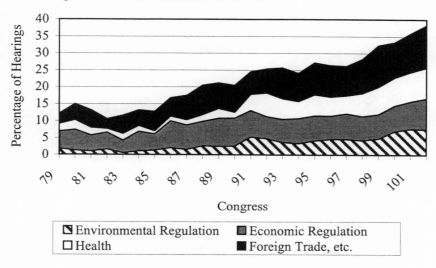

policy areas in figure 12.3. As will be shown later, these events generated the sharp drop in the index of topic concentration at this time. Also, this large group of policy areas reached its largest share of the agenda space from the 93d to the 98th Congress. This occurred during the 1970s and was largely the result of the sharp temporary rise in the number of hearings devoted to energy policy in the face of the oil crises during that time. Since then energy issues have occupied a decreasing percentage of the agenda space. All in all, we can say that Congress has not only become more active over the postwar period, but that it has diversified its attention in an especially dramatic fashion, boldly asserting itself into a great number of previously uncharted issue areas.

Just as the agenda of Congress has shifted from some areas to others over the postwar period, the same can be seen in the decisions of the Court. Figure 12.4 shows that the Supreme Court once devoted a large share of its agenda space to four policy areas — taxes; transportation; Indian affairs, immigration, and public lands and water management; and economic regulation — comprised slightly more than 35 percent of the Supreme Court's agenda during the early period. These peaked in the 83d Congress at 40 percent of the Court's issue space. Since then they have declined to about 18 percent of the Court's agenda. Taxes and economic regulation have seen the largest percentage decline, while transportation has all but disappeared from the agenda.

These four areas have been more than replaced by the rise to dominance of

FIGURE 12.4 THE DECLINE OF OLD ISSUES IN THE SUPREME COURT

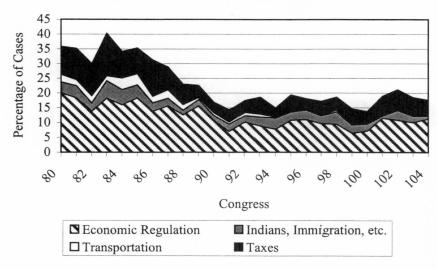

five other policy areas — criminal justice; civil liberties; social welfare and family issues; civil rights; and federalism, intergovernmental relations, and government operations. Figure 12.5 shows that these have grown from about 40 percent of the Court's agenda to over 60 percent of the decisions in the later years. These areas peaked in the 99th Congress at close to 70 percent of the Court's agenda space. These findings support Pacelle's findings that the Court has gone from a focus on economic matters to a concern with civil rights and liberties and social welfare matters (1991).

As in Congress, there are a number of policy areas that have occupied a relatively stable part of the Supreme Court's agenda. The largest and most important of these is judicial power. This area has consistently occupied about 12–20 percent of the Court's agenda space. This makes sense in that regulating the activity of courts and attorneys logically rests with the highest court in the country. The data show that Congress has played a significantly smaller role than the Court in this issue area. Congress appears willing to allow the judicial system wide latitude to regulate its own affairs.

To sum up, congressional hearings have moved from a focus on the three areas of defense, federalism, intergovernmental relations and government operations, and Indian affairs, immigration, and public lands to focusing on economic and environmental regulation, health policy, and foreign trade, international affairs, and foreign aid. At the same time Congress has increased

FIGURE 12.5 THE RISE OF NEW ISSUES IN THE SUPREME COURT

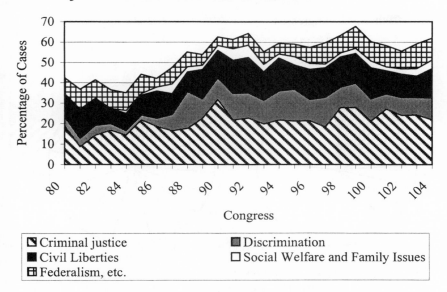

Criminal justice · Civil Liberties · Federalism, etc. · Discrimination · Social Welfare and Family Issues

the total number of hearings and spread out its attention across a greater number of policy areas. The Supreme Court has moved out of economic matters to focus more on matters of civil rights and liberties, social welfare, and criminal justice. Judicial matters, including the regulation of attorneys, have occupied a large and relatively stable share of the Court's agenda.

While both the Court and the Congress have changed their focus, they have not done so in the same way. The issues that concern the two institutions are different, as we have seen. Also, and perhaps more importantly, the two institutions have differed dramatically in their willingness to spread themselves thin. Congress has become increasingly involved in a greater and greater variety of different areas, whereas the Court has narrowed the range of areas in which it operates. We turn to the diversity of each institution's agenda next.

MEASURES OF CONCENTRATION

To understand the dispersion of Congress's and the Supreme Court's attention across policy areas, we first present simple pie charts to display the proportion of the agenda devoted to each of our twenty-one policy areas. For each issue area we present the average percentage of the agenda space across five congressional sessions at the start and end of the time periods of each data set. The numbers on the figures correspond to the policy area codes in table 12.1.

FIGURE 12.6 CONGRESS'S ATTENTION TO ISSUE AREAS

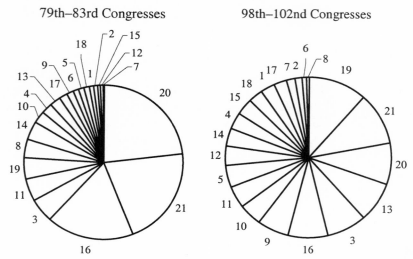

79th–83rd Congresses

98th–102nd Congresses

Note: Each pie chart presents the proportion of hearings during the period indicated in each of twenty-one topic areas. See table 12.1 for a list of topics and appendix 4 for a complete description of each one.

FIGURE 12.7 SUPREME COURT'S ATTENTION TO ISSUE AREAS

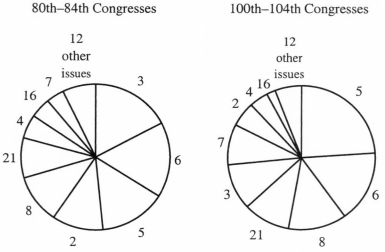

80th–84th Congresses

100th–104th Congresses

Note: Each pie chart presents the proportion of cases heard during the period indicated in each of twenty-one topic areas. See table 12.1 for a list of topics and appendix 4 for a complete description of each one.

Figure 12.6 displays the spread of congressional attention. The first chart covers the 79th through 83d Congresses and shows a tight focus on three areas, with remaining attention broadly spread across eighteen other topics, with none of those other areas being the focus of a substantial proportion of the total. In the second chart, we see the more recent period, where the situation could not be more contrasting: attention is spread broadly across all twenty-one issue areas, with no single area predominating. Figure 12.6 shows vividly how congressional attention has moved from a predominant concern with only three issue areas to an almost equal level of attention across all the issue areas we have studied. In figure 12.7, we see the comparable information for the Court, but the contrast could hardly be starker.

Figure 12.7 shows a dramatic difference between the Court and the Congress. While Congress's attention has become increasingly diverse, the Court's was about as focused at the end as it was at the beginning. Echoing the findings in figures 12.4 and 12.5, we see changes in the specific issues the Court has chosen to address, but no change in the overall diversity of the Court's agenda. Some issues have increased dramatically, some have decreased significantly, and others have not changed very much. The overall dispersion of attention appears roughly similar in the two periods. So Congress appears to have spread itself increasingly thin whereas the Court has simply altered, not diversified, its agenda.

TOPIC CONCENTRATION

We can measure the diversity of an agenda by calculating an index based on the sum of the squared proportions of attention to each issue area: a Herfindahl score. These are used by various social scientists to study such issues as market concentration in economics, party competition in comparative politics, and in other areas where one wants a simple indicator of the degree of concentration of a variable across categories. Economists therefore use the index to assess whether a given firm has established a monopolistic position or whether there is great competition in a given area; comparative political scientists use the same index (there called Rae's index of party competition) to assess the degree of competition among political parties active in a given country's electoral system; and we can use the same formula to get a systematic summary of the diversity of the agendas of the two institutions of interest here (see Hardin 1998a; Hardin, chapter 5 of this volume; Baumgartner, Jones, and MacLeod 2000).

We calculated an index of topic concentration for Congress and the Supreme Court for the entire time period; the results are presented in figure 12.8.

FIGURE 12.8 SPREAD OF ATTENTION ACROSS ISSUE AREAS IN THE SUPREME COURT AND CONGRESS

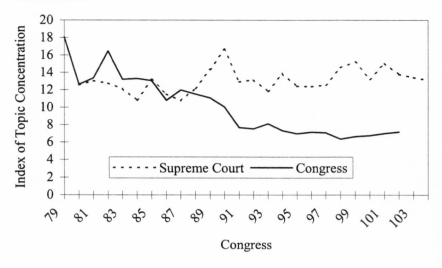

The higher the index score, the more attention is focused in a few issue areas; the lower the score, the more attention is spread across many issues. Changes over time in the index of topic concentration can show systematically what we observed piecemeal in figures 12.2 through 12.7: increasing scores would indicate that the institution is increasingly focusing its attention on a smaller number of issues, whereas decreasing scores over time would indicate that the institution is increasingly spreading its attention across a greater and greater number of distinct topics. Since we are using the same set of policy areas and the scores are a function of the percentage of the agenda space to each area, we can compare the scores for Congress and the Supreme Court. The Herfindahl scores were multiplied by 100 for ease of presentation.

Congress's index fluctuates across a wider range and moves in a more coherent trend than does the index for the Court. Starting at a high of about 18, it drops by more than half to 8 in the 91st Congress, around which it has fluctuated ever since. From the 79th to the 90th Congress, hearing topics spread out among the issue areas into a more diffuse set of policy areas. This combined with the rise in the number of hearings shows Congress reaching more extensively into a greater variety of policy areas. The stable index of topic concentration since the 91st Congress shows no dramatic diffusion or concentration of hearing attention to issues; however, this does not mean nothing was happening. The previous discussion shows that important changes have continued in the shape of the policy agenda. Still, the diversity of the congressional agenda has been steady at a very great level of diversity since about the 91st Congress.

The index of topic concentration for the Supreme Court provides evidence for a narrower policy focus for the Court than for Congress. Starting at a score of about 12, there was a general upward trend to a high above 16 for the 90th Congress. Since then it has dropped to and stabilized at a level of about 13. The trend for the Court from the 83d to the 99th Congress corresponds with the dramatic rise in the number of cases the Court decided. This means that the growth was increasingly concentrated in fewer policy areas. Likewise, the decline in the total number of cases since then corresponds to the decreasing policy concentration of the Court's agenda. As the previous data showed, the drop in numbers took place from cuts in the dominant issue areas, which in turn produced the decline in policy concentration.

CONCLUSION

The point of the foregoing discussion is to show important differences and similarities in the activities of Congress and the Supreme Court. While Congress has generally increased the number of committee hearings over the last fifty years, it has also spread its attention across an increasingly diverse set of policy areas. In other words, the dynamic changes in American society have been reflected in changes in the topics addressed in Congress. The same cannot be said for the Court. While the Court has seen its agenda change over the years, it has not become more diverse; on the contrary, its attention has grown increasingly focused over the years.

Two time periods stand out as especially important. For the Court this is the 83d through 94th Congresses, covering 1953–75. These years cover the entire Warren Court and the majority of the Burger Court. Following Eisenhower's appointment of Earl Warren as chief justice, there was a dramatic rise in the number of cases the Court decided each term. The low topic concentration in the 83d and 84th Congresses changed dramatically until reaching its peak for the entire time period in the 90th Congress. Interestingly, the subsequent drop in the index of topic concentration corresponds with the appointment of Chief Justice Warren Burger in 1969 and the Court's decreasing activity in the civil liberties and criminal justice areas. The time of the Warren Court witnessed the most dramatic increase in the rising issue areas from about 36 percent of the Court's agenda to over 60 percent of the agenda. This corresponded with the sharpest decline in the old issues from 40 percent in the 83d Congress to 15 percent in the 91st Congress.

There was a corresponding, though lagged, change in Congress's activity during this time. From the 86th to the 96th Congress the number of committee hearings rose dramatically. There was also a dramatic decline in the index of topic concentration from the 82d to the 91st Congress. This is due to the fact that the new issues in Congress rose most dramatically from the 82d to 91st Congress while the old issues experienced their sharpest decline during that same period.

The second time period that especially stands out is the 99th Congress, covering 1985–86. The decline in Court activity that started after the 97th Congress became precipitous after the 99th. Since then, the index of topic concentration has declined from about 15 to about 13. In this two-year span, the four rising issues reached their highest level of agenda space. These changes correspond with the coming to majority of Republican appointments to the Supreme Court.

It is especially interesting to note that overall levels of activity show no consistent pattern with diversity of attention. Whereas an increase in levels of congressional activity was generally associated with an increasing spread of that attention, the Court shows the opposite pattern. When its activity level grew, it focused its attention more narrowly. As the Court cut back on the number of decisions it made per year in the recent period, it spread out these decisions into more issue areas. These contrasting patterns suggest that internal characteristics of the two institutions, not only exogenous social factors, play important roles in determining the size and composition of the governmental agenda.

The Supreme Court's activity is a function of its internal characteristics, which differ from those of Congress. The Court has been more focused than Congress since the 87th Congress in the issues it has chosen to address. In the most recent years, while the number of committee hearings has increased or stayed the same, the Court has very actively reduced the number of cases it decides. Not only has the Court held tight control over the size of its agenda, refusing to rule in all but a dwindling proportion of the cases presented to it, but the Court has also refused to allow its agenda to spread more broadly in each successive year. Congress has increasingly legislated in a broader and broader range of areas; the Court has reduced not only the number of decisions it makes, but also the range of those decisions over time.

In the congressional committee structure there is no centralized control over the agenda. Committee chairs have wide discretion in selecting issues they want to hold hearings about. Also, members of Congress are driven by constituent concerns to address topics as they rise in prominence. The Supreme Court is a less representative institution than Congress and has a more centralized agenda setting process. As a result, the Court has focused on a narrower set of issues than Congress, and in the most recent sessions has dramatically decreased the amount of its activity. We can safely say that the institutions of government are not forced to react to social changes in any common ways. Rather, their reactions to transformations occurring around them due to social, technological, military, and economic changes are largely driven by internal characteristics as well. The agenda of the Supreme Court has changed over the postwar period, to be sure, but it has changed in a very different pattern than that of Congress. This suggests that analysts should be wary of treating institutions as pure black boxes reacting to social trends. A full understanding of the dynamics of the policy process requires an understanding of those social trends but this chapter has shown clearly that institutional practices also shape the policy process. As we think of the coevolution of issues and institutions in politics, it is important to note that the same set of issues affecting society reacting with different institutional structures can have differing consequences. Clearly then, a complete understanding of the process by which issues rise onto the governmental agenda must be sensitive to social forces pushing these issues to the fore as well as to endogenous institutional factors that also affect if, and how, the institution responds.

PART FOUR
CONCLUSIONS

The preceding chapters have introduced a great variety of evidence in support of the ideas that public policies are complex and that government responses to them have inevitably been subject to changing attention, positive and negative feedback processes, and alternating periods of stable attention and dramatic alterations in public response to various social issues. We have looked at the multidimensional nature of a number of public policies, and seen a variety of examples of institutional response to those complicated social questions. Institutional design, we have shown, is intimately related to issue definition; issues and structures reinforce each other, and and each affects how the other evolves over time. We have seen important long-term implications of the rise of new issues in American politics just as we have seen numerous examples of how individual policy areas have been affected by the politics of punctuated equilibrium.

In this last section, we consider a number of implications of these findings. Rather than focus on any particular policy issues or particular questions of institutional design, we take a step back and consider what positive and negative feedback processes mean for the structure of American government more broadly. We consider the nature of the political system and also the nature of political science. That is, our conclusions have many things to say about what we can and cannot expect of our political system. American political life simultaneously harbors the opportunities for specialized groups of policy experts to exert powerful control over those issue domains on which they are considered to be endowed with some special expertise as well as the chance that radical disruptions will be made in who controls what policies and toward what ends. We have both entrenched interests and powerful conservative forces as well as radical possibilities that are occasionally realized by various forces not necessarily easily predicted in advance.

At the same time, our study has many implications for political science, and it is on this note that we end the book. Students of positive feedback processes focus on such different elements of the political process from those focusing on negative feedback processes that it is easy for each group to consider the other to be engaged in an entirely alien enterprise. In our view, each must make significant room for the other, since each is involved in explaining and understanding an important part of the political system, but neither can tell the complete story. We end the book with a discussion of what questions we have answered here, but more importantly perhaps what questions we have raised that future scholars may continue to seek to answer.

13

PUNCTUATIONS, IDEAS, AND PUBLIC POLICY

BRYAN D. JONES AND

FRANK R. BAUMGARTNER

We asked the authors of the chapters in this volume to focus on two themes and to illustrate them using the data sets of the Policy Agendas Project. First, we were interested in detecting real-world evidence about the operation of positive and negative feedback systems in public policy processes. Second, we wanted to examine in more detail how policy making institutions evolve under the combined pressure of exogenous events (such as war, recession, and other factors outside of the control of policy makers themselves), and endogenous changes (that is, things having to do with the behaviors and attitudes of policy makers themselves, such as their frames of reference, levels of attention, relations with each other, and other institutional factors). In this chapter we put the essays in perspective, drawing some general lessons from them and pointing to possible paths for future research.

In doing this, we address four topics. The first is the role of the study of equilibrium-breaking events in the policy process; the second is the coevolution of policy making structures and issues; the third is how positive feedback actions in public policy come to stop; and last is the analysis of buttressing and challenging ideas in the study of the policy process.

EXTREME VALUES AND PUNCTUATIONS

A major lesson of the work presented in this volume is the limited utility of equilibrium-based concepts in explaining policy change. We are careful to note that these ideas are of "limited utility" because they are very useful indeed in explaining limited parts of the process, but cannot be the basis for an understanding of all elements of the policy process. Important parts of the process, in particular those that are subject to positive feedback and dramatic change, cannot be explained by the same equilibrium-based analyses that are so useful in explaining other parts of the same process. Equilibrium implies continual adjustment and balance. The old Newtonian law expressed as "for every action there is an equal and opposite reaction" summarizes such equilibrium processes. We term these "negative feedback systems" because each action is damped down or counterbalanced by a subsequent action — each feedback effect is smaller than the one preceding it. In classic physics, such systems can be called dissipative — that is, the friction in the system dampens the effects of any change. The world is unchanging in its basic structure, in balance, and it is fundamentally predictable and relatively stable. Once one knows the negative feedback process that is in play, then one can predict the bounds within which the system will always operate.

In the natural sciences of today, the old static concept of equilibrium is being supplemented by the notion that physical systems are often characterized "by rare but extreme events often dominating the long-term balance" of the system (Sornette 2000, 12). Work in statistics, physics, and geology has resulted in a statistical theory of these large-scale fluctuations, termed *extreme value theory*. Extreme values occur only occasionally, but when they do happen, they wreak havoc with and change the basic structure of a physical system. Omitting the extreme values from our theories, or treating them as anomalies best ignored for the sake of simplicity, would be like having a theory of earthquakes with no concern for predicting the "big one."

For social scientists, extreme value theory carries two important lessons. First, a single extreme value (or set of associated extreme values) can change the dynamics of a system. Geophysicist Didier Sornette (2000, 12) notes that the single largest earthquake in California accounts for as much as one-third of the total long-term tectonic deformation in the state. Yet some social scientists still eliminate "outliers" from their data analyses because they are "unrepresentative" of the data — anomalies that are best ignored rather than explored. A major reason that we use the case method (among other methods) in studying public policy is exactly this reason: extreme values may affect the course of public policy in fundamental ways. If we do not study the particulars of policy change, then we cannot grasp this nonincremental dynamics. Of course, one may decide that one wants to understand "most" policy changes, or that extreme values are unusual and possibly idiosyncratic. This is certainly true: the positive feedback processes that lead to extreme values are quite different from the negative feedback processes that lead to more routine outcomes. Our point throughout this book has been, however, to point out that a complete understanding must include both the relatively easy-to-understand smooth functioning of negative feedback processes and a recognition of the inevitability and massive impacts of such positive feedback processes as those that lead to the creation and the destruction of massive government institutions that then structure policies for decades to come. One sets an easy course for oneself as an analyst by arguing that it is "good enough" only to focus on the periods of smooth functioning of stable policy subsystems. Where did the subsystem come from? That's a much harder question to answer, but without addressing it one can only have a limited understanding of the policy process. Equilibrium-based theories, therefore, can be useful, but not universally: their utility is limited, or incomplete.

The second lesson that follows from extreme value theory is that the automatic functioning of the normal distribution should not be assumed. Increasingly, scientists in many areas of research have discovered that the normal distribution, with its characteristic bell-shaped curve, does not correctly describe the distribution of outcomes. To a casual observer, any generally symmetric curve may appear to be a normal curve. Closer inspection, however, often shows that large distributions of data exhibit a greater proportion of extremely large values than would be expected from a normal distribution. In change distributions, the set of outcomes described by "fat-tailed" or leptokurtotic, distributions is more common than one might expect. Compared to the normal curve, a leptokurtotic distribution has a taller central peak, weaker shoulders, and greater numbers of extreme values. In change data, the tails of the distribution are extreme changes — punctuations. This is not the case for many variables that people are generally familiar with, such as heights, weights, or intelligence. In distributions of height, the tails represent very tall and very short people. Heights are normally distributed and hence the variable occurs within strict limits. You are unlikely ever to meet someone twice your height, no matter how short you are. But policy change data often is not normally distributed — it is easy to find a budget increase that doubles the commitment of government to an objective, or a cut that reduces the commitment of government to an objective by half. The policy world is far "wilder" than the "mildness" of the world of heights or of many other distributions of outcomes with which we are all familiar. Because the normal distribution is so common, social scientists often assume it to be universal. But in fact, many social and political phenomena (like many physical phenomena) are not normally distributed at all. Among these are policy changes as they are reflected in the U.S. federal budget.

There are two particular advantages in the developments in extreme value theory for students of public policy. First, we are able to make predictions about *whole distributions,* not particular points in time at which a punctuation will occur. As any student of policy activity has doubtless experienced, it is easier to observe past punctuations than to predict future ones. (On the other hand, it is easy to predict future stability or incrementalism; one will be right most of the time, and wrong only when it matters most!) By studying whole distributions, we can predict that, in the future, punctuations will occur, even if we do not know exactly when or in which area.

Second, the study of statistical distributions allows us to pool data in a different way: pooling across policy categories, for example, allows us to study whole policy processes in one conceptual framework. Compared to experimental data sets in the natural sciences, or economics, where monthly or daily measures are available, policy making as measured here occurs on an annual basis. This periodicity corresponds to federal budgeting decisions and to the rhythm of government in general. The Policy Agendas Project data sets employed by the authors in this book monitor policy making over a fifty-year period, but this is a short time series compared to those used in many natural sciences. By pooling data across policy content categories, we can study distributions in a way that is not possible with time series data.

In our studies of such policy measures as budgets, statutes, and the scheduling of hearings, the typical distribution has extreme tails (Jones 2001; Jones, Baumgartner, and True 1996). Extreme values imply punctuations. It is possible that a single punctuation will disrupt a system, leaving it to drift incrementally afterward. More probable is that the extreme values will be correlated — when one extreme value occurs, several others will also occur. One might think of earthquake activity. Prior to a major quake, there is seismic activity, and afterward there is the potential for moderate to severe aftershocks. Similarly in social systems, bandwagons in politics, fads in social fashions, and bubbles and crashes in stock markets all follow this kind of dynamic, known as a positive feedback system, at least for a time.

In policy making systems, major punctuations involve changes in attention and thought patterns among the participants. Some have contended that such shifts in thought patterns are not the critical component of policy change. Rather, some external event — war, recession, public opinion change — triggers a policy response. The authors in this volume do not agree, though of course, they recognize that these are part of the process. In his study of defense expenditures in chapter 7, James True notes that budgetary punctuations cannot always be associated with war or other external challenges. He writes that the defense expenditure system is attention driven: "Some aspects of the domestic and international environments must be emphasized and some ignored." Once a major change in a frame of reference is established, it tends to endure for a time, but "no one logic and no single frame of reference lasts forever." Replacing a dominant frame, however, is not a smooth and straight-forward process. People become cognitively and emotionally attached to a frame adapted in an earlier era, and this can make proper responses to existing events difficult. It is true, as William Riker was fond of pointing out, that institutions are "sticky" — they make change more difficult and stability more likely by locking in past policy choices. But human cognition is also sticky, causing allegiances to frames of reference that are not relevant for today's challenges.

A major area for research, then, is how ideas and policy punctuations are related, and how both are filtered through the existing institutional structure. The punctuated equilibrium perspective directs our attention to how governmental institutions and policy ideas interact — sometimes yielding stability, sometimes yielding punctuations. But the particular network of causation has not been fully analyzed. More than anything else, we need case studies of particular policy arenas cast within a framework that is sensitive to institutional constraints and incentives and the nature of the ideas and arguments put forth by the participants. We also need more analyses of distributions of outcomes though this has not been a favored mode of analysis in political science or public policy.

EVOLUTION OF POLICY MAKING INSTITUTIONS

Policy making institutions evolve under the pressure of policy dynamics. It is simply not the case that a policy making system stays at equilibrium until someone formally changes the rules. Of course it can happen that formal rule changes alter existing policy arrangements — witness the drafting of the U.S. Constitution, or the drafting of almost any piece of major legislation. One distinguishing facet of major legislation is the creation of new bureaus or intergovernmental regulations that cause other actors to change how they do business.

On the other hand, under the pressures of day-to-day policy demands, policy making systems may evolve, sometimes in unexpected ways. A major finding to emerge from our studies of policy dynamics is that the complexity of issues is related to the evolution of policy making systems. In a study of the committee system of the U.S. Congress, we found that as new issues were brought into the legislative arena, committee jurisdictions became less clear.

That is, fewer issues could easily be assigned to a single committee because of the complex nature of the new issues (Baumgartner, Jones, and MacLeod 2000). The committee system in Congress operates differently when facing the challenges of multiple issues whose structure is complex than it does in a simpler world where issues are easily categorized and assigned to committees. Compared to the early postwar period, we found that in the 1970s and beyond congressional committees increasingly share jurisdictions, receive multiply referred bills, and are in conflict with one another. The key to understanding how issue complexity affects the evolution of policy making systems is to note that issues may be characterized by several attributes. That allows policy entrepreneurs to stress one attribute in a policy debate, but other participants are free to try to focus attention on a second, third, or even fourth attribute of the issue.

If every issue could be characterized by one and only one attribute, then there would be far less propensity for policy structures to evolve or to change radically after a shift in frame. The reason is that it would be simple to design a nonconflictual policy system in which all issues with Attribute 1 are assigned to Policy Venue 1, all issues with Attribute 2 are assigned to Policy Venue 2, and so forth. Years ago Shepsle (1979) recognized such a system as a "structure-induced equilibrium." It was a system in which congressional committees each reached equilibrium among affected interests, then bargained among themselves for inclusion in budget and other legislation. Because the system involved positive sum gains for all parties, the system resembled trade among nations. And indeed, Congress in the quarter century after World War II operated according to such a system to a greater extent than it does today.

The system, however, could not survive the onslaught of new issues that assaulted the system in the 1960s and 1970s. These issues could not be easily compartmentalized into the existing committee system because they emerged in between or across the jurisdictions of more than one committee. Nuclear power and pesticide-intensive agriculture were not just issues of economic progress; they also involved health and environmental issues. The resulting battles over incorporation of the new issues produced a confusing set of overlapping committee jurisdictions as committee chairs attempted to define issues so that they would fall into their own bailiwicks. Clearly there were limits to this struggle, limits set by the rules of the chamber, but nevertheless attempts to clarify committee jurisdictions did not have their desired effects (King 1997). This set of overlapping jurisdictions meant that advocates of new issues have an easier time in getting a hearing on their preferred issue, but are less likely to get something done about it. The old system excluded many issues that needed attention, but it could forge solutions to the issues it did handle.

Congress does most of its legislative business in committees, so understanding how they work is of intrinsic interest. But we began our studies of the committee structure for a different reason (Jones, Baumgartner, and Talbert 1993). It is emblematic of policy making systems characterized by a tension between decentralized forces (the committees) and centralizing ones (the chamber). Further, the committees often represent, in gross terms, different approaches or perspectives toward the issue: they are institutionalized frames. As the frames change, the related institutions must be affected.

As a consequence, the point that issue complexity both opens more venues for policy action and makes action more difficult is a general one. It applies to any policy making system that harbors multiple venues having some independence of policy action. It applies to the U.S. federal system, and increasingly characterizes the European Union. Where issues are complex, more policy making bodies in a system may find reason to intervene. But the potential consequences are gridlock — unless, that is, some system of deference emerges similar to that envisioned by Shepsle and the students of the old committee system in Congress. In chapter 4, Valerie Hunt explores systems of deference and attention among policy making institutions — particularly the House of Representatives and the Senate, in the making of immigration policy. Deference itself is subject to dynamics — the relationship among institutions may change where one institution is assertive and others are inattentive or passive. In recent years, for example, the U.S. Supreme Court has increasingly felt emboldened to declare acts of Congress unconstitutional — even though all three branches of government possess constitutional views on the law. In effect, by not challenging the Court's claims, Congress and the president have deferred to the Court in this very important matter.

Students of policy dynamics have shown that multiple venues harboring independent policy activity do not result invariably in gridlock, because they offer access points for excluded groups and their ideas. On the other hand, our studies of legislative jurisdictions indicate that too many ideas chasing a limited number of policy venues can result in something akin to overload, where little is done because attention is not focused, as John Hardin shows in chapter 5, on health care reform. Under what conditions then do multiple access points provide dynamism, and under what conditions do they yield gridlock? This is certainly a question for much future analysis, much of which we hope will be done by readers of this book using our new data resources at least as a place to start.

THE LIMITS OF PUNCTUATED CHANGE

In human systems, seldom do positive feedback processes last long enough to destroy the system. Partly this is a matter of definition; we showed in *Agendas and Instability in American Politics* (1993) that policy subsystems can be destroyed in periods of democratic mobilization. But it is not typical for Congress or the presidency to be destroyed, and infrequently during U.S. history have political parties disappeared. On the other hand, as the experience of Canada indicates, it is not unheard of for parties to be virtually destroyed through electoral procedures in other democratic countries. Because the U.S. federal government has been so stable, in fact, American theorists may sometimes have a tendency to downplay radical or transforming changes. But these do occur, we have shown, in particular policy areas, all of the time. A look around the world shows how unusual the United States is in the stability of its institutional structures. Our institutions have changed over the years, to be sure. But in other countries, more far-reaching institutional reforms or even constitutional collapse and revolution have been much more common. All are part of similar processes.

Kenneth Arrow (1999, 54) writes,

> In economic systems, the stock market certainly has violent fluctuations, most usually sudden drops. Yet there is a sense in which these falls, large as they may seem at the time, are in the long run bounded in magnitude. Is there some similar sense in which the accidents of legislative history may lead to results that differ, but, broadly considered, are similar in nature and structure?

Arrow asks under what circumstances a period of positive feedback may stop, in essence exhausting itself before destroying the system in which it is embedded. We will have no full theoretical answer until more cases of positive feedback processes are recognized for what they are, and are studied in detail. But we have a few suggestions of where students might pursue answers.

1. Systems with more regular feedback processes built in are less likely to suffer extreme disruptions. To the extent that a system receives minor shocks on a frequent basis, it may be able to avoid major shocks (Jones 1994). Berkman and Reenock (2000) have shown exactly this in a study of institutional reforms within the fifty states. Where small-scale reforms are continually adopted, large-scale omnibus agency consolidations are less likely. Where reforms are rare, they are more global when they finally do occur.

2. Systems designed to activate dormant interests when a system is under threat are more likely to survive more or less intact. The reason that most of the time stock market crashes are reversible is that the price of stocks will strike some as tempting, and they will begin to buy stocks. When one side in an interest-group struggle wins, the other side has the motive to organize. Observing the relative mobilizational capacity of various interests surrounding a given issue can yield a prediction about how well each one might be able to mobilize, or how far a rival might be able to push a positive feedback process before it reaches an end.

3. Attention is always a major scarce resource in politics. Sustained attention has the capacity of destroying what Roger Cobb and Charles Elder years ago so aptly termed "systems of limited participation." To the extent that collective attention ebbs, the system is more likely to survive.

4. Decentralized decision making systems, in which many venues for policy making exist, provide both dynamism to policy processes and a potential limitation for out-of-control positive feedback processes. On the one hand, more limited policy venues are more likely to be captured by interests challenging the status quo. On the other hand, the existence of many venues means that to change the entire system all of them will have to be captured.

ANALYZING BUTTRESSING AND CHALLENGING IDEAS

In his book about his experiences in trying to regulate the tobacco industry, David Kessler, commissioner of the U.S. Food and Drug Commission under Presidents George H. W. Bush and Bill Clinton, criticizes political scientists for failing to appreciate the role of individual leadership in public policy change. He writes:

> Political scientists have traditionally believed that it is almost impossible for individuals in large bureaucracies to make a difference. Bureaucratic routines, the influence of interest groups, and the divided nature of government are seen as placing insurmountable obstacles in the way of people trying to tackle large public issues. In my view, this pessimistic conclusion needlessly discourages people from entering public service. (Kessler 2001, 461)

Kessler goes on to cite a sizable number of books and articles authored by political scientists that "help answer how individuals, both within and outside of government, can bring about effective change" (461).

The punctuated equilibrium perspective, along with the broader agenda setting perspective increasingly common in political science, was in part designed to illuminate how individual entrepreneurship can alter prevailing patterns of privilege. Rather than viewing the currently accepted set of ideas, groups, and institutions as unchanging, our perspective sees all prevailing arrangements as potentially fragile. In such a world, public debate matters.

If public debate matters, then how people involved in politics interpret messages matters. As we write these conclusions in the summer of 2001, many centrist Democrats have concluded that gun control is an "albatross" for their party, costing them many rural votes. After the election of November 2000, even President Clinton acknowledged the effectiveness of the National Rifle Association: "They probably had more to do than anyone else in the fact that we didn't win the House this time, and they hurt Al Gore" (Dao 2001, 4-1).

Yet the reality of gun control politics is, as usual, multifaceted. The Republican Party did score big wins in rural regions in 2000. But the Democrats cut heavily into traditional Republican advantages in the suburbs. In doing so, they won a national majority of more than five hundred thousand votes. Yielding rural regions for suburbs may not be a bad bargain, even according to electoral college calculations. The news on other fronts for anti–gun control forces was similarly mixed. Of the seven U.S. Senate races where the NRA spent the most money, five candidates lost. In Colorado and Oregon, citizens supported antigun ballot measures, despite extraordinary efforts by the NRA to defeat them. So the second "story line" about the 2000 election is that the Democrats' more moderate stance on gun control helped to forge a national popular majority and a tie in the Senate.

It is not entirely clear why so many Democrats have cast their lots with the "gun control was fatal to our cause" story line given the very mixed message the election sent. Nor can our perspective help to decide such debates. But it can make us sensitive to the naïveté of the notion that any causal story that accompanies a political outcome is necessarily true. The fact that most commentators and elected official have their own perspectives and biases on these issues should also give one pause. Once a given story such as "don't touch guns — it's political suicide" becomes the accepted political wisdom, it can be self-perpetuating. Accepted wisdoms are not necessarily either wise nor true, though they can be powerful if they are accepted by enough participants in the policy debate.

Prevailing systems of power have associated with them an underlying idea, theme, or causal story that acts to deter concerted action for change (Baumgartner and Jones 1993; D. Stone 1989). Challenge the causal story and you challenge the entire prevailing system of power. Naturally, not all causal stories are wrong, but some are. When they are wrong, often they had considerable

validity in the past, but continue to buttress a system of power and deter intervention and change. These prevailing systems have gone by a number of
names — policy subsystems, policy monopolies, and systems of limited participation, to name but a few.

It is now clear that systems of limited participation don't survive without
buttressing ideas. We know that the relationship between ideas and traditional
sources of power — interest group contributions to political fortunes, the
division of party opinion and ideology in the country and in policy making
branches, and class, race, gender, and ethnic divisions — interact with the interplay of ideas to produce patterns of policy stability and change. But we are
only beginning to understand how this works.

In any case, we must start with the incontrovertible fact that systems of
limited participation will form in democratic systems as well as authoritarian
ones. Fundamental to human cognition is what Herbert Simon termed the
"bottleneck of attention": human short-term memory makes it impossible
to focus on multiple aspects of a complex situation at a single point in time
(Jones 1994, 2001). There is a collective analogue to the bottleneck of attention
in organizations, including government: the policy agenda.

Second, humans assume things exist because they are caused by a single
identifiable force. While this assumption of causation is correct in simple
worlds, it may not be so straightforward in complex worlds, where cause and
effect can be separated by large differences in time. A system of limited participation may have been politically powerful twenty years ago but may exist
today simply because no one has reexamined its justification for continued existence. As a consequence, change in democracies as elsewhere hinges on the
activities of the committed few, whose success is contingent on the fragility of
prevailing arrangements.

A major factor limiting change in policy subsystems is the power of underlying ideas to stop creative thinking. When we meet a powerful, appealing
idea, we tend to stop analysis. One example will suffice. In the western United
States, there is a powerful tradition stemming from the Progressive movement
in the first quarter of the twentieth century supportive of citizen initiative to
break up powerful business-government alliances. The process was used vig-
orously at first, then fell into virtual disuse until the late 1970s. Then it was
reinvented as an antigovernment device.

What happens, however, when the initiative process spawns its own industry? Today, firms in this industry will write your initiative, will hire paid signature gatherers to get your proposal on the ballot, will provide a public relations campaign to promote your proposal, and will design and implement a

fund-raising plan to pay for all of the above. We see the emergence of a classic system of limited participation (Meyer 2001; Gerber 1999). Yet the rhetoric of the initiative process remains captured in the old Progressive ideas of using the initiative to limit the actions of the powerful and their access to the councils of government. As soon as the words "citizen democracy" are uttered, people throughout the west cease any questioning of the system (if, indeed, they ever started).

Prevailing supportive ideas of systems of limited participation are like the dog that did not bark during the night, signaling that an insider perpetrated the crime. We don't examine these ideas because they seem so right. If prevailing systems of power are to be altered, it is critical that buttressing ideas be recognized for what they are. It would be a mistake to think that these buttressing ideas are wrong; indeed, they are often correct in the abstract. But they often conflict with other ideas that are just as appealing that, for one reason or another, are not brought into the analysis. We have no simple proposals for dealing with the need for continual creative destruction of policy monopolies in democratic nations. At present, we only warn against the acceptance of a prevailing opinion that may operate to perpetuate systems of limited participation beyond their usefulness in the governing process.

In the not too distant past, economic and scientific progress were justifications for abuses of the environment, energy, public health and safety, and consumers (Baumgartner and Jones 1993). The 1950s saw X-ray machines in shoe stores and glow-in-the-dark radium-laced watch dials as our faith in things nuclear went a little bit too far (see Weart 1988). These problems still exist, but they are fought out in the world of normal politics. Today, two major generally accepted ideas seem particularly dangerous in regard to their abilities to reinforce systems of privilege. They both stem from the same source: the traditional American suspicion of electoral democracy. The first, discussed above, is that somehow "citizens" can govern better than the "political elite." Elected officials are subject to pressures from corrupting forces — basically interest groups. The solution is to let citizens govern — through the direct determination of public policy by public opinion. Today we have proposals for extending the initiative and referendum process, internet issue voting, and proportional representation.

The second is the elevation of the rule of law as a principle superior to electoral democracy. The rule of law, like citizen input into democratic governance, is an important principle. But unchecked it empowers some participants at the expense of others. How the acceptance of a prevailing idea as some sort of absolute can damage democratic governance is most strongly brought home by the U.S. Supreme Court's decision in *Bush v. Gore,* where the Court abandoned utterly and completely its aversion to "political questions" best left up to the elected branches of government to decide a presidential election for the first time in the nation's history. The manipulation of the image of the judge as representative of the rule of law (rather than ideological policy maker, a conception that has considerable support in the judicial behavior literature) is exemplified by Chief Justice Renquist's addition of gold chevrons to his black robes — a subtle claim of authority that is intended to reinforce the superiority of the Court to Congress and the president in determining the course of public policy in the country.

Again, it must be emphasized that there is something fundamental about citizen democracy and the rule of law. Like scientific and economic progress, they are critical values in a well-governed human society. The problem enters when we fail to see the democratic trade-offs inherent in any value system. At present, we know of no stronger antidote to one-dimensional thinking in politics than in the very courses that we teach. Instead of teaching the traditional view in political science that interest groups and the operation of conservative governing institutions lock in prevailing patterns of power, we urge our colleagues and students to join the editors and authors of this volume in teaching the importance of the interaction of ideas and institutions in politics. The public debate is important, but not determinative, in democratic politics, because institutions are important. Institutions are important, but not determinative, in democratic politics, because ideas are important. The result is a punctuated, episodic pattern of change in which individuals, and political science courses, can matter.

GLOOM, DOOM, AND DEMOCRACY

Not so long ago, many journalists and social scientists were doing a great deal of hand wringing about the state of democracy in the world. So many predictions, so certain, have ended up on the ash heap of history, often to be replaced by new gloom-and-doom predictions about the ability of people to govern themselves. In 1975, economist William Nordhaus was certain that democracies would be unable to contain inflation. In 1978, economists Allen Meltzer and Scott Richard predicted that democracies would unable to stop redistributing income. Others saw the problem not as one of redistribution, with the lower classes using the vote to confer benefits on themselves at the expense of economic vitality, but as one of freedom of association. Not the vote, but interest groups corroded good government. In 1994, journalist Jonathan Rauch popularized a thesis developed some years before by economist Mancur Olson (1982). Democracies, claimed Olson and Rauch, could not avoid becoming old and tired because enough groups would be part of the process to make sure that no changes inimical to them could occur, while continuing to divide up the spoils of politics. Olson's theory about the relative abilities of business vs. citizens to organize for collective action and to place demands on government led him to argue in *The Rise and Decline of Nations* that countries must inevitably decline as they age because an ever-growing set of special interest groups would demand ever-greater subsidies, and politicians would simply give in. The result would be greater and greater inefficiencies built into the economy through various government programs, income transfers, and subsidies until finally the nation declined as its economy became too inefficient. This is what Rauch called "Demosclerosis" in a widely cited book in 1994.

Quite obviously, none of this happened. These scholars were not wrong in isolating important social and political forces. Not at all. But they were dead wrong in not appreciating the manner in which feedback works in democratic systems. It is true that voters are capable of shortsightedness. But they are also capable of approving of approaches commensurate with long-term investment. How else can one explain the popularity of using government surpluses to pay down the national debt? Indeed, how can one explain the existence of surpluses at all?

Olson and Rauch clearly isolate a problem with the open nature of democratic systems. But they completely underestimate the ability of democratic forces to rent asunder cozy interest-group arrangements. It is neither simple nor easy, but it does occur.

Democratic systems, unlike any other form of government, provide complex feedback processes that have the potential (but not always the realized potential) of error correction. But that feedback is disjointed, sporadic, and not always successful when it occurs. In comfortable behind-the-scenes policy subsystems, government by the interested and active can cause demosclerosis. In high-agenda, high-profile policy making, issues can be simplified and distorted, resulting in poor policies. Errors, even large-scale errors, are inevitable in any system composed of human beings. In the end, democratic policy making is to be judged not by the errors it makes, but the errors it corrects.

APPENDICES

APPENDIX 1

Complete List of Topics and Subtopics Used in the Policy Agendas Project

Code   Title

1. Macroeconomics

- 100   General Domestic Macroeconomic Issues (includes combinations of multiple subtopics)
- 101   Inflation, Prices, and Interest Rates
- 103   Unemployment Rate
- 104   Monetary Supply, Federal Reserve Board, and the Treasury
- 105   National Budget and Debt
- 107   Taxation, Tax policy, and Tax Reform
- 108   Industrial Policy
- 110   Price Control and Stabilization
- 199   Other

2. Civil Rights, Minority Issues, and Civil Liberties

- 200   General
- 201   Ethnic Minority and Racial Group Discrimination
- 202   Gender and Sexual Orientation Discrimination
- 204   Age Discrimination
- 205   Handicap or Disease Discrimination
- 206   Voting Rights and Issues
- 207   Freedom of Speech
- 208   Right to Privacy
- 209   Anti-Government Activities
- 299   Other

3. Health

- 300   General
- 301   Health Care Reform, Health Care Costs, Insurance Costs and Availability
- 303   Medicare and Medicaid
- 306   Regulation of Prescription Drugs, Medical Devices, and Medical Procedures
- 307   Health Facilities Construction and Regulation, Public Health Service
  See also: 311 nursing home regulation
- 309   Mental Illness and Mental Retardation
- 310   Medical Fraud, Malpractice, and Physician Licensing Requirements
- 311   Elderly Health Issues
  See also: 303 elderly and Medicare; 1303 elderly assistance programs

798   Research and Development
799   Other

8. Energy

800   General
       See also: 2104 for energy and water development projects
801   Nuclear Energy and Nuclear Regulatory Commission Issues
       See also: 501 nuclear worker safety; 1614 defense related nuclear waste;
       704 nuclear waste
802   Electricity and Hydroelectricity
803   Natural Gas and Oil (Including Offshore Oil and Gas)
       See also: 2103 public lands management (including mineral resources of
       the outer continental shelf); 710 oil spills
805   Coal
806   Alternative and Renewable Energy
807   Energy Conservation
898   Research and Development
899   Other

10. Transportation

1000   General
       See also: 1003 budget requests and appropriations for FAA and CAB
1001   Mass Transportation and Safety
1002   Highway Construction, Maintenance, and Safety
1003   Airports, Airlines, Air Traffic Control and Safety
1005   Railroad Transportation and Safety
1006   Truck and Automobile Transportation and Safety
       See also: 705 automobile emissions regulation; 806 automobile CAFE
       standards
1007   Maritime Issues
       See also: 1902 international fishing agreements; 1915 Panama Canal;
       2104 port development and construction
1010   Public Works (Infrastructure Development)
       See also: 800 energy project; 2104 water resources development
1098   Research and Development
1099   Other

12. Law, Crime, and Family Issues

1200   General
1201   Executive Branch Agencies Dealing With Law and Crime
       See also: 1800 U.S. Customs appropriations

1202   White Collar Crime and Organized Crime
        See also: 1203 drug related money laundering

1203   Illegal Drug Production, Trafficking, and Control

1204   Court Administration
        See also: 1205 parole issues; 1210 criminal sentencing requirements and
        civil suit guidelines

1205   Prisons

1206   Juvenile Crime and the Juvenile Justice System

1207   Child Abuse and Child Pornography

1208   Family Issues

1209   Police, Fire, and Weapons Control

1210   Criminal and Civil Code

1211   Riots and Crime Prevention
        See also: 1208 domestic violence

1299:   Other

13. Social Welfare

1300   General
        See also: 300 HHS appropriations specific to health; 300 HEW
        appropriations specific to health; 600 HEW appropriations specific
        to education

1301   Food Stamps, Food Assistance, and Nutrition Monitoring Programs
        See also: 349 the role of diets in disease prevention

1302   Poverty and Assistance for Low-Income Families
        See also: 508 child care; 1204 legal assistance for the poor

1303   Elderly Issues and Elderly Assistance Programs (Including Social Security
        Administration)
        See also: 311 elderly health issues; 1301 elderly nutrition assistance programs;
        1408 elderly housing

1304   Assistance to the Disabled and Handicapped
        See also: 205 handicapped access to federal buildings

1305   Social Services and Volunteer Associations
        See also: 1929 Peace Corps

1399   Other

14. Community Development and Housing Issues

1400   General

1401   Housing and Community Development
        See also: 1403 urban economic development; 1405 rural economic
        development

19. International Affairs and Foreign Aid

20. Government Operations

See also: 201 racial discrimination in the USPS; 2008 construction of post
office buildings

2004   Government Employee Benefits, Civil Service Issues
See also: 200 discrimination in the federal government employment;
2003 postal employees; 2012 political activities of federal employees

2005   Nominations and Appointments

2006   Currency, Commemorative Coins, Medals, U.S. Mint
See also: 104 monetary policy

2007   Government Procurement, Procurement Fraud and Contractor
Management
See also: 1610 military procurement; 1617 military contractor oversight

2008   Government Property Management

2009   IRS Administration
See also: 107 taxation

2010   Nixon Impeachment

2011   Federal Government Branch Relations and Administrative Issues

2012   Regulation of Political Campaigns, Political Advertising, PAC regulation,
Voter Registration, Government Ethics

2013   Census

2014   District of Columbia Affairs

2015   Relief of Claims Against the U.S. Government

2030   Federal Holidays

2099   Other

21. Public Lands and Water Management

2100   General

2101   National Parks, Memorials, Historic Sites, and Recreation
See also: 2103 public lands management

2102   Native American Affairs

2103   Natural Resources, Public Lands, and Forest Management
See also: 709 animal and forest protection; 803 oil and gas leasing;
805 coal leasing; 2101 land conveyance for national parks

2104   Water Resources Development
See also: 711 water and soil conservation; 802 hydroelectricity;
1007 navigation and maritime issues

2105   U.S. Dependencies and Territorial Issues

2199   Other

APPENDIX 2

Complete List of Topics and Subtopics Used by OMB

Code   Title

050   National Defense

     051   Department of Defense-Military

     053   Atomic Energy Defense Activities

     054   Defense-related Activities

150   International Affairs

     151   International Development and Humanitarian Assistance

     152   International Security Assistance

     153   Conduct of Foreign Affairs

     154   Foreign Information and Exchange Activities

     155   International Financial Programs

250   General Science, Space, and Technology

     251   General Science and Basic Research

     252   Space Flight, Research, and Supporting Activities

270   Energy

     271   Energy Supply

     272   Energy Conservation

     274   Emergency Energy Preparedness

     276   Energy Information, Policy, and Regulation

300   Natural Resources and Environment

     301   Water Resources

     302   Conservation and Land Management

     303   Recreational Resources

     304   Pollution Control and Abatement

     306   Other Natural Resources

350   Agriculture

     351   Farm Income Stabilization

     352   Agricultural Research and Services

370   Commerce and Housing Credit

     371   Mortgage Credit

     372   Postal Service

     373   Deposit Insurance

     376   Other Advancement of Commerce

400   Transportation

     401   Ground Transportation

     402   Air Transportation

403 Water Transportation

407 Other Transportation

450 Community and Regional Development

    451 Community Development

    452 Area and Regional Development

    453 Disaster Relief and Insurance

500 Education, Training, Employment, and Social Services

    501 Elementary, Secondary, and Vocational Education

    502 Higher Education

    503 Research and General Education Aids

    504 Training and Employment

    505 Other Labor Services

    506 Social Services

550 Health

    551 Health Care Services

    552 Health Research and Training

    554 Consumer and Occupational Health and Safety

570 Medicare

    571 Medicare

600 Income Security

    601 General Retirement and Disability Insurance (excluding social security)

    602 Federal Employee Retirement and Disability

    603 Unemployment Compensation

    604 Housing Assistance

    605 Food and Nutrition Assistance

    609 Other Income Security

650 Social Security

    651 Social Security

700 Veterans Benefits and Services

    701 Income Security for Veterans

    702 Veterans Education, Training, and Rehabilitation

    703 Hospital and Medical Care for Veterans

    704 Veterans Housing

    705 Other Veterans Benefits and Services

750 Administration of Justice

    751 Federal Law Enforcement Activities

    752 Federal Litigative and Judicial Activities

753   Federal Correctional Activities
754   Criminal Justice Assistance
800   General Government
801   Legislative Functions
802   Executive Direction and Management
803   Central Fiscal Operations
804   General Property and Records Management
805   Central Personnel Management
806   General Purpose Fiscal Assistance
808   Other General Government
809   Deductions for Offsetting Receipts
900   Net Interest
901   Interest on the Public Debt
902   Interest Received by On-budget Trust Funds
903   Interest Received by Off-budget Trust Funds
908   Other Interest
950   Undistributed Offsetting Receipts
951   Employer Share, Employee Retirement (On-budget)
952   Employer Share, Employee Retirement (Off-budget)
953   Rents and Royalties on the Outer Continental Shelf
954   Sale of Major Assets

Sources: *Budget of the United States Government for Fiscal Year 1995* (1996, U.S. Department of Commerce), CD-ROM; see also OMB technical staff paper FAB 79-1, *The Functional Classification in the Budget,* dated February 22, 1979. Criteria for functional classification may be found in "The Budget System and Concepts of the United States Government" in the *FY 1995 BUSG* and in the *FY 1996 BUSG.* Additional information was drawn from the *Budget of the United States Government* (serial, fiscal years 1948 through 1996) and from the *Report of the President's Commission on Budget Concepts* (U.S. Government Printing Office, October 1967).

APPENDIX 3
United States Supreme Court Judicial Data Base Codes Used by Spaeth (Spaeth 1997, 1998)
Code   Title
1 Criminal Procedure
010   Involuntary Confession
013   Habeas Corpus

3 First Amendment

911   Federal Pre-emption of State Regulation: Rarely Involves Union Activity.
      Does not Involve Constitutional Interpretation.

920   Submerged Lands Act

930   Commodities

931   Intergovernmental Tax Immunity

932   Marital Property, Including Obligation of Child Support

933   Natural Resources

934   Pollution, Air or Water

935   Public Utilities

936   State Tax

939   Miscellaneous

949   Miscellaneous Federalism

11 Interstate Relations

950   Boundary Dispute Between States

951   Non-real Property Dispute Between States

959   Miscellaneous Interstate Relations Conflict

12 Federal Taxation

960   Federal Taxation (except as pertains to 970 and 975): Typically under
      Provisions of the Internal Revenue Code

970   Federal Taxation of Gifts, Personal, and Professional Expenses

975   Priority of Federal Fiscal Claims: Over Those of the States or Private Entities

979   Miscellaneous Federal Taxation

13 Miscellaneous

980   Legislative Veto

989   Miscellaneous

APPENDIX 4
Linking the Policy Agenda Topic Codes with Those Used by Spaeth
(Spaeth 1997, 1998)

Policy Area	Policy Agendas Project Codes	Supreme Court Codes
1. Macroeconomics	100, 103, 104, 105, 108, 110, 199	No Issue Areas
2. Taxes	107, 2009	173, 626, 936, 960, 970, 975, 979
3. Economic Regulation: Banking, Finance, and Domestic Commerce	1500, 1501, 1502, 1504, 1505, 1507, 1520, 1521, 1522, 1523, 1524, 1525, 1526, 1599	601, 605, 611, 614, 615, 617, 618, 631, 636, 653, 656, 661, 662, 663, 664, 699

4. Employment and Labor Issues	500, 501, 502, 503, 504, 505, 506, 508, 529, 599	Issue Area 7, covering: 553, 555, 557, 559, 561, 563, 575, 576, 577, 578, 579, 581, 582, 583, 584, 585, 586, 587, 588, 589, 599. And 621
5. Criminal Justice	1200, 1201, 1202, 1203, 1205, 1206, 1207, 1209, 1210, 1211, 1299	010, 013, 014, 015, 016, 017, 018, 020, 021, 022, 023, 030, 040, 041, 050, 060, 070, 100, 101, 102, 103, 104, 105, 106, 107, 110, 111, 112, 113, 114, 115, 116, 117, 118, 119, 120, 161, 162, 163, 164, 165, 166, 167, 168, 169, 171, 174, 175, 176, 177, 178, 180, 181, 190, 191, 199
6. Judicial Power and Regulation of Attorneys	1204	Issue Area 9, covering: 701, 702, 703, 704, 705, 706, 707, 708, 712, 715, 717, 721, 731, 741, 751, 752, 753, 754, 755, 759, 801, 802, 803, 804, 805, 806, 807, 808, 809, 810, 811, 851, 852, 853, 854, 855, 856, 857, 858, 859, 860, 861, 862, 863, 864, 865, 866, 867, 868, 869, 870, 899. And Issue Area 6, covering: 542, 544, 546, 548
7. Civil Rights: Voting and Discrimination	200, 201, 202, 204, 205, 206, 299	210, 211, 212, 220, 221, 222, 223, 230, 250, 261, 283, 284, 301, 321, 331, 341, 391, 399
8. Civil Liberties	207, 208, 209	Issue Area 3, covering: 401, 411, 415, 416, 421, 422, 430, 431, 432, 433, 434, 435, 441, 444, 451, 455, 461, 462, 471, 472. And Issue Area 4, covering 501, 502, 503, 504, 505, 506, 507. And Issue Area 5, covering 531, 533, 534, 537

9. Environmental Regulation	Topic code 7, covering: 700, 701, 703, 704, 705, 707, 708, 709, 710, 711, 798, 799	638, 933, 934
10. Energy	Topic Code 8, covering: 800, 801, 802, 803, 805, 806, 807, 898, 899	674, 681, 682, 683, 684, 685, 935
11. Transportation	Topic Code 10, covering: 1000, 1001, 1002, 1003, 1005, 1006, 1007, 1010, 1098, 1099	671, 672, 673, 675
12. Space, Science, Technology and Communications	Topic Code 17, covering: 1700, 1701, 1704, 1705, 1706, 1707, 1708, 1709, 1798, 1799	686, 687, 688
13. Health	Topic Code 3, covering: 300, 301, 303, 306, 307, 309, 310, 311, 312, 313, 315, 331, 332, 333, 334, 349, 398, 399	No Issue Area Codes
14. Agriculture	Topic Code 4, covering: 400, 401, 402, 403, 404, 405, 498, 499	No Issue Area Codes
15. Social Welfare and Family Issues	1208. Topic Code 13, covering: 1300, 1301, 1302, 1303, 1304, 1305, 1399	311, 312, 381, 382, 383, 384, 385, 386, 387, 388
16. Indians, Immigration, Public Lands and Water Management	Topic Code 21, covering: 2100, 2101, 2102, 2103, 2104, 2105, 2199	172, 271, 272, 293, 294, 371, 372, 373, 374, 375, 376
17. Housing and Community Development	Topic Code 14, covering: 1400, 1401, 1403, 1404, 1405, 1406, 1407, 1408, 1409, 1410, 1499	652
18. Education (excluding constitutional issues such as desegregation, etc.)	Topic Code 6, covering: 600, 601, 602, 603, 604, 606, 607, 609, 698, 699	No Issue Area Codes
19. Foreign Trade, International Affairs, and Foreign Aid	Topic Code 18, covering: 1800, 1802, 1803, 1804, 1806, 1807, 1808, 1809. Topic	179

	Code 19, covering: 1900, 1901, 1902, 1905, 1906, 1907, 1908, 1909, 1910, 1911, 1912, 1914, 1915, 1919, 1920, 1925, 1926, 1927, 1929, 1999	
20. Defense	Topic Code 16, covering: 1600, 1602, 1603, 1604, 1605, 1606, 1608, 1609, 1610, 1611, 1612, 1614, 1615, 1616, 1617, 1619, 1620, 1699	361, 362, 363
21. Federalism, Intergovernmental Relations and Government Operations	Topic Code 20, covering: 2000, 2001, 2002, 2003, 2004, 2005, 2006, 2007, 2008, 2009, 2010, 2011, 2012, 2013, 2014, 2015, 2030, 2099	616, 650, 900, 910, 911, 920, 903, 931, 932, 939, 949. Issue Area 11, covering: 950, 951, 959. And 980, 989

REFERENCES

Aberbach, Joel D. 1990. *Keeping a Watchful Eye: The Politics of Congressional Oversight.* Washington: Brookings.

Adler, E. Scott. Forthcoming. *Why Congressional Reforms Fail: Reelection and the Committee System.* Chicago: University of Chicago Press.

Adler, E. Scott, and John Lapinski. 1997. "Demand-side Theory and Congressional Committee Composition: A Constituency Characteristics Approach." *American Journal of Political Science* 41:895–918.

Aldrich, John, and David Rohde. 1997. "Balance of Power: Republican Party Leadership and the Committee System in the 104th House." Paper presented at the Annual Meeting of the Midwest Political Science Association, Chicago.

Allison, Graham T. 1971. *Essence of Decision: Explaining the Cuban Missile Crisis.* Boston: Little Brown.

Alvarez, R. Michael, and Jason Saving. 1997. "Deficits, Democrats, and Distributive Benefits: Congressional Elections and the Pork Barrel in the 1980s." *Political Research Quarterly* 50:809–32.

"An act making appropriations for the civil and diplomatic expenses of Government for the fiscal year ending the thirtieth day of June, eighteen hundred and forty-five, and for other purposes." 1844. 28 Cong. Ch. 105, 5 Stat. 691.

"An act to provide for surveying the coasts of the United States." 1807. 9 Cong. Ch. 8, 2 Stat. 413.

"An act to repeal part of the act, entitled 'An act to provide for surveying the coasts of the United States.'" 1818. 15 Cong. Ch. 58, 3 Stat 425.

Annals of Congress. 1806. 9th Congress, 2d session, 151–53.

Arnold, R. Douglas. 1979. *Congress and the Bureaucracy: A Theory of Influence.* New Haven: Yale University Press.

Arrow, Kenneth. 1999. Comments on the Commentaries. In *Competition and Cooperation: Conversations with Nobelists about Economics and Political Science,* ed. James E. Alt, Margaret Levi, and Elinor Ostrom. New York: Russell Sage.

Arthur, W. Brian. 1994. *Increasing Returns and Path Dependence in the Economy.* Ann Arbor: University of Michigan Press.

Axelrod, Donald. 1988. *Budgeting for Modern Government.* New York: St. Martin's Press.

Axelrod, Robert. 1997. *The Complexity of Cooperation.* Princeton: Princeton University Press.

Bach, Stanley, and Steven S. Smith. 1988. *Managing Uncertainty in the House of Representatives: Adaptation and Innovation in Special Rules.* Washington: Brookings.

Bader, John B. 1997. *Taking the Initiative: Leadership Agendas in Congress and the "Contract with America."* Washington: Georgetown University Press.

Baird, Vanessa A. 1998. "The Expanding Issue Agenda of the United States Supreme Court." Paper presented at the Annual Meeting of the American Political Science Association, Boston.

Ball, Robert M. 1995. "What Medicare Architects Had in Mind." *Health Affairs* 14 (4): 62–72.

Banerjee, Abhijit V. 1992. "A Simple Model of Herd Behavior." *Quarterly Journal of Economics* 107:797–817.

Barker, Lucius. 1967. "Third Parties in Litigation: A Systematic View of the Judicial Function." *Journal of Politics* 29:41–69.

Bartels, Larry M. 1988. *Presidential Primaries and the Dynamics of Public Choice.* Princeton: Princeton University Press.

———. 1987. "Candidate Choice and the Dynamics of the Presidential Nominating Process." *American Journal of Political Science* 31:1–30.

Baum, Lawrence. 1998. *The Supreme Court.* 6th ed. Washington: CQ Press.

Baumgartner, Frank R. 1989. *Conflict and Rhetoric in French Policymaking.* Pittsburgh: University of Pittsburgh Press.

Baumgartner, Frank R., and Bryan D. Jones. 1993. *Agendas and Instability in American Politics.* Chicago: University of Chicago Press.

Baumgartner, Frank R., Bryan D. Jones, Glen S. Krutz, and Michael C. Rosenstiehl. 1997. "Trends in the Production of Legislation, 1949–1994." Paper presented at the American Political Science Association Meetings, Washington.

Baumgartner, Frank R., Bryan D. Jones, and Michael C. MacLeod. 1997. "It Doesn't Get Any Worse Than This: Institutional Dilemmas of Policymaking in Health Care." Typescript, University of Washington, Center for American Politics and Public Policy.

———. 1998a. "Lessons from the Trenches: Ensuring Quality, Reliability, and Usability in the Creation of a New Data Source." *Political Methodologist* 8 (2): 1–10.

———. 1998b. "Policymaking, Jurisdictional Ambiguity, and the Legislative Process." Discussion Paper 4, Center for American Politics and Public Policy, University of Washington.

———. 2000. "The Evolution of Legislative Jurisdictions." *Journal of Politics* 62:321–49.

Baumgartner, Frank R., Bryan D. Jones, and Michael C. Rosenstiehl. 1997. "New Issues and Old Committees: Jurisdictional Change in Congress, 1947–1993." Paper presented at the Midwest Political Science Association Meetings, Chicago.

Baumgartner, Frank R., and Beth L. Leech. 1998. *Basic Interests: The Importance of*

Groups in Politics and in Political Science. Princeton: Princeton University Press.

Bendor, Jonathan, and Terry M. Moe. 1985. "An Adaptive Model of Bureaucratic Politics." *American Political Science Review* 79:755–74.

Bentley, Arthur. 1908. *The Process of Government.* Chicago: University of Chicago Press.

Berelson, Bernard, Paul Lazarsfeld, and William McPhee. 1954. *Voting.* Chicago: University of Chicago Press.

Berkman, Michael B., and Christopher Reenock. 2000. "Building the American States: Executive Branch Reorganization and Reform, 1952–1992." Presented at the Annual Midwest Political Science Association Meetings, Chicago.

Berman, Larry. 1982. *Planning a Tragedy: The Americanization of the War in Vietnam.* New York: Norton.

Bianco, William T. 1994. *Trust: Representatives and Constituents.* Ann Arbor: University of Michigan Press.

Bikhchandani, Sushil, David Hirshleifer, and Ivo Welch. 1992. "A Theory of Fads, Fashion, Custom, and Cultural Change as Informational Cascades." *Journal of Political Economy* 100:992–1026.

Binder, Sarah A. 1995. "Partisanship and Procedural Choice: Institutional Change in the Early Congress, 1789–1823." *Journal of Politics* 57:1093–118.

———. 1996. "The Partisan Basis of Procedural Choice: Allocating Parliamentary Rights in the House, 1789–1990." *American Political Science Review* 90:8–20.

———. 1997. *Minority Rights, Majority Rule: Partisanship and the Development of Congress.* Cambridge: Cambridge University Press.

Birkland, Thomas. 1997. *After Disaster: Agenda-Setting, Public Policy, and Focusing Events.* Washington: Georgetown University Press.

Black, Duncan. 1958. *The Theory of Committees and Elections.* London: Cambridge University Press.

Bond, Jon R., and Richard Fleisher. 1990. *The President in the Legislative Arena.* Chicago: University of Chicago Press.

Borjas, George J. 1990. *Friends or Strangers: The Impact of Immigrants on the U.S. Economy.* New York: Basic Books.

———. 1999. *Heaven's Door: Immigration Policy and the American Economy.* Princeton: Princeton University Press.

Bosso, Christopher J. 1987. *Pesticides and Politics: The Life Cycle of a Public Issue.* Pittsburgh: University of Pittsburgh Press.

———. 1994. Review of *Agendas and Instability in American Politics,* by Frank R. Baumgartner and Bryan D. Jones. *American Political Science Review* 88:752–53.

Boynton, G.R. 1989. "The Senate Agriculture Committee Produces a Homeostat." *Policy Sciences* 22:51–80.

Brady, David W. 1988. *Critical Elections and Congressional Policymaking.* Palo Alto: Stanford University Press.

Brady, David W., and Craig Volden. 1998. *Revolving Gridlock: Politics and Policy from Carter to Clinton.* Boulder: Westview.

Brock, Gerald. 1994. *Telecommunications Policy for the Information Age: From Monopoly to Competition.* Cambridge: Harvard University Press.

Browne, William P. 1995. *Cultivating Congress: Constituents, Issues, and Interests in Agricultural Policymaking.* Lawrence: University Press of Kansas.

Bullock, Charles. 1976. "Motivations for U.S. Congressional Committee Preferences: Freshmen of the 92nd Congress." *Legislative Studies Quarterly* 1:201–12.

Bush, George, and Brent Scowcroft. 1998. *A World Transformed.* New York: Knopf.

Calavita, Kitty. 1984. *U.S. Immigration Law and the Control of Labor: 1820–1924.* London: Academic Press.

———. 1992. *Inside the State: The Bracero Program, Immigration, and the I.N.S.* New York: Routledge.

———. 1994. "U.S. Immigration and Policy Responses: The Limits of Legislation." In *Controlling Immigration: A Global Perspective,* ed. Wayne Cornelius, Philip L. Martin, and James F. Hollifield. Stanford: Stanford University Press.

———. 1996. "The New Politics of Immigration: 'Balanced-Budget Conservatism' and the Symbolism of Proposition 187." *Social Problems* 43:284–306.

Caldeira, Gregory, and John R. Wright. 1988. "Organized Interest and Agenda-Setting in the U.S. Supreme Court." *American Political Science Review* 82:1109–28.

———. 1990. "Amici Curiae before the Supreme Court: Who Participates, When, and How Much?" *Journal of Politics* 52:782–806.

Cameron, Charles, William Howell, Scott Adler, and Charles Riemann. 1997. "Divided Government and the Legislative Productivity of Congress, 1945–1994." Paper presented at the American Political Science Association Meetings, Washington.

Canon, David, Garrison Nelson, and Charles Stewart. 1994. "Committees in the United States Congress, 1946–94." Data file. Department of Political Science, University of Wisconsin, Madison.

Canon, David, and Martin Sweet. 1998. "Informational and Demand-Side Theories of Congressional Committees: Evidence from the Senate, 1816–1993." Paper presented at the Annual Meeting of the American Political Science Association, Boston.

Caraley, Demetrios. 1992. "Washington Abandons the Cities." *Political Science Quarterly* 107:1–30.

Carpenter, Daniel P. 1996. "Adaptive Signal Processing, Hierarchy, and Budgetary Control in Federal Regulations." *American Political Science Review* 90:283–302.

Carter, James E. 1980. "State of the Union Address." *Current Policy,* no. 132.

Cater, Douglass. 1964. *Power in Washington.* New York: Random House.

Chaffee, Steve H., and D. G. Wilson. 1977. "Media Rich, Media Poor: Two Studies of Diversity in Agenda-Holding." *Journalism Quarterly* 54:466–76.

Chong, Dennis. 1991. *Collective Action and the Civil Rights Movement.* Chicago: University of Chicago Press.

Cobb, Roger W., and Charles D. Elder. 1983. *Participation in American Politics: The Dynamics of Agenda-Building.* 2d ed. Baltimore: Johns Hopkins University Press.

Cobb, Roger W., Jeannie-Keith Ross, and Marc Howard Ross. 1976. "Agenda Building as a Comparative Political Process." *American Political Science Review* 70:126–38.

Committee on Science and Technology, U.S. House of Representatives. 1980. *Toward the Endless Frontier: History of the Committee on Science and Technology, 1959–79.* Committee print. Washington: Government Printing Office.

Congressional Quarterly. 1950–96 (annual). *Congressional Quarterly Almanac.* Washington: Congressional Quarterly.

Conlan, Timothy. 1998. *From New Federalism to Devolution: Twenty-Five Years of Intergovernmental Reform.* Washington: Brookings.

Converse, Philip E., and Roy Pierce. 1986. *Political Representation in France.* Cambridge: Harvard University Press.

Cooper, Joseph. 1977. "Congress in Organizational Perspective." In *Congress Reconsidered,* ed. Lawrence Dodd and Bruce Oppenheimer. New York: Praeger.

Cooper, Joseph, and Cheryl D. Young. 1989. "Bill Introduction in the Nineteenth Century: A Study of Institutional Change." *Legislative Studies Quarterly* 14:67–105.

Cornelius, Wayne, Philip L. Martin, and James F. Hollifield, eds. 1994. *Controlling Immigration: A Global Perspective.* Stanford: Stanford University Press.

Correa, Hector, and Ji-Won Kim. 1992. "A Causal Analysis of the Defense Expenditures of the USA and the USSR." *Journal of Peace Research* 29:161–74.

Cox, Gary W., and Mathew D. McCubbins. 1993. *Legislative Leviathan: Party Government in the House.* Berkeley and Los Angeles: University of California Press.

Crenson, Matthew A. 1987. "The Private Stake in Public Goods: Overcoming the Illogic of Collective Action." *Policy Sciences* 20:259–76.

Culbertson, H. M. 1992. "Measuring Agenda Diversity in an Elastic Medium: Candidate Position Papers." *Journalism Quarterly* 69:938–46.

Cusack, Thomas R. 1992. "On the Domestic Political-Economic Sources of American Military Spending." In *The Political Economy of Military Spending in the United States,* ed. Alex Mintz. London: Routledge.

Cusack, Thomas R., and Michael D. Ward. 1981. "Military Spending in the United States, Soviet Union, and the People's Republic of China." *Journal of Conflict Resolution* 25:429–69.

Danziger, James N. 1998. *Understanding the Political World.* 4th ed. New York: Longman.

Dao, James. 2001. "New Gun Control Politics: A Whimper, Not a Bang." *New York Times,* March 11, 4-1.

David, Paul A. 1985. "Clio and the Economics of QWERTY." *American Economic Review* 75:332–37.

Davidson, Roger H., and Walter J. Oleszek. 1994. *Congress and Its Members.* 5th ed. Washington: Congressional Quarterly.

———. 1998. *Congress and Its Members.* 6th ed. Washington: Congressional Quarterly.

Davis, Otto A., M. A. H. Dempster, and Aaron Wildavsky. 1966. "A Theory of the Budget Process." *American Political Science Review* 60:529–47.

———. 1974. "Toward a Predictive Theory of Government Expenditure: U.S. Domestic Appropriations." *British Journal of Political Science* 4:419–52.

Deering, Christopher J., and Steven S. Smith. 1997. *Committees in Congress.* 3d ed. Washington: Congressional Quarterly.

Demkovich, Linda. 1980. "Reagan's Cure for Health Care Ills — Keep the Government's Hand Off." *National Journal,* December 13, 2124–27.

Derthick, Martha, and Paul J. Quirk. 1985. *The Politics of Deregulation.* Washington: Brookings.

DeSipio, Louis, and Rodolfo de la Garza. 1998. *Making Americans, Remaking America: Immigration and Immigration Policy.* Boulder, Colo.: Westview.

Dion, Douglas. 1997. *Turning the Legislative Thumbscrew: Minority Rights and Procedural Change in Legislative Politics.* Ann Arbor: University of Michigan Press.

Dodd, Lawrence C. 1994. "Political Learning and Political Change: Understanding Development across Time." In *The Dynamics of American Politics,* ed. Lawrence C. Dodd and Calvin Jilson. Boulder, Colo.: Westview.

Donovan, Mark. 1993. "The Social Construction of People with AIDS: Target Populations and U.S. Policy, 1981–90." *Policy Studies Review* 12 (4): 3–29.

Downs, Anthony. 1957. *An Economic Theory of Democracy.* New York: Harper.

———. 1972. "Up and Down with Ecology: The Issue Attention Cycle." *Public Interest* 28:38–50.

Dulles, John Foster. 1954. "Foreign Policies and National Security." *Vital Speeches of the Day,* February 1, 232–35.

Easterlin, Richard. 1980. "Immigration: Economic and Social Characteristics." In *Encyclopedia of American Ethnic Groups,* ed. Stephan Thernstrom. Cambridge: Harvard University Press.

Edwards, George C., III. 1989. *At the Margins: Presidential Leadership of Congress.* New Haven: Yale University Press.

Edwards, George C., III, Andrew Barrett, and Jeffrey Peake. 1997. "The Legislative Impact of Divided Government." *American Journal of Political Science* 41:545–63.

Edwards, George C., III, and B. Dan Wood. 1999. "Who Influenced Whom? The President, Congress, and the Media." *American Political Science Review* 93: 327–44.

Eisenhower, Dwight David. 1953. "Atoms for Peace" speech before U.N. General Assembly, December 8. http://www.tamu.edu/scom/pres/speeches/ikeatoms.html.

Epstein, Lee, and Jack Knight. 1998. *The Choices Justices Make.* Washington: Congressional Quarterly.

Epstein, Lee, Jeffrey A. Segal, Harold J. Spaeth, and Thomas G. Walker. 1996. *The Supreme Court Compendium: Data, Decisions, and Developments.* 2d ed. Washington: Congressional Quarterly.

Espenshade, Thomas J. and Charles A. Calhoun. 1993. "An Analysis of Public Opinion toward Undocumented Immigration." *Population Research and Policy Review* 12:189–224.

Evans, C. Lawrence. 1995. "Committees and Health Jurisdictions in Congress." In *Intensive Care: How Congress Shapes Health Policy,* ed. Thomas Mann and Norman Ornstein. Washington: Brookings.

Evans, Diana. 1994. "Congressional Oversight and the Diversity of Members' Goals." *Political Science Quarterly* 109:669–87.

Feeley, T. Jens. 1999a. "Punctuated Equilibrium Theory: Exploring the Influences of Committee Competition, Party Control, and Issue Salience on U.S. Science and Technology Policy." Paper presented at the Annual Meeting of the Midwest Political Science Association, Chicago.

———. 1999b. "Punctuated Equilibrium Theory: Toward an Understanding of U.S. Science and Technology Policy, 1949–1993." Paper prepared for delivery at the Annual Meeting of the American Political Science Association, Atlanta.

Fenno, Richard. 1966. *The Power of the Purse.* Boston: Little, Brown.

———. 1973. *Congressmen in Committee.* Boston: Little, Brown.

Fetzer, Joel S. 2000. *Public Attitudes toward Immigration in the United States, France, and Germany.* Cambridge: Cambridge University Press.

Fiorina, Morris P. 1974. *Representatives, Roll Calls, and Constituencies.* Lexington, Mass.: Lexington.

———. 1977. *Congress: Keystone of the Washington Establishment.* New Haven: Yale University Press.

Flemming, Roy B., John Bohte, and B. Dan Wood. 1997. "One Voice among Many: The Supreme Court's Influence on Attentiveness to Issues in the United States, 1947–92." *American Journal of Political Science* 41:1224–50.

Flemming, Roy B., B. Dan Wood, and John Bohte. 1999. "Attention to Issues in a System of Separated Powers: The Macrodynamics of American Policy Agendas." *Journal of Politics* 61:76–108.

Freeman, Gary. 1995. "Modes of Immigration Politics in Liberal Democratic States." *International Migration Review* 29:881–902.

Fuchs, Lawrence. 1990. *The American Kaleidoscope: Race, Ethnicity, and the Civic Culture.* Middletown: Wesleyan University Press.

Futrell, Robert Frank. 1974. *Ideas, Concepts, and Doctrine: A History of Basic Thinking in the United States Air Force 1907–1964.* Maxwell Air Force Base, Ala.: Air University.

Gamm, Gerald, and Kenneth Shepsle. 1989. "Emergence of Legislative Institutions: Standing Committees in the House and Senate, 1810–1825." *Legislative Studies Quarterly* 14:39–66.

General Accounting Office. 1996. "Executive Guide: Effectively Implementing the Government Performance and Results Act" (GAO/GGD–96–118). Washington: Government Printing Office.

Gerber, Elizabeth. 1999. *The Populist Paradox.* Princeton: Princeton University Press.

Gibson, James L. 1997. *United States Supreme Court Judicial Data Base, Phase II: User's Guide.* New York: P. Lang.

Gimpel, James G., and James R. Edwards Jr. 1999. *The Congressional Politics of Immigration Reform.* Boston: Allyn and Bacon.

Gittenger, Ted. 1997. *Vietnam: The Early Decisions.* Austin: University of Texas Press.

Granovetter, Mark. 1978. "Threshold Models of Collective Behavior." *American Journal of Sociology* 83:1420–43.

Greene, William H. 1993. *Econometric Analysis.* 2d ed. New York: Macmillan.

Griffin, Larry J., Joel A. Devine, and M. Wallace. 1982. "Monopoly Capital, Organized Labor, and Military Expenditures in the U.S., 1949–1976." *American Journal of Sociology* 88:113–53.

Griffith, Ernest S. 1939. *The Impasse of Democracy.* New York: Harrison-Hilton.

Groseclose, Tim. 1994. "Testing Committee Composition Hypotheses for the U.S. Congress." *Journal of Politics* 56:440–58.

Groseclose, Tim, Steve Levitt, and Jim Snyder. 1999. "Comparing Interest Group Scores across Time and Chambers: Adjusted ADA Scores for the U.S. Congress." *American Political Science Review* 93:33–50.

Gujarati, Damodar N. 1988. *Basic Econometrics.* New York: McGraw-Hill.

Hacker, Jacob. 1997. *The Road to Nowhere.* Princeton: Princeton University Press.

Hager, George. 1998. "House Passes Spending Bill." *Washington Post,* October 21, sec. A, p. 1.

Haig, Alexander. 1981. "Relationship of Foreign and Defense Policies." *Current Policy,* no. 302.

Haines, David W. 1996. *Refugees in America in the 1990s.* Westport, Conn.: Greenwood.

Hakman, Nathan. 1966. "Lobbying the Supreme Court: An Appraisal of Political Science 'Folklore.'" *Fordham Law Review* 35:15–50.

Hall, Richard L. 1996. *Participation in Congress*. New Haven: Yale University Press.

Hall, Richard L., and Bernard Grofman. 1990. "The Committee Assignment Process and the Conditional Nature of Committee Bias." *American Political Science Review* 84:1149–66.

Hall, Richard L., and Frank Wayman. 1990. "Buying Time: Moneyed Interests and the Mobilization of Bias in Congressional Committees." *American Political Science Review* 84:797–820.

Hansen, John M. 1991. *Gaining Access: Congress and the Farm Lobby, 1919–1981*. Chicago: University of Chicago Press.

Hardin, John W. 1994. "Congressional Activity on National Health Insurance Proposals: How Political Change Influences Legislative Organization." Presented at the Annual Meeting of the Midwest Political Science Association, Chicago.

———. 1998a. "Advocacy versus Certainty: The Dynamics of Committee Jurisdiction Concentration." *Journal of Politics* 60:374–97.

———. 1998b. "An In-Depth Look at Congressional Committee Jurisdictions Surrounding Health Issues." *Journal of Health Politics, Policy, and Law* 23:517–50.

Harlow, Ralph V. 1917. *The History of Legislative Methods in the Period Before 1835*. New Haven: Yale University Press.

Harper, Donald. 1982. *Transportation in America*. Englewood Cliffs, N.J.: Prentice Hall.

Hartmann, Frederick H., and Robert L. Wendzel. 1985. *To Preserve the Republic: United States Foreign Policy*. New York: Macmillan.

Hasbrouck, Paul. 1927. *Party Government in the House of Representatives*. New York: Macmillan.

Henck, Fred, and Bernard Strassberg. 1988. *A Slippery Slope: The Long Road to the Breakup of AT&T*. New York: Greenwood.

Himelfarb, Richard. 1995. *Catastrophic Politics: The Rise and Fall of the Medicare Catastrophic Coverage Act of 1988*. University Park: Penn State University Press.

Hinich, Melvin J., and Munger, Michael C. 1997. *Analytical Politics*. New York: Cambridge University Press.

Hitch, Charles J., and Roland N. McKean. 1960. *The Economics of Defense in the Nuclear Age*. Cambridge: Harvard University Press.

Huckfeldt, Robert, and John D. Sprague. 1995. *Citizens, Politics, and Social Communication*. New York: Cambridge University Press.

Huntington, Samuel P. 1961. *The Common Defense: Strategic Programs in National Politics*. New York: Columbia University Press.

Hurley, Patricia, David Brady, and Joseph Cooper. 1977. "Measuring Legislative Potential for Policy Change." *Legislative Studies Quarterly* 2:385–98.

Hutchinson, Edward P. 1981. *Legislative History of American Immigration Policy 1798–1965*. Philadelphia: University of Pennsylvania Press.

Iglehart, John. 1978a. "The Cost of Keeping the Elderly Well." *National Journal,*
October 28, 1728–31.

———. 1978b. "Congress Has a Feeling of Malaise about Health Care." *National
Journal,* May 20, 805–9.

Immigration and Naturalization Service. 1999. *Annual Report: Refugees, Fiscal Year
1997.* July, no. 4. Prepared by the Office of Policy and Planning, Statistics Branch.

Jenkins, Jeffery A. 1998. "Property Rights and the Emergence of Standing Committee
Dominance in the Nineteenth-Century House." *Legislative Studies Quarterly*
23:493–520.

Jones, Bryan D. 1994. *Reconceiving Decision-Making in Democratic Politics.* Chicago:
University of Chicago Press.

———. 2001. *Politics and the Architecture of Choice.* Chicago: University of Chicago Press.

Jones, Bryan D., Frank R. Baumgartner, and Jeffery C. Talbert. 1993. "The Destruction
of Issue Monopolies in Congress." *American Political Science Review* 87:657–71.

Jones, Bryan D., Frank R. Baumgartner, and James L. True. 1996. "The Shape of Change:
Punctuations and Stability in U.S. Budgeting, 1947–94." Presented at the Annual
Meeting of the Midwest Political Science Association, Chicago.

———. 1998. "Policy Punctuations: U.S. Budget Authority, 1947–1995." *Journal of
Politics* 60:1–33.

Jones, Charles O. 1975. *Clean Air.* Pittsburgh: University of Pittsburgh Press.

Jones, Charles O., and Randall Strahan. 1985. "The Effects of Energy Politics on
Congressional and Executive Organization in the 1970s." *Legislative Studies
Quarterly* 10:151–79.

Kahan, Jerome. 1975. *Security in the Nuclear Age.* Washington: Brookings.

Kahneman, Daniel, and Amos Tversky. 1984. "Choices, Values, and Frames." *American
Psychologist* 39:341–50.

———. 1985. "Prospect Theory: An Analysis of Decision-Making under Risk."
Econometrica 47:263–91.

Kamlet, Mark S., and David C. Mowery. 1987. "Influences on Executive and Congressional
Budgetary Priorities, 1955–1981." *American Political Science Review* 81:155–78.

Katz, Jonathan N., and Brian R. Sala. 1996. "Careerism, Committee Assignments, and
the Electoral Connection." *American Political Science Review* 90: 21–33.

Kegley, Charles W., Jr. 1995. *Controversies in International Relations: Realism and the
Neoliberal Challenge.* New York: St. Martins.

Kennan, George [Mr. X]. 1947. "The Sources of Soviet Conduct." *Foreign Affairs*
26:506–82.

Kennedy, John F. 1962. "Inaugural Address." In *Public Papers of the Presidents: John F.
Kennedy.* Washington: Government Printing Office.

Kennedy, Peter. 1992. *A Guide to Econometrics.* 3d ed. Cambridge: MIT Press.

Kessler, David. 2001. *A Question of Intent: A Great American Battle with a Deadly Industry.* New York: Public Affairs.

Kiel, L. Douglas, and Euel Elliott. 1996. *Chaos Theory in the Social Sciences.* Ann Arbor: University of Michigan Press.

Kiewiet, Roderick, and Matthew McCubbins. 1991. *The Logic of Delegation: Congressional Parties and the Appropriations Process.* Chicago: University of Chicago Press.

Kindleberger, Charles P. 1996. *Manias, Panics, and Crashes.* 3d ed. New York: Wiley.

King, David C. 1994. "The Nature of Congressional Committee Jurisdictions." *American Political Science Review* 88: 48–62.

———. 1997. *Turf Wars: How Congressional Committees Claim Jurisdiction.* Chicago: University of Chicago Press.

King, Desmond. 2000. *Making Americans: Immigration, Race, and the Origins of the Diverse Democracy.* Cambridge: Harvard University Press.

Kingdon, John W. 1981. *Congressmen's Voting Decisions.* 2d ed. New York: Harper and Row.

———. 1984. *Agendas, Alternatives, and Public Policies.* Boston: Little, Brown.

———. 1989. *Congressmen's Voting Decisions.* 3d ed. Ann Arbor: University of Michigan Press.

———. 1995. *Agendas, Alternatives, and Public Policies.* 2d ed. New York: HarperCollins.

———. 1997. Presentation at Texas A&M University, February 19.

Kinsella, David. 1994. "Conflict in Context: Arms Transfers and Third World Rivalries." *American Journal of Political Science* 38:557–81.

Kissinger, Henry. 1979. *The White House Years.* Boston: Little, Brown.

Korb, Lawrence J., and Melvin Laird. 1981. "A $200 Billion Defense Budget . . ." *Washington Star,* January 21, 17.

Kosterlitz, Julie. 1988. "The Coming Crisis." *National Journal,* August 6,2029–32.

———. 1989. "Focuses: Gray Power." *National Journal,* July 29.

Krehbiel, Keith. 1991. *Information and Legislative Organization.* Ann Arbor: University of Michigan Press.

Krugman, Paul. 1997. "How the Economy Organizes Itself in Space: A Survey of the New Economic Geography." In *The Economy as an Evolving Complex System II,* ed. W. Brian Arthur, Steven N. Durlauf, and David A. Lane. Reading, Mass.: Addison Wesley.

Krutz, Glen S. 2001. "Tactical Meneuvering on Omnibus Bills in Congress." *American Journal of Political Science* 45:210–23.

Krutz, Glen S., Richard Fleisher, and Jon R. Bond. 1998. "From Abe Fortas to Zoë Baird: Explaining Why Some Presidential Nominations Fail in the Senate." *American Political Science Review* 92:871–81.

Larocca, Roger. 1995. "Measuring Presidential Influence on the Congressional

Agenda." Paper presented at the Midwest Political Science Association Meetings, Chicago.

LeMay, Michael C. 1994. *Anatomy of a Public Policy: The Reform of Contemporary American Immigration Law.* Westport, Conn.: Praeger.

Levitt, Steven D., and James M. Snyder Jr. 1997. "The Impact of Federal Spending on House Election Outcomes." *Journal of Political Economy* 105:30–53.

Lieb, Robert. 1981. *Transportation: The Domestic System.* Reston, Va.: Reston Publishing.

Liebowitz, Stanley, and Stephen E. Margolis. 1999. *Winners, Losers, and Microsoft: Competition and Anti-trust in High Technology.* Oakland, CA: Independent Institute.

Lindblom, Charles E. 1960. "The Science of 'Muddling Through.'" *Public Administration Review* 19:79–88.

———. 1977. *Politics and Markets.* New York: Basic Books.

Logsdon, John M., ed. 1995. *Exploring the Unknown: Selected Documents in the History of the U.S. Civil Space Program.* Vol. 1. Washington: NASA History Office.

Lohmann, Susanne. 1994. "The Dynamics of Informational Cascades: The Monday Demonstrations in Leipzig, East Germany, 1989–1991." *World Politics* 47:42–101.

Lowi, Theodore J. 1969. *The End of Liberalism.* New York: Norton.

Lyden, Fremont J., and Ernest G. Miller, eds. 1967. *Planning Programming Budgeting: A Systems Approach to Management.* Chicago: Markham.

MacKuen, Michael, Robert S. Erikson, and James A. Stimson. 2001. *The Macro Polity.* New York: Cambridge University Press.

Majeski, Stephen J. 1983. "Mathematical Models of the U.S. Military Expenditure Decision-Making Process." *American Journal of Political Science.* 27:485–514.

———. 1992. "Defense Budgeting, Fiscal Policy, and Economic Performance." In *The Political Economy of Military Spending in the United States,* ed. Alex Mintz. London: Routledge.

Malbin, Michael. 1980. "Big Government or Small Government: The Candidates Give Their Views." *National Journal,* January 26, 136–43.

Maltzman, Forrest. 1997. *Competing Principals: Committees, Parties, and the Organization of Congress.* Ann Arbor: University of Michigan Press.

Mandelbrot, Benoit B. 1982. *The Fractal Geometry of Nature.* San Francisco: Freeman.

March, James G., and Johan P. Olsen. 1989. *Rediscovering Institutions.* New York: Free Press.

Marmor, Theodore. 1970. *The Politics of Medicare.* London: Routledge.

———. 1994. "The Politics of Universal Health Insurance: Lessons from Past Administrations." *Political Science and Politics* 27:194–99.

Marra, Robin F., and Charles W. Ostrom, Jr. 1992. "Issues in Defense Spending:

Plausibility and Choice in Soviet Estimates." In *The Political Economy of Military Spending in the United States,* ed. Alex Mintz. London: Routledge.

Massey, Douglas S. 1990. "The Social and Economic Origins of Immigration." *Annals of the American Academy of Political and Social Science* 510 (July): 60–73.

———. 1995. "The New Immigration and Ethnicity in the United States." *Population and Development Review* 21:631–35.

Mayer, Kenneth R. 1992. "Elections, Business Cycles, and the Timing of Defense Contract Awards in the United States." *The Political Economy of Military Spending in the United States,* ed. Alex Mintz. London: Routledge.

Mayhew, David R. 1974. *Congress: The Electoral Connection.* New Haven: Yale University Press.

———. 1991. *Divided We Govern.* New Haven: Yale University Press.

McCombs, Maxwell, and Jian-Hua Zhu. 1995. "Capacity, Diversity, and Volatility of the Public Agenda: Trends from 1954 to 1994." *Public Opinion Quarterly* 59:495–525.

McConachie, Lauros. 1898. *Congressional Committees.* New York: Crowell.

McCubbins, Mathew, and Thomas Schwartz. 1984. "Congressional Oversight Overlooked: Police Patrols versus Fire Alarms." *American Journal of Political Science* 28:165–79.

McDonald, Kim A. 1995. "Too Many Co-authors?" *Chronicle of Higher Education* 41 (33): A35–A36.

Meernick, James, Eric L. Krueger, and Steven C. Poe. 1998. "Testing Models of U.S. Foreign Policy: Foreign Aid during and after the Cold War." *Journal of Politics* 60:63–85.

Melese, Francois. 1999. "The Latest in Performance Budgeting: The Government Performance and Results Act (GPRA)." *Armed Forces Comptroller* 44 (spring): 19–22.

Melnick, R. Shep. 1994. *Between the Lines: Interpreting Welfare Rights.* Washington: Brookings.

Meltzer, Allen, and Scott Richard. 1978. "Why Government Grows (and Grows) in a Democracy." *Public Interest* 52: 109–26.

Memory, J. D., J. F. Arnold, D. W. Stewart, and R. E. Fornes. 1985. "Physics as a Team Sport." *American Association of Physics Teachers* 53:270–71.

Meyer, Alexandra. 2001. "The Initiative Process as Policy Subsystem." Unpublished paper, Department of Political Science, University of Washington, Seattle.

Mintz, Alex, ed. 1992. *The Political Economy of Military Spending in the United States.* London: Routledge.

Moise, Edwin E. 1996. *Tonkin Gulf and the Escalation of the Vietnam War.* Chapel Hill: University of North Carolina Press.

Morgenthau, Hans J. 1951. *In Defense of the National Interest.* New York: Knopf.

Morone, James A. 1990. *The Democratic Wish: Popular Participation and the Limits of Popular Government.* New York: Basic Books.

Mucciaroni, Gary. 1995. *Reversals of Fortune.* Washington: Brookings.

Murphy, James. 1974. "Political Parties and the Porkbarrel: Party Conflict and Cooperation in House Public Works Committee Decision Making." *American Political Science Review* 68:169–85.

Murphy, Walter F. 1964. *Elements of Judicial Strategy.* Chicago: University of Chicago Press.

Nickels, Ilona B. 1994. *Guiding a Bill through the Legislative Process.* Washington: Congressional Research Service, Library of Congress.

Nimmen, Jane Van, and Leonard C. Bruno, with Robert L. Rosholt. 1988. *NASA Historical Data Book, Volume 1 (NASA SP-4012).* Washington: NASA Scientific and Technical Information Division.

Nincic, Miroslav, and Thomas R. Cusack. 1979. "The Political Economy of U.S. Military Spending." *Journal of Peace Research* 16:101–14.

Nixon, Richard M. 1970. *U.S. Foreign Policy for the 1970s.* Washington: Government Printing Office.

Nordhaus, William. 1975. "The Political Business Cycle." *Review of Economic Studies* 42:169–90.

North, Douglas C. 1990. *Institutions, Institutional Change and Economic Performance.* New York: Cambridge University Press.

NSC-20/1. 1948 [1975]. "United States Objectives with Respect to Russia." Top secret paper prepared by the Policy Planning Staff of the Department of State in connection with NSC-20, "Appraisal of the Degree and character of Military Preparedness Required by the World Situation." Declassified August 1, 1975.

NSC-68. 1950 [1975]. "A Report to the National Security Council." Reprinted in *Naval War College Review* 27 (May/June 1975): 51–108.

NSC-162. 1953 [1971]. "Review of Basic National Security Policy." Signed October 30, 1953. Reprinted in *The Pentagon Papers* (New York: Quadrangle).

Nuechterlein, Donald E. 1978. *The Setting of National Priorities.* Boulder, Colo.: Westview.

O'Brien, David M. 1993. *Storm Center.* 3d ed. New York: Norton.

Oleszek, Walter J. 1989. *Congressional Procedures and the Policy Process.* 3d ed. Washington: Congressional Quarterly.

———. 1996. *Congressional Procedures and the Policy Process.* Washington: Congressional Quarterly.

Olson, Mancur. 1965. *The Logic of Collective Action.* Cambridge: Harvard University Press.

———. 1982. *The Rise and Decline of Nations.* New Haven: Yale University Press.

Ornstein, Norman J., Thomas E. Mann, and Michael J. Malbin, eds. 1992. *Vital Statistics on Congress: 1991–1992.* Washington: Congressional Quarterly.

———. 1996. *Vital Statistics on Congress, 1995–1996.* Washington: Congressional Quarterly.

Osborne, David, and Ted Gaebler. 1993. *Reinventing Government: How the Entrepreneurial Spirit Is Transforming the Public Sector.* New York: Plume.

Ostrom, Charles W., Jr. 1977. "Evaluating Alternative Foreign Policy Decision-Making Models." *Journal of Conflict Resolution* 21:235–65.

———. 1978. "A Reactive Linkage Model of the U.S. Defense Expenditure Policymaking Process." *American Political Science Review* 72:941–57.

Ostrom, Charles W., Jr., and Robin F. Marra. 1986. "U.S. Defense Spending and the Soviet Estimate." *American Political Science Review* 80:819–42.

Pacelle, Richard L., Jr. 1991. *The Transformation of the Supreme Court's Agenda: From the New Deal to the Reagan Administration.* Boulder, Colo.: Westview.

———. 1995. "The Dynamics and Determinants of Agenda Change in the Rehnquist Court." In *Contemplating Courts,* ed. Lee Epstein. Washington: Congressional Quarterly.

Padgett, John F. 1980. "Bounded Rationality in Budgetary Research." *American Political Science Review* 74:354–72.

Peltason, Jack W. 1955. *Federal Courts in the Political Process.* New York: Doubleday.

Peltzman, Sam. 1976. "Toward a More General Theory of Regulation." *Journal of Law and Economics* 19:211–40.

Perry, H. W., Jr. 1991. *Deciding to Decide: Agenda Setting in the United States Supreme Court.* Cambridge: Harvard University Press.

Peterson, Geoffrey, and J. Mark Wrighton. 1998. "The Continuing Puzzle of Committee Outliers: A Methodological Reassessment." *Congress and the Presidency* 25:67–78.

Peterson, Mark A. 1990. *Legislating Together.* Cambridge: Harvard University Press.

———. 1993. "Political Influence in the 1990s: From Iron Triangles to Policy Networks." *Journal of Health Politics, Policy, and Law* 18:395–438.

———. 1994. "Health Care and the Hill: Why Is This Year Different from All Others?" *Political Science and Politics* 27:202–7.

Polsby, Nelson W. 1968. "The Institutionalization of the U.S. House of Representatives." *American Political Science Review* 62:144–68.

Poole, Keith T., and Howard Rosenthal. 1997. *Congress: A Political-Economic History of Roll Call Voting.* New York: Oxford University Press.

Price, David. 1979. *Policymaking in Congressional Committees: The Impact of "Environmental" Factors.* Tucson: Institute of Governmental Research, University of Arizona.

Provine, Doris Marie. 1980. *Case Selection in the United States Supreme Court.* Chicago: University of Chicago Press.

Putnam, Robert D. 1993. *Making Democracy Work.* Princeton: Princeton University Press.

Quattrone, George A., and Amos Tversky. 1988. "Contrasting Rational and Psychological Analyses of Political Choice." *American Political Science Review* 83:719–36.

Rauch, Jonathan. 1987. "Swing toward Spending." *National Journal,* April 18, 922–26.

———. 1994. *Demosclerosis.* New York: Times Books.

Reagan, Ronald W. 1981. "Address to U.S. Military Academy." *New York Times,* May 28, D-10.

———. 1982. "Budget Message of the President." *Budget of the United States Government for FY 1983.* Washington: Government Printing Office.

Redford, Emmette S. 1969. *Democracy in the Administrative State.* New York: Oxford University Press.

Reimers, David M. 1998. *Unwelcome Strangers. American Identity and the Turn against Immigration.* New York: Columbia University Press.

Reports. 1987. "Some Catastrophic Coverage Likely." *National Journal,* February 7, 310.

Rich, Spencer. 2001. "Congress: Return of Catastrophic." *National Journal,* February 24, 560–61.

Riker, William H. 1980. "Implications from the Disequilibrium of Majority Rule for the Study of Institutions." *American Political Science Review* 74:432–46.

———. 1984. "The Heresthetics of Constitution-Making: The Presidency in 1787, with Comments on Determinism and Rational Choice." *American Political Science Review* 78:1–16.

———. 1986. *The Art of Political Manipulation.* New Haven: Yale University Press.

Rochefort, David A., and Roger W. Cobb. 1994. *The Politics of Problem Definition: Shaping the Public Agenda.* Lawrence: University Press of Kansas.

Rohde, David W. 1991. *Parties and Leaders in the Postreform House.* Chicago: University of Chicago Press.

———. 1992. "Agenda Change and Partisan Resurgence in the House of Representatives." In *The Atomistic Congress: An Interpretation of Congressional Change,* ed. A. Hertzke and R. Peters. Armonk, N.Y.: Sharpe.

Rose, Mark. 1990. *Interstate: Express Highway Politics, 1939–1989.* Knoxville: University of Tennessee Press.

Rundquist, Barry, and John Ferejohn. 1975. "Observations on a Distributive Theory of Policymaking: Two American Expenditure Programs Compared." In *Comparative Public Policy: Issues, Theories, and Methods,* ed. C. Kiske, W. Loehr, and J. McCamant. New York: Wiley.

Sabatier, Paul A. 1988. "An Advocacy Coalition Framework of Policy Change and the Role of Policy-Oriented Learning Therein." *Policy Sciences* 21 (1): 129–68.

Sabatier, Paul A., and Hank C. Jenkins-Smith. 1993. *Policy Change and Learning. An Advocacy Coalition Approach.* Boulder, Colo.: Westview.

Salisbury, Robert H., and Kenneth A. Shepsle. 1981. "U.S. Congressman as Enterprise." *Legislative Studies Quarterly* 6:559–76.

Sarasohn, Judy. 1982. "Airport Program Slipped into Tax Bill." *Congressional Quarterly Weekly Report,* September 25, 2382–83.

Schattschneider, E. E. 1960. *The Semi-sovereign People.* New York: Holt.

Schauffler, Helen Halpin, and John D. Wilkerson. 1997. "National Health Care Reform, 103rd Congress: A Description of the Activities and Influence of Public Health Activists." *American Journal of Public Health* 87(7): 1107–12.

Schelling, Thomas C. 1978. *Micromotives and Macrobehavior.* New York: Norton.

Schick, Allen. 1966. "The Road to PPB: The Stages of Budget Reform." *Public Administration Review* 26:243–58.

———. 1995a. "From the Old Politics of Budgeting to the New." In *Budgeting, Policy, Politics: An Appreciation of Aaron Wildavsky,* ed. Naomi Caiden and Joseph White. New Brunswick, N.J.: Transaction.

———. 1995b. *The Federal Budget: Politics, Policy, Process.* Washington: Brookings.

Schickler, Eric. 1998. "Institutional Change in the House of Representatives, 1867–1986: A Test of Partisan and Median Voter Models." Paper presented at the Midwest Political Science Association Meetings, Chicago.

Schiller, Wendy. 1995. "Senators as Political Entrepreneurs: Using Bill Sponsorship to Shape Legislative Agendas." *American Journal of Political Science* 39:186–203.

Schilling, Warner R., Paul Y. Hammond, and Glenn H. Snyder. 1962. *Strategy, Politics, and Defense Budgets.* New York: Columbia University Press.

Schlozman, Kay Lehman, and John T. Tierney. 1986. *Organized Interests and American Democracy.* New York: Harper.

Schneider, William. 1987. "Democrats Seeking Social Justice on the Cheap." *National Journal,* March 21, 710.

Schubert, Glendon. 1959. *Quantitative Analysis of Judicial Behavior.* New York: Free Press.

———. 1962. "Policy without Law: An Extension of the Certiorari Game." *Stanford Law Review* 14:284–327.

Schulzinger, Robert D. 1984. *American Diplomacy in the Twentieth Century.* New York: Oxford University Press.

Segal, Jeffrey A., and Harold J. Spaeth. 1993. *The Supreme Court and the Attitudinal Model.* New York: Cambridge University Press.

Shaw, Donald, and Maxwell McCombs. 1977. *The Emergence of American Political Issues.* Saint Paul: West.

Shepsle, Kenneth A. 1979. "Institutional Arrangements and Equilibrium in Multidimensional Voting." *American Journal of Political Science* 23:27–60.

Shepsle, Kenneth A., and Barry R. Weingast, eds. 1995. *Positive Theories of Congressional Institutions.* Ann Arbor: University of Michigan Press.

———. 1987. "The Institutional Foundations of Committee Power." *American Political Science Review* 81:85–104.

Shipan, Charles. 1992. "Individual Incentives and Institutional Imperatives: Committee Jurisdiction and Long-Term Health Care." *American Journal of Political Science* 36:877–95.

Simon, Herbert A. 1947. *Administrative Behavior: A Study of Decision Making Processes in Administrative Organizations.* New York: Macmillan.

———. 1983. *Reason in Human Affairs.* Stanford: Stanford University Press.

———. 1985. "Human Nature in Politics: The Dialogue of Psychology with Political Science." *American Political Science Review* 79:293–304.

———. 1997. *Administrative Behavior.* 4th ed. New York: Free Press.

Simon, Rita J., and Susan H. Alexander. 1993. *The Ambivalent Welcome: Print Media, Public Opinion, and Immigration.* Westport, Conn.: Praeger.

Sinclair, Barbara. 1986. "The Role of Committees in Agenda Setting in the U.S. Congress." *Legislative Studies Quarterly* 11:35–45.

———. 1992. "The Emergence of Strong Leadership in the 1980s House of Representatives." *Journal of Politics* 54:657–84.

———. 1995. *Legislators, Leaders, and Lawmaking: The U.S. House of Representatives in the Postreform Era.* Baltimore: Johns Hopkins University Press.

———. 1997. *Unorthodox Lawmaking: New Legislative Processes in the U.S. Congress.* Washington: Congressional Quarterly.

Skocpol, Theda. 1997. *Boomerang: Health Care Reform and the Turn against Government.* New York: Norton.

Smith, James F. 1999. "The Benefits and Threats of PBB: An Assessment of Modern Reform." *Public Budgeting and Finance* 19:3–15.

Smith, James P., and Barry Edmonston, eds. 1997. *The New Americans: Economic, Demographic, and Fiscal Effects of Immigration.* Washington: National Academy Press.

Smith, Rogers. 1993. *Civic Ideals: Conflicting Visions of Citizenship in U.S. History.* New Haven: Yale University Press.

Smith, Steven S. 1989. *Call to Order: Floor Politics in the House and Senate.* Washington: Brookings.

Sniderman, Paul, Richard Brody, and Philip Tetlock. 1991. *Reasoning and Choice.* Cambridge: Harvard University Press.

Sornette, Didier. 2000. *Critical Phenomena in Natural Sciences.* Berlin: Springer.

Spaeth, Harold J. 1997. *United States Supreme Court Judicial Database, 1953–1996*

Terms. Computer File #9422. 8th ICPSR Version. Produced by Michigan State University, Department of Political Science. Ann Arbor, Mich.: Inter-university Consortium for Political and Social Research.

————. 1998. *Expanded United States Supreme Court Judicial Database, 1946–1968 Terms.* Computer File #6557. 4th ICPSR Version. Produced by Michigan State University, Deptartment of Political Science. Ann Arbor, Mich.: Inter-university Consortium for Political and Social Research.

Spanier, John. 1988. *American Foreign Policy since World War II.* 11th ed. Washington: Congressional Quarterly.

Starr, Paul. 1984. *The Social Transformation of American Medicine.* New York: Basic Books.

Stein, Robert, and Kenneth Bickers. 1994. "Congressional Elections and the Pork Barrel." *Journal of Politics* 56:377–99.

Steinbruner, John D. 1974. *The Cybernetic Theory of Decision: New Dimensions of Political Analysis.* Princeton: Princeton University Press.

Stern, Robert H., Eugene Gressman, and Stephen M. Shapiro. 1986. *Supreme Court Practice.* 6th ed. Washington: Bureau of National Affairs.

Stone, Alan. 1989. *Wrong Number.* New York: Basic Books.

Stone, Deborah. 1989. "Causal Stories and the Formation of Policy Agendas." *Political Science Quarterly* 104: 281–300.

Su, Tsai-Tsu, Mark S. Kamlet, and David Mowery. 1993. "Modeling U.S. Budgetary and Fiscal Outcomes: A Disaggregated, Systemwide Perspective." *American Journal of Political Science* 37:213–45.

Talbert, Jeffery C., Bryan D. Jones, and Frank R. Baumgartner. 1995. "Nonlegislative Hearings and Policy Change in Congress." *American Journal of Political Science* 39:383–406.

Tanenhaus, Joseph, Marvin Schick, Matthew Muraskin, and Daniel Rosen. 1963. "The Supreme Court's Certiorari Jurisdiction: Cue Theory." In *Judicial Decision Making,* ed. Glendon Schubert. New York: Free Press.

Taylor, Andrew J. 1998. "Domestic Agenda-Setting, 1947–1994." *Legislative Studies Quarterly* 23:373–98.

Taylor, Maxwell D. 1959. *The Uncertain Trumpet.* New York: Harper.

Teixeira, Roy A. 1992. *The Disappearing American Voter.* Washington: Brookings.

Temin, Peter. 1987. *The Fall of the Bell System.* New York: Cambridge University Press.

Tichenor, Daniel J. 1994. "The Politics of Immigration Reform in the United States, 1981–1990." *Polity* 26(3):333–362.

Trager, Frank N. 1977. "The National Security Act of 1947." *Air University Review* (November–December 1977): 2–15.

True, James L. 1995. "Is the National Budget Controllable?" *Public Budgeting and Finance* 15:18–32.

———. 1997. "Agenda-Setting Politics, Policy Punctuations, and the Avalanche Budget Model." Ph.D. diss., Department of Political Science, Texas A&M University.

True, James L., Bryan D. Jones, and Frank R. Baumgartner. 1999. "Punctuated Equilibrium Theory: Explaining Stability and Change in American Policymaking." In *Theories of the Policy Process,* ed. Paul Sabatier. Boulder, Colo.: Westview.

Truman, David. 1951. *The Governmental Process.* New York: Knopf.

Truman, Harry S. 1948. "Special Message to the Congress on Greece and Turkey: The Truman Doctrine," March 12, 1947. In *Public Papers of the Presidents.* Washington: Government Printing Office.

Tversky, Amos, and Daniel Kahneman. 1986. "Rational Choice and the Framing of Decisions." *Journal of Business* 59:251–78.

U.S. Arms Control and Disarmament Agency. [serial] *World Military Expenditures and Arms Transfers.* Washington: Government Printing Office.

U.S. Bureau of the Census. 1996. *Statistical Abstract of the United States, 1996.* Washington: Government Printing Office.

———. 1973. *Congressional District Data Book, 93d Congress.* Washington: Government Printing Office.

U.S. Office of Management and Budget. [serial] *Budget of the United States Government.* Washington: Government Printing Office.

———. 1979. *The Functional Classification in the Budget.* Technical Staff Paper BRD/FAB 79-1. Washington: Office of Management and Budget.

Vance, Cyrus. 1980. "U.S. Foreign Policy: Our Broader Strategy." *Current Policy,* no. 153.

Vose, Clement E. 1959. *Caucasians Only.* Berkeley and Los Angeles: University of California Press.

Ward, Michael D., David R. Davis, and Corey L. Lofdahl. 1995. "A Century of Tradeoffs: Defense and Growth in Japan and the United States." *International Studies Quarterly* 39:27–50.

Wawro, Greg. 2000. *Legislative Entrepreneurship in the U.S. House of Representatives.* Ann Arbor: University of Michigan Press.

Weart, Spencer. 1988. *Nuclear Fear: A History of Images.* Cambridge: Harvard University Press.

Weaver, R. Kent. 1986. "The Politics of Blame Avoidance." *Journal of Public Policy* 6:371–98.

Weigley, Russell F. 1973. *The American Way of War.* New York: Macmillan.

Wells, Samuel F., Jr. 1979. "Sounding the Tocsin: NSC-68 and the Soviet Threat." *International Security* 4:116–58.

White, Kenneth J. 1997. *Shazam User's Reference Manual.* Vancouver, B.C.: McGraw-Hill.

Wildavsky, Aaron. 1964. *The Politics of the Budgetary Process.* Boston: Little, Brown.

————. 1992. *The New Politics of the Budgetary Process.* 2d ed. New York: HarperCollins.

Wilkerson, John D., T. Jens Feeley, Nicole S. Schiereck, and Christi Sue. 1999a. "Bill Introductions as Indicators of Issue Salience: Health Legislation 1987–1990." Paper presented at the Annual Meeting of the Western Political Science Association, Seattle.

————. 1999b. "Policy Interest and Legislative Responsiveness: Bill Introductions as Indicators of Issue Salience." Paper prepared for delivery at the 1999 Annual Meeting of the American Political Science Association, Atlanta.

Willand, Jennifer R. 1998. "Forecasting Budget Theory for the 21st Century through a Local Lens." Paper presented at the 1998 Meeting of the American Society for Public Administration, Seattle.

Wlezien, Christopher. 1995. "The Public as Thermostat: Dynamics of Preferences for Spending." *American Journal of Political Science* 39:981–1000.

Wolfinger, Raymond, and Steven Rosenstone. 1980. *Who Votes?* New Haven: Yale University Press.

Wolman, Harold, and Lisa Marckini. 1998. "Changes in Central-City Representation and Influence in Congress since the 1960s." *Urban Affairs Review* 34:291–312.

Woolley, John T. 2000. "Using Media-Based Data in Studies of Politics." *American Journal of Political Science* 44:156–73.

Worsham, Jeff. 1998. "Wavering Equilibriums, Subsystem Dynamics, and Agenda Control." *American Politics Quarterly* 26:485–512.

Wright, Fiona M. 1997. "The House in an Era of Fiscal Austerity: Institutional and Strategic Responses to the New Deficit Politics, 1974–1996." Paper presented at the Annual Meeting of the American Political Science Association, Washington.

Zaller, John R. 1992. *The Nature and Origins of Mass Opinion.* New York: Cambridge University Press.

Zhu, Jian-Hua. 1992. "Issue Competition and Attention Distraction: A Zero-Sum Theory of Agenda-Setting." *Journalism Quarterly* 69:825–36.

Zuk, Gary, and Nancy R. Woodbury. 1986. "U.S. Defense Spending, Electoral Cycles, and Soviet-American Relations." *Journal of Conflict Resolution* 30:445–68.

INDEX